Study Guide

D1462373

for Rathus's

Psychology
Concepts and Connections

Seventh Edition
Brief Version

Lisa Valentino
Seminole County Community College

THOMSON

WADSWORTH

Australia • Canada • Mexico • Singapore • Spain • United Kingdom • United States

Printer: Patterson Printing Company

ISBN: 0-534-61239-3

For more information about our products, contact us at:
Thomson Learning Academic Resource Center
1-800-423-0563

For permission to use material from this text, contact us by:
Phone: 1-800-730-2214
Fax: 1-800-731-2215
Web: http://www.thomsonrights.com

Wadsworth/Thomson Learning
10 Davis Drive
Belmont, CA 94002-3098
USA

Asia
Thomson Learning
5 Shenton Way #01-01
UIC Building
Singapore 068808

Australia/New Zealand
Thomson Learning
102 Dodds Street
Southbank, Victoria 3006
Australia

Canada
Nelson
1120 Birchmount Road
Toronto, Ontario M1K 5G4
Canada

Europe/Middle East/South Africa
Thomson Learning
High Holborn House
50/51 Bedford Row
London WC1R 4LR
United Kingdom

Latin America
Thomson Learning
Seneca, 53
Colonia Polanco
11560 Mexico D.F.
Mexico

Spain/Portugal
Paraninfo
Calle/Magallanes, 25
28015 Madrid, Spain

INTRODUCTION

Welcome to the study of Psychology!

This Study Guide was prepared with you, the student, in mind. It is designed to help you understand and apply the material in Spencer Rathus's Psychology: Concepts and Connections 7th edition Brief Version. This guide is not intended for use alone – it is for you to use alongside your textbook. My hope is that it will help you structure your study time and efforts so that you develop a better understanding of the textbook materials.

Good Luck,

Lisa Valentino
Seminole Community College

TABLE OF CONTENTS

Chapter One: The Science of Psychology

PowerPreview: *Skim the major headings in this chapter in your textbook. Jot down anything that you are surprised or curious about. After this write down four or five questions that you have about the material in this chapter.*

Things that surprised me/I am curious about from Chapter 1:

Questions that I have about Psychology, its History and Methods of Study:

- •
- •
- •
- •

QUESTION: *These are some questions that you should be able to answer after you finish studying this chapter:*

What Is Psychology?
- ❖ *What is the best definition for psychology? And what else?*
- ❖ *What are the four goals of psychology?*
- ❖ *What are theories, and how do psychologists use them?*

What Psychologists Do: Fields of Psychology
- ❖ *How are clinical psychologists different from counseling psychologists? How are they the same? How are psychiatrists different from psychologists?*
- ❖ *How are school and educational psychologists different?*
- ❖ *What are the differing concerns for developmental, personality, social and experimental psychologists?*
- ❖ *How are the interests of Industrial/Organizational, Human Factors, and Consumer psychologists different?*
- ❖ *What aspects of behavior might a health psychologist examine? How is it different from the interests of a sports psychologist?*
- ❖ *What is Critical Thinking, and why is it important for psychologists?*

Where Psychology Comes From: A History
- ❖ *How did the ancient Greeks influence psychology? When and where did psychology begin? Who is the founder of psychology?*
- ❖ *What is structuralism? What are its basic beliefs?*
- ❖ *What is functionalism? What are its basic beliefs? How do they differ from those of structuralism?*
- ❖ *What is behaviorism? What are its basic beliefs? How do they differ from those of structuralism and functionalism?*

- ❖ *What is Gestalt psychology? How do the beliefs of Gestalt psychology differ from those of behaviorism?*
- ❖ *Who is Sigmund Freud? What is psychoanalysis, and what are the basic beliefs of psychodynamic psychology?*

How Today's Psychologists View Behavior and Mental Processes
- ❖ *What are the basic beliefs of the Biological, Evolutionary, Cognitive, Humanistic-Existential, Psychodynamic, Learning and Sociocultural Perspectives? How do each of these views differ? How are they the same?*

How Psychologists Study Behavior and Mental Processes
- ❖ *Is psychology a science? What is the scientific method? How is it used in psychology?*
- ❖ *How do psychologists use samples to reach conclusions about people in general?*
- ❖ *What three methods do psychologists use to observe subjects? How are case studies, survey and naturalistic observation different?*
- ❖ *What is a correlation? What type of question would psychologists ask in correlational studies? What are the limitations of correlation research?*
- ❖ *What is an experiment? What type of research questions would a psychologist ask in an experimental study?*
- ❖ *What are independent and dependent variables? What is a placebo? How do psychologists use blind and double blind experiments?*

Ethical Issues in Psychological Research and Practice
- ❖ *What ethical issues are psychologists concerned with when researching on human subjects? How do psychologists assure that they are not violating any of these ethical issues in research?*
- ❖ *What ethical issues are psychologists concerned with when researching on animal subjects?*

Life Connections: Critical Thinking, Science & Pseudoscience
- ❖ *What is Critical Thinking?*

Reading for Understanding/Reflect: *The following section provides you with the opportunity to check your understanding of your reading of the text by filling in the blanks in the brief paragraphs that relate to each of the preview questions. You will also be prompted to rehearse your understanding of the material with periodic Reflection breaks. Remember it is better to study in more frequent, short sessions then in one long "cram session." Be sure to reward yourself with short study breaks before each of the Reflection exercises.*

Reading for Understanding about "What Is Psychology?"
What is psychology? Psychology is best defined as the (1)_____study of (2)_____ and (3)_____ processes. Psychologists study all aspects of living organisms from the (4)_____ system, to learning and (5)_____, as well as personality and the behavior of people in (6)_____ settings.

What are the four goals of psychology? What are theories and how do psychologists use them? Psychologists have four goals. They seek to (7)_____, (8)_____, (9)_____ and (10)_____ behavior and mental processes. Psychologists use (11)_____, or formulations of apparent relationships among observed events, to develop explanations and predictions.

Reflection Break # 1:

Goals of psychology: *Described below are some activities of psychologists—identify which of the four goals is being pursued.*

_____ 1. A psychologist is observing a group of four-year-olds in a playroom and counting the number of times they talk to another child.

_____ 2. A psychologist counts the number of times a person of different ages visits specific web sites to see if a person's age is related to their internet interests.

_____ 3. A psychiatrist gives some of his depressed patients sugar pills and others a new drug to see if the new drug will help them to experience less depression.

_____ 4. Another psychologist examines the relationship between an athlete's anger and their win/loss record.

_____ 5. A student is interested in whether there is a gender difference in the neatness of office space.

_____ 6. An industrial psychologist is interested in whether a change in temperature will increase the productivity of assembly line workers.

_____ 7. A researcher is interested in whether too much sugar in the diet is the cause of hyperactivity in young boys.

_____ 8. An organizational psychologist is interested in why employees who work for one division of a company are more likely to quit than those who work at another division.

Reading for Understanding on "What Psychologists Do?"

Just what do psychologists do? Psychologists can be found in almost any employment setting. Psychologists engage in (12)_____ and (13)_____. Research that has no immediate application is said to be (14)_____ research whereas (15)_____ research seeks solutions to specific problems. (16)_____ psychologists help people by applying psychological knowledge to help people change their behaviors.

How are clinical psychologists different from counseling psychologists? How are they the same? How are psychiatrists different from either psychologist? (17)_____ psychologists help people with psychological disorders adapt to the demands of life, they may help their client to resolve their problems that range from anxiety and (18)_____, to sexual dysfunction. (19)_____ differ from clinical psychologists in that they are medical doctors who specialize in the study and treatment of psychological disorders. The clients of (20)_____ psychologists are often less serious then those of clinical psychologists, although they tend to use the same methods to diagnose and treat. Although more then half of doctoral students in psychology are enrolled in counseling or (21)_____ psychology programs, there are many other specializations in psychology.

How are school and educational psychologists different? (22)_____ psychologists are employed by school systems to identify and assist students with learning problems. They differ from (23)_____ psychologists in that the school psychologist will make decisions about the (24)_____ of students; working directly with the student. The educational psychologist, on the other hand, will attempt to facilitate learning by focusing on course (25)_____ and development of instructional methods.

What are the differing concerns for developmental, personality, social and experimental psychologists? (26)_____ psychologists study physical, (27)_____, social and personality changes that occur throughout the life span. Psychologists that attempt to define human traits and determine influences on thoughts, feelings, and behavior are known as (28)_____ psychologists. Social psychologists are primarily concerned with the (29)_____ of an individual's thoughts, feelings, and behaviors in (30)_____ settings. Finally, (31)_____ psychologists specialize in conducting research into basic processes such as sensation and perception, or learning and memory.

How are the interests of Industrial/Organizational; Human Factors and Consumer psychologists different? Psychologists that focus on the behavior of people in businesses and organizations are known as (32)_____ psychologists, while (33)_____ psychologists study the relationship between people and work. (34)_____ psychologists are more technically oriented in their jobs and focus on people-friendly design of equipment. Department stores and supermarkets are more likely to hire a (35)_____ psychologist to examine and predict the behaviors of shoppers.

What aspects of behavior might a health psychologist examine? How is it different from the interests of a sports psychologist? (36)_____ psychologists are likely to spend much of their time studying the effects of stress on health problems like headaches and cancer, while a professional football team would be most interested in having a (37)_____ psychologist on staff to help their athletes improve overall performance.

Reflection Break # 2:
Types of psychologists: *Match the description of the psychologist with their proper title.*

a. **Counseling**
b. **Clinical**
c. **Applied Research**
d. **Basic Research**
e. **Psychiatrist**
f. **School**
g. **Educational**
h. **Developmental**
i. **Personality**
j. **Consumer**
k. **Social**
l. **Industrial**
m. **Organizational**
n. **Health**
o. **Sport**

_____1. Working with a young gymnast player to help her use visualization to complete a flip on the balance beam.

_____2. Works with a new Internet start up company to target their market audience.

_____3. Works in an elementary school, developing programs for children with special needs, and administering assessment tests.

_____4. Works at a university, spends most of their time researching processes involved in learning and designing new teaching methods.

_____5. Spends most their time researching general questions on animal behavior.

_____ 6. This specialist is a medical doctor who specializes in the study and treatment of psychological disorders.

_____ 7. This sub specialist might work to define the characteristics or traits that define an individual's unique personality.

_____ 8. A psychologist who may work to advise clients to help them clarify their goals or overcome obstacles.

_____ 9. This psychologist would be interested in social pressures or influences that might change an individual behavior.

_____ 10. This specialist would most likely work to help people with more severe psychological disorders adjust to the demands of life.

_____ 11. This psychologist might be interested in examining the effects of stress on headaches or cardiovascular disease.

_____ 12. This psychologist might work with a Fortune 500 company to improve its employee relations.

_____ 13. This researcher would be interested in designing research studies to find solutions to specific real-life problems.

_____ 14. This psychologist would be interested in identifying how the thinking of a three-year-old might differ from that of a seven-year-old.

_____ 15. This psychologist would most likely study the behavior of people in different business organizations.

Reading for Understanding about "Psychology's History"

How did the ancient Greeks influence psychology? When and where did psychology begin? Who is the founder of psychology? **Peri Psyches**, or about the Psyche, was written by (38)_____. This book began with a history of psychological thought and the nature of the (39)_____ and behavior. Aristole was a proponent of (40)_____, the view that science could rationally treat only information gathered by the senses. Aristotle argued that human behavior is subject to (41)_____ and laws. Other Greek philosophers that contributed to psychology's early development included, (42)_____, who was the first to raise the question of whether there is free will and (43)____who argued that we could not attain reliable self-knowledge through our senses. He argued that we should rely on rational thought and (44)_____, a careful examination of one's own thoughts and emotions, to achieve self-knowledge. Although the early Greeks are considered to have influenced the thinking of psychology, most historians set the modern debut of psychology as a lab science in the year (45)_____, when (46)_____ established the first psychological laboratory in Leipzig, Germany. Wundt saw the (47)_____ as a natural event that could be studied scientifically.

What is structuralism? What are its basic beliefs? Wundt and his students attempted to break the conscious experience into (48)_____ sensations, (49)_____ feelings and mental images. This approach was known as (50)_____, and argued that the mind functioned by combining objective and subjective elements of experience.

What is functionalism? What are its basic beliefs? How do they differ from those of structuralism? Toward the end of the 19th century, an American psychologist adopted a broader view of psychology. William (51)_____ argued that there was a relationship between conscious experience and behavior, that the stream of consciousness is fluid and continuous and that (52)_____ could not be used to study this experience. (53)_____, another early school of psychology placed more emphasis on the way in which our experience allows us to function more adaptively. Whereas, (54)_____ would ask, "What pieces make up that experience?" the (55)_____ would ask, "What is the purpose of this behavior or mental process?"

What is behaviorism? What are its basic beliefs? How do they differ from those of structuralism and functionalism? Around the turn of the 20th century, Functionalism was the dominate view in psychology, however, John (56)_____ believed that if psychology was to be a natural science, it must limit it self to the study of (57)_____—observable, measurable events. This belief that psychology should not study mental processes or stream of consciousness, but that it should be the scientific study of behavior was known as (58)_____.

Although (59)_____ is considered the founder of behaviorism, he was not the only major contributor to behaviorism. Harvard University psychologist, B.F. (60)_____ was also a leading behaviorist. He believed that organisms learn to behave in certain ways because they have been (61)_____, or encouraged by the positive outcomes of their behavior. Both Watson and Skinner believed that behavior occurred because it was (62)_____.

What is Gestalt psychology? How do the beliefs of Gestalt psychology differ from behaviorism? Another school of psychology developed in Germany. This school of psychology argued that we cannot hope to understand human nature by focusing on overt behavior only, and was known as (63)_____ psychology. These psychologists focused on human (64)_____ and argued that the "(65)_____ was more then the sum of the parts". Gestalt psychologists demonstrated that much learning, especially in problem solving, is accomplished by (66)_____, not mechanical repetition.

Who is Sigmund Freud? What is psychoanalysis and what are the basic beliefs of psychodynamic psychology? Freud is the founder of the school of psychology known as (67)_____. This approach differs from all of the other schools in that it places emphasis on the role of the (68)_____ in our behavior. Freud was a (69)_____, not a psychologist. He was astounded as to how little insight his patients had into their motives. He argued that most of the (70)_____ is unconscious-a seething cauldron of conflicting (71)_____, urges, and wishes. Because of this belief in the notion of underlying forces, this theory is referred to as (72)_____ psychology.

Reflection Break # 3:
Key Figures in the History of Psychology: *Match the person with the description of their significance to psychology.*

a. Aristotle
b. B. F. Skinner
c. Gustav Fechner
d. Wilhelm Wundt
e. William James
f. Charles Darwin
g. John Watson
h. Socrates
i. Wertheimer, Koffka & Kohler
j. Sigmund Freud
k. Christine Ladd Franklin
l. Margaret Floy Washburn
m. Helen Bradford Thompson
n. Mary Whiton Calkins
o. Gilbert Haven Jones
p. J. Henry Alston
q. Robert Williams
r. Kenneth B. Clark
s. Stanley Sue
t. Jorge Sanchez

_____ 1. Author of *Peri Psyches*.
_____ 2. Greek philosopher who claimed that one could not attain reliable self-knowledge through our senses.
_____ 3. Founder of the structuralism school of thought.
_____ 4. Published his landmark book *Elements of Psychophysics* in 1860.
_____ 5. Chief proponent of functionalism; author of *The Principles of Psychology*.
_____ 6. Considered to be one of the first behaviorists, he had an affair with a student, which led him to resign from his post at John Hopkins and begin a career in advertising.
_____ 7. Leading proponents of Gestalt psychology.
_____ 8. A Harvard University professor; one the major contributors to behaviorism; believed that organisms learn to do things because they are reinforced.
_____ 9. A Viennese physician who is the founder of the Psychodynamic school of psychology; believed in the importance of the unconscious.
_____ 10. Originator of the idea of evolution; argued the principle of "survival of the fittest"; was a strong influence on William James.
_____ 11. Psychologist who is sometimes referred to as the "father of Ebonics".
_____ 12. First African American to receive his Ph.D. in psychology.
_____ 13. Psychologist whose research was cited when the U.S. Supreme Court overturned the "separate but equal" schools doctrine.
_____ 14. First African American psychologist to be published in a major psychology journal.
_____ 15. First female president of the American Psychological Association.
_____ 16. Early female psychologist, taught at Johns Hopkins and Colombia Universities and formulated a theory of color vision.
_____ 17. The first psychologist to study gender differences; she authored *The Mental Traits of Sex*.
_____ 18. First women to receive her Ph.D. in psychology; she wrote *The Animal Mind*.
_____ 19. He was among the first psychologists to show that intelligence tests are culturally biased—to the detriment of Mexican-American children.
_____ 20. A contemporary psychologist interested in discrimination and its connection to racial differences in intelligence and achievement.

Reading for Understanding on "Psychology Today"

What are the basic beliefs of the Biological, Evolutionary, Cognitive, Humanistic-Existential, Psychodynamic, Learning and Sociocultural Perspectives? How do each of these views differ? How are they the same? Today, psychology has many perspectives. These include: biological, evolutionary, cognitive, humanistic-existential, psychodynamic, learning, and sociocultural perspectives. Each approach has its own beliefs about behavior and mental processes. (73)_____ psychologists are psychologists that are especially interested in the role of evolution in behavior and mental processes. This type of psychologist suggests that most of human social behavior has a (74)_____ basis. Psychologists with a (75)_____ perspective believe that our thoughts and behavior are made possible by the nervous system and the activities in our body. This type of psychologist sees the links between events in the (76)_____ and behavior and mental processes. They are also concerned with the influence of (77)_____ and heredity.

7

Psychologists with a (78)_____ perspective investigate the ways in which we perceive and mentally represent a world. These types of psychologists, in short, study those things we refer to as the (79)_____. The humanistic-existential perspective is similar to the cognitive perspective. However, humanism stresses the human capacity for (80)_____ and the central roles of the consciousness, self-awareness, and decision-making. (81)_____ psychology considers personal or subjective experience to be the most important event in psychology. (82)_____ views people as free to choose and be responsible for choosing ethical conduct. In contrast to other theories, Freud's (83)_____ theory argues that the unconscious is more important in explaining behavior and mental processes. Contemporary psychologists who follow Freud are likely to call themselves (84)_____; Karen Horney and Eric Erickson are two of these.

Many psychologists today study the effects of (85)_____ on behavior. To them (86)_____ is the essential factor in describing, predicting, explaining, and controlling behavior. John Watson, a (87)_____, argued that people do things because of their learning histories, their situations, and the rewards; not because of their (88)_____ choice. Watson and other behaviorists emphasize environmental influences and the learning of habits through repetition and (89)_____. Learning theorists that suggest that people can modify or even create their environments are known as (90)_____ theorists. They note that people engage in intentional learning by (91)_____ others.
The psychological perspective that focuses on the many ways in which people differ from one another by studying the influences of ethnicity, gender, culture, and socioeconomic status is known as the (92)_____ perspective. This type of psychologist may examine the effects of cultural heritage, race and language of various (93)_____ groups on their behavior.

Reflection Break # 4:
Psychology Today: *Identify the current perspective from the descriptions.*

_____1. Someone who might look at the relationship between an individual's cultural heritage and the frequency of specific psychological disorders.

_____2. A psychologist who might argue that the reason that males may exhibit more aggressive behavior is due to their hormonal make-up.

_____3. A psychologist who would focus on how we mentally represent the world to explain behaviors.

_____4. A psychologist who would tend to attribute dreams to unconscious processes.

_____5. A psychologist who might argue that your behavior is the result of your freedom to make choices in life.

_____6. A psychologist who argues that children who are shy and withdrawn engage in this behavior because of environmental influences and reinforcement.

Reading for Understanding about "How Psychologists Study Behavior and Mental Processes"
Is psychology a science? What is the scientific method? How is it used in psychology?
Sir Francis Galton's fascination with (94)_____ led to many positive innovations in the field of psychology, such as the use of questionnaires and twin studies. Galton invented the use of the (95)_____ method, a mathematical way to examine the relationship between variables.

Modern psychology is an (96)_____ science. This means that assumptions about the behavior of people must be supported by (97)_____. In science, strong (98)_____, reference to authority figures, or tightly knitted theories are not considered to be (99)_____ scientific evidence.

Psychologists are scientists because they use the (100)_____ method to solve problems. The scientific method is an organized way of using experience and (101)_____ of ideas to expand knowledge. Research psychologists begin by formulating a research (102)_____. These can come from anywhere: daily experiences, common knowledge, or psychological (103)_____. A research question is often reworded as (104)_____, or a specific statement about behavior and mental processes that can be tested. After formulating the hypothesis, the researcher would then (105)_____ the hypothesis through controlled methodology. Once the research tests are concluded the psychologist will draw a (106)_____ on the accuracy of their hypothesis based on the findings of the test. Research psychologists are guided by the principles of (107)_____ thinking; they are (108)_____, they examine all possible explanations for a behavior. For example, they try not to confuse (109)_____ between findings with cause and effect. Once their research is completed, researchers are obligated to (110)_____, or repeat their study to see if the findings will hold up over time. Finally, many researchers will (111)_____ their findings in professional journals to allow the whole scientific community to evaluate the methods and conclusions of their research.

How do Psychologists use samples to reach conclusions about people in general? Psychologists use a (112)_____, or a segment of the targeted group, to represent the (113)_____, or targeted group, when conducting psychological research. They must be drawn so that they accurately (114)_____ the population they are intended to reflect. Only the use of a representative sample allows us to (115)_____, or extend our findings. Too often psychologists may have problems in obtaining a (116)_____ sample. Much early research in psychology relied on samples that were exclusively (117)_____, and they under represented members of ethnic (118)_____ groups. This presents a problem in (119)_____ early findings to women and ethnic minorities.

One method used by researchers to try to obtain a representative sample is to use (120)_____ sampling, so that each member of the population has an equal chance of being selected to participate. Another sampling method is to use a (121)_____ sample in which identified groups in the population are represented proportionately. Often haphazardly drawn samples, like those taken by magazines, may show a (122)_____ bias, where the people who willingly participate in the study may be systematically different from those who did not. Obviously, (123)_____ is an important concern for psychologists.

What three methods do psychologists use to observe subjects? How are case studies, survey and naturalistic observation different? Unscientific accounts of people's behavior are referred to as (124)_____. Scientists have devised controlled methods of (125)_____ others. (126)_____ studies, or information we collect about individuals and small groups, are often used to investigate rare occurrences. Although they can provide compelling portraits of individuals, case studies often have many sources of (127)_____. For example, people may

(128)_____ or misrepresent their pasts, interviewers may have (129)_____ and encourage subjects to fill in gaps with information that is consistent with them. Psychologists use questionnaires and interviews to conduct (130)_____. This method of observing subjects has the advantage of allowing psychologists to study (131)_____ of people at one time. Survey research, however, also has its problems. People may recall their behavior inaccurately or purposely (132)_____ themselves. Some people try to ingratiate themselves to their interviewer by answering in what they perceive to be a more (133)_____ desirable response; others may (134)_____ attitudes and exaggerate problems to draw attention to themselves. When psychologists observe subjects in their natural environment they are said to have used (135)_____. This approach has the advantage of allowing psychologists to (136)_____ behavior as it happens. Researchers conducting naturalistic observation use methods that try to avoid interfering with the behaviors they are observing; they try to be (137)_____.

What is a correlation? What type of question would psychologists ask in correlational studies? What are the limitations of correlation research? Questions that address therapeutic relationships between variables are answered using the (138)_____ method. A number called the correlation (139)_____ is used to indicate the direction and size of the correlation between the variables. The numerical value of the correlation may vary between −1.00 and (140)_____. When variables are (141)_____ correlated, one variable increases as the other variable increases; when variables are (142)_____ correlated, as one variable increases the other variable decreases. The most significant limitation of correlational research is that it does not prove cause and (143)_____.

What is an experiment? What type of research questions would a psychologist ask in an experimental study? The best research method for answering cause and effect questions is considered to be an (144)_____. In this method a group of subjects receives a (145)_____, such as a medication, or drug. The subjects are then carefully (146)_____ to determine whether the treatment makes a difference in their behavior. Experiments are used because they allow psychologists to (147)_____ the experiences of subjects and allow the experimenter to draw conclusions about (148)_____ and effect.

What are independent and dependent variables? What is a placebo? How do psychologists use blind and double blind experiments? In an experiment, the researcher manipulates the (149)_____ variable so that its effect may be determined. The measured results, or outcomes in the experiment, are called (150)_____ variables. It is believed that the appearance of the (151)_____ variable depends on the (152)_____ variable. In most experimental studies there are at least two groups of subjects. Subjects in the (153)_____ group receive the treatment whereas subjects in the (154)_____ group do not. In good experiments every effort is made to ensure that all other (155)_____ are kept constant for subjects in both groups. In this way researchers have confidence that the differences between the control and experimental groups is not due to (156)_____.

Sometimes in experiments it is unclear whether the results of the study are due to the subjects (157)_____ about the effects of the independent variable. Therefore, it is sometimes important for the subjects to be (158)_____ the treatment they have received. This is accomplished through the use of a (159)_____, or a "sugar pill." Studies in which the subjects are unaware of the treatment they have obtained are known as (160)_____ studies. Studies in which both subjects and experimenters are unaware of who was obtained the treatment are called (161)_____ studies.

Reflection Break # 5:

Briefly list and describe the basic principles (procedures) of the scientific method followed by psychologists.

*

*

*

*

*

Reading for Understanding on "Ethical Issues in Psychological Research and Practice"
What ethical issues are psychologists concerned with when researching on human subjects? How do psychologists assure that they are not violating any of these ethical issues in research?
Psychologists adhere to a number of ethical standards that are intended to promote individual (162)_____, human welfare, and scientific (163)_____. These standards are also intended to ensure that psychologists do not undertake research methods or treatments that are (164)_____. In almost all institutional settings (165)_____ committees help researchers consider the potential harm of their methods and review proposed studies according to (166)_____ guidelines. In order to avoid harming subjects, when psychologists conduct research with human subjects, the subjects must give (167)_____ consent before they participate in research programs. Additionally psychologists treat the records of research subjects and clients as (168)_____. Psychologists do this because they respect people's (169)_____ and because people are more likely to express their true thoughts and feelings when researchers or therapists keep their disclosures private. Ethical guidelines also limit the type of research that psychologists may conduct. Many experiments like the Milgram study cannot be run without (170)_____ subjects. Psychological ethics require that subjects who are deceived be (171)_____ afterward to help eliminate misconceptions and anxieties about the research.

What ethical issues are psychologists concerned with when researching on animal subjects?
Psychologists and other scientists frequently turn to (172)_____ to conduct harmful or potentially harmful research that cannot be carried out on humans. Although the studies are carried out with animals, psychologists still face the (173)_____ dilemma of subjecting study participants to harm. As with people, psychologists follow the principal that animals should be subjected to (174)_____ only when there is no alternative and they believe that the benefits of the research will justify the harm.

Reading for Understanding about "Life Connections: Critical Thinking, Science and Pseudoscience"

What is Critical thinking and why is it important for psychologists? Psychologists are (175)_____ and as such they use critical thinking when examining problems. Critical thinking means having a (176)_____ attitude. This means taking nothing for granted. Critical Thinking refers to a process of thoughtfully (177)_____ and probing the arguments of others. Critical thinkers examine (178)_____ of terms, they examine the (179)_____, or premises of arguments, and they are (180)_____ in drawing conclusions. Critical thinkers consider (181)_____ interpretations of research evidence and are careful not to (182)_____ or overgeneralize.

Psychologists rely on (183)_____ before they will accept any claims or arguments about what is true. Psychologists apply critical thinking when examining the claims of (184)_____, or false sciences. (185)_____, or the claim that you are able to predict someone's personality based on the positions and movements of stars and planets is one such area that psychologists approach with skepticism. Since psychology is an (186)_____ science, it's beliefs about behavior must be supported by evidence; persuasive arguments and reference to (187)_____ figures are NOT considered scientific evidence.

Reflection Break # 6:

1. What does your textbook author mean when he says that critical thinkers are "skeptical"? Think about some questions that you might ask if you were using a skeptical approach and share them with your study group

---

REVIEW: Key Terms and Concepts

Psychology	4	associationism	8	Sociocultural perspective	16
theories	4	introspection	8	ethnic group	16
pure research	5	structuralism	9	gender	17
applied research	5	Elements of Psychophysics	9	correlational method	20
clinical psychologist	5	The Principles of Psychology	9	scientific method	20
counseling psychologist	5	Functionalism	10	hypothesis	21
school psychologists	6	behaviorism	10	selection factor	21
educational psychologists	6	reinforced	11	replicate	21
developmental psychologist	6	Gestalt psychology	11	generalize	22
personality psychologists	6	insight	12	sample	22
social psychologists	6	psychoanalysis	12	population	22
experimental psychologist	6	psychodynamic	13	random sampling	22
industrial psychologist	6	genes	14	stratified sample	22
organizational psychologist	6	biological perspective	14	volunteer bias	23
human factors psychologists	6	evolutionary perspective	14	case studies	23
consumer psychologists	7	cognitive perspective	14	survey	24
health psychologists	7	humanism	15	Naturalistic observation	24
sports psychologists	7	existentialism	15	correlation coefficient	24
Peri Psyches	8	neoanalysts	15	positive correlation	25
empiricism	8	social cognitive theory	16	negative correlation	25

FINAL CHAPTER REVIEW

Recite:

Visit the Recite section on pages 34-37 of your textbook. Use the card provided with your textbook to cover the answers of the Recite section. Read the questions aloud and recite the answers.

Multiple Choice Questions

1. Which of the following statements BEST defines Psychology today?
   a. The empirical study of the behavior of the unconscious mind.
   b. The scientific treatment of social deviants.
   c. The scientific study of behavior and mental processes.
   d. The empirical study of behavior.

2. When a psychologist conducts research into a problem with no immediate application to personal or social problems, the researcher is conducting_____ research.
   a. applied
   b. pure
   c. case study
   d. experimental

3. Professor Smith is interested in characterizing the attitudes of the graduating class of 2003 towards premarital sex. Which goal of psychology is professor Smith's research addressing?
   a. explanation
   b. control
   c. description
   d. prediction

4. Shonda helps people with psychological disorders adjust to the demands of life. She is most likely a(n) _____ psychologist.
   a. industrial/organizational
   b. clinical
   c. educational
   d. health

5. _____ psychologists work to assist students who have problems that interfere with learning, whereas _____ psychologists focus on course planning and development of instructional methods.
   a. Developmental, School
   b. Educational, Developmental
   c. School, Educational
   d. Educational, School

6. Bill is a psychologist who works in the aerospace industry designing cockpit instrument panels. Bill is a
   a. consumer psychologist.
   b. engineering psychologist.
   c. industrial psychologist.
   d. human factors psychologist.

7. *Peri Psyches*, which translates as "about the Psyche," is an ancient work that began with a history of psychological thought and included historical perspectives on the nature of the mind and was written by
   a. Socrates
   b. Aristotle
   c. Plato
   d. Fechner

8. This women psychologist completed all of the requirements for the Ph.D at Harvard University, but was denied a Harvard degree because of a ban on admitting women. Even without a degree, she went on to become a pioneer in memory research and became the first female president of the American Psychological Association. This description best describes the life and career of
   a. Christine Ladd-Franklin.
   b. Margaret Floy Washburn.
   c. Mary Whiton Calkins.
   d. Helen Bradford Thompson.

9. In a discussion with a friend about what the focus of psychological study should be you argue that psychology should attempt to break conscious experience down into objective sensations such as sight and taste and subjective feelings. This view most closely resembles which of the following historical schools of psychology?
   a. functionalism
   b. gestalt
   c. structuralism
   d. humanism

10. Which of the following pairs are NOT correctly matched?
    a. Wundt—Structuralism
    b. Watson—Behaviorism
    c. James—Gestalt
    d. Skinner—Behaviorism

11. Gestalt psychology is to patterns as psychoanalysis is to
    a. learning.
    b. sensation.
    c. unconscious processes.
    d. genetics.

12. Your psychology professor suggests that species tend to evolve in adaptive direction and that human behavior has a hereditary basis. Which perspective in psychology is he likely to be a proponent of?
    a. biological
    b. behavioral
    c. evolutionary
    d. cognitive

13. Psychologists who ascribe to a(n) _____ perspective investigate ways in which we perceive and mentally represent the world, whereas those how ascribe to a _____ perspective tend to attribute desires and unusual ideas to unconscious process.
    a. cognitive, psychoanalytic
    b. behavioral psychoanalytic
    c. biological, cognitive
    d. evolutionary, behavioral

14. Dr. Johnson is conducting research into bilingual education. She believes that bilingual education will benefit the intellectual development of children and designs a research study to test this statement. The statement that bilingual education will benefit the intellectual development of children is her
    a. selection factor.
    b. independent variable.
    c. dependent variable.
    d. hypothesis.

15. When researchers conduct scientific research, the people that are studied are referred to as a _____ and the group that is targeted by the study is referred to as the _____.
    a. population, sample
    b. selection factor, population
    c. case study, selection factor
    d. sample, population

16. Last weekend when you were at the local shopping mall a woman approached you and asked you to answer a few questions about your preferences in brands of coffee. This researcher was using the _____ method.
    a. correlational
    b. survey
    c. experimental
    d. naturalistic observational

17. Professor Rogers is interested in measuring the relationship between her use of humor in her lectures and her students' understanding of math concepts. Which research method would she be most likely to use?
    a. case study
    b. experiment
    c. random sampling
    d. correlation

18. Dr. Jones is interested in determining whether a specific brand of face cream causes acne pimples to shrink. He conducts an experiment in which he gives one group of patients the new cream and a second group an inert cream. The independent variable in the study is
    a. whether the pimples shrink.
    b. the type of cream the subjects get.
    c. the number of new pimples the subjects have.
    d. the age of the subjects.

19. Dr. Jones is interested in determining whether a specific brand of face cream causes acne pimples to shrink. He conducts an experiment in which he gives on group of patients the new cream and a second group an inert cream. The dependent variable in the study is
    a. whether the pimples shrink.
    b. the type of cream the subjects get.
    c. the number of new pimples the subjects have.
    d. the age of the subjects.

20. When the subjects and the researchers in a psychological experiment are unaware of who obtained treatment, the study is said to be
    a. blind.
    b. random.
    c. a stratified sample.
    d. double-blind.

Essay Questions:
1. Imagine that you are the president of a large corporation that designs and manufactures different cosmetic products. Describe three types of psychologists you would hire to work in your company. What would a typical day at work for each of them consist of and why would having them on staff benefit your company?

2. Compare how each of the current perspectives of psychology would view the same problem. Provide an example of a question, or a claim that each perspective would make about the problem.

3. Pretend that you are in a discussion with friends and the topic is what is a science. It is argued that psychology is not a true science like chemistry and physics. How would you defend the proposition that psychology is it true science?

4. You are researcher interested in and whether students enrolled introduction college courses learn more about the subject than students enrolled a self-study study course. Design an experiment that will examine this question. Be sure to identify your independent and dependent variables. Who will be your control group and who will be your treatment group? Discuss how you will measure your dependent variable and the procedures you will use to conduct the experiment.

5. Explain the difference between correlational and experimental research studies. Be sure to explain how each type of study is conducted and what type of conclusions can be drawn from each. What are the limitations of each type of study?

CONNECT & EXPAND:

1. **Careers in Psychology:** Search the following Internet resources for information about an area of specialization in psychology, for example clinical work or experimental psychology. Write a summary of the information included. Information such as degree requirements necessary, any skills necessary for that specialization, and any other important information should be provided. (*Your instructor will provide specific requirements such as length, and formatting. Be sure to include the URL or web address of the source for your information.*)
   - ❖ American Psychological Association   http://www.apa.org
   - ❖ *American Psychological Society* http://www.psychologyscience.org/about.htm
   - ❖ *Frank Fullerton's web site*   http://www.wiu.edu/users/mffef
   - ❖ *Marky Lloyd's Careers in Psychology*
           http://www.psychwww.com/careers/index.htm
   - ❖ *Indiana State's Careers in psychology*   http://web.indstate.edu/psych/toc.htm

2. **History of Psychology:** Visit the following web site on the history of psychology: http://www.cwu.edu/~warren/today.html
   Pick three dates and note any important events that occurred on that day. Share your results with three or four of your classmates and compile a master list of dates and important events in the history of psychology. Present this information to the rest of the class in a visual format.

3. **APA and APS:** Visit the websites of the two professional psychological associations. Explain for the class what the acronyms APA and APS stand for. What are the goals of each association? How are they the same and how do they differ? When were they each founded and how many members does each association currently have?

4. **Scientific Journals in Psychology:** Visit Psychweb at http://www.psywww.com/journals and get an idea of the variety of journals available in psychology. Visit the home page for four different journals. Answer the following questions:
           What kind of articles does the journal publish?
           How often is the journal published?

Who is the journal's target audience?

What is the journal's goal?

Share your results with your classmates in a format specified by your instructor.

5. **Reading and Identifying Scientific Research in Psychology:** Locate one of the following published scientific research studies (or find one of your own) and read the study for an understanding of the scientific methods used.

   As you read the study answer the following questions:
   1. What topical area of psychology is represented by the study?
   2. What is the target population of the study?
   3. What are the characteristics of the sample? (For example, number of subjects, demographics, etc.)
   4. What type of research is this study? (Experimental, correlational, case study, survey)
   5. If the study is an experimental study, what are the independent and dependent variables? The control and treatment groups?
   6. Describe the procedures used to observe the subjects?
   7. What does the author conclude is the outcome of the study?

Suggested articles:

   Milgram, S. (1963). Behavioral study of obedience. Journal of Abnormal and Social Psychology, 67, 371-378.

   Milgram, S. (1964). Group pressure and action against a person. Journal of Abnormal and Social Psychology, 69, 137-143.

   Steele, K., Bass, K. & Crook, M. (1999). The mystery of the Mozart effect: Failure to replicate. Psychological Science, 10, 366-369.

   Vasta, R., Rosenberg, D., Knott, J.A. & Gaze, C.E. (1997). Experience and the water-level task revisited: Does experience exact a price? Psychological Science, 8, 336-339.

6. *Life Connections:* **Critical Thinking, Science and Pseudoscience:** Try critically thinking about current issues in psychology yourself. Find an article from a recent issue of *Psychology Today* (Psychology Today is available on line at http://www.psychologytoday.com)

   Pick a feature article and read it using the perspective of a skeptical, or critical thinker. Evaluate the claim made in the article from the viewpoint of a critical thinker using the following series of questions. Present this information to your classmates in the format specified by your instructor.
   a. What is the claim being made by the author?
   b. What evidence does the author use to support the claim?
      Does the author use empirical research?
      Does the author use reference to authority opinion?
   c. Does the author oversimplify or overgeneralize in making their argument?
   d. Is there enough good evidence to support the argument's claim?
   e. Should a critical thinker "buy" the claim being made by the author?

Chapter Two: Biology and Behavior

PowerPreview: *Skim the major headings in this chapter in your textbook. Jot down anything that you are surprised or curious about. After this write down four or five questions that you have about the material in this chapter.*

Things that surprised me/I am curious about from Chapter 2:

Questions that I have about Biology and Behavior:

-
-
-
-

QUESTION: *These are some questions that you should be able to answer after you finish studying this chapter:*

Evolution and Evolutionary Psychology: "Survivor" Is More Than Just a Game
- ❖ *Who was Charles Darwin? What did he do?*
- ❖ *What are the basic beliefs of the theory of evolution?*
- ❖ *What is Evolutionary Psychology?*
- ❖ *What is meant by the concept "instinct"?*

Heredity: The Nature of Nature
- ❖ *What is meant by the concept of heredity? What is meant by the concepts "genetics," "behavioral genetics," and "molecular genetics"?*
- ❖ *What are the roles of genes and chromosomes in heredity?*
- ❖ *What are kinship studies and how do they help psychologists study the role of heredity in behavior?*
- ❖ *What is selective breeding?*

The Nervous System: On Being Wired
- ❖ *What are neurons?*
- ❖ *What are Neural Impulses? What happens when a neuron fires?*
- ❖ *What is a synapse?*
- ❖ *Which neurotransmitters are of interest to psychologists? What do they do?*
- ❖ *What are the parts of the nervous system?*
- ❖ *What are the divisions and functions of the peripheral nervous system?*
- ❖ *What are the divisions and functions of the central nervous system?*

The Brain: The Star of the Human Nervous System
- ❖ *How do researchers learn about the functions of the brain and nervous system?*
- ❖ *What are the structures and functions of the brain?*

- *What are the parts of the cerebral cortex? What parts of the cerebral cortex are involved in thinking and language?*
- *What does it mean to be "right-brained" or "left-brained"? Does it matter if one is left or right handed? Why are people right-handed or left-handed?*
- *What happens when the brain is split in two?*

The Endocrine System: Chemicals in the Blood
- *What is the endocrine system?*

Life Connections: "Raging Hormones" ("More Please?")
- *PMS, Manopause, Menopause, Andropause and Viropause what are they and how do they effect our behaviors?*

Reading for Understanding/Reflect: *The following section provides you with the opportunity to perform 3 of the R's of the PQ4R study method. In this section I will encourage you to check your understanding of your reading of the text by filling in the blanks in the brief paragraphs that relate to each of the preview questions. You will also be prompted to rehearse your understanding of the material with periodic Rehearsal/Reflection breaks. Remember it is better to study in more frequent, short session then in one long "cram session." Be sure to reward yourself with short study breaks before each of the Rehearsal/Reflection exercises.*

Reading for Understanding on "Evolution and Evolutionary Psychology"
Who was Charles Darwin? What did he do? A cousin of Sir Francis (1)_____, Darwin enjoyed collecting and (2)_____plants, minerals and animals. After graduating from (3)_____ University he undertook a five-year volunteer position aboard the HMS (4)_____. When the ship stopped in the (5)_____ Islands he observed how plants and animals varied from island to island. These observations convinced him that although the organisms shared common ancestors, they had (6)_____ into different organisms. Darwin originally did not want his ideas published until after his death because he feared the (7)_____they would bring to his family. However in 1859 when he heard that Alfred Russel (8)_____was about to present similar ideas, he presented and published his *"On the Origin of Species by Natural Selection"* and in 1871 he published *"The Descent of Man"* in which he made the case that (9)_____, like other species were a product of evolution.

What are the basic beliefs of the theory of evolution? According to Darwin's theory of (10)_____, there is a struggle for survival as various species and individuals compete for the same territories. There are small random genetic variations called (11)_____ that lead to differences in physical traits. Species that are (12)_____ manage to survive, or are naturally selected; their numbers (13)_____ and they transmit their traits to future generations. Species that do not adapt dwindle in numbers and may eventually become (14)_____.

What is Evolutionary Psychology? What is meant by the concept "instinct"? Evolutionary psychology is the field of psychology that studies ways in which (15)_____ and (16)_____ are connected with mental processes and behavior. One of the key concepts of evolutionary psychology is that not only are physical traits genetically transmitted, so are patterns of (17)_____, like aggression and strategies of mate selection. These behavior-patterns are termed (18)_____, or species-specific, because they evolve within certain species. An (19)_____ is a stereotyped pattern of behavior that is triggered in a specific situation and tends to resist modification.

Reflection Break # 1:
Evolution and Evolutionary Psychology

- In 2-3 sentences summarize the basic tenets of Darwin's Theory of evolution.

Reading for Understanding on "Heredity: The Nature of Nature"
What is meant by the concept of heredity? What is meant by the concepts "genetics," "behavioral genetics", and "molecular genetics"? Heredity is the transmission of traits from generation to generation by means of (20)_____ and chromosomes. (21)_____ is involved in almost all human traits and behavior. Behavioral genetics bridges the sciences of (22)_____ and biology and is concerned with the genetic transmission of traits that give rise to patterns of (23)_____. The field of (24)_____ looks at both species-specific behavior patterns and individual differences among the members of a species. One answer may be found in an individual's genetic code. (25)_____ genetics attempts to identify specific genes that are connected with behavior and mental processes.

What are the roles of genes and chromosomes in heredity? (26)_____, which consist of DNA, are the building blocks of heredity. A thousand or more genes make up each (27)_____. Each cell in the body contains (28)_____ chromosomes, arranged in 23 (29)_____. The sequence of the (30)_____ in the DNA molecule is the genetic code that will cause the organism to develop. Behavioral geneticists are attempting to sort out the relative importance of (31)_____, or heredity, and (32)_____, or environmental influences on the origins of behavior.

What are kinship studies? The more closely people are related the more (33)_____ they have in common. If genes are involved in a trait or behavior, then people who are closely related are (34)_____ likely to show similar traits or behavior. (35)_____ studies are studies of the distribution of traits, or behavior patterns, among related people. Examples of kinship studies are (36)_____ studies and (37)_____ studies. In twin studies, the presence of traits and behavior patterns are compared in monozygotic, or (38)_____, and dizygotic, or (39)_____, twins. When identical twins, or close blood relatives share certain behaviors, it is suggested that the behavior may have a (40)_____ component. This is especially true when the behavior is shared by close blood relatives are raised in different (41)_____ from an early age.

What is selective breeding? Under (42)_____ selection, traits that enable organisms to adapt to their environment are likely to be preserved, in selective (43)_____ we breed plants and animals to enhance desired physical and behavioral traits.

Reflection Break # 2:
Heredity: The Nature of Nature
1. Briefly explain what is meant by heredity and how genetics can play a role in behavior.

2. Explain how kinship studies like twin and family studies can help researchers answer questions on the role of biological versus environmental influences on behavior. Be sure to discuss both the advantages and disadvantages of this type of research.

Reading for Understanding on "The Nervous System: On Being Wired"

What are neurons? What kinds of neurons are found in the human body? What is their role in human behavior? Neurons are (44)_____ that have branches, trunks and roots. Neurons lie end to end and (45)_____ messages from a number of sources such as light, other (46)_____ and pressure on the skin. They can also pass along messages. Neurons communicate by releasing chemicals called (47)_____ which are taken up by other neurons, muscles and glands. Neurotransmitters cause (48)_____ changes in the receiving neuron so that the messages, or neural (49)_____ can travel along the "trunk" of the neuron.

The nervous system also contains (50)_____ cells that remove dead neurons and waste products from the nervous system. Glial cells also (51)_____ and (52)_____ neurons and direct their growth. (53)_____, however, are the most important cells in the nervous system. They vary as to their function and location, but all contain (54)_____, or short fibers that extend like roots from the cell body to receive incoming messages, and an (55)_____, the trunk that extends from the cell body. Neuronal axons end in small bulb like structures named (56)_____.

Neurons carry messages in (57)_____ direction. Within a neuron, the information flows from the (58)_____, through the (59)_____ to the (60)_____. Neuronal axons are wrapped tightly with a white, fatty substance called (61)_____, that insulates the axon from the electrically charged atoms found in the fluids that surround the nervous system. Myelin is part of the maturation process and minimizes the leakage of the (62)_____ current being carried along the axon, thus allowing the messages to be carried more (63)_____. Neurons that transmit the sensory information from the body to the nervous system are known as (64)_____ neurons and (65)_____ neurons send messages back to the muscles and sensory organs.

What are Neural Impulses? What happens when a neuron fires? Luigi Galvani demonstrated that neural messages are (66)_____ in nature. This process involves (67)_____ changes that cause an electrical charge to be transmitted along the lengths of neuronal axons. This electrical charge results from a process that allows positively charged (68)_____ to enter the cell. The entry of these (69)_____ charged ions into the cell cause the cell to become (70)_____ with respect to the outside. Once the cell is depolarized, the positively charged ions are (71)_____ out of the cell and the cell returns to its negative (72)_____ potential. Most neurons have a (73)_____ potential of –70 millivolts and an (74)_____ potential of +40 millivolts, thus it takes approximately 110 millivolts of charge to create an all-or-none neural message that will travel the length of the axon. This explains the "(75)_____" portion of neural communication, but this is not the whole story. Neural messages also travel via chemical messengers called (76)_____.

The conduction of the electrical neural messages is what is being referred to when biological psychologists say a neuron has "(77)_____." Once a neuron fires and its electrical impulse travels to the end of the axon it releases (78)_____. In accordance with the (79)_____ principle each time a neuron fires it transmits an impulse of the same strength. Thus neurons will fire more frequently when they have been stimulated by a (80)_____ number of neurons. Also, for a brief period of time, a few (81)_____ of a second, after the neuron fires it is insensitive to messages from other neurons. This is known as the (82)_____ period.

What is a synapse? Neurons relay their messages across junctions known as (83)_____, they consist of an axon terminal from the (84)_____ neuron; a (85)_____ from the receiving neuron and a fluid filled gap called the (86)_____. Although the neuronal impulse is (87)_____ it does not jump the synaptic cleft; instead the axon terminals release (88)_____ into it.

Which neurotransmitters are of interest to psychologists? What do they do? Neurotransmitters are the chemical keys to neural communication; they are released from the (89)_____ into the synaptic cleft and from there they influence the receiving neuron. Dozens of neurotransmitters have been identified; each has it own (90)_____ structure and can fit into a specific (91)_____ on the receiving cell. Unused neurotransmitters are either broken down or reabsorbed by the axon terminal in a process known as (92)_____.

Some neurotransmitters act to (93)_____, or cause other neurons to fire; others act to (94)_____, or keep other receiving neurons from firing. Neurotransmitters have been shown to be involved in all kinds of processes from muscle (95)_____ to thoughts and (96)_____. Excesses or (97)_____ of neurotransmitters have also been linked to psychological disorders such as (98)_____ and schizophrenia. Some neurotransmitters of interest to psychologists include: (99)_____, which controls muscle contractions; dopamine, which has been shown to be involved in voluntary movements, (100)_____ and memory and (101)_____ arousal and has been linked to schizophrenia and (102)_____ disease; (103)_____, produced largely in the brain stem and acts as both a neurotransmitter and a hormone it is believed to be involved in general arousal, learning, memory and eating; serotonin, primarily an (104)_____ neurotransmitter, deficiencies have been linked to (105)_____ disorders, alcoholism, (106)_____, aggression and insomnia; and the (107)_____, which occur naturally in the brain, may increase our sense of competence, enhance the functioning of the immune system and have been linked to the pleasurable "runner's high" reported by long distance runners.

What is the nervous system? The nervous system is a bundle of (108)_____ and (109)_____; it is the system that regulates the body and is involved in (110)_____ processes, (111)_____ responses, heartbeat control, and visual-motor coordination and so on. The nervous system consists of the (112)_____, spinal cord and the (113)_____ linking them to the sensory organs, muscles and glands. The nervous system is divided into two major divisions. The brain and (114)_____ cord make up the (115)_____ nervous system; while the (116)_____ (afferent) and motor ((117)_____) neurons make up the (118)_____ nervous system.

What are the divisions and functions of the peripheral nervous system? The (119)_____ nervous system allows us to receive information from the outside world. The peripheral nervous system consists of two main divisions: (120)_____ and (121)_____. The somatic nervous system contains (122)_____ (afferent) and (123)_____ (efferent) neurons and transmits messages about skeletal muscles, (124)_____, and joints to the (125)_____ nervous system. It also controls (126)_____ muscular activity. The (127)_____ nervous system (ANS) regulates the glands and activities such as heartbeat, (128)_____, and dilation of the pupils. The ANS also has two branches. The (129)_____ division helps the body expend the body's resources from stored resources during a fight or flight response to a predator. The (130)_____ branch or division of the autonomic nervous system has the opposite effect from that of the (131)_____, it helps the body (132)_____ the body's reserves of energy.

What are the divisions and functions of the central nervous system? Your (133)_____ nervous system (CNS) enables you to use symbols and language and to adapt to and create new environments. The CNS consists of the (134)_____ cord and the (135)_____. The spinal cord is a true "information superhighway," it consists of a column of (136)_____ that transmit messages from sensory (137)_____ to the brain and from the brain to muscles and (138)_____ throughout the body. Spinal (139)_____ are unlearned responses to stimuli that involve only two neurons. Spinal reflexes do not involve the (140)_____.

The brain and spinal cord both contain (141)_____ matter, which is composed of short, nonmyelinated neurons and (142)_____ matter, which contains bundles of longer, myelinated axons.

Reflection Break # 3:
"The Nervous System: On Being Wired"
I. Neurons: Into the Fabulous Forest: *Label neuronal diagram*:

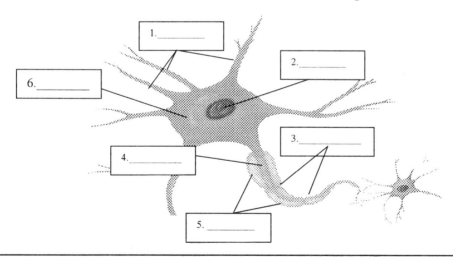

II. Neurotransmitters: The Chemical Keys to Communication: *Name the neurotransmitter from a description of its actions.*

_____1.   Neurotransmitter that causes muscle contractions and is involved in the formation of memories.

_____2.   These neurotransmitters work to inhibit pain by blocking pain causing chemicals out of their receptor sites.

_____ 3. Neurotransmitter involved in muscle contraction, learning and memory, and emotional response.

_____ 4. Neurotransmitter that accelerates the heart rate, affects eating and has been linked with activity levels, learning and remembering.

_____ 5. Neurotransmitter involved in psychological problems including obesity, depression and insomnia, alcoholism and aggression.

_____ 6. Imbalances of this neurotransmitter are linked with mood disorders such as depression and bipolar disorder.

_____ 7. Neurotransmitter found at synapses between motor neurons and muscles; deficiencies of this neurotransmitter have been linked with Alzheimer's disease.

_____ 8. Drugs that block the re-uptake of this neurotransmitter are helpful in the treatment of depression.

_____ 9. Low levels of this neurotransmitter have been linked to the tremors of Parkinson's disease.

III. The Parts of the Nervous System: *Fill in the blanks in the nervous system organizational chart.*

Nervous System

1. _____ Nervous System	2. _____ Nervous System

| 3. _____ | 4. _____ | 5. _____ Nervous System | 6. _____ Nervous System |

| 7. _____ Nervous System | 8. _____ Nervous System |

Reading for Understanding on "The Brain: The Star of the Human Nervous System"
How do researchers learn about the functions of the brain and nervous system? Historically researchers have learned about the brain by studying the effects of (143)_____, but they provide uncontrolled opportunities. The cases of Phineas (144)_____ and Leborgne are two examples of how scientists have learned about the functions of the brain as a result of an accidental damage.

Scientists have also used experimental methods like purposeful (145)_____ to the brain, electrical (146)_____ of certain brain structures and brain (147)_____. When scientists purposely damage a specific section of the brain they are said to create a (148)_____. Studies have shown that lesions of a monkey's (149)_____ create a rage response, while lesions of a rat's hypothalamus leads them to stop (150)_____. Surgeon Wilder (151)_____ used electrical stimulation rather then lesions to study the brain. Researchers have also used the (152)_____ (EEG) to record the natural electrical activity of the brain. The EEG has been used to locate the areas of the (153)_____ that respond to certain stimuli and to diagnose types of abnormal behavior and to help locate (154)_____.

In recent years new technology has allowed scientists to use the (155)_____ to generate images of the brain from different sources of radiation; these methods include the (156)_____, or CAT, the (157)_____, or PET and the (158)_____, or MRI. The CAT scan passes a narrow (159)_____ beam through the head and measures the structures that reflect the x-rays from various angles generating a (160)_____-dimensional image of the brain. The PET scan forms computer based images of parts of the brain by tracing the amount of (161)_____ used and has been used by researchers to see which parts of the brain are most (162)_____ during various activities. The MRI uses a powerful (163)_____ field, and (164)_____ waves that cause parts of the brain to emit signals that are measured from various angles.

What are the structures and functions of the brain? The (165)_____, where the spinal cord rises to meet the brain, consists of three major structures: the (166)_____, which regulates the heart rate, blood pressure and respiration; the (167)_____, which is involved in movement, attention and respiration; and the (168)_____, which is involved in balance and coordination. Also beginning in the hindbrain and ascending through the midbrain into the lower portion of the forebrain is the (169)_____ system that is vital to the functions of attentions, sleep and arousal.

The important structures of the forebrain include: the (170)_____, which serves as a relay station for sensory stimulation; the (171)_____, which regulates body temperature and various aspects of motivation and emotion, as well as eating and drinking behaviors; the limbic system which is involved in memory, (172)_____ and motivation and the (173)_____ which is the brain's center of thinking and language.

The limbic system of the brain is made up of several structures, including the (174)_____, which studies have shown is involved in aggressive behavior, vigilance and learning and memory; the (175)_____, which has been shown to be involved in memory.

What are the parts of the cerebral cortex? What parts of the cerebral cortex are involved in thinking and language? The (176)_____, or cerebral cortex, is the crowning glory of the brain; it is responsible for the (177)_____ abilities of thinking and language. It's surface is wrinkled, or (178)_____, with ridges and valleys that allow a great deal of surface to be packed into the brain. The valleys in the cortex are called (179)_____, and a key one divides the cerebrum in to two halves, or (180)_____, which are connected by the (181)_____, a bundle of some 200 million nerve fibers.

Each of the cerebral hemispheres are divided in to four (182)_____; the (183)_____ lobe, is located in front of the central fissure, while the (184)_____ lobe lies behind it. The (185)_____ lobe lies on the side of the brain, below the lateral fissure; and the (186)_____ lobe lies in the back of the brain, behind and below the parietal lobe. The (187)_____ cortex is found in the occipital lobe, and the (188)_____ cortex is found in the temporal lobe. The (189)_____ cortex is found in the parietal lobe and the (190)_____ cortex, the executive center of the brain, is found in the frontal lobe along with the (191)_____ cortex.

In some ways the left and right (192)_____ of the brain are alike; however, when is comes to speech and language the two hemispheres (193)_____. For nearly all right-handed people and most left-handed people the (194)_____ hemisphere controls language function. Two key language centers lie within this "language" hemisphere, they are (195)_____ area, an egg sized area located in the left frontal lobe near the section of the motor cortex that controls the muscles of the tongue, throat and other areas of the face; and (196)_____ area, an area in the temporal lobe near the auditory cortex that responds mainly to auditory information. Damage to either area results in (197)_____, or a disruption of the ability to understand or produce language. In Broca's aphasia the individual would be unable to (198)_____ speech, whereas an individual with Wernicke's aphasia would have difficulty in (199)_____ speech. (200)_____, a serious reading impairment, appears to result from problems in the angular gyrus, which lies between the visual cortex and Wernicke's area.

What does it mean to be "right-brained" or "left-brained"? Does it matter if one is left or right handed? Why are people right-handed or left-handed? When we refer to a person as either "left or right-brained" we are referring to the notion that the (201)_____ of the brain are involved in very different kinds of functions. According to this view, (202)_____-brained people would be primarily logical and intellectual since the left hemisphere has been shown to be more involved in cognitive functions involving (203)_____ analysis and (204)_____ solving. "(205)_____-brained" individuals would, on the other hand, tend to be more intuitive, creative and emotional due to the right hemisphere's superiority in visual spatial functions, and (206)_____, emotional and creative mathematical (207)_____. However, this notion is (208)_____; research does not support it and it is erroneous to think that the hemispheres of the brain act (209)_____.

We usually label individuals as right or left handed on the basis of their (210)_____ preferences, yet some people write with one hand and throw with another. About 1 person in 10 is (211)_____. Being left-handed appears to be connected with (212)_____ problems such as dyslexia and (213)_____. Learning disabilities and some health problems, like (214)_____ headaches and allergies, are also somewhat more common in left-handers, but so is (215)_____. Handedness appears to have a (216)_____ component, but Daniel Geschwind of UCLA suggests that it is not likely to be a single (217)_____ characteristic.

What happens when the brain is split in two? For the most part, the behavior of people who have had split brain operations, where their (218)_____ is severed, is perfectly (219)_____. However they may be able to (220)_____ describe an unseen object such as a pencil held in the hand connected to the hemisphere that contains (221)_____ functions, yet they (222)_____ describe it when the object is held in the other hand.

Reflection Break # 4:
The Brain and Cerebral Cortex: *Match the brain structure to its function.*
Brain Structures:

a.	Electroencephalograph	c.	Magnetic resonance	f.	Cerebellum
b.	Computerized axial		imaging	g.	Reticular activating
	tomograph	d.	Medulla		system
		e.	Pons	h.	Thalamus

i.	Hypothalamus	q.	temporal lobe	y.	Angular gyrus
j.	Limbic system	r.	occipital lobe	z.	Aphasia
k.	Amygdala	s.	somstosensory cortex	aa.	Positron emission tomography
l.	Cerebrum	t.	motor cortex		
m.	Corpus callosum	u.	association cortex	bb.	Fissure
n.	cerebral cortex	v.	prefrontal region	cc.	hippocampus
o.	frontal lobe	w.	Broca's area		
p.	parietal lobe	x.	Wernicke's area		

Functions:

_____ 1. It's name comes from the Latin words meaning bark; it is involved in almost every bodily activity; the surface of the cerebrum.

_____ 2. Language center that is essential to understanding relationships between words and meanings.

_____ 3. When this structure is damaged people usually understand language well enough but speak slowly and laboriously.

_____ 4. Brain imaging technique that can reveal deformities in shape or structure by passing a narrow X-ray beam through the head and measures the structures that reflect the x-rays.

_____ 5. A disruption of the ability to understand or produce language.

_____ 6. Lies in the frontal lobe just across the valley of the central fissure from the somatosensory cortex; activity in this area causes parts of the body to move.

_____ 7. Located in the frontal lobe, near the forehead; is known as the brain's executive center.

_____ 8. Lies between the visual cortex and Wernicke's area; translates visual information into auditory information.

_____ 9. Areas of the cortex not primarily involved in sensation or motor activity.

_____ 10. Lies just behind the central fissure from the parietal lobe and receives messages from the skin senses all over the body.

_____ 11. Used by neuroscientists to record the natural electrical activity of the brain.

_____ 12. Brain imaging technique where a computer generated image of the activity of the parts of the brain by tracing the amount of glucose used.

_____ 13. The cortical lobe that lies in front of the central fissure and contains the motor cortex.

_____ 14. The cortical lobe that lies below the side, or lateral, fissure and contains the auditory cortex.

_____ 15. The cortical lobe that lies in the back of the brain and contains the visual cortex.

_____ 16. The cortical lobe that lies behind the central fissure and contains the somatosensory cortex.

_____ 17. Brain imaging technique in which the patient lies in a powerful magnetic field and is exposed to radio waves that cause parts of the brain to emit signals.

_____ 18. The crowning glory of the brain, it is responsible for the cognitive abilities of thinking and language.

_____ 19. A valley in the cortex.

_____ 20. Hindbrain structure that regulates vital functions like heart rate, blood pressure and respiration.

_____ 21. The thick bundle of nerve fibers that connect the two hemispheres of the cortex.

_____ 22. A bulge in the hindbrain that contains bundles of nerves that transmit information about body movement and is involved in functions related to attention, sleep, alertness and respiration.

_____ 23. Limbic structure that is connected with aggressive behavior, fear and vigilance.

_____ 24. Made up of several structures including the amygdala, hippocampus and parts of the hypothalamus; it is involved in memory and emotion and in the drives of hunger, sex and aggression.

_____ 25. Damage to this limbic structure leads to an inability to store new memories.

_____ 26. Begins in the hind-brain and ascends through the mid-brain into the lower part of the forebrain and is vital to the functions of attention, sleep and arousal; injury may result in coma.

_____ 27. Lies below the thalamus and above the pituitary gland and is vital in the regulation of body temperature, concentration of fluids, storage of nutrients and aspects of motivation and emotion.

_____ 28. Located near the center of the brain and serves as a relay station for sensory stimulation.

_____ 29. Means "little brain" in Latin; has two hemispheres that are involved in maintaining balance and in controlling motor behavior.

Reading for Understanding on "The Endocrine System"

What is the endocrine system? The body contains two types of (223)_____, ducted, or those glands with (224)_____ that carry substances to specific locations, and (225)_____. The (226)_____ system consists of the ductless glands that secrete (227)_____, chemicals that are released into the bloodstream. Like (228)_____, hormones have specific receptor sites and they only act in certain locations. The (229)_____ releases a number of releasing hormones that influence only the pituitary gland; other hormones are released by the (230)_____ gland and influence other areas of the body.

What functions of hormones are of interest to psychologists? Much (231)_____ action helps the body maintain steady state, such as fluid and blood sugar levels. The pituitary gland is so central to the body's functioning that it is known as the "(232)_____ gland;" it lies below the (233)_____ and is connected to it by a dense network of blood vessels. The pituitary gland secretes (234)_____ hormone, which regulates the growth of muscles, bones and glands; (235)_____, which regulates maternal behavior in lower mammals and stimulates milk production in women; (236)_____, which inhibits production of urine when body fluid levels are low; and (237)_____, which stimulates labor in pregnant women and is connected with maternal behavior.

The (238)_____ gland secretes the hormone melatonin, which helps regulate the (239)_____ cycle, and may affect the onset of (240)_____. The thyroid gland produces (241)_____, a hormone that affects the body's metabolism. Deficiencies in thyroxin, or

(242)_____ can result in obesity and sluggishness in adults, or (243)_____, characterized by stunted growth and mental retardation, if it occurs in children. Too much thyroid hormone, (244)_____, is characterized by excitability and weight loss.

The adrenal (245)_____ of the adrenal gland produces corticosteriods, which help to increase resistance to (246)_____, promote muscle development, and encourage the liver to release stored (247)_____. The adrenal (248)_____ of the adrenal gland produces the hormones, adrenaline and noradrenaline. (249)_____, or epinephrine, is produced solely by the adrenal medulla and has been shown to intensify most (250)_____, and to be critical to the experience of fear and (251)_____. (252)_____, helps (along with adrenaline) the body cope with threats and stress, it also raises blood pressure and acts as a neurotransmitter.

The male sex hormone, (253)_____, is responsible for prenatal sexual differentiation. During puberty it also encourages the growth of (254)_____ and bone and the development of primary and secondary (255)_____ characteristics. The (256)_____ sex hormones, estrogen and progesterone, are produced in the (257)_____ and together regulate the female menstrual cycle. (258)_____ fosters female reproductive capacity and secondary sex characteristics, while (259)_____ stimulates the growth of the female reproductive organs and prepares the uterus to maintain pregnancy. The female sex hormones have also been connected with (260)_____ functioning and psychological (261)_____ in women.

Reflection Break # 5:
Review on "Hormones and the Endocrine System:" *Match the hormone with the description of its action.*
Hormones:

a. Prolactin
b. Corticosteroids
c. Oxytocin
d. Noreadrenaline.

e. Growth Hormone
f. Testosterone
g. Melatonin
h. Thyroxin

i. Adrenaline
j. Progesterone
k. Antidiuretic hormone
l. Estrogen

Actions:
_____1. Hormone released by the pituitary gland responsible for regulation of the growth of muscles, bones and glands.
_____2. Hormone that stimulates the growth of female reproductive organs and prepares the uterus to maintain pregnancy.
_____3. Pituitary hormone that regulates maternal behavior and stimulates production of milk in women.
_____4. Released by the pituitary gland that inhibits the production of urine when body fluids are low.
_____5. The male sex hormone; is responsible for the development of both primary and secondary sex characteristics.
_____6. When released by the pituitary gland this hormone stimulates labor in pregnant women.
_____7. These hormones are released by the adrenal glands and have been shown to increase resistance to stress, promote muscle development and cause the liver to release stored sugar.

_____ 8. Produced by the adrenal medulla, this hormone is exclusively produced by the adrenal glands. It is of interest to psychologists since it intensifies most emotions and is crucial to the experience of fear and anxiety.

_____ 9. Hormone secreted by the adrenal medulla, but also produced elsewhere in the body. Also acts as a neurotransmitter.

_____ 10. Female sex hormone produced by both the ovaries and the testes. This hormone fosters reproductive capacity and development of secondary sex characteristics.

_____ 11. This hormone affects the body's metabolism. Too little of it leads to obesity, and sluggishness; too much is characterized by insomnia, excitability and weight loss.

_____ 12. Produced by the pineal gland, this hormone helps to regulate the sleep-wake cycle.

Reading for Understanding on "Life Connections: "Raging Hormones" ("More Please"?)"

(262)_____ have always been assumed to be the only sex prone to hormone related changes in behavior. They have historically been assumed to be more likely to commit suicide or crimes, call in sick or develop physical and emotional problems just prior to and during (263)_____. This is known as PMS, or (264)_____ syndrome. A (265)_____ ago PMS was something a woman must tolerate; this is no longer true. Although the causes of PMS are not fully understood, the current view suggests that PMS has a (266)_____ basis. Treatment options include (267)_____, diet, (268)_____ replacement and medications that affect levels of (269)_____ in the nervous system.

(270)_____, or the cessation of menstruation, is caused by a drop-off in female sex hormones. Menopause usually occurs during the late 40's or 50's, although there are wide variations. It is the final stage of the (271)_____, which is caused by a falling off in the secretion of the hormones estrogen and progesterone. Although menopause is a highly meaningful life change for women, most women get through it (272)_____ any problems. For those women who do experience physical distress (273)_____ therapy (HRT) can be used to reduce hot flashes and other symptoms.

Historically more research has been done on (274)_____ health problems than (275)_____, except in the area of problems related to low levels of male sex hormones. (276)_____ is a term used to describe a cluster of psychological problems that are apparently connected with the normal age-related male decline in the sex hormone testosterone. (277)_____ refers to a decline in virility, but is not a scientific term and (278)_____ is another unscientific term used for a male menopause.

In men, unlike women, the age-related decline of the production of sex hormones is (279)_____ and it is not uncommon to find a man in his 70's fathering a child. However, some men do experience (280)_____ symptoms of declining sex hormones in their 50's & 60's. These symptoms include difficulty in achieving and maintaining an (281)_____, a loss of muscle and bone mass and loss of about 2 inches of height. (282)_____ and diet have been shown to help slow or reverse some of these changes and hormone replacement, although (283)_____, may also help.

Irritable male syndrome, first observed in (284)_____, is a term used by Gerald Lincoln to refer to behavioral changes that result from a drop in (285)_____ levels. He suggests that when presented with a man who is grumpy and irritable physicians prescribe (286)_____ medications when hormone replacement might be needed. Research suggests that (287)_____ replacement often does boost strength, energy and the sex drive; however, it is also connected with increased risk of (288)_____ cancer and (289)_____ disease.

Reflection Break # 6:
Life Connections: "Raging Hormones" ("More Please"?)

1. Discuss the pros and cons of Hormone Replacement Therapy (HRT) for women during menopause.

2. Briefly discuss the problems with controversy surrounding andropause and irritable male syndrome. What treatment options are available for men who experience physical and psychological discomfort associated with a decline in testosterone?

REVIEW: Key Terms and Concepts

FINAL CHAPTER REVIEW

Recite:
Visit the Recite section on pages 82-85 of your textbook. Use the card provided with your textbook to cover the answers of the Recite section. Read the questions aloud and recite the answers.

Multiple Choice Questions

1. The concepts of adaptation and natural selection are key concepts in
   a. biological psychology.
   b. cognitive psychology.
   c. evolutionary psychology.
   d. clinical psychology.

2. The field of _____ is concerned with the genetic transmission of traits that give rise to patterns of behavior and bridges the sciences of psychology and biology .
   a. genetics
   b. evolutionary psychology
   c. behavioral genetics
   d. molecular genetics

3. _____ are the basic building blocks of heredity and are carried on 23 pairs of
   _____.
   a. Chromosomes, genes
   b. Mutations, genes
   c. Genes, deoxyribonucleic acid
   d. Genes, chromosomes

4. Dr. Small is interested in comparing the presence of shyness in people who are biologically related with those who are unrelated to determine whether genetic factors play a role in shyness. What type of study would she be most likely to conduct?
   a. a twin study
   b. an adoption study
   c. all of the above
   d. none of the above

5. Cells found in the nervous system that remove dead neurons and waste products and insulate, nourish and direct the growth of neurons are known as
   a. glial cells.
   b. neurotransmitters.
   c. dendrites.
   d. efferents.

6. In the disease multiple sclerosis the _____ is replaced with a hard fibrous tissue that throws off the timing of nerve impulses and disrupts motor control.
   a. axon
   b. neurotransmitter
   c. dendrite
   d. myelin

7. Your co-worker, like Michael J Fox, has Parkinson's disease. Deficiencies of which neurotransmitter have been associated with the progressive loss of muscle control associated with his disease?
   a. achetylcholine
   b. dopamine
   c. norepinephrine
   d. endorphins

8. Brian is a cross-country runner. He claims that he really enjoys running because he gets a wonderful "high" after running long distances. Since he knows you are taking a psychology class he asks you to explain what causes this. You tell him that as he runs
   a. serotonin blocks the pain receptors in his skin.
   b. dopamine prevents his muscles from tightening up and causing pain.
   c. endorphins block the chemicals that transmit pain to the brain.
   d. acetylcholine is depleted in the hippocampus, blocking the formation of a pain memory.

9. The _____ nervous system contains the brain and spinal cord, while the sensory and motor neurons that transmit messages to the muscles and glands make up the _____ nervous system.
   a. central, peripheral
   b. peripheral, sympathetic
   c. parasympathetic, sympathetic
   d. sympathetic, central

10. On the way home from the library last night you heard the footsteps of someone following you. You turned and saw the shadow of a large man heading towards you. You ran to your car faster then you had ever run. When you were finally in the car your heart rate was highly elevated, your breathing was rapid and you were sweating. This fight or flight response was most likely the result of activity in your
    a. parasympathetic nervous system.
    b. somatic nervous system.
    c. sympathetic nervous system.
    d. none of the above.

11. You touch a hot stove and pull your hand back. This reflexive action was most likely the result of activity in your
    a. spinal cord.
    b. brain.
    c. hypothalamus.
    d. hippocampus.

12. Norma's physician suspects that she has a brain tumor. Which brain-imaging technique is he most likely to use to confirm his diagnosis?
    a. An electroencephalograph
    b. A CAT scan
    c. A PET SCAN
    d. An fMRI

13. Which of the following brain structures, when damaged, would lead your heartbeat and respiration to stop instantly?
    a. pons
    b. medulla
    c. cerebellum
    d. limbic system

14. The brain structure vital to the regulation of body temperature, concentration of fluids, storage of nutrients and other aspects of motivation and emotion is the
    a. hippocampus.
    b. amygdala.
    c. thalamus.
    d. hypothalamus.

15. Your grandmother recently had a small stoke that has left her unable to move her right side. Most likely the stroke caused damage in which lobe of her cerebral cortex?
    a. frontal
    b. parietal
    c. temporal
    d. occipital

16. Damage to the cerebral cortex in the occipital lobe would most likely lead to a loss of
    a. the sensations of warmth, cold, touch and pain.
    b. vision.
    c. the ability to produce spoken language.
    d. hearing.

17. Which area of the brain is known as the brain's executive center?
    a. The hippocampus
    b. The prefrontal cortex
    c. Broca's area
    d. Wernicke's area

18. Which of the following pairings are correct?
    a. Broca's area--speech production; Wernicke's area--language comprehension
    b. Prefrontal area—vision; Occipital area—executive function
    c. Broca's area--language comprehension; Wernicke's area--speech production
    d. Temporal area—hearing; Parietal area—vision

19. Lola is pregnant and is ready to deliver her child. Which of the following hormones will her physician use to stimulate her labor?
    a. Epinephrine
    b. Growth hormone
    c. Thyroxin
    d. Oxytocin

20. Deficiencies in _____ affect the body's metabolism and can cause cretinism in children.
    a. Melatonin
    b. Testosterone
    c. Thyroxin
    d. Estrogen

Essay Questions:
1. Imagine meeting four different people who have each sustained injury to different sections of their brain. Person A has irreversible damage to her frontal lobe. Person B has irreversible damage to his parietal lobe. Person C has irreversible damage to her temporal lobe and person D as irreversible damage to his occipital lobe. In general, what would be the effects of each of these injuries?

2. Imagine taking a bite of a juicy apple. Briefly discuss the role that each part of the brain plays in this simple act.

3. What is the advantage of knowing that a mental illness is caused by a neuro-chemical problem? How might a better understanding of brain chemistry help psychologists develop a better definition of mental illness?

4. Design experiments using each of the following methods to learn something about the brain:
    a. MRI
    b. PET
    c. CAT

   In each case think about what your research question would be and how you would go about answering it. Specify your subject population, your research question and the design of your experiment. How would the information gained from the different studies be different?

5. Design an experiment in which you test whether language is only localized in the left hemisphere by using split-brain subjects. Explain how you would resolve the controversy concerning the localization of language with your experimental design.

CONNECT AND EXPAND:

1. **Neurons:**
    A: Visit John Krantz's Internet page at {http://psych.hanover.edu/Krantz/tutor.html} and complete the Neuron and Synapse Tutorials.
    B. Visit http://faculty.washington.edu/chudler.color/pic1.html to color a neuron on-line. Or http://faculty.washington.edu/chudler/colorbook.html and print out the pages.

2. **Neuroscience:** Visit http://faculty.washington.edu/chudler/hunt3.html and participate in the Neuroscience Treasure Hunt. See if you can be the first in your class to win the Golden Neuron Award.

3. **Spinal Cord and Nervous System:** Draw a diagram demonstrating the sensory (afferent) and motor nerve pathways involved when you touch a hot stove. Share your pictures with your study mates and note any differences. Together with your study mates review each of the pictures with the material in your textbook to correct any inaccuracies.

4. **Cerebral Cortex:**
    A. Revisit http://faculty.washington.edu/chudler.color/pic1.html to color the different lobes of the cortical tissue.
    B. Visit http://www.pbs.org/wgbh/aso/tryit/brain. Probe the motor cortex and observe the movements that arise as a result of the probing.

5. **Drugs and their actions:** Pick a popular drug, medication, or herb and research its neurochemical actions. What neurotransmitters or hormone does it effect? What are its actions? How does the information that you find fit with the information presented in your textbook? Present your findings to your classmates in a format specified by your instructor.

6. **Life Connections: Raging Hormones:** Research the benefits and risks associated with Hormone Replacement Therapy. Read what the American Medical Association says about the use of HRT at

http://www.medem.com/search/article_display.cfm?path=n:&mstr=/ZZZ596TUCKC.html&soc=AMA&srch_typ=NAV_SERCH
and then conduct a further search of your own using your favorite search engine (www.google.com, www.ask.com, www.dogpile.com). Based on the information you find, what would advice would you give your mother about the use of Hormone Replacement Therapy during menopause? How would your advice be different if it was your father?

Chapter Three: Voyage Through the Lifespan

PowerPreview: *Skim the major headings in this chapter in your textbook. Jot down anything that you are surprised or curious about. After this write down four or five questions that you have about the material in this chapter.*

Things that surprised me/I am curious about from Chapter 3:

Questions that I have about Voyage Through the LifeSpan:
-
-
-
-

QUESTION: *These are some questions that you should be able to answer after you finish studying this chapter:*

Prenatal Development: The Beginning of Our Life Story
- ❖ *What developments occur from conception through birth?*

Childhood: Physical, Cognitive, and Social Development
- ❖ *What physical developments occur during childhood?*
- ❖ *Controversy in Psychology: Is development continuous or discontinuous?*
- ❖ *What are Jean Piaget's views of cognitive development?*
- ❖ *How do children reason about what is right and wrong?*
- ❖ *What are Erikson's stages of psychosocial development?*
- ❖ *How do feelings of attachment develop? What kinds of experiences affect attachment?*
- ❖ *What types of parental behavior are connected with variables such as self-esteem, achievement motivation, and independence in children?*

Adolescence: Physical, Cognitive, and Social Development
- ❖ *What physical developments occur during adolescence?*
- ❖ *What cognitive developments occur during adolescence?*
- ❖ *Controversy in Psychology: Are there gender differences in moral development?*
- ❖ *What social and emotional developments occur during adolescence?*

Adulthood: Physical, Cognitive, and Social Development
- ❖ *What physical developments occur during adulthood?*
- ❖ *Why do we age?*
- ❖ *What cognitive developments occur during adulthood?*
- ❖ *What is Alzheimer's disease? What are its origins?*
- ❖ *What social and personality developments occur during young adulthood?*

- ❖ *What social and personality developments occur during middle adulthood?*
- ❖ *Controversy in Psychology: Do women experience an "Empty Nest Syndrome" when the youngest child leaves home?*
- ❖ *What social and personality developments occur during late adulthood?*
- ❖ *How do people in the United States age today?*

On Death and Dying
- ❖ *What are psychological perspectives on death and dying?*

Life Connections: Day Care—Blessing, Headache, or Both?
- ❖ *How does Day care affect bonds of attachment?*
- ❖ *How Does Day care influence social and cognitive development?*

Reading for Understanding/Reflect: The *following section provides you with the opportunity to perform 2 of the R's of the PQ4R study method. In this section I will encourage you to check your understanding of your reading of the text by filling in the blanks in the brief paragraphs that relate to each of the preview questions. You will also be prompted to rehearse your understanding of the material with periodic Reflection breaks. Remember it is better to study in more frequent, short sessions then in one long "cram session." Be sure to reward yourself with short study breaks before each of the Reflection exercises.*

Reading for Understanding about "Prenatal Development: The Beginning of Our Life Story"

What developments occur from conception through birth? Within nine (1)_____ a child develops from a nearly microscopic cell to a (2)_____. The period from conception to implantation is known as the (3)_____ stage. The major organ systems are formed during the (4)_____ stage, which lasts from implantation until about the eighth week of development. During the fourth (5)_____ a primitive heart begins to beat and pump blood and it will continue to beat without rest for the remainder of the life of the organism. By the end of the (6)_____ month the nervous system begins to transmit messages and the sex organs begin to differentiate. The embryo is suspended in the (7)_____ sac and exchanges nutrients and wastes with the mother through the (8)_____. The (9)_____ stage, which lasts from the beginning of the third month until birth, is characterized by maturation and gains in (10)_____. It is during the fetal period that the mother will detect the first fetal (11)_____.

Reflection Break # 1:
Prenatal Development: *Review prenatal developmental changes by filling in the chart below:*

	Time period	**Major characteristics**
Germinal		
Embryonic		
Fetal		

Reading for Understanding about "Childhood: Physical, Cognitive and Social Development"

What physical developments occur during childhood? Childhood begins at (12)_____.
(13)_____ development includes gains in height and weight, maturation of the nervous system and development of bones, muscles and organs. The most dramatic gains in height and weight occur during (14)_____. Most babies usually double their birth weight in about (15)_____ months and (16)_____ it by their first birthday. (17)_____ are simple, unlearned, inborn responses to stimuli that in many cases are essential to the survival of the infant. Examples include sucking, rooting and swallowing.

Perceptually, newborn babies can (18)_____ quite well and prefer visual stimuli that resemble the human (19)_____ over other stimuli. Infants are capable of (20)_____ perception by the time they can crawl. Newborns can (21)_____ and show a preference for their (22)_____'s voice. Newborns show preferences for (23)_____ odors and (24)_____ foods. Finally, newborn babies are sensitive to (25)_____, which is an extremely important avenue of learning and communication.

Controversy in Psychology: Is Development Continuous or Discontinuous? Does development occur gradually or in stages? An important controversy in developmental psychology concerns the question as to whether developmental changes tend to occur gradually (26)_____ or in major leaps (27)_____. (28)_____ theorists, like Watson, tend to view psychological development as a more (29)_____ process. (30)_____ theorists, on the other hand, view development as discontinuous. Some aspects of development, such as the adolescent growth spurt, or prenatal development occur in stages and are (31)_____. There still remains controversy as to whether (32)_____ development, attachment and gender typing are continuous or discontinuous.

What are Jean Piaget's views of cognitive development? The ways in which children mentally represent and think about the world is their (33)_____ development. The Swiss biologist and psychologist Jean (34)_____ saw children as budding scientists who actively strive to make sense of the perceptual world. He hypothesized that children's cognitive processes develop in an orderly sequence of (35)_____. He defined intelligence as involving the processes of (36)_____ (responding to events according to existing schemes) and (37)_____ (changing schemes to permit effective responses to new events). (38)_____ were a pattern of action or a mental structure involved in acquiring or organizing knowledge. Piaget's view of cognitive development includes a series of stages. During the first stage, known as the (39)_____ stage, the infant begins to coordinate perception of self with motor activity. Also occurring during this stage is the establishment of (40)_____, in which infants show a realization that objects removed from sight still exist. The second of Piaget's stages, known as the (41)_____ stage is characterized by the use of words and symbols to represent objects. However, preoperational thought is one-(42)_____ and a consequence of this is (43)_____, in which children cannot understand that others do not see things the way they do. Preoperational children also show (44)_____, or the attribution of life and consciousness to physical objects and (45)_____, the belief that environmental events like rain and thunder are human inventions. Additionally, preoperational children show an inability to center on more than one aspect of a situation and thus are unable to understand the law of (46)_____. Piaget's third stage of cognitive development is termed the (47)_____ stage and it is characterized by conservation, less egocentrism, (48)_____, or the recognition that many processes can be reversed, and subjective moral judgments.

How do children reason about what is right and wrong? Lawrence (49)_____ hypothesized that children's moral reasoning develops through three levels, each of which consists of two stages. The stage in which moral judgments are based on the consequences of behavior is known as the (50)_____ level. In the (51)_____ level moral decisions develop from conformity to conventional standards of right and wrong through necessity to maintain the social order. Reliance on one's own conscience is characteristic of the (52)_____ level. Not all individuals reach the (53)_____ level.

What are Erikson's stages of psychosocial development? (54)_____ relationships are crucial to children. Erik (55)_____ hypothesizes that there are eight stages of psychosocial development. Each represents a life (56)_____. The first of these is "(57)_____," during which the crisis centers on the child's learning that the world is a good place that can meet its needs. The second occurs in early childhood when the child begins to explore the environment and develops (58)_____ (self-direction) or its opposite, feelings of (59)_____ and (60)_____. The third stage, occurring in later childhood, encourages us to develop (61)_____ or feelings of inferiority.

How do feelings of attachment develop? What kinds of experiences affect attachment? Mary (62)_____ defines attachment as an emotional tie that is formed between a person and another specific person. (63)_____ keeps organisms together and are vital to the survival of infants. Ainsworth developed the (64)_____ method to study attachment and identified three types of attachment: secure attachment, avoidant attachment and ambivalent attachment. In the strange-situation (65)_____ attached infants mildly protest their mothers departure seek interaction and are readily comforted. (66)_____ attached infants are least distressed by their mother's departure and ignore their mothers when they return. (67)_____ attached infants show the signs of distress when their mother leaves and shows ambivalence when she returns by alternately clinging to her and pushing her away. According to Ainsworth, there are three stages of attachment: the initial-preattachment phase, which is characterized by (68)_____ attachment; the attachment-in-the-making phase, which is characterized by preference for (69)_____ figures; and the clear-cut-attachment phase, which is characterized by intensified dependence on the (70)_____.

(71)_____ have argued that children become attached to their mothers through conditioning because their mothers feed them and attend to their other needs. Harry (72)_____'s studies with rhesus monkeys suggest an innate motive, (73)_____, may be more important than conditioning in the development of attachment. Konrad Lorenz, an (74)_____, notes that attachment is (75)_____, or inborn. He notes that there are (76)_____ periods during which animals such as geese and ducks will become attached instinctively (or (77)_____ on) to an object that they follow.

What types of parental behavior are connected with variables such as self-esteem, achievement motivation, and independence in children? Many psychologists have been concerned with relationships between (78)_____ styles and personality development in children. Diana Baumrind has been interested in the development of (79)_____, or the ability of the child to manipulate the environment, in relation to parenting behavior. Styles of (80)_____ behavior include the authoritative, authoritarian, and permissive styles. (81)_____ parents are restrictive and demand mature behavior but temper their strictness with love and support. (82)_____ parents view obedience as a virtue, they have strict guidelines about what is right and wrong and rely on force and poor communication. (83)_____ parents are generally easy going with their children; they are warm and supportive, but poor at communication. (84)_____ parents tend to leave their children on their own; they make few demands and show little warmth or encouragement. Research shows that (85)_____ in parenting is superior in rearing children; but that (86)_____ also pays off. The children of (87)_____ parents are the most achievement-oriented and well adjusted. The incidence of child abuse is generally (88)_____. Many factors contribute to child abuse; they include (89)_____, a history of child abuse, failure to become attached to the children, substance abuse and (90)_____ attitudes toward child rearing. Child abuse (91)_____ tend to run in families. Children who are (92)_____ are likely to develop personal, psychological and social problems.

Reflection Break # 2:
Childhood: Physical, Cognitive and Social Development
1. Review the Sensory capabilities of the Newborn by filling in the chart below.

Sense	Capabilities:
Vision	
Hearing	
Taste & Smell	
Touch	

2. Match the cognitive concept with its proper description.

a. ambivalent/resistant attachment
b. concrete operational
c. trust vs. mistrust
d. assimilation
e. Authoritarian parenting
f. sensorimotor
g. decentration
h. secure attachment
i. preoperational
j. egocentrism
k. intial preattachment phase
l. preconventional stage
m. attachment in the making phase
n. accommodation

o. autonomy vs. shame & doubt
p. artificialism
q. center
r. clear-cut attachment
s. reversibility
t. Authoritative parents
u. object permance
v. avoidant attachment
w. scheme
x. Permissive parenting
y. Animism
z. Conservation
aa. conventional stage
bb. indiscriminate attachment

41

_____1. Erikson's stage of psychosocial development in which we depend on our primary caregivers and come to expect that the environment will---or will not---meet our needs.

_____2. Responding to a new stimulus through a reflex or existing habit.

_____3. A pattern of action or mental structure involved in acquiring or organizing knowledge.

_____4. The creation of new ways of responding to objects or looking at the world.

_____5. Stage of attachment characterized by preference for familiar figures.

_____6. This cognitive stage in which thought is characterized by the use of words and symbols to represent objects; thought is limited and tends to be one dimensional.

_____7. The belief that environmental events like rain and thunder are human inventions.

_____8. The recognition that many processes can be undone, or restored to their previous condition.

_____9. The inability of preoperational children to understand that other people do not see things the same way they do.

_____10. Stage of moral reasoning in which judgments are based on expectations of rewards and punishments.

_____11. Stage of attachment characterized by intensified dependence on the primary caregiver.

_____12. Type of parenting in which parents are restrictive and demand mature behavior but temper their strictness with love and support. The children of these parents are most achievement-oriented and well-adjusted.

_____13. The realization that objects removed from sight still exist.

_____14. Stage of psychosocial development where children explore the environment actively and try new things.

_____15. The attribution of life and consciousness to physical objects like the sun.

_____16. This laws holds that basic properties of substances such as mass, weight and volume remain the same when you change superficial properties such as their shape or arrangement.

_____17. Type of attachment demonstrated when infants show sever signs of distress when the mother leaves, but alternately clings and pushes her away when she returns.

_____18. The inability to think about two aspects of a situation at once.

_____19. The stage of cognitive development in which children show the beginnings of the capacity for adult logic.

_____20. The first stage of cognitive development in which the infant is capable of assimilating novel stimuli using reflexes and develops object permanence.

_____21. Type of parenting in which parents view obedience as a virtue, they have strict guidelines about what is right and wrong, and they rely on force and have poor communication skills.

_____22. Type of attachment demonstrated when infants mildly protest their mother's departure, yet seek interaction upon reunion and are easily comforted.

_____23. Attachment in which infants show no preference for particular people.

_____24. Stage of reasoning on moral behavior in which right and wrong are judges by conformity to familial, religious or societal standards.

_____25. The ability of concrete operational children to focus, or center on two dimensions of a problem at once.

_____26. Type of parenting in which the parents are generally easygoing with their children; they are warm and supportive but poor at communication.

_____27. Type of attachment demonstrated when infants are least distressed by their mother's departure.

_____28. Stage of attachment characterized indiscriminate attachment.

Reading for Understanding about "Adolescence: Physical, Cognitive, and Social Development"

What physical developments occur during adolescence? (93)_____ is a time of transition from childhood to adulthood that begins at puberty and ends with assumption of adult responsibilities. During the adolescent (94)_____, young people may grow 6 or more inches in a year. (95)_____ begins with the appearance of secondary sex characteristics and is the period during which the body becomes sexually mature. In boys, pituitary hormones stimulate the increase output of (96)_____ and in girls a cascade of hormones causes the (97)_____ to secrete higher levels of estrogen. (98)_____ production becomes cyclical in females and regulates the menstrual cycle. The beginning of menstruation is known as (99)_____.

What cognitive developments occur during adolescence? (100)_____ thinking appears in adolescence, but not everyone reaches this stage. Formal operation thought is characterized by the ability to deal with the (101)_____ and the hypothetical. Adolescent thought is also marked by a form of (102)_____, in that they can understand the thoughts of others, but still have trouble separating things that are of concern to others and those that are concerns only to themselves. Two consequences of adolescent egocentrism are the imaginary audience and the (103)_____. The (104)_____ refers to the adolescent beliefs that they are the center of attention and that other people are as concerned with their appearance and behavior as they are. The (105)_____ refers to the adolescent belief that one's feelings and ideas are special, even unique, and that one is invulnerable.

A number of questions have been raised concerning the (106)_____ of Piaget's views. These include: timing, (107)_____, and sequencing. Some critics argue that children are more (108)_____ then Piaget thought, that he underestimated the abilities of children. Other critics argue that events like egocentrism and conservation appear to develop more (109)_____ than Piaget thought and still others question the consistency of the (110)_____ of development. In the end, although Piaget's theory has been questioned, it has not been (111)_____.

Another aspect of cognitive development in the adolescent includes changes in (112)_____. Although none of Kohlberg's levels are tied to age, most adolescents and adults reason (113)_____. When (114)_____ thought does emerge, it does so in adolescence. Post conventional moral reasoning is based on person's own moral (115)_____; moral judgments are derived from (116)_____, rather then from conventional standards. Research seems to (117)_____ Kolhberg's developmental sequences of moral development.

Controversy in Psychology: Are There Gender Differences In Moral Development?
A number of studies using Kholberg's moral dilemmas have found that boys show (118)_____ levels of moral reasoning then girls. However, researcher Carol (119)_____ argues that this

gender difference reflects patterns of socialization, not gender differences in morality. A meta-analysis of the research, however, show there is only a slight tendency for males to favor a (120)_____ approach and for girls to show a (121)_____ approach.

What social and personality developments occur during adolescence? In terms of social and personality development, adolescence has been associated with (122)_____. Stanley Hall attributed the conflicts and distress of adolescence to (123)_____ changes, however research evidence suggests that (124)_____ influences have a relatively greater impact. Adolescents and parents are often in (125)_____ because adolescents desire more (126)_____ and may experiment with things that can jeopardize their health. However, despite bickering, most adolescents continue to love and respect their (127)_____.

According to Erik Erikson, adolescents strive to forge an (128)_____, or a sense of who they are and what they stand for. Adolescents who do not develop ego identity may experience (129)_____; they spread themselves too thin, running down one blind alley after another. Sexually, the changes of (130)_____ prepare the body for sexual activity, and high (131)_____ levels also stir interest in sex. But most sexually active adolescents do not use (132)_____ reliably. There is however, good news from the CDC that shows a (133)_____ in the teenage pregnancy rate in the final decade of the 20th century.

Reflection Break # 3:
Adolescence: Physical, Cognitive and Social Development
Part I. Matching: *Match the term with its proper description.*

a. Adolescence
b. Puberty
c. Secondary sex characteristics
d. Menarche
e. Testosterone
f. Estrogen and androgens
g. Formal operations
h. Egocentrism

i. Imaginary audience
j. Personal fable
k. Conventional morality
l. Post conventional morality
m. *Sturm und Drang*
n. Ego identity
o. Role diffusion

_____1. Erikson's term for adolescents who spread themselves too thin and place themselves at the mercy of leaders.

_____2. A time of transition from childhood to adulthood.

_____3. The period during which the body becomes sexually mature.

_____4. A firm sense of one who is and what one stands for.

_____5. The appearance of body hair, deepening of the voice in males and rounding of hips and breasts in females.

_____6. The final stage in Piaget's theory characterized by abstract thinking.

_____7. The inabilities of adolescents to separate things that are of concern to others and those of concern only to themselves.

_____8. The belief of adolescents that other people are concerned with their thoughts and behavior as they are.

_____9. G. Stanley Hall's term used to characterize the storm and stress of adolescence.
_____10. The beginning of menstruation.
_____11. The belief of adolescents that their feelings and ideas are special, even unique, and that we are invulnerable.
_____12. Male sex hormone.
_____13. Moral reasoning based on a person's own moral standards and personal values.
_____14. Female sex hormones.
_____15. Moral reasoning governed by social rules and conventions.

Part II.

Briefly describe how the physical, cognitive and social/personal aspects of adolescence contribute to an ego identity.

Reading for Understanding about "Adulthood: Physical, Cognitive and Social Development"

What physical developments occur during adulthood? Development continues throughout the (134)_____. The most obvious aspects of development during adulthood are (135)_____. People are usually at the (136)_____ of their physical powers during young adulthood. Middle adulthood is characterized by a gradual (137)_____ in strength. (138)_____, or the cessation of menstruation, usually occurs in the late 40's or early 50's and has been thought to depress many women, but research suggests that most women go through this passage without great (139)_____. Older people show less sensory (140)_____, and their reaction time (141)_____. The (142)_____ system weakens and changes occur that eventually result in death.

Why do we age? (143)_____ plays a role in longevity. One theory ((144)_____) suggests that aging and death are determined by our genes. Another theory ((145)_____) holds that factors such as pollution, disease, and ultraviolet light weaken the body so that it loses the ability to repair itself. (146)_____ factors such as exercise, proper nutrition, and not smoking also contribute to longevity.

What cognitive developments occur during adulthood? People are usually at the height of their (147)_____ powers during early adulthood, but people can be (148)_____ for a lifetime. (149)_____ functioning declines with age, but the declines are not usually as large as people assume. People tend to retain (150)_____ ability, as shown by vocabulary and general knowledge, into advanced old age. (151)_____ intelligence, or one's vocabulary and accumulated knowledge, generally increases with age; while (152)_____ intelligence, the ability to process information rapidly, declines more rapidly. However, workers' (153)_____ with solving specific kinds of problems is often more important than their fluid intelligence.

What is Alzheimer's disease? What are its origins? (154)_____ disease is characterized by a general, gradual cognitive deterioration in memory, language, and problem solving. On a biological level, it is connected with reduced levels of (155)_____ in the brain and with the build-up of (156)_____ in the brain. Alzheimer's disease does not reflect the normal aging

45

process. There are, however, normal, more gradual (157)_____ in intellectual functioning and memory among older people.

Changes in (158)_____ and (159)_____ development during adulthood are most likely the most fluid. Research evidence does suggest that people tend to grow psychologically (160)_____ as they advance from adolescence through middle adulthood.

What social and personality developments occur during young adulthood? (161)_____ adulthood is generally characterized by efforts to advance in the business world and the development of intimate ties. Erikson characterized young adulthood as the stage of (162)_____. According to Daniel Levinson many young adults reassess the directions of their lives during the "(163)_____." Often we find that the lifestyles that we adopted during our 20's do not fit as comfortably as we had expected, and the later thirties are characterized by (164)_____.

What social and personality developments occur during middle adulthood? Erikson labeled the life (165)_____ of middle age as generativity vs. stagnation. (166)_____ involves doing things that we believe are worthwhile and enhances and maintains self-esteem. (167)_____ means trading water, or moving backwards and has powerful destructive effects on self-esteem. Many theorists view middle adulthood as a time of crisis (the "(168)_____") and further reassessment. Many adults try to come to terms with the (169)_____ between their achievements and the dreams of their youth during middle adulthood. Research suggests that there are (170)_____ differences in the experience of a midlife transition in that women undergo their transition a number of years (171)_____.

Controversy in Psychology: Do Women Experience an "Empty Nest Syndrome" When the Youngest Child Leaves Home?
In earlier decades, psychologists placed a great emphasis on a concept referred to as "empty nest syndrome" and the concept was applied most often to (172)_____. Current research paints a more (173)_____ picture. Certainly, *some* middle-aged adults become depressed when their youngest child leaves home (the so-called (174)_____ syndrome), but many report increased satisfaction, stability, and self-confidence.

What social and personality developments occur during late adulthood? Erikson characterizes late adulthood as the stage of (175)_____. He saw the basic challenge as maintaining the belief that life is worthwhile in the face of (176)_____. Ego integrity derives from (177)_____, which can be defined as expert knowledge about the meaning of life, balancing one's own needs and those of others and striving for excellence in one's behavior and achievements. Other views of late adulthood stress the importance of creating new (178)_____; however (179)_____ and (180)_____ realities may require older people to become more selective in their pursuits.

How do people in the United States age today? Many (181)_____ about aging are growing less prevalent. Most older Americans report being generally (182)_____ with their lives.

Those who experience "(183)_____" reshape their lives to focus on what they find to be important, maintain a positive outlook, and find new challenges.

Reflection Break # 4:

Adulthood: Physical, Cognitive and Social Development: *Briefly describe the physical, cognitive and social changes that occur during these periods of adulthood by filling in the chart below:*

	Physical	**Cognitive**	**Psychosocial**
Early adulthood			
Middle adulthood			
Later adulthood			

Reading for Understanding about "On Death and Dying"

What are psychological perspectives on death and dying? (184)_____ has identified five stages of dying among people who are terminally ill: denial, anger, (185)_____, depression, and final acceptance. However, other investigators find that psychological reactions to approaching (186)_____ are more varied than Kubler-Ross suggests.

Reading for Understanding on "Life Connections: Day Care—Blessing, Headache, or Both?"

How does Day care affect bonds of attachment? Many parents wonder if day care will affect their children's (187)_____ to them and this issue has been hotly debated. Some studies have show that children in full-time day care are (188)_____ likely to show an insecure attachment than those children not in day care. However this likelihood is (189)_____ and the majority of infants in day care are (190)_____ attached.

How does Day care influence social and cognitive development? Day care has (191)_____ effects on social and cognitive development. Infants with day care experience are more (192)_____ oriented and play at a (193)_____ developmental levels then home reared infants. (194)_____ children are more likely to share and are more independent, self confident, outgoing, and affectionate. Day care participation during elementary school years is associated with (195)_____ school performance, especially in (196)_____ socioeconomic families. A recent study by the National Institute on Child Health and Human Development concluded that children in (197)_____ quality day care (defined by the richness of the learning environment and ratio of caregivers) were (198)_____ than children reared at home with their mothers. A Swedish study found that the children in the high quality day care

(199)_____ those in home care on tests of (200)_____ and (201)_____ skills. However, in 2001 another study was published suggesting that children who spent time away from their (202)_____ were more likely to be rated as defiant, aggressive and disobedient in kindergarten. Yet, the researchers suggested (203)_____ in interpreting the data, since the differences between the groups were very (204)_____ and very few of the children exhibited above average behavior problems.

REVIEW: Key Terms and Concepts

FINAL CHAPTER REVIEW

Recite:
Visit the Recite section on pages 133-135 of your textbook. Use the card provided with your textbook to cover the answers of the Recite section. Read the questions aloud and recite the answers. This will help you cement your knowledge of key concepts.

Multiple Choice Questions
1. Dr. Wong is a developmental psychologist. He will most likely be interested in studying
   a. the role of early life influences on adult behavior
   b. the effects of genetic factors on traits.
   c. the causes of developmental abnormalities.
   d. all of the above.

2. Which of the following represents the correct sequence of development of the conceived organism during the prenatal period?
   a. neonate, zygote, embryo, fetus
   b. embryo, fetus, zygote, neonate
   c. fetus, neonate, embryo, zygote
   d. zygote, embryo, fetus, neonate

3. During the _____ stage of prenatal development the mother detects the first movements, the organs continue to mature, and the heart and lungs become increasingly capable of sustaining independent life.
   a. fetal
   b. embryonic
   c. period of the ovum
   d. germinal

4. Susan strokes the cheek of her newborn infant and the infant turns her head to the side where she was stroked. Which reflex did Susan's infant demonstrate?
   a. withdrawal
   b. rooting
   c. babinski
   d. moro

5. Jean Piaget is to _____ as John Waston is to _____.
   a. continuous; biological
   b. biological; discontinuous
   c. behavioral, biological
   d. discontinuous, continuous

6. Sam has recently expanded his scheme of the concept "doggie" to include big and little dogs. According to Jean Piaget, Sam has engaged in
   a. accommodation
   b. sensorimotor development
   c. assimilation
   d. conservation

7. Sakira is able to play peek-a-boo with her 8 month old son because, according to Piaget he has acquired
   a. conservation.
   b. object permanence.
   c. egocentrism.
   d. animism.

8. Tanya makes moral judgments according to familial, religious and societal standards of right and wrong. She feels that moral behavior is defined by what the majority does or what is "normal". According to Lawrence Kohlberg, Tanya is reasoning at a _____ level of moral reasoning.
   a. pre-conventional
   b. conventional
   c. post-conventional
   d. pre-operational

9. When in a strange situation, Erin shows severe signs of distress when her mother leaves; yet when her mother returns, she alternately pushed her away and clings to her. Mary Ainsworth would say that Erin is
   a. securely attached.
   b. avoidantly attached.
   c. indiscriminately attached.
   d. ambivalently/resistantly attached.

10. According to ethologist Konrad Lorenz attachment is
    a. acquired due to the need for contact comfort.
    b. learned by observing the relationship between mother and father.
    c. instinctual and inborn.
    d. the result of proper parenting style.

11. Andrew and Sasha are strict parents. They demand mature behavior from their children, yet they temper their strictness and demands with love and support. Samuel and Leslie, on the other hand, are warm and easygoing with their children, but they are not very good at communicating. Baumrind would say that Andrew and Sasha's parenting style is _____, where as Samuel and Leslie are _____ parents.
    a. authoritarian, uninvolved
    b. authoritative, permissive
    c. authoritarian, permissive
    d. authoritarian, authoritative

12. Keshia is 11, she has grown approximately 8 inches in the last year, her hips have begun to widen and her breasts have begun to develop. She has also noticed the growth of hair in her underarm and pubic areas, and last month she experienced her menarche. Which developmental period would psychologists say that she is in?
    a. childhood
    b. adolescence
    c. puberty
    d. both b & c.

13. The major achievements of this final stage of cognitive development according to Piaget are the development of classification, the ability to think about ideas as well as objects, abstract thinking and the ability to hypothesize. This stage is known as
    a. concrete operations.
    b. formal operations.
    c. sensorimotor operations.
    d. post-formal operations.

14. Justin is 16. He spends a long hours grooming and worries that people will stare at him whenever he gets a pimple. Justin's behavior is indicative of the concept of the
    a. personal fable.
    b. egotistical behavior of adolescents.
    c. imaginary audience.
    d. concrete operational thinking of adolescents.

15. According to Erik Erikson the fifth stage of psychosocial development occurs during adolescence. This stage is known as
    a. trust vs. mistrust.
    b. integrity vs. despair.
    c. ego identity vs. role diffusion.
    d. generativity vs. stagnation.

16. Renee is in her late 40's. She has stopped ovulating and begun to experience hot flashes, loss of sleep and some anxiety and depression. She is mostly likely in
    a. menopause.
    b. puberty.
    c. climax.
    d. manopause.

17. You ask your physician why humans age. She tells you that aging is determined by a biological clock that ticks at a rate governed by your genes. Which theory of aging does your physician ascribe to?
    a. The wear-and-tear theory.
    b. The programmed senescence theory.
    c. The free radical theory.
    d. Both b and c.

18. Lifetime attainments, vocabulary and accumulated facts are to _____ intelligence as the ability to process information rapidly and mental flexibility are to _____ intelligence
    a. fluid, componential
    b. crystallized, contextual
    c. crystallized, fluid
    d. fluid, crystallized

19. A progressive form of mental deterioration that is characterized by general, gradual decline in cognitive functioning best describes
    a. crystallized intelligence.
    b. fluid intelligence.
    c. Alzheimer's disease.
    d. normal aging.

20. Which of the following lists the correct sequence of Kubler-Ross's five stages of dying?
    a. anger, denial, bargaining, depression, acceptance
    b. depression, anger, denial, bargaining, acceptance
    c. denial, anger, bargaining, depression, acceptance
    d. bargaining, anger, denial depression, acceptance

Essay Questions:

1. Create a booklet that illustrates examples of the Piagetian concepts of assimilation and accommodation. You might want to use examples from your experience of learning about psychology. In your booklet also provide examples of your own use of egocentrism, animism or artificialism in thinking?

2. How would you characterize your parents' parenting style? Were they warm, cold, restrictive or permissive? How did the parenting style you experienced affect your feelings and behavior? After studying this chapter, how will your own parenting style be similar to your parents? How will it be different? In a one-page essay characterize your parents parenting style and compare it with your own. Are you (or will you be) an authoritative parent? How do you know? Provide specific examples of your behavior to support your answer.

3. Did you undergo puberty early or late as compared to your peers? How did your experience with puberty affect your popularity and your self-esteem? Compare your experience with what is considered "typical" by psychologists in a one-page essay.

4. How do changes in cognitive development during adolescence contribute to the desire for privacy and risk taking? Did you have an intense need for privacy as an adolescent? Do you know adolescents who act as if they believe that they will live forever? Why do you think that adolescents think like this? Does Piaget's theory explain these behaviors? What do you think can be done – based on what you have learned about the thinking of adolescents – to decrease risk-taking behavior in today's adolescents? Prepare a two-page report that describes your recommendations; be sure to support your ideas with evidence from developmental theory.

5. Think of the older people that you know. In a three or four paragraph essay describe how the concepts of crystallized and fluid intelligence applies to their lives. What kind of cognitive changes can you look forward to as you age? Do you think that you will follow the "typical" pattern? Why or why not?

6. Erik Erikson wrote that one aspect of wisdom is the ability to visualize one's role in the march of history and to accept one's own death. Do you believe that acceptance of death is a sign of wisdom? Why or why not? Present your views in a two-page essay.

CONNECT & EXPAND:

1. **Prenatal Development: The Beginning of Our Life Story**

   Prenatal Screening. What tests and screening measures are available for pregnant women? Which ones are recommended as routine? When would a woman need alternative tests? Investigate the tests recommended for pregnant women and create a one-page summary of your findings. You might want to visit http://www.stanford.edu/~holbrook/. This site provides technical, but interesting information about a variety of prenatal tests used to diagnose many different conditions in both the unborn child and the mother. Includes ultrasound, amniocentesis, Percutaneous Umbilical Blood Sampling, and Rh Disease.

2. **Childhood: Cognitive Development**

   Have each member of your study group give the following Piagetian conservation tests to a four-year old and an eight-year-old child. Summarize the results and report your findings to your whole class in a format specified by your instructor.

   Conservation of number: Place two rows of 10 objects (M&M's or Skittles candies work great) so that they line up. Ask the child if the two rows have the same number of candies. (They should say yes.) In front of the child spread out one of the rows of candies so that there is about ½ inch of space between each candy. Ask the child if the two rows contain the same number of candies now. Record the child's response. Return the candies to their original position and repeat.

   Conservation of length: Cut two pieces of string so that they both are exactly 10 inches ling. Place both pieces of string one beneath the other so that the ends line up. Ask the child if the two strings are the same length. (They should say yes.) In front of the child scrunch up one of the strings so that it is looped over itself. Ask the child if the two strings are the same length now. Record the child's response. Return the strings to their original position and repeat.

   Conservation of substance: Take two identical balls of playdoh. Roll them in to balls until the child agrees that they are the same size. Now take one of the balls and roll it into a "hot dog" shape. Ask the child if the two pieces of playdoh have the same amount of playdoh. Record the child's response. Return the balls to their original shape and repeat.

3. **Childhood: Social and Personality Development**

   Child Temperament. Visit http://www.preventiveoz.org/ and use this program to develop a profile of yourself, your own child or a fictional one. To start using this program, click on **"Image of Your Child"** and complete the short, temperament questionnaire.   You will then see an on-line profile of your child's temperament. Using the further links research general strategies for managing the highs or lows of your child's temperament and what specific behavioral issues are normal for your child's temperament. Compare your "child's temperament" to those of the other members of your study group. Report the similarities and differences to your whole class in a format specified by your instructor.

4. **Adolescence: Physical Development**

Sex and sexuality are important issues for adolescents, yet American parents generally give their children little information about sex. Although both teenagers and parents express the need to talk freely about sex, parents are often reluctant and claim that they lack the knowledge and communication skills to talk openly about sex. One source of information about sex is popular magazines like *Parents*, Parenting.com, *Ladies Home Journal*, *Redbook* and for teens *YM* and *Seventeen* magazines.

Search the most recent issues of three of these magazines for information on adolescent sexuality. What kind of information is presented? Are issues like homosexuality, contraception and sexually transmitted diseases discussed? What about values are they addressed? How are the approaches of the "parent"-orient magazines different from those directed at teens? Share your findings with your study group. Report your study group's findings to your class in a format specified by your instructor.

5. **Adolescence: Social and Personality Development**

Consider the stereotype of adolescents as a time of "storm and stress". What findings or occurrences prompted this stereotype? Does this stereotype fit your own experience? How or how not? What does the psychological research suggest—is adolescence a time of "storm and stress?" Visit a teen chat room (http://www.chatweb.net) and pose this question to those present. Report your findings to your class in a format specified by your instructor.

6. **Adulthood: Physical Development**

Northwestern Mutual's Longevity Game. This is an interactive lifestyle and health awareness quiz, to get a general idea of how long you may live past retirement. Take the quiz. How long does the site suggest that you will live? The site also claims that you can learn the secrets of longevity, by finding out what their Centenarians have to say. Are there any behavior patterns that you could change that might add to your life expectancy? What factors may contribute to differences in health and longevity among people in different ethnic groups and gender? How would you explain different patterns of aging in different ethnic groups? Explain your views on this issue in a two-page essay.
URL: http://www.northwesternmutual.com/nmcom/NM/longevitygameintro/toolbox--calculator--longevitygameintro--longevity_intro

7. **Life Connections: Day Care—Blessing, Headache, or Both?**

Read more about the Psychological effects of Day Care. You can begin with the APA Monitor article @ http://www.apa.org/monitor/mar00/childcare.html.
What more is presented about the psychological effects of day care? Does the evidence suggest that a day care experience benefits or harms children? How? If you were a parent, how would (did) you choose the specific day care you use? How does your opinion of day care compare to that of the American Psychological Associations? Prepare a report of your findings for new parents in a format specified by your instructor.

Chapter Four: Sensation and Perception

PowerPreview: *Skim the major headings in this chapter in your textbook. Jot down anything that you are surprised or curious about. After this write down four or five questions that you have about the material in this chapter.*

Things that surprised me/I am curious about from Chapter 4:

Questions that I have about Sensation and Perception:

- •
- •
- •
- •

QUESTION: *These are some questions that you should be able to answer after you finish studying this chapter:*

Sensation and Perception: Your Tickets of Admission to the World Outside
- ❖ *What are sensation and perception?*
- ❖ *How do we know when something is there? How do we know when it has changed?*
- ❖ *What is signal-detection theory?*
- ❖ *What are feature detectors?*
- ❖ *How do our sensory systems adapt to a changing environment?*

Vision: Letting the Sun Shine In
- ❖ *Just what is this stuff called light?*
- ❖ *How does the eye work?*
- ❖ *What are some perceptual dimensions of color?*
- ❖ *How do we perceive color?*
- ❖ *Controversy in Psychology: What happens in the brain when lights with different wavelengths stimulate the retina? How many kinds of color receptors are there?*
- ❖ *What is color blindness? Why are some people colorblind?*

Visual Perception: How Perceptive?
- ❖ *How do we organize bits of information like perceptions into meaningful wholes?*
- ❖ *How do we perceive movement?*
- ❖ *How do we perceive depth?*
- ❖ *What are perceptual constancies? Why do we perceive a door to be a rectangle even when it is partly open?*

Hearing: Making Sense of Sound
- ❖ *What is sound?*

- ❖ *How does the ear work? How do we locate sounds?*
- ❖ *How do we perceive loudness and pitch?*
- ❖ *Controversy in Psychology: How Do We Explain Pitch Perception? What happens when the basilar membrane runs out of places to vibrate? What happens when it cannot vibrate fast enough?*
- ❖ *What is deafness? What can we do about it?*

The Chemical Senses: Smell and Taste
- ❖ *How does the sense of smell work?*
- ❖ *How does the sense of taste work?*

The Skin Senses (Yes it Does)
- ❖ *What are the skin senses? How do they work?*

Kinesthesis and the Vestibular Sense
- ❖ *What is kinesthesis?*
- ❖ *How does the vestibular sense work?*

Extrasensory Perception: Is There Perception Without Sensation?
- ❖ *Is there really such as thing as extrasensory perception? (ESP)*

Life Connections: Pain, Pain, Go Away—Don't Come Again Another Day
- ❖ *What is pain? What can we do about it?*

Reading for Understanding/Reflect: The *following section provides you with the opportunity to perform 3 of the R's of the PQ4R study method. In this section I will encourage you to check your understanding of your reading of the text by filling in the blanks in the brief paragraphs that relate to each of the preview questions. You will also be prompted to rehearse your understanding of the material with periodic Rehearsal/Reflection breaks. Remember it is better to study in more frequent, short sessions then in one long "cram session." Be sure to reward yourself with short study breaks before each of the Rehearsal/Reflection exercises.*

Reading for Understanding about "Sensation and Perception: Your Tickets of Admission to the World Outside"

What are sensation and perception? (1)_____ is a mechanical process that involves the stimulation of sensory receptors (neuron) and the transmission of sensory information to the (2)_____ nervous system. Sensory receptors are located in (3)_____ organs such as eyes and ears. Stimulation of the senses results from sources of (4)_____ like light and sound or from the presence of chemicals. (5)_____ is the active organization of sensations into a representation of the outside world and it reflects (6)_____ and expectations.

How do we know when something is there? How do we know when it has changed? The discipline that deals with the ways in which we translate physical events into psychological experiences is known as (7)_____. Energy sources like light and sound are converted to neural impulses by the sensory receptors, a process known as (8)_____. The absolute threshold is the term used by Gustav (9)_____ to refer to the (10)_____ intensity at which the stimulus can be detected. (11)_____ determine the absolute threshold of the senses by exposing subjects to progressively stronger stimuli until they find the minimum stimuli that the person cannot detect no less then half the time. It has been discovered that these absolute threshold are not really absolute; that is, some people are more (12)_____ than others.

Psychophysicist Ernst (13)_____ discovered that the threshold for perceiving differences in intensity is about 1/60th of their intensity and this constant carries his name. The difference threshold is the (14)_____ difference in intensity that can be discriminated. Difference thresholds are expressed as (15)_____'s constants. Closely related to difference thresholds is the concept of (16)_____ (17)_____ difference, or the minimal amount by which a source of energy must be increased, or decreased, so that a difference in intensity will be perceived.

What is signal-detection theory? According to signal (18)_____ theory, the intensity of the signal is just one factor that determines whether people will perceive sensory stimuli. The theory explains the ways in which stimuli (19)_____, background noise and (20)_____ factors like motivation, familiarity with a stimulus and attention, interact to influence whether a stimulus will be detected.

What are feature detectors? Feature detectors were first discovered by David (21)_____ and Torsten (22)_____ and are neurons that fire in response to specific (23)_____ of sensed stimuli. Feature detectors in the visual cortex respond to particular features of visual input such as lines sensed at various (24)_____, or specific colors and (25)_____ feature detectors respond to the pitch and loudness of sound stimuli.

How do our sensory systems adapt to a changing environment? We become more (26)_____ to stimuli of low magnitude and less sensitive to stimuli that remain the same. Sensory (27)_____ refers to these processes of adjustment. Growing more sensitive to stimulation is referred to as (28)_____, or positive adaptation. Growing less sensitive to continuous stimulation is called (29)_____, or negative adaptation.

Reflection Break # 1:
1. Without using the terms "sense" or "perceive," clearly differentiate between the processes of sensation and perception.

2. Using the principles of signal detection theory explain why for the first few nights after moving from the country to the city you might first notice all of the street noise, but your roommate who has lived the city all their life, would not. What might happen if you take your "city slicker" roommate to the country?

Reading for Understanding about "Vision: Letting the Sun Shine In"
Just what is this stuff called light? Visible light triggers visual sensations and is part of the spectrum of (30)_____ energy. Light is made up of (31)_____ of energy; different colors have different (32)_____. The wavelength of light determines its color, or (33)_____. The color violet has the (34)_____ wavelength and red has the (35)_____. White sunlight can be broken down into the colors of the rainbow by the means of a (36)_____.

How does the eye work? The eye senses and transmits visual stimulation to the (37)_____ lobe of the cerebral cortex. Light first passes through the (38)_____, or the transparent covering of the eye's surface. The size of the (39)_____ determines the amount that can pass through the cornea. The pupil is an opening of the muscle known as the (40)_____, or the colored part of the eye. Once light passes through the pupil, it encounters the (41)_____. The lens focuses light into the (42)_____ by changing its thickness. The retina is composed of (43)_____, or neurons that are sensitive to light, called rods and cones. (44)_____ permit perception of color. (45)_____ transmit sensations of light and dark only.

Light is transmitted from the retina to the brain via the (46)_____ nerve, which is made up of the axons of retinal (47)_____ cells. In the (48)_____, or most sensitive area of the retina, the photoreceptor cells are densely packed. The (49)_____ spot, or the area of the retina where the axons of the ganglion cells collect to form the optic nerve, is insensitive to visual stimulation. Visual (50)_____, or sharpness of vision, is connected with the (51)_____ of the eye and age. As we age, our lenses grow brittle, making it difficult to focus; this condition is called (52)_____.

The fovea of the retina is made up almost exclusively of (53)_____. Rods are nearly absent from the (54)_____ and are more sensitive than cones to lowered lighting. The process of adjusting to lower lighting conditions is called (55)_____ adaptation; adaptation to bright lighting conditions takes place more rapidly then dark adaptation. Dark adaptation takes longer because (56)_____ continue to adapt to darkness once cones have reached their peak adaptation.

What are some perceptual dimensions of color? There are three perceptual dimensions of color; they are hue, (57)_____ and saturation. The (58)_____ of light determines its hue. The (59)_____ of a color is its degree of lightness or darkness. (60)_____ refers to the intensity of a color. Colors can also have (61)_____ associations within various cultural settings. If we blend the colors of the spectrum into a (62)_____ a color wheel is created. Colors on the green blue side of a color wheel are considered to be (63)_____ in temperature; those on the red orange side are considered (64)_____. Colors across from one another on the color wheel are labeled (65)_____ colors. Red-(66)_____ and blue-(67)_____ are the major complementary color pairs. When lights of complementary colors are mixed they dissolve to (68)_____. (69)_____ result when there has been as persistent sensation of one color of a complementary pair; you perceive the complementary color when the first color is removed.

How do we perceive color? Our ability to perceive (70)_____ depends on the eye's transmission of different messages to the brain when lights of different (71)_____ stimulate the cones in the retina.

Controversy in Psychology: What happens in the eye and the brain when lights with different wavelengths stimulate the retina? There are (72)_____ theories as to how we perceive color. According to the (73)_____ theory, there are three types of cones—some of which are sensitive to (74)_____, others to (75)_____, and still others to (76)_____. Research shows that there are indeed (77)_____ that are sensitive to blue, green and red. The (78)_____ theory proposes three types of color receptors: (79)_____-green, (80)_____-yellow and light-(81)_____. Opponent process theory is supported by the appearance of (82)_____. Research suggests that (83)_____ theories are at least partially correct.

What is color blindness? Why are some people color-blind? People with normal color vision are called (84)_____. (85)_____ see no color and (86)_____ are blind to some parts of the spectrum. (87)_____ color blindness is rare. (88)_____ color blindness is more common and is a sex-linked trait that affects mostly (89)_____.

Reflection Break # 2:

a. red light
b. violet light
c. cornea
d. iris
e. pupil
f. sclera
g. lens
h. retina
i. rods

j. cones
k. dark adaptation
l. acuity
m. optic nerve
n. fovea
o. blind spot
p. value
q. saturation
r. complementary colors

s. afterimage
t. trichromatic theory
u. opponent process
    theory
v. tichromat
w. monochromat
x. dichromat
y. hue
z. warm colors

_____1.   Individuals able to discriminate among all color of the visible spectrum.
_____2.   The colored part of the eye.
_____3.   Colors that are located directly across from one another on the color wheel.
_____4.   Individuals who are sensitive to only lightness and darkness; fully color blind.
_____5.   Photoreceptors that provide color vision.
_____6.   An image that is the result of persistent sensation of colors; contains the
            complementary colors of the original image.
_____7.   The part of the eye that focuses the light by adjusting its thickness.
_____8.   Colors on the yellow/orange/red side of the color wheel.
_____9.   The opening in the eye that allows light to pass through.
_____10.   Individuals that can discriminate among red and green, or blue and yellow, but not
            all.
_____11.   This term is used to refer to the intensity of a color.
_____12.   Light with the longest wavelength
_____13.   The hard, protective "white" of the eye.
_____14.   The degree of lightness or darkness of a color.
_____15.   Made up of the axons of the ganglion cells; travels from the eye to the occipital lobe
            of the brain.
_____16.   States that color vision results from action of blue-yellow, red-green and brightness
            cells.
_____17.   Cells that are only sensitive to the intensity of light.
_____18.   The photoreceptive part of the eye.
_____19.   The transparent surface that covers the front of the eyes surface.
_____20.   Proposes that there are three types of color receptors, red, green and blue-violet.
_____21.   Term used to refer to the sharpness of vision.
_____22.   The portion of the retina that is insensitive to visual stimulation.
_____23.   The wavelength of light.
_____24.   The process of adjusting to lower light conditions.
_____25.   The most sensitive area of the retina; contains densely packed cones.
_____26.   Light with the shortest wavelength.

Reading for Understanding about "Visual Perception: How Perceptive!"

How do we organize bits of information like perceptions into meaningful wholes? Perceptual organization involves (90)_____ patterns and processing information about (91)_____ between parts and the whole. Whereas sensation may be thought of as a (92)_____ process, (93)_____ is an active process through which we interpret the world around us. The rules of (94)_____ involve figure-ground relationships, proximity, similarity, continuity, common fate and closure. The principle of (95)_____ refers to our tendency to perceive a complete, or whole, figure, even when there are gaps in the sensory input. (96)_____ refers to the fact that when you look out your window and see many things; these objects tend to be perceived as figures against backgrounds. If the figure-ground relationship is (97)_____ our perceptions tend to be unstable. The (98)_____ vase and the (99)_____ cube are two of psychologists' favorite examples of perceptual shifts that result from an ambiguous figure-ground.

The perceptual law of (100)_____ refers to our tendency to group objects that are close together, or near one another as a perceptual unit. (101)_____ refers to our tendency to perceive objects that are like one another as belonging together. The rule of (102)_____ refers to our tendency to perceive a series of points or broken lines as having unity. According to the law of (103)_____, elements seen moving together are perceived as belonging together. Perception of a whole followed by perception of parts is termed (104)_____ processing whereas; perception of the parts that leads to perception of a whole is termed (105)_____ processing.

How do we perceive movement? The visual perception of movement is based on a change of (106)_____ relative to other objects. In addition to studying real movement psychologists also study three types of (107)_____ movement: the autokinetic effect, stroboscopic motion, and the phi phenomenon. The (108)_____ effect refers to the tendency to perceive a stationary point of light in a dark room as moving. (109)_____ motion, responsible for the illusion of motion pictures, occurs through the presentation of a rapid progression of images of stationary objects, or (110)_____. The (111)_____ refers to the apparent motion of a series of lights turned on and off.

How do we perceive depth? (112)_____ perception involves monocular and binocular cues. (113)_____ cues, rely on the use of one eye and include the (114)_____ cues of perspective, relative size, clearness, interposition, shadows, and texture gradient, and the (115)_____ cues of: motion parallax and accommodation. Distant objects stimulate (116)_____ areas on the retina than those nearby, as a result, (117)_____ occurs, that is parallel lines appear to come closer together as they recede from us. (118)_____ refers to the fact that distant objects look smaller then nearby objects; (119)_____ refers to the fact that closer objects provide more detail than distant objects. The monocular cue of (120)_____ refers to the fact that nearby objects will overlap and block our view of distant objects. (121)_____ refers to the fact that we learn that an opaque object blocks light and produces shadows and this gives us information about the dimensionally of objects. Another monocular cue is the use of (122)_____, in this cue we learn the closer objects are perceived as having rougher textures. Motion cues are also (123)_____ cues, the tendency of objects to seem to move backward or forward as a function of their distance is known as (124)_____.

(125)_____ cues, or cues that involve the use of both eyes to judge depth include retinal disparity and convergence. (126)_____ refers to the fact that the retina of each eye receives a different image of an object. The degree of (127)_____ in these images is the retinal disparity. (128)_____ objects have greater retinal disparity. (129)_____ refers to the tension in the eye muscles that occurs when we attempt to maintain a single image of a nearby object by turning our eyes inward.

What are perceptual constancies? Why do we perceive a door to be a rectangle even when it is ajar? How can the principles of visual perception be used to trick the eye? Perceptual (130)_____ are acquired through experience and make the world a stable place. There are a number of perceptual constancies including size, color, brightness and shape. We (131)_____ to assume that objects retain their size, shape, brightness and color despite their (132)_____ from us, or changes in (133)_____ conditions. Visual (134)_____ such as the Hering-Helmholtz and Muller-Lyer tend to trick the eye because they play with perceptual constancies.

Reflection Break # 3:
Gestalt Laws of Perceptual Organization: *Label each of the following examples as to which Gestalt Law of Perceptual organization they illustrate.*

_____1.   XXXXXXXXX
              OOOOOOOOO
              XXXXXXXXX
              OOOOOOOOO

_____2.   X   O   X   O
              X   O   X   O
              X   O   X   O
              X   O   X   O

_____3. ----------------|----------|----------

_____4.   XXXXXXXXXXX
              OOOOOOOOOOOOO
              YYYYYYYYYYYYYY
              QQQQQQQQQQQQQQQQQ

Perceptual Organization, Movement, Depth, Constancies and Illusions:

a. top-down processing
b. bottom-up processing
c. auto-kinetic effect
d. stroboiscopic motion
e. phi phenomenon
f. monocular cues
g. binocular cues
h. perspective
i. relative size
j. interposition
k. shadowing
l. texture gradient
m. motion parallax
n. retinal disparity
o. convergence
p. clearness
q. pictorial cues
r. color constancy
s. brightness constancy
t. shape constancy
u. visual illusions

v. size constancy

_____1. Images that trick the eye because of our tendency to use perceptual rules that do not apply.

_____2. The tendency for us to perceive objects as retaining their color, even if lighting conditions alter their appearance.

_____3. An example of apparent motion in which movement is provided by the presentation of a rapid progression of images of stationary objects.

_____4. The perception of larger objects as being closer to us.

_____5. The tendency to perceive a stationary point of light in a dark room as moving.

_____6. The perception of objects with greater detail as being closer to us.

_____7. Perception of shadows and highlights as giving depth to two-dimensional objects.

_____8. Perception of objects with tougher texture as being closer to the observer.

_____9. Perceptual processes that relies on knowledge of the "big" picture to organize a perception.

_____10. Perception of objects that seem to move forward with us as distant, and those that move backwards as nearby.

_____11. The tendency to perceive objects as maintaining their shape, even if they look different.

_____12. An example of apparent motion in which an on/off process is perceived as movement.

_____13. The tendency to perceive one color as brighter or darker due to our expectations of that color.

_____14. Perceptual processing that begins with smaller units and works toward the whole.

_____15. Perceiving objects that cast large differences in retinal images on the retina as being closer.

_____16. Perception of objects that require greater inward movement of the eyes as being closer.

_____17. The perception of overlapping objects as being dimensional.

_____18. Perceptual cues commonly used by artists to create an impression of a third dimension in two-dimensional works.

_____19. The tendency to perceive objects as the same size even though the size of it image on retina varies.

_____20. Perceptual cues that involve both eyes.

_____21. Perceptual cues that rely on the input from one eye.

_____22. The perception of parallel lines coming closer together, or converging, as they recede from us.

Reading for Understanding about "Hearing: Making Sense of Sound"

What is sound? Sound waves, also called (135)_____ stimulation, require a medium such as air or water in order to be transmitted. Sound (136)_____ alternately compress and expand molecules of the medium, creating (137)_____. The human ear can hear sounds varying in (138)_____ from 20 to 20,000 cycles per second (Hz). Pitch and (139)_____ are two psychological dimensions of sound. The (140)_____ of a sound is determined by its (141)_____, or the number of cycles per second, and are expressed in the unit hertz. One cycle per second is (142)_____ Hz. The greater the frequency, the (143)_____ the sound's pitch. The loudness of a sound corresponds to the (144)_____, or height, of sound waves as measured in (145)_____(dB). (146)_____ dB is equivalent to the threshold of hearing; the lowest sound that the typical person can hear. We can experience hearing (147)_____ if we are exposed to protracted sounds of 85 to 90 dB or more.

How does the ear work? The (148)_____ is shaped and structured to capture sound waves and has three parts, the (149)_____ ear, the (150)_____ ear and the (151)_____ ear. The outer ear is shaped to funnel sound waves to the (152)_____, a thin membrane that vibrates in response to sound waves. The middle ear functions as an (153)_____ and contains the eardrum and three small (154)_____, the hammer, the anvil and the stirrup, which also transmit sound by (155)_____. The stirrup is attached to another vibrating membrane, the (156)_____ window. The oval window transmits vibrations into the inner ear, which is composed of the bony tube known as the (157)_____. The cochlea is divided into three fluid filled (158)_____ by membranes. One of the membranes is the (159)_____ membrane and vibrations in the fluid of the cochlea press against this membrane. Attached to the basilar membrane is the organ of (160)_____. The organ of Corti contains some 16,000 receptor, or (161)_____ cells that dance in response to vibrations of the (162)_____ membrane. The up and down movements of these hair cells generate neural impulses that are carried via the (163)_____ nerve to the temporal lobes of the brain.

How do we locate sounds? When sounds come from the right or left we locate sounds by determining in which ear they are (164)_____. It is more difficult for us to locate sounds that come from directly in (165)_____ or behind us; in this case, we might (166)_____ our heads to pin down the directional information.

How do we perceive loudness and pitch? The (167)_____ of sounds appear to be related to the number of, and how often the receptor neurons in the organ of (168)_____ fire. Sounds are perceived as (169)_____ when more sensory neurons fire.

Controversy in Psychology: What happens when the basilar membrane runs out of places to vibrate? Explaining (170)_____ perception appears, like color vision, to take at least two processes. The (171)_____ theory of pitch perception holds that the pitch of a sound is sensed according to the place along the basilar membrane that vibrates in response to it; it accounts for sounds whose frequencies exceed 4,000 Hz. (172)_____ theory states that pitch perception depends on the stimulation of neural impulses that match the frequency of the sound waves, and accounts for frequencies of 20 to 1,000 Hz. The (173)_____ principle states that groups of neurons take turns firing and accounts for pitch discrimination between a few hundred and 4,000 cycles per second.

What is deafness? What can we do about it? There are two major types of (174)_____. (175)_____ deafness-common among older people-is caused by damage to the middle ear and is often ameliorated by (176)_____, which amplify sounds. (177)_____ deafness is usually caused by damage to neurons in the inner ear, and can sometimes be corrected by (178)_____ implants.

Reflection Break # 4:
1. Summarize the processes involved in the transduction of sound waves by the ear.

2.	Describe the claims of the place, frequency and volley theories of pitch perception. Explain why all three theories are needed to account for pitch discrimination.

Reading for Understanding about "The Chemical Senses: Smell and Taste"

How does the sense of smell work? The sense of smell is a (179)_____ sense. It samples molecules of substances called (180)_____ through the olfactory membrane in each nostril. Receptor neurons fire when a few drops of a substance in a (181)_____ form come in contact with them. The firing of the receptor neurons is then transmitted to the brain via the (182)_____ nerve. Smell makes a key contribution to the (183)_____ of foods.

How does the sense of taste work? (184)_____ is the other chemical sense. There are four primary taste qualities: sweet, (185)_____, salty, and (186)_____. Flavor involves the odor, (187)_____, and temperature of food, as well as its taste. Taste is sensed through taste cells, which are located in taste buds on the (188)_____. Taste buds appear to specialize; some appear to be more responsive to (189)_____ whereas others react to several tastes. People live in different taste worlds; those of us with low sensitivity for sweet taste may require (190)_____ the sugar to sweeten our food, people who enjoy bitter food may actually be taste (191)_____ to them. These types of taste sensitivities appear to have a strong (192)_____ component. Although older people often complain that their food has no (193)_____, it is more likely to be a result in a decline in the sense of (194)_____, and thus the flavor of food, then a decline in taste.

Reading for Understanding about "The Skin Senses (Yes it Does)"

What are the skin senses? How do they work? The (195)_____ senses include touch, pressure, warmth, cold, and pain. We have distinct sensory receptors for pressure, (196)_____ and pain, but some nerve endings may receive more than one type of sensory input. (197)_____ and (198)_____ are sensed by receptors located around the roots of hair cells below the surface of the skin. Psychophysicists use methods like the (199)_____ threshold, where the subject is touched at two different points until they report that there are two rods, to determine sensitivity to pressure. This type of research has shown that the fingertips, lips, nose and cheeks are (200)_____ sensitive then other areas of the body. The receptors for temperature are located just beneath the (201)_____. We have (202)_____ receptors for warmth and cold.

Reading for Understanding about "Kinesthesis and the Vestibular Sense

What is kinesthesis? How does the vestibular sense work? (203)_____ is the sensation of body position and movement. It relies on sensory organs in the joints, (204)_____, and muscles that is fed back to the brain. The (205)_____ sense is housed primarily in the semicircular canals of the ears and tells us whether we are in an upright position.

Reading for Understanding about " Extrasensory Perception: Is There Perception Without Sensation?"

Extrasensory perception, or (206)_____, refers to the perception of objects or events through means other than sensory organs. If you had (207)_____would be able to perceive future events in advance; on the other hand if you were able to mentally manipulate or move objects you would have (208)_____. Both of these concepts are associated with ESP. Two other theoretical forms of ESP are (209)_____, or the direct transmission of thoughts from one person to another, and (210)_____, or the perception of objects that do not stimulate the sensory organs.

Is there really such as thing as extrasensory perception (ESP)? Many psychologists do not believe that ESP is an appropriate area for (211)_____ study. The ganzfeld procedure studies (212)_____ by having one person (the sender) try to mentally transmit visual information to a receiver in another room. Because of the (213)_____ problem and lack of replication of positive results, there is no reliable evidence for the existence of ESP.

Reflection Break # 5:

1. Using the material presented in this section explain why food often "tastes" funny when you have a stuffy nose or cold.

2. Explain why some parts of the body are more sensitive to touch an pressure than others.

3. What is the general opinion of the psychological community as to whether ESP exists? Why?

Reading for Understanding about "Life Connections: Pain, Pain, Go Away--Don't Come Again Another Day"

What is pain? What can we do about it? (214)_____ means there is something wrong in the body. We can sense pain throughout most of the body, but it is usually (215)_____ where nerve endings are densely packed. Pain (216)_____ at the point of contact and is transmitted to the brain by various (217)_____, including prostaglandins, and bradykinin and substance P. (218)_____ facilitate transmission of the pain message to the brain and heighten circulation to the injured area causing the redness and swelling we know as (219)_____. Analgesic drugs like (220)_____ and ibuprofen alleviate pain by inhibiting the production of prostaglandins.

Melzack's theory of the "(221)_____" suggests that perception of pain also involves other aspects of our physiology and psychology and reflects our cognitive interpretation of the situation, our emotional response, and the ways in which we respond to stress. Melzack also proposes a "(222)_____" theory of pain. Amputees often experience pain in "(223)_____" limbs. Rubbing or scratching painful areas can (224)_____ perception of pain by transmitting additional messages that have the effect of shutting down a "gate" in the (225)_____.

Traditional (226)_____ believe that the practice balances the body's flow of energy, but research reveals that it stimulates nerves that reach the (227)_____ and may decrease pain by causing release of (228)_____. Coping with pain has traditionally been a (229)_____ issue, however more recently psychology has provided expanded method of fighting pain. Psychological research has show that giving people accurate (230)_____ about their condition often helps them manage pain. Distraction and fantasy, hypnosis, and relaxation and biofeedback training have also proved (231)_____ in pain management.

REVIEW: Key Terms and Concepts

FINAL CHAPTER REVIEW
Recite:

Visit the Recite section on pages 175-177 of your textbook. Use the card provided with your textbook to cover the answers of the Recite section. Read the questions aloud and recite the answers. This will help you cement your knowledge of key concepts.

Multiple Choice Questions

1. Sensation is best defined as
   a. the active process in which sensations are organized and interpreted to form an inner representation of the world.
   b. the use of needles to relieve pain.
   c. the stimulation of sensory receptors and the transmission of sensory information to the CNS.
   d. both a & c.

2. A candle flame viewed from 30 miles on a clear, dark night, a watch ticking from about 20 feet away in a quiet room and 1 teaspoon of sugar dissolved in 2 gallons of water are examples of
   a. the j. n. d.
   b. sensation.
   c. perception.
   d. absolute thresholds.

3. Hubel and Wiesel discovered neurons in the visual cortex of the brain that fire in response to particular features of visual input. These cells are known as
   a. receptor cells.
   b. signal detection cells.
   c. feature detectors.
   d. sensory adapters.

4. When you first apply perfume or cologne you are able to smell it. However, after a period of time, you no longer smell it. This is an example of
   a. sensory adaptation.
   b. sensitization.
   c. Signal detection theory.
   d. absolute threshold.

5. Which of the following indicates the correct sequence of visual processing?
   a. cornea, pupil, lens, retina, bipolar cells, ganglion cells, optic nerve to the brain
   b. retina, cornea, pupil, lens, bipolar cells, ganglion cells, optic nerve to the brain
   c. pupil, cornea, lens, retina, ganglion cells, bipolar cells, optic nerve to the brain
   d. cornea, pupil, lens, bipolar cells, retina, ganglion cells, optic nerve to the brain

6. Natasha has recently begun experiencing difficulty with her vision and is able to see things at a distance, but has difficulty focusing on objects close to her. You explain to her that the shape of her eye has changed and has affected her

   _____.
   a. nearsightnedness.
   b. visual acuity.
   c. color-blindness.
   d. bipolar cells.

7. Which theory of color vision explains color best?
   a. The trichromatic theory.
   b. The opponent-process theory.
   c. The Young-Helmholtz theory.
   d. All of the above.

8. Deon is unable to discriminate among colors of the visible spectrum and is sensitive to only lightness and darkness. Deon is
   a. a monochromat.
   b. a dicromat.
   c. a trichromat.
   d. congenitally blind.

9. When you perceive the figure below as a three columns of X's and three columns of O's, you are relying on the perceptual rule of

X O X O X O
X O X O X O
X O X O X O
X O X O X O

a. continuity.
b. common fate.
c. proximity.
d. similarity.

10. Brad solves puzzles by looking at the cover picture and then looking for pieces to fill in the picture. Brad is using _____ to solve the puzzle.
a. continuity
b. bottom-up processing
c. top down processing
d. figure ground

11. Cues like perspective, relative size, clearness and texture gradient create an illusion of depth that can be perceived by _____ are known as _____ cues.
a. one eye, monocular
b. two eyes; binocular
c. one eye; binocular
d. two eyes, monocular

12. Objects that are nearer are perceived with greater detail then distant objects. Thus artists can suggest that objects are closer to the viewer by depicting them with greater detail. This is an example of the use of the monocular depth cue of
a. perspective.
b. relative size.
c. interposition.
d. clearness.

13. As you try to maintain a single image of an object moving closer to you, your eyes must turn inward, making you cross-eyed. The tension in the eye muscles provides a binocular cue for depth known as
a. interposition.
b. convergence.
c. retinal disparity.
d. motion parallax.

14. How do psychologists explain pitch perception?
a. Place theory is used to explain pitches below 4,000 Hz; frequency theory is used to explain pitches between 20 and a few thousand cycles per second, and the volley principle is used to explain pitch discrimination between a few hundred and 4,000 cycles per second.
b. Place theory is used to explain pitches above 4,000 Hz; frequency theory is used to explain pitches between 20 and a few hundred cycles per second, and the volley principle is used to explain pitch discrimination between a few hundred and 4,000 cycles per second.
c. Place theory is used to explain pitches above 4,000 Hz; frequency theory is used to explain pitches between a few hundred and 4,000 cycles per second, and the volley principle is used to explain pitch discrimination between 20 and a few hundred cycles per second.
d. Place theory is used to explain pitches below 4,000 Hz; frequency theory is used to explain pitches between a few hundred and 4,000 cycles per second, and the volley principle is used to explain pitch discrimination between 20 and a few hundred cycles per second.

15. Dustin recently sustained damage to the structures of his middle ear and is now deaf. Dustin's deafness is known as _____ deafness.
    a. conductive
    b. sensorineural
    c. cochlear
    d. acoustic trauma

16. Smell is to _____ as taste is to _____.
    a. olfactory neuron; taste bud
    b. odors; flavors
    c. Both a & b.
    d. None of the above.

17. The method used by psychophysicists to assess sensitivity to pressure is known as
    a. two-point threshold.
    b. acupuncture.
    c. pressure adaptation.
    d. gate theory.

18. Kinesthesis is to _____ as vestibular is to _____.
    a. semicircular canals; joints & tendons
    b. joints & tendons; semicircular canals
    c. skin; semicircular canals
    d. joints & tendons; tongue

19. Madame Lola claims that she is able to perceive future events in advance of them occurring. Madame Lola is claiming she has
    a. telepathy.
    b. precognition.
    c. psychokinesis.
    d. clairvoyance.

20. You are studying telepathy having one person act as a "sender" by randomly viewing selected visual stimuli while a person in another room acts as a "receiver" and tries to mentally tune in the sender. The procedure you are using is known as the
    a. File drawer problem procedure.
    b. Rhine card deck procedure.
    c. Ganzfeld procedure.
    d. Psychokinesis procedure.

Essay Questions:
1. You have been hired by an appliance company to develop a print advertising campaign for a washing machine. Your consumer research tells you that the public perceives the machine as "big" and "clunky," and the dials "cheap" looking. Describe how you would use your knowledge of perceptual organizing principles to create the illusion of a smaller, less cheap looking machine that would sell better.

2. Explain why it would be more difficult for a one-eyed golfer to judge the distance to the pin then it would be for a two-eyed golfer.

3. Compare and contrast Conductive and Sensorineural deafness. How do people with each type cope with the impairment?

4. Sports require great sensory and perceptual skill. Think about your favorite sport and identify the sensory input needed to perform. Describe the actions of the various sense organs during play. How does the brain help to coordinate the activities of all of the sensory systems?

5. When some people have limbs amputated due to accidents or disease, they often feel pain from their "phantom" limb. Based on your knowledge of pain sensation and brain functions how would you account for this phenomenon?

CONNECT & EXPAND:

1. **Sensations:** With a partner, blindfold yourself and walk around a familiar room. Note the sensory experiences that you have. How are they different then those you normally experience? Now visit an unfamiliar room. How is your sensory experience different? What sensory information did you rely on to avoid tripping and bumping in to things? How is this different from the information that you use all the time? Now cover your ears and repeat the experiences, how is your sensory experience different without auditory versus visual experience?

2. **Laws of Perceptual Organizations:**
Similarity, proximity, and common fate: Examine magazines, newspaper or children's books for illustrations that depict the above gestalt organizational principles.

Closure and continuity: Make line drawings of familiar objects by tracing pictures from children's coloring books leaving out sections of the drawing. Ask your study partners, or friends to identify the objects in the pictures. See how incomplete the drawings can be and still be identified.

Present your illustrations of each of the laws on a poster board. Do not label them. Share your board with your classmates and see of they can identify the principles.

3. **Perceptual Illusions:** Visit the illusion website at
http://www.ritsumei.ac.jp/~akitaoka/cataloge.html and at
http://dragon.uml.edu/psych/illusion.html
Examine some of the illusions. Try to describe which of the perceptual organizing principles and constancies are being used to create these illusions. Present your findings to your classmates.

4. **Taste versus Flavor:** Do this with a partner.
    Prepare slices of apple and other fruits of different textures, an onion, and different varieties of potato chips (sour cream & onion, salt & vinegar and plain).
    Blindfold your partner.
    Begin with the potato chips. Have your partner pinch their nose closed. Place a potato chip inside their mouth. Can they tell you which flavor it is? Once they have guessed allow them to unplug their nose. What happens to their experience of taste?
    Repeat the same procedure with the rest of the chips, the fruit and onion.
When the objects were placed in your mouth with your nose closed was it more difficult to identify what you tasted? Why?
What where you able to tell about the objects with your nose plugged? Does the texture of some of the food tell you anything?

5. **ESP:** Do you think that you might have psychic abilities? For one week keep track of the times when you have special feelings about something that is about to happen or when you try to make something happen. At the end of the week examine your report. Do the events that you predict actually happen like you predict they will? Were able to successfully wish things into being? Does the week's data support the fact that you have psychic ability?

6. **Life Connections: Pain, Pain Go Away –Gender Differences in Pain.** Table 4.3 on page 172 of your textbook describes data obtained by the Arthritis Foundation in 2000 indicating gender differences in men and women's experience of pain. More recently there has been an increased interest in gender related factors that might impact pain sensitivity and the higher prevalence of pain conditions in women. Research the current views on gender differences in pain perception and management and report your findings to your classmates in a format specified by your instructor.

Chapter Five: Consciousness

PowerPreview: *Skim the major headings in this chapter in your textbook. Jot down anything that you are surprised or curious about. After this write down four or five questions that you have about the material in this chapter.*

Things that surprised me/I am curious about from Chapter 5:

Questions that I have about Consciousness:

-
-
-
-

QUESTION: *These are some questions that you should be able to answer after you finish studying this chapter:*

Just What Is Consciousness?
- ❖ *What is consciousness?*

Sleep and Dreams
- ❖ *What is a circadian rhythm?*
- ❖ *What occurs during sleep?*
- ❖ *Why do we sleep?*
- ❖ *What are dreams? Why do we dream what we dream?*
- ❖ *What kinds of sleep disorders are there?*

Altering Consciousness Through Hypnosis: On Being Entranced
- ❖ *What is hypnosis?*
- ❖ *What changes in consciousness are induced by hypnosis?*
- ❖ *How do modern psychologists explain the effects of hypnosis?*

Altering Consciousness Through Meditation: Letting Your World Fade Away
- ❖ *What is meditation?*
- ❖ *What are the effects of meditation?*

Altering Consciousness Through BioFeedback: Getting in Touch with the Untouchable
- ❖ *What is biofeedback training?*
- ❖ *How is biofeedback training used?*

Altering Consciousness Through Drugs
- ❖ *What are substance abuse and dependence?*
- ❖ *What are the causes of substance abuse and dependence?*
- ❖ *What are the effects of alcohol?*

- *Controversy in Psychology: Is a Drink a Day Good for you?*
- *What are the effects of opiates?*
- *What are the effects of barbiturates and methaqualone?*
- *What are the effects of amphetamines?*
- *What are the effects of cocaine?*
- *What are the effects of nicotine?*
- *What are the effects of marijuana?*
- *Controversy in Psychology: Is marijuana harmful? Should it be available as a medicine?*
- *What are the effects of LSD and other kinds of hallucinogenic drugs?*

Life Connections: Getting to Sleep—and Elsewhere-Without Drugs

Reading for Understanding/Reflect: The *following section provides you with the opportunity to perform 2 of the R's of the PQ4R study method. In this section I will encourage you to check your understanding of your reading of the text by filling in the blanks in the brief paragraphs that relate to each of the preview questions. You will also be prompted to rehearse your understanding of the material with periodic Rehearsal/Reflection breaks. Remember it is better to study in more frequent, short sessions then in one long "cram session." Be sure to reward yourself with short study breaks before each of the Reflection exercises.*

Reading for Understanding about "What Is Consciousness?"
Controversy in Psychology: Is consciousness a proper area of psychological study?
(1)_____ has not always been an acceptable topic of study in psychology. Early psychologists like William (2)_____ and John (3)_____ felt that consciousness was not a proper area of study because it could not be directly observed or measured. Today however, many psychologists believe that consciousness lies within the (4)_____ and that we cannot capture the richness of human experience without referring to consciousness.

What is consciousness? The term *consciousness* is a psychological (5)_____, or a concept that has been devised to help understand our observations of behavior, that has several meanings, including sensory (6)_____, the selective aspect of (7)_____, direct inner awareness; personal unity, or the sense of (8)_____, and the (9)_____ state.

(10)_____ as sensory awareness refers to our ability to be (11)_____, or conscious of the environment around us. Sometimes, however, we are (12)_____ of sensory stimulation, that is, unless we pay attention. Focusing on a particular stimulus is referred to as (13)_____, a concept important to self-control. To adapt to our environment we must (14)_____ which stimuli to pay attention to and which to ignore. Our ability to pick out what one person is saying in a noisy room is selective attention, also, adeptly termed the (15)_____ effect.

We can also be conscious, or have direct (16)_____, of thoughts, images, emotions and memories without sensory stimulation. This aspect of consciousness is difficult to measure (17)_____. Sigmund Freud, the founder of (18)_____, differentiated between thoughts that are conscious and those that are (19)_____. Material that is not currently in awareness, but is readily available is said to be (20)_____ material. According to (21)_____ some painful memories and unacceptable sexual and aggressive impulses are automatically ejected from our conscious awareness. (22)_____ of these memories and impulses allows us to avoid feelings of anxiety, shame and guilt. When we choose to stop thinking about unacceptable ideas, he argued that we are engaging in (23)_____.

Reflection Break # 1:

1. What is a psychological construct?

2. Contrast the five different meanings for the psychological construct of consciousness presented in your textbook.

3. Is consciousness an appropriate area of study for psychologists? What do you think? Explain.

Reading for Understanding about "Sleep and Dreams"

What is a circadian rhythm? A (24)_____ is a cycle that is connected with the 24-hour period of the earth's rotation, such as the sleep-wake cycle. A cycle of wakefulness and sleep is normally 24 (25)_____ long.

What occurs during sleep? We undergo several (26)_____ of sleep during a normal sleep period. According to (27)_____ (EEG) records, the brain emits waves of different frequencies and amplitudes during each stage of sleep. Waves high in frequency are associated with (28)_____. There are (29)_____ stages of non-rapid-eye-movement (NREM) sleep and one stage of (30)_____ sleep. Stage 1 sleep is the (31)_____, and stage 4 is the (32)_____ phase of sleep.

As we begin to relax before going to sleep, our brains emit (33)_____ waves. As we enter stage one sleep, our brain waves slow down to a pattern of (34)_____ waves that are accompanied by slow, rolling (35)_____ movements. During the transition from an alpha wave state to a theta wave the individual may also experience a (36)_____ state in which they experience brief dream-like images that resemble vivid photographs. After approximately 30 to 40 minutes in stage (37)_____ the sleeper undergoes a steep decline into stages 2, 3, and 4. In stage 2, brain waves are medium in (38)_____, 4 to 7 cycles in (39)_____ and are punctuated by sleep (40)_____. During stages 3 and 4 our brains produce (41)_____ waves, with stage 4 being the (42)_____ stage of sleep. After about a half hour of stage 4 sleep we begin a relatively rapid journey back up through stage 3 and 2 into a (43)_____ movement (REM) state characterized by rapid, low amplitude brain waves resembling those of stage one and the rapid movements of eyes beneath the closed lids. REM sleep has also been called (44)_____ sleep because the EEG patterns resemble those of the waking state; however it is extremely difficult to awaken a person during REM. Each 8-hour period of sleep is characterized by approximately (45)_____ trips through the stages of sleep.

Why do we sleep? Sleep apparently serves a (46)_____ function, but we do not know exactly how sleep restores us or how much sleep we need. When we are (47)_____ of sleep for several nights research has shown that several aspects of psychological functioning deteriorate, most notably (48)_____, learning and (49)_____. The National Sleep Foundation estimates that sleep (50)_____ is connected with 100,00 crashes and 1500 vehicular deaths each year. Animals and people who have been deprived of (51)_____ sleep learn more slowly and forget what they have learned more rapidly. It has been suggested that REM sleep may foster the (52)_____ of the brain before birth and may also help maintain (53)_____ in adults by exercising them at night. Additionally individuals who have been deprived of REM sleep also show (54)_____; they spend more time in REM during subsequent sleep periods.

What are dreams and why do we dream what we dream? (55)_____ are a form of cognitive activity that occurs mostly while we are sleeping. Most dreaming occurs during (56)_____ sleep. Freud believed that dreams reflected (57)_____ wishes and "protected sleep" by keeping unacceptable ideas out of (58)_____. This theory has been challenged by the observation that our dream behavior is generally (59)_____ with our waking behavior. The (60)_____ hypothesis, a more biological view on the meaning of dreams, suggests that dreams largely reflect automatic biological activity by the pons and the synthesis of subsequent sensory stimulation by the frontal part of the brain. Another view of dreams is that with the brain cut off from the outside world, (61)_____ are replayed and consolidated during sleep. Still another suggestion is that REM is a way of testing whether the individual has benefited from the (62)_____ functions of sleep. When restoration is adequate, the brain (63)_____. The content of most dreams is an extension of the events of the (64)_____ day. (65)_____ are also dreams that occur during REM sleep.

What kinds of sleep disorders are there? A common sleep disorder is (66)_____, which is most often encountered by people who are anxious and tense. Deep sleep disorders also include narcolepsy, (67)_____, sleep terrors, bed-wetting, and (68)_____.

According to the National Sleep Foundation more than (69)_____ of American adults are affected by insomnia in any given year, with it more prevalent in (70)_____ than (71)_____. Factors contributing to insomnia include (72)_____, pain, children, (73)_____, bedding, nasal congestion and (74)_____. A person with (75)_____ falls asleep suddenly and irresistibly. The "attack" generally lasts approximately 15 (76)_____ are which the person awakens feeling refreshed and may be accompanied by sleep (77)_____ in which the individual experiences a sudden collapse of muscle groups or even the entire body. Narcolepsy afflicts as many as 100,000 people in the United States and is considered to be a disorder of (78)_____ sleep functioning. (79)_____ and (80)_____ drugs have proved useful in treating narcolepsy.

(81)_____ is a dangerous sleep disorder in which the air passages are obstructed and the individual stops breathing periodically. The (82)_____ may cause the individual to suddenly sit up, gasping for air before falling back to sleep. Apnea is associated with (83)_____ and chronic loud (84)_____ and can lead to high blood pressure, heart attacks and (85)_____. Causes of apnea include anatomical (86)_____ such as thick palate and problems in the breathing centers in the brain and treatments include (87)_____, surgery and continuous positive airway pressure.

The deep–sleep disorders include (88)_____, bed-wetting and sleepwalking all occur during stage 3 or 4 and are more common in (89)_____. Sleep terrors are similar to (90)_____, but more severe. In them the dreamer (91)_____ fully wakes up and may recall a vague image of someone pressing on his or her chest. (92)_____ is often seen as a stigma that reflects parental harshness but may result from an immaturity of the nervous system. In most cases it resolves itself before (93)_____. Finally, (94)_____ affects about 15 % of children. Sleepwalkers may roam about but typically do not (95)_____ their excursions.

Reflection Break # 2:
Stages of Sleep: *Fill in the following chart describing the stages of sleep.*

Stage One	Stage Two	Stage Three	Stage Four	REM Stage
• **Type of Sleep?:** • **Brain Waves?:** • **Eye Movements?:** • **Dreams?:**	• **Type of Sleep?:** • **Brain Waves?:** • **Eye Movements?:** • **Dreams?:**	• **Type of Sleep?:** • **Brain Waves?:** • **Eye Movements?:** • **Dreams?:.**	• **Type of Sleep?:** • **Brain Waves?:** • **Eye Movements?:** • **Dreams?:**	• **Type of Sleep?:** • **Brain Waves?:** • **Eye Movements?:** • **Dreams?:** • **Other?:**

Sleep Disorders: *Match the sleep disorder with its description.*

a. insomnia   c. apnea   e. bed-wetting
b. narcolepsy   d. Sleep terrors f. sleep walking

_____1. Often seen as a stigma that reflects parental harshness, or the child's attempt to punish parents, but may result from immaturity of the nervous system.
_____2. Person falls asleep suddenly and irresistibly; attack may last 15 minutes after which person awakes refreshed.
_____3. Often occurs in deep sleep; similar to, but less severe than nightmares.
_____4. Disorder in which individual may stop breathing periodically; has been linked to obesity, anatomical deformities, such as a thick palate and chronic loud snoring.
_____5. People with this disorder show greater restlessness and muscle tension and are more likely to worry and report racing thoughts.
_____6. Contrary to myth, there is no evidence that waking individuals with this sleep disturbance leads them to become violent; although they may be confused.

Reading for Understanding about "Altering Consciousness Through Hypnosis: On Being Entranced"
What is hypnosis? (96)_____ is an altered state of consciousness in which people are suggestible and behave as though they are in a trance. Modern hypnosis seems to have begun in the 18th century with the ideas of Joseph (97)_____ but has only recently become a respectable subject of psychological study. Hypnosis has been used as an (98)_____ in dentistry, childbirth and even surgery and has also been used to teach clients how to reduce

(99)_____ or overcome fears, lose weight and prompt the memory of witnesses.

What changes in consciousness are induced by hypnosis? The hypnotic trance is not sleep as is demonstrated by differences between the (100)_____ recordings between the two. People who are hypnotized may show (101)_____, narrowed attention, (102)_____ (false memories), (103)_____ (heightened memory), suggestibility, assumption of unusual roles, perceptual distortions including (104)_____ and delusions, posthypnotic (105)_____, and posthypnotic suggestion.

Controversy in Psychology: How do modern psychologists explain the effects of hypnosis? Current theories of hypnosis deny the existence of a special trance (106)_____. Rather, they emphasize people's ability to (107)_____ the "trance" (role theory), to do what is expected of them ((108)_____ theory), and to divide their consciousness ((109)_____ theory) as directed by the hypnotist.

Reading for Understanding about "Altering Consciousness Through Meditation: Letting Your World Fade Away"
What is meditation? According to psychologists, (110)_____ refers to the various ways of focusing one's consciousness to alter one's relationship to the world. In Transcendental meditation (TM), one focuses "passively" on an object or a (111)_____. In this way, (112)_____ (that is, the normal focuses of attention) is altered. (113)_____ Meditation is a simplified form of Far Eastern mediation that was brought to the US by the Maharishi Mahesh Yogi and often has the effect of inducing (114)_____. In TM the mantras, can be (115)_____ or (116)_____ that are claimed to help the person achieve an altered state of consciousness.

What are the effects of meditation? In early research Herbert (117)_____ found no scientific evidence that TM expands consciousness. However, TM did appear to reduce the respiration, and blood pressure of (118)_____ individuals and produced a (119)_____ response. Meditation also produced more frequent (120)_____ waves and increases the nighttime concentrations of the hormone (121)_____. More recent research found that TM was significantly (122)_____ effective at reducing high blood pressure than progressive relaxation or a placebo.

Reading for Understanding about "Altering Consciousness Through BioFeedback: Getting in Touch with the Untouchable"
What is biofeedback training? How is biofeedback training used? Biofeedback is a method for increasing consciousness of (123)_____ functions. In (124)_____, the organism is continuously provided with information about a targeted biological response such as heart rate or emission of alpha waves. People and lower animals can learn to control (125)_____ functions such as heart rate, blood pressure, and even the emission of certain brain (126)_____ through biofeedback training.

Reflection Break # 3:
1. Briefly describe the changes in consciousness induced by hypnosis discussed in your textbook.

2.   How are meditation, biofeedback and hypnosis different?

Reading for Understanding about "Altering Consciousness Through Drugs"
What are substance abuse and dependence? Substance (127)_____ is repeated use that persists even though it impairs one's social, occupational or physical functioning. (128)_____ is more severe and has both behavioral and physiological aspects. Dependence may be characterized by (129)_____ one's life around getting and using the substance and by the development of (130)_____, or the body's habituation to the substance so that higher amounts are needed to obtain similar effects, (131)_____ symptoms, or both. An (132)_____ syndrome often results when level of usage suddenly drops off and may include anxiety, tremor, restlessness, weakness, rapid pulse and high blood pressure.

What are the causes of substance abuse and dependence? People usually try drugs out of (133)_____, peer pressure, (134)_____, escape from boredom or pressure and the seeking of (135)_____. Social-cognitive theorists suggest that usage can be (136)_____ by anxiety reduction, feelings of euphoria, and other positive sensations. People are also motivated to avoid (137)_____ symptoms once they become physiologically dependent on a drug. Biological views on drug uses suggest that people may have (138)_____ predispositions to become physiologically dependent on certain substances.

What are the effects of alcohol? Depressant drugs generally act by (139)_____ the activity of the CNS. Alcohol, the most widely used drug, is a (140)_____. Excessive drinking has been linked to lower (141)_____, loss of (142)_____ and downward movement in social status. The effects of (143)_____ vary with the dose and duration of use. Low doses of alcohol may be (144)_____, while higher doses have a (145)_____ effect. Alcohol is also (146)_____ and can lead to physiological (147)_____. It provides an (148)_____ for failure or for antisocial behavior, but it has not been shown to induce such behavior directly.

Controversy in Psychology: Is a Drink a Day Good for You? Some research has shown that drinking lightly may actually be (149)_____, reducing the risk of cardiovascular and Alzheimer's disease; however, health professionals are (150)_____ to advise that people drink regularly. Negative aspects of alcohol usage include (151)_____, due to its interference in the body's absorption of vitamins and disorders like (152)_____ of the liver and Wernicke-Korsakoff syndrome. (153)_____ treatment has shown effective in teaching problem drinkers how to cope with temptations but (154)_____ is the most widely used program to treat alcoholism.

What are the effects of opiates? Opiates are (155)_____ that are derived from the opium poppy; (156)_____ are synthesized in a laboratory, but have a similar chemical structure. The opiates morphine and heroin are (157)_____ that reduce pain, but they are also bought on the street because of the (158)_____ "rush" they provide. (159)_____ use can lead to physiological dependence. It was originally thought that the use of (160)_____ would help those addicted to morphine over come their physiological dependence; today, (161)_____ a synthetic opiod, helps heroine addicts avert the symptoms caused by withdrawal. (162)_____withdrawal syndromes often begin with flu-like symptoms and progress through tremor, cramps, chills alternating with sweating, rapid pulse, high blood pressure, insomnia, vomiting and diarrhea.

What are the effects of barbiturates and methoaqualone? Barbiturates and a similar drug, (163)_____, are also depressants. Barbiturates have medical uses, including relaxation, (164)_____, and treatment of epilepsy, high blood pressure, and insomnia. (165)_____ are popular street drug because they are relaxing and produce a mild euphoria; however, they lead rapidly to physiological and psychological dependence.

What are the effects of amphetamines? (166)_____ are substances that act by increasing the activity of the nervous system. (167)_____, called speed, are stimulants that produce feelings of euphoria when taken in high doses. But high doses may also cause (168)_____, insomnia, psychotic symptoms, and a "crash" upon (169)_____. Amphetamines and a related stimulant, (170)_____, are commonly used to treat hyperactive children. (171)_____ for amphetamines develops rapidly and users can be come dependent on them. Regular use of (172)_____ may be physically addictive, but the extent to which amphetamines cause physical addiction has been a subject of (173)_____.

What are the effects of cocaine? Psychologically speaking, the stimulant (174)_____ provides feelings of euphoria and bolsters self-confidence. Physically, it causes sudden rises in (175)_____ and constricts blood vessels. (176)_____ can lead to restlessness, insomnia, psychotic reactions, and cardiorespiratory collapse.

What are the effects of nicotine? (177)_____ is an addictive stimulant that can paradoxically help people relax. Nicotine stimulates discharge of the hormone (178)_____ and release of many (179)_____ including dopamine and acetylcholine. Nicotine is the drug found in (180)_____ smoke, but cigarette smoke also contains carbon monoxide and (181)_____. Symptoms of (182)_____ from nicotine include nervousness, drowsiness, loss of energy, insomnia, and various other symptoms that resemble (183)_____. Cigarette smoking has been linked to death from (184)_____ disease and cancer, and to other health problems. Even (185)_____ smoking has also been connected with respiratory illness, asthma and other health problems.

What are the effects of marijuana? (186)_____ substances produce distorted sensations and perceptions. Marijuana is a (187)_____, or hallucinogenic, substance whose active ingredients, including THC, that often produces relaxation, heightened and distorted perceptions, feelings of empathy, and reports of new insights. (188)_____ may occur. (189)_____ elevates the heart rate and the smoke is likely to be harmful.

Controversy in Psychology: Is marijuana harmful? Should it be available as a medicine? There are many controversies concerning marijuana. Although it has some (190)_____ uses, it impairs learning and memory and may affect the growth of adolescents. Psychiatrist Lester (191)_____ calls marijuana an inexpensive, versatile and reasonably safe medicine, however, others disagree.

What are the effects of LSD and other kinds of hallucinogenic drugs? (192)_____ is a hallucinogenic drug that produces vivid hallucinations. Some LSD users have "(193)_____," or distorted perceptions or hallucinations that mimic the LSD "trip", but occur days or weeks later. Other hallucinogenic drugs include (194)_____, and (195)_____ (PCP). Regular use of hallucinogenic drugs may lead to tolerance and psychological (196)_____.

Reflection Break # 4:
Altering Consciousness Through Drugs
Drugs
Match the description with the drug name.

a.	LSD	f.	Ampetamines	k.	substance abuse
b.	Marijuana	g.	Barbiturates	l.	tolerance
c.	Nicotine	h.	Opiod	m.	abstinence syndrome
d.	Mescaline	i.	Opiates	n.	substance dependence
e.	Cocaine	j.	Alcohol		

Descriptions

_____1. A stimulant that produces euphoria, reduces hunger deadens pain and bolsters self-confidence; is derived from the coca plant and gave *Coca-Cola* its name.

_____2. A hallucinogenic drug, often smoked by mouth; produces relaxation, perceptual distortions and enhancement of experiences; major psychedelic substance is THC.

_____3. Synthetic substance similar in chemical structure to opiates; most well known is methadone.

_____4. A depressant often taken in via the mouth; produces relaxation, euphoria and lower inhibitions has been connected with aggressive behavior, poor grades and sexual promiscuity.

_____5. Repeated use of a substance despite the fact that it is causing the individual to experience social, occupational, psychological or physical problems.

_____6. The body's habituation to a substance such that with regular use the individual requires higher doses to achieve similar effects.

_____7. Depressants with several medical uses including relief of pain, anxiety and tension, treatment of epilepsy, high blood pressure and insomnia.

_____8. Group of narcotics including morphine, heroin codeine, and Demerol, derived from the opium poppy; often injected, or smoked by mouth; produces relaxation euphoria, and relief from anxiety and pain.

_____9. A hallucinogenic drug derived from the peyote cactus often taken by mouth that may lead to tolerance and psychological dependence.

_____10. Characteristic withdrawal symptoms that occur when the level of usage of a substance suddenly drops off.

_____11. A stimulant found in tobacco; stimulates the discharge of the hormone adrenaline and the release of dopamine and acetylcholine.

_____12. A group of stimulants first used by soldiers in WWII to help them stay alert, called speed, uppers, bennies and dexies; side effects include restlessness, loss of appetite and psychotic symptoms.

_____13. A powerful synthetic hallucinogenic that produces vivid and colorful hallucinations; some users have flashbacks or distorted perceptions that mimic the original 'trip' but occur days, or weeks later.

_____14. Most severe of the substance use disorders; has both behavioral and biological aspects and is behaviorally characterized by loss of control over one's use of the substance.

Reading for Understanding about "Life Connections Getting to Sleep—and Elsewhere – Without Drugs"

The most common method of fighting insomnia in the US is with sleeping (197)_____.
Sleeping pills generally work by (198)_____ arousal, but this is often a short lasting effect
and gradually the individual will develop a (199)_____ for many types of sleeping pills,
meaning they will require higher doses to achieve the same effects. (200)_____ methods for
coping with insomnia include relaxation exercises, biofeedback training, challenging
exaggerated fears, establishing a regular routine and fantasizing.

There are physiological and psychological aspects to (201)_____with the temptation of
drugs. (202)_____ approaches to substance abuse focus on modifying abusive and
dependent ideas and behavior patterns and helping the individual to maintain a (203)_____ to
do without the drugs. These strategies include (204)_____ or mediation, seeking assistance
from a friend or counselor and prioritizing your expectations.

REVIEW: Key Terms and Concepts

Construct	180	Hypnosis	190	Opiates	199
Selective attention	180	Franz Mesmer	190	Narcotics	199
Cocktail party effect	180	Hypnotic trance	190	Opioids	199
Direct inner awareness	181	Hypnotic suggestibility	191	Barbiturates	201
Preconscious	181	Role theory	191	Methaqualone	201
Unconscious	181	Response set theory	192	Amphetamines	201
Repression	181	Neodissociation theory	192	Attention deficit/hyperactivity	
Suppression	181	Mediation	193	disorder	201
Nonconscious	181	Transcendental meditation	193	Cocaine	202
Circadian rhythm	182	Mantras	193	Nicotine	202
Non-rapid-eye movement	183	Relaxation response	193	Hydrocarbons	203
Rapid-eye movement	183	Biofeedback training	194	Passive smoking	204
Alpha waves	183	Electromyograph	195	Hallucinogenic	204
Theta waves	183	Psychoactive substances	195	Marijuana	204
Hypnagogic state	183	Depressants	195	Psychedelic	204
Delta waves	183	Stimulants	195	Hashish	204
Paradoxical sleep	183	Substance abuse	196	LSD	206
Activation-synthesis	187	Tolerance	196	Flashbacks	206
Insomnia	188	Abstinence syndrome	196	Mescaline	207
Narcolepsy	188	Delirium tremens	196	Phencyclidine	207
Sleep paralysis	188	Cirrhosis of the liver	199	Ecstasy	207
Apnea	188	Wernicke-Korsakoff			
Sleep terrors	189	syndrome	199		

FINAL CHAPTER REVIEW

Recite:

Visit the Recite section on pages 213-214 of your textbook. Use the card provided with your textbook to cover the answers of the Recite section. Read the questions aloud and recite the answers. This will help you cement your knowledge of key concepts.

Multiple Choice Questions

1. Which of the following is <u>NOT</u> an accepted meaning of the psychological construct "consciousness"?
    a. Consciousness is sensory awareness of the environment.
    b. Consciousness is selective attention.
    c. Consciousness is direct inner awareness.
    d. Consciousness is repression of memories.

2. The 25 hour cycle of wakefulness and sleep that is connected with the earth's rotation is known as our
    a. REM.
    b. Circadian rhythm.
    c. NREM.
    d. Consciousness.

3. Your roommate has been asleep for about 30 –40 minutes, her brain waves are medium in amplitude with a frequency of about 4-7 cycles per second and are punctuated by sleep spindles. Which stage of sleep is your roommate likely to be in?
    a. REM
    b. Stage 1
    c. Delta sleep
    d. Stage 2

4. Your roommate has been asleep has been asleep for about 70 minutes. Her brain waves are relatively rapid, low-amplitude waves similar to those of the waking state and are punctuated by observable eye movements under the closed eyelids. Which stage of sleep is your roommate likely to be in?
    a. REM
    b. Stage 1
    c. Delta sleep
    d. Stage 2

5. Your roommate is deeply asleep. His brain waves show slow waves (about .5 to 2 cycles per second) with a great amplitude. Which stage of sleep is your roommate likely to be in?
    a. REM
    b. Stage 1
    c. Stage 4
    d. Stage 2

6. As you tuck your son into bed one night he asks you why he needs to sleep. Which one of the following explanations would be <u>incorrect</u>?
    a. You need REM sleep to learn and store new memories.
    b. Babies need REM sleep to encourage brain development before birth.
    c. REM sleep helps to maintain neurons by exercising them at night.
    d. NREM sleep is needed for dreaming.

7. Your roommate knows that you are studying sleep in your psychology class and asks you to explain why he dreams when he sleeps at night. You tell him that the neurotransmitter acetylcholine and the brain structure the pons stimulate activation of the reticular activating system. The RAS stimulates neural activity in the cortical areas of the brain involved in memory and the cortex then synthesizes the stimulation into a dream. Which theoretical explanation of dreaming have you have just given your roommate?
   a. Repression of unconscious urges
   b. Wish fulfillment
   c. Synthesis-activation
   d. Activation-synthesis

8. Nightmares are to _____ as sleep terrors are to _____.
   a. REM; NREM
   b. NREM; REM
   c. childhood trauma; adulthood stressors
   d. less vivid memories; more vivid recollection

9. Sandy experiences "sleep attacks" that last approximately 15 minutes. During these attacks she often experiences a sudden collapse of muscle groups and an inability to move. She almost always awakes feeling refreshed. Most likely Sandy's symptoms are indicative of
   a. sleep terrors
   b. Narcolepsy
   c. Sleep apnea
   d. Insomnia

10. Harvey's doctor has encouraged him to lose weight and has prescribed a continuous positive airway pressure treatment for him while he sleeps. Which sleep disorder does Harvey most likely have?
    a. Sleep terrors
    b. Narcolepsy
    c. Sleep apnea
    d. Insomnia

11. Hypnosis is best defined as
    a. a form of animal magnetism.
    b. an altered state of consciousness in which people appear to be highly suggestible and behave as if they are in a trance.
    c. an altered state of consciousness in which the person experiences a sleep attack that may last about 15 minutes, after which they awaken refreshed.
    d. a state in which a person may experience brief dreamlike images that resemble vivid photographs.

12. Hypnosis is used today
    a. in nightclub acts.
    b. as an anesthetic in childbirth and surgery.
    c. as an aid in relaxation training.
    d. all of the above.

13. Your mother has recently undergone hypnosis for dental surgery and asks you to explain the effects of hypnosis to her. You explain to her that we can selectively focus our attention on one thing and dissociate ourselves from the other things going on around us. Which theory of hypnosis did you use?
    a. Role theory
    b. Neodissociation theory
    c. Response set theory
    d. Activation-synthesis theory.

14. Kira has recently learned a new method to achieve an altered state of consciousness that involves repeating and concentrating on a word or sound. Kira has most likely learned
   a. hypnosis.
   b. transcendental meditation.
   c. biofeedback.
   d. progressive relaxation.

15. Stephen has recently learned a new procedure that allows him to combat stress and tension by voluntarily lowering his heart rate and blood pressure. What technique is Stephen using?
   a. Hypnosis
   b. Transcendental Meditation.
   c. Biofeedback
   d. Progressive Relaxation.

16. Repeated use of a substance despite the fact that it causes or compounds a social, occupational, psychological or physical problem is defined by the American Psychiatric Association as
   a. tolerance.
   b. abstinence syndrome.
   c. substance dependence.
   d. substance abuse.

17. The depressant that is abused by ten to twenty million Americans and has been linked to lower productivity, sexual promiscuity, loss of employment and a downward movement in social status is
   a. opiates.
   b. barbiturates.
   c. methaqualone.
   d. alcohol.

18. Which class of drug is most likely to be used by a student who needs to stay up all night to cram for an exam?
   a. barbituates
   b. alcohol
   c. opiates
   d. amphetamines

19. The agent in tobacco products that creates the physiological dependence is
   a. cocaine.
   b. nicotine.
   c. dexedrine.
   d. the hydrocarbons.

20. Marijuana, Mescaline, PCP and Ecstasy all belong to the class of drugs known as the
   a. stimulants.
   b. depressants.
   c. opiates.
   d. hallucinogenics.

Essay Questions:
1. What are circadian rhythms? Why is it important for businesses and industry to have a good understanding of circadian rhythms?

2. You come home from school and want to take a real nap (not a "power nap") in which you get the most out of your sleep. If you are going to go into a deep sleep, based on your knowledge of the sleep cycle, what is the best length of time for you to nap? What would be the worst amount of time for you to sleep?

3. What evidence does your textbook give to support the argument that sleep is a restorative process? What are some of the arguments presented in the text used to explain *why* we sleep?

4. Compare Freud's view and that of the Activation-Synthesis hypothesis on why we dream.

5. Briefly describe the actions of the psychoactive drugs discussed in your textbook. Should our society place more control on the availability of alcohol and nicotine? Should marijuana be legalized? Explain your position.

CONNECT & EXPAND:

1. **Circadian Rhythms:** Monitor your circadian rhythm by mapping the times that you are awake and the times that you sleep for two weeks. Take your body temperature at 7 AM, 11AM, 3 PM, 7 PM and 11 PM and graph this data as well. Be sure to record your temperature to the nearest tenth of a degree.

    Do your sleep/waking times show a cyclic nature? How long does your cycle appear to be? 24 hours? 25 hours?

2. **Sleep Disorders:** Take the Sleep test at http://www.sleepnet.com/sleeptest.html
    ▪ Do your results suggest that you maybe at risk for any of the sleep disorders. If so, research them and their treatments.
    ▪ Share your findings with your study group.

3. **Dreams:** Dreaming: describe a recent dream of yours to your study partner and have your study partner describe a recent dream to you.
    • What would a Freudian psychologist say about the content of this dream? How would they interpret the content?
    • Compare your analysis of your partner's dream to their analysis of your dream? Did you both interpret the "symbolism" in the dream in the same way?
    • Now, contrast the Freudian interpretation of the meaning of the dreams with the view presented by those biological theorists who ascribe to the activation-synthesis model? How would these theorists interpret the content of the dream?

4. **Hypnosis:** Read the information on Hypnosis and its use presented at http://www.hypnosis.com/faq/faq0.html#contens
    Prepare an oral report for your class on Hypnosis.
    ▪ What is it?
    ▪ How accurate are memories recalled under hypnosis?
    ▪ Does the evidence suggest that hypnosis can enhance the testimony of eyewitnesses?
    ▪ How effective has hypnosis been shown to be as a pain control method?

5. **Altering Consciousness through the Use of Drugs:** Visit http://faculty.washington.edu/chudler/introb.html and research the effects of five psychoactive drugs. Prepare a poster comparing the actions and side effects.

6. **Life Connections: Getting to Sleep—and Elsewhere—Without Drugs**
    Create an information brochure for college students about the dangers of sleep deprivation. Include an assessment tool for determining whether someone is sleep deprived and suggestions for coping with insomnia without the use of sleeping pills.

Chapter Six: Learning

PowerPreview: *Skim the major headings in this chapter in your textbook. Jot down anything that you are surprised or curious about. After this write down four or five questions that you have about the material in this chapter.*

Things that surprised me/I am curious about from Chapter 6:

Questions that I have about Learning:

-
-
-
-

QUESTION: *These are some questions that you should be able to answer after you finish studying this chapter:*

Learning: Experience, Change, Adaptation and...
- ❖ *What is learning?*

Classical Conditioning: Learning What Comes After What
- ❖ *What is classical conditioning?*
- ❖ *What is the contribution of Ivan Pavlov to the psychology of learning?*
- ❖ *Controversy in Psychology: Why did Pavlov's dogs learn to salivate in response to the bell?*
- ❖ *What are taste aversions? Why are they of special interest to psychologists?*

Factors in Classical Conditioning
- ❖ *What are the roles of extinction and spontaneous recovery in classical conditioning?*
- ❖ *What are the roles of generalization and discrimination in classical conditioning?*
- ❖ *What is higher-order conditioning?*

Operant Conditioning: Learning What Does What to What
- ❖ *What is the contribution of B. F. Skinner to the psychology of learning?*
- ❖ *What is operant conditioning?*
- ❖ *What are the various kinds of reinforcers?*

Factors in Operant Conditioning
- ❖ *What are the roles of extinction and spontaneous recovery in operant conditioning?*
- ❖ *Why did Skinner make a point of distinguishing between reinforcers on the one hand, and rewards and punishments on the other?*
- ❖ *Why do many psychologists disapprove of punishment?*
- ❖ *Controversy in Psychology: Should children be punished for misbehavior?*
- ❖ *What are discriminative stimuli?*
- ❖ *What are the various schedules of reinforcement? How do they affect behavior?*
- ❖ *How can we use shaping to teach complex behavior patterns?*

Cognitive Factors in Learning
- ❖ *How do we explain what happens during classical conditioning from a cognitive perspective?*
- ❖ *What is the evidence that people and lower organisms form cognitive maps of their environments?*
- ❖ *How do people learn by observing others?*

Life Connections: Violence in the Media and Aggression

Reading for Understanding/Reflect: *The following section provides you with the opportunity to perform 2 of the R's of the PQ4R study method. In this section I will encourage you to check your understanding of your reading of the text by filling in the blanks in the brief paragraphs that relate to each of the preview questions. You will also be prompted to rehearse your understanding of the material with periodic Reflection breaks. Remember it is better to study in more frequent, short session then in one long "cram session." Be sure to reward yourself with short study breaks before each of the Reflection exercises.*

Reading for Understanding about "Learning: Experience, Change, Adaptation and..."
What is learning? (1)_____ is the process by which experience leads to modified representations of the environment (the (2)_____ perspective) and relatively permanent changes in behavior (the (3)_____ perspective). Changes associated with (4)_____ changes, like growth, do not reflect learning.

Reading for Understanding about "Classical Conditioning: Learning What Comes After What"
What is classical conditioning? What is the contribution of Ivan Pavlov to the psychology of learning? Classical conditioning is a simple form of (5)_____ learning that enables organisms to (6)_____ events. The Russian physiologist Ivan (7)_____ happened upon conditioning by chance, as he was studying (8)_____ in laboratory dogs. The salivation in response to meat powder is a (9)_____, or an unlearned response to a stimulus. Pavlov discovered that reflexes can be learned, or (10)_____, through association. Pavlov called his trained salivary responses "(11)_____ reflexes" because they were "conditional" upon the repeated pairing of a previously neutral stimulus and a (12)_____ that predictably elicited the target response. Today Pavlov's conditional reflexes are referred to as (13)_____ responses.

Controversy in Psychology: Why did Pavlov's dogs learn to salivate in response to the bell? Behavioral and cognitive psychologists explain classical conditioning very (14)_____. Behavioral psychologists explain the outcome of this process in terms of the publicly (15)_____ conditions of learning. The organism forms associations between stimuli because the stimuli are (16)_____, that is, they occur at the same time. Cognitive psychologists, on the other hand, view classical conditioning as the learning of (17)_____ among events; in other words the focus is on the (18)_____ gained by the organism.

In (19)_____ conditioning a previously neutral stimulus (the conditioned stimulus, or (20)_____ comes to elicit the response evoked by a second stimulus (the (21)_____ stimulus, or US) as a result of repeatedly being paired with the second stimulus. The response to the CS is a learned or conditioned (22)_____.

What are taste aversions? Why are they of special interest to psychologists? (23) _____ are examples of classical conditioning in which organisms learn that a food is noxious on the basis of nauseating experience. Taste aversions are of special interest because they differ from other kinds of (24)_____ conditioning in two ways. First, learning may occur on the basis of a (25)_____ association and second, because the unconditioned stimulus (in this case, (26)_____) can occur (27)_____ after the conditioned stimulus (in this case, the flavor of food). Psychologists believe that taste aversions may provide organisms with an (28)_____ advantage because they motivate organisms to avoid potentially harmful foods.

Reading for Understanding about "Factors in Classical Conditioning"

What are the roles of extinction and spontaneous in recovery in classical conditioning?
Extinction and spontaneous (29)_____ help organisms adapt to environmental changes by updating their (30)_____ or revising their representations of the changing environment. (31)_____ is the process by which conditioned stimuli (CSs) lose their ability to elicit conditioned responses (CRs) because the CS is no longer associated with the US. According to the cognitive perspective, extinction teaches the organism to change its (32)_____ of the environment because the learned, or conditioned stimulus (CS), no longer allows it to make (33)_____. Extinguished responses may show (34)_____ as a function of the time that has elapsed since extinction occurred. Thus, it appears that extinction of a conditioned response is not a permanent eradication, but an (35)_____ of the response. (36)_____ psychologists argue that both spontaneous recovery and extinction are adaptive processes that allow organisms to successfully handle situations that recur from time to time.

What are the roles of generalization and discrimination in classical conditioning?
Generalization and discrimination are also (37)_____. (38)_____ helps organisms adapt to new events by responding to a range of stimuli similar to the CS. In (39)_____, organisms learn to show a CR in response to a more limited range of stimuli by pairing only the limited stimulus with the US.

What is higher-order conditioning? In (40)_____ conditioning, a previously neutral stimulus comes to serve as a CS after being paired repeatedly with a stimulus that has already become a CS.

Reflection Break # 1:
1. Briefly define learning from the perspective of a behavioral psychologist. How would the definition of a cognitive psychologist be different?

2. Identify the unconditioned stimulus (US), unconditioned response (UR), conditioned stimulus (CS) and conditioned response (CR) in the following scenario:
   Tasha is a one-year-old child. Since she was born, every time her parents go out they leave her with Aleshia, a babysitter. On every occasion as soon as Aleshia arrives, Tasha's parents leave. Every time Tasha's parents leave, she cries. At her birthday party, as soon as Tasha sees Aleshia arrive, she begins to cry.

   (US)_____   **(UR)**_____
   (CS)_____   **(CR)**_____

3. **Matching:**

a. spontaneous recovery
b. discrimination
c. higher-order conditioning

d. taste aversions
e. extinction
f. generalization

_____1. The tendency for a conditioned response to be evoked by stimuli that are similar to the original CS.
_____2. Adaptive conditioned responses in which an organism will avoid a potentially harmful food after a single exposure.
_____3. The tendency for an organism to elicit a CR to only a narrow range of stimuli.
_____4. A process by which CSs lose the ability to elicit CRs because the CSs are no longer associated with a US.
_____5. Conditioning in which a previously neutral stimulus comes to serves as a CS after being paired with another CS.
_____6. The return of a previously extinguished CR as a function of the passage of time.

Reading for Understanding about "Operant Conditioning: Learning What Does What to What"

Pavlov's classical conditioning focused on how organisms form (41)_____ about their environments. (42)_____ conditioning, as you will see in this section, focuses on what they do about them.

The historic work of Edward (43)_____ at Columbia University was psychology's first formal study of the effects of rewards and punishments on learning. Thorndike studied cats in puzzle boxes and found that with (44)_____ it took progressively less time for the cat to solve the puzzle. Thorndike explained the cats learning in terms of the Law of (45)_____, which stated that a response is "stamped in" or strengthened in a particular situation by a reward. (46)_____, on the other hand, "stamp out" stimulus response connections.

What is the contribution of B. F. Skinner to the psychology of learning? B.F. Skinner developed the concept of (47)_____, encouraged the study of discrete behaviors such as lever pressing by rats, and innovated many techniques for studying (48)_____ conditioning such as the "Skinner box" and the (49)_____ recorder. He was also involved in the development of behavior (50)_____ and programmed learning. During World War II, Skinner was responsible for "Project Pigeon" in which he proposed that pigeons be trained to guide (51)_____ to their targets. Unfortunately, for Skinner, and fortunately for the pigeon population, the defense department scraped the project.

What is operant conditioning? Operant conditioning is a simple form of learning in which organisms learn to engage in behavior because of the (52)_____ of that behavior. Organisms learn to engage in voluntary behavior, or (53)_____ that result in desirable consequences. Operant behaviors that are (54)_____ occur with greater frequency.

To study operant behavior efficiently, Skinner devised an animal cage, or operant (55)_____ . The operant chamber, or "(56)_____," allows for careful experimentation because experimental conditions can be carefully introduced and removed. In the box an animal (usually a rat or pigeon) is reinforced for (57)_____ a lever. According to John Garcia, Skinner's "greatest contribution to the study of behavior was the marvelously efficient (58)_____ methodology."

What are the various kinds of reinforcers? Any stimulus that increases the (59)_____ that responses preceding it will be repeated serves as a reinforcer. (60)_____ include positive, negative, immediate, delayed, primary, and secondary reinforcers. Positive reinforcers (61)_____ the probability that an operant will occur when they are applied. Negative reinforcers also (62)_____ the probability that operants will occur, but by their removal. (63)_____ reinforcers are more effective than delayed reinforcers. Primary reinforcers have their value because of the organism's (64)_____ makeup. (65)_____ reinforcers such as money and approval acquire their value through association with established reinforcers and are also known as (66)_____ reinforcers.

Reading for Understanding about "Factors in Operant Conditioning"

What are the roles of extinction and spontaneous recovery in operant conditioning? (67)____ and spontaneous recovery are also adaptive in operant conditioning. In operant conditioning, learned responses are (68)_____ as a result of repeated performance in the absence of reinforcement. (Why continue to engage in a response that goes (69)_____?) And, as in classical conditioning, (70)_____ occurs as a function of the passage of time, which is adaptive because things may return to the way they were.

Why did Skinner make a point of distinguishing between reinforcers on the one hand, and rewards and punishments on the other? Reinforcers are defined as stimuli that (71)_____ the frequency of behavior. Rewards and punishments are defined, respectively, as pleasant and aversive (72)_____ that affect behavior. Reinforcers are known by their (73)_____, whereas (74)_____ and (75)_____ are know by how they feel. (76)_____, like reinforcers, tend to increase the frequency of behavior. Skinner preferred the concept of (77)_____ to that of reward because its definition does not rely on getting inside the head of the organism. Instead, lists of reinforcers are obtained empirically, by observing their (78)_____ on behavior. (79)_____ are defined as aversive events that decrease, or suppress the frequency of the behavior they follow.

Why do many psychologists disapprove of punishment? Many psychologists recommend not using punishment because it (80)_____, it does not suggest (81)_____ behavior, it may create feelings of (82)_____, it may only suppress behavior in the (83)_____ situation in which it is used, it may (84)_____ to the suppression of wide varieties of behavior, and it may suggest that recipients punish others as a way of coping with (85)_____. Psychologists suggest that it is preferable to focus on (86)_____ desirable behavior, or by using (87)_____ from positive reinforcement for unwanted behavior by ignoring the unwanted behavior.

What are discriminative stimuli? (88)_____ stimuli (such as a colored light) indicate when operants (such as pecking a button) will be reinforced. Discriminative stimuli act as (89)_____; they provide information about when an operant will be reinforced.

What are the various schedules of reinforcement? How do they affect behavior? (90)_____ reinforcement, in which every response is reinforced, leads to the most rapid (91)_____ of new responses; but operants are maintained most economically through (92)_____, or intermittent reinforcement. Responses acquired, or maintained via partial reinforcement are said to be (93)_____ to extinction. A cognitive theorist would argue that this occurs because the organism does not (94)_____ reinforcement every time, therefore they persist in the absence of reinforcement.

There are (95)_____ basic schedules of reinforcement schedules. In a (96)_____ schedule, a specific amount of time must elapse after a previous correct response before reinforcement again becomes available. In a (97)_____ schedule, the amount of time between reinforcements is allowed to vary. In a (98)_____ schedule, a fixed number of correct responses must be performed before one is reinforced. In a (99)_____ schedule, this number is allowed to vary. (100)_____ schedules maintain high response rates and fixed interval schedules result in characteristic upward moving waves on a cumulative recorder known as a "fixed interval (101)_____".

How can we use shaping to teach complex behavior patterns? In shaping, (102)_____ of the target response are reinforced, leading to the performance of a complex sequence of behaviors. (103)_____ can be used for teaching behaviors ranging from dancing to driving a car.

Reflection Break # 2:

1. How are classical and operant conditioning different? How are they the same?

2. Fill in this summary chart on reinforcement and punishment.

	Stimulus is desired (wanted, pleasant)	Stimulus is undesired (not wanted, unpleasant)
Stimulus is applied	Example: *Dog is given a treat when he obeys a command.* Does behavior increase or decrease? ———————— Is this reinforcement or punishment? ———————— If it is reinforcement, is it positive or negative? _____	Example: *You cursed, so you must do extra chores.* Does behavior increase or decrease? ———————— Is this reinforcement or punishment? ———————— If it is reinforcement, is it positive or negative? _____
Stimulus is removed	Example: *A student gets an F on a test, so they cannot go to Friday nights party.* Does behavior increase or decrease? ———————— Is this reinforcement or punishment? ———————— If it is reinforcement, is it positive or negative? _____	Example: *Your headache goes away when you take aspirin.* Does behavior increase or decrease? ———————— Is this reinforcement or punishment? ———————— If it is reinforcement, is it positive or negative? _____

3. **Matching:**
   a. shaping
   b. punishments
   c. variable interval schedule

   d. discriminative stimuli
   e. fixed ratio schedule
   f. continuous reinforcement

   g. partial reinforcement
   h. fixed interval schedule
   i. variable ratio schedule

_____ 1. Schedule of reinforcement that a piecemeal worker is on when they are told that they will be paid for every 5 items they produce.

_____ 2. Aversive events that suppress or decrease the frequency of the behavior they follow.

_____ 3. A method of learning that assumes that any complex task can broken down into a number of smaller steps.

_____ 4. A light or sound that acts as a cue in operant conditioning.

_____ 5. Schedule of reinforcement used by a car dealer offering cash rebates for car buying only in the months of January, April, July, and October.

_____ 6. Conditioning in which every response is followed by reinforcement.

_____ 7. Schedule of reinforcement used by a professor who gives unpredictable pop quizzes.

_____ 8. Conditioning in which only some responses are followed by reinforcements.

_____ 9. Schedule of reinforcement often used by casinos in their slot machines, payoff can come at anytime, the more responses you make, the more rewards, but you never know when it will come.

Reading for Understanding on "Cognitive Factors in Learning"

How do we explain what happens during classical conditioning from a cognitive perspective? Cognitive psychologists see people as searching for (104)_____, weighing evidence and making (105)_____. They use concepts such as mental structures, (106)_____, templates and information processing to explain learning. According to (107)_____ theory, in classical conditioning organisms learn associations between stimuli only when stimuli provide new information about each other. From this perspective, classical conditioning does not occur mechanically, but because it provides (108)_____.

What is the evidence that people and lower organisms form cognitive maps of their environments? Some evidence is derived from Tolman's research on (109)_____learning. He demonstrated that rats can modify their cognitive map of the environment in the absence of (110)_____. Tolman differentiated between learning and (111)_____. He argued that organisms "learn," or acquire information about the environment, without being (112)_____ for doing so. This learning remains hidden, or latent, until the reinforcement provides the (113)_____ for the organism to perform what it has learned.

How do people learn by observing others? Albert (114)_____ has shown that people can learn to do things simply by observing others; it is not necessary that they emit responses that are reinforced in order to learn. Learners may then choose to perform the behaviors they have (115)_____ "when the time is ripe"-that is, when they believe that the learned behavior is appropriate or is likely to be (116)_____. (117)_____ learning may actually account for most human learning. In observational learning the person who engages in a response to be imitate is a (118)_____. When the observers see the model being reinforced for displaying a behavior the observer is said to be (119)_____ reinforced.

Reading for Understanding about "Life Connections: Violence in the Media and Aggression"

What do we know about the effects of media violence?

Media violence can contribute to violent behavior by providing violent (120)_____, disinhibiting (121)_____ impulses, increasing the viewer's level of (122)_____, priming aggressive thoughts and memories, and (123)_____ the viewer to violence. Since the emphasis of observational learning is on (124)_____ processes, it appears that the effects of exposure to violent behavior can be toned down in children by (125)_____ them that the behavior does not represent the behavior of most people; that the behavior is not real and that the real life (126)_____ for violent behavior are harmful to both the victim and aggressor.

Reflection Break # 3:

1. In the first reflection break of this chapter you were asked to Identify the unconditioned stimulus (US), unconditioned response (UR), conditioned stimulus (CS) and conditioned response (CR) in the following scenario:

   Tasha is a one-year-old child. Since she was born, every time her parents go out they leave her with Aleshia, a babysitter. On every occasion as soon as Aleshia arrives, Tasha's parents leave. Every time Tasha's parents leave, she cries. At her birthday party, as soon as Tasha sees Aleshia arrive, she begins to cry.

   Now, that you have finished this last section on the cognitive factors in learning explain why Tasha cried when Aleshia arrived at the birthday party in terms of Rescorla's contiguity theory.

2. How do the results of research into cognitive factors in learning challenge behaviorist principles? In your answer be sure to discuss the impact of contingency theory and latent and observational learning.

REVIEW: Key Terms and Concepts

FINAL CHAPTER REVIEW
Recite:

Go to the Recite section for this chapter on pages 247-248 in your textbook. Use the tear-off card provided at the back of the book to cover the answers of the Recite section. Read the questions aloud and recite the answers. This will help you cement your knowledge of key concepts.

Multiple Choice Questions:

1. A relatively permanent change in behavior that arises from practice or experience is the behavioral definition for
   a. hypnosis
   b. learning
   c. memory
   d. personality

2. Learning defined as a mental change is to a _____ view, as learning defined as a change in behavior is to a _____ view.
   a. behavioral; cognitive
   b. psychoanalytic; behavioral
   c. cognitive; psychoanalytic
   d. cognitive; behavioral

3. Anticipation of events is to _____ conditioning, as learning what to do is to _____ conditioning.
   a. classical; operant
   b. skinnerian; pavlovian
   c. operant; classical
   d. classical; pavlovian

4. Erin's mother is always anxious when she drives on a snow-covered road. After a few weeks of driving with her mother on snow-covered roads, Erin shows anxiety whenever she sees snow. This is an example of what type of conditioning?
   a. Classical
   b. Skinnerian
   c. Operant
   d. Reflexive

5. Hannah always baby-sits for the Smith's. As soon as Hannah arrives the Smith's leave the house and their infant son cries. At his first birthday party the Smith's son cries as soon as he sees Hannah arrive at the party. In this scenario Hannah serves as a
   a. conditioned response.
   b. unconditioned stimulus.
   c. conditioned stimulus.
   d. unconditioned response.

6. Hannah always baby-sits for the Smith's. As soon as Hannah arrives the Smith's leave the house and their infant son cries. At his first birthday party the Smith's son cries as soon as he sees Hannah arrive at the party. In this scenario the baby crying at the sight of Hannah is an example of a
   a. conditioned response.
   b. unconditioned stimulus.
   c. conditioned stimulus.
   d. unconditioned response.

7. When he was 16 years old, Matt was dared to eat 40 hot dogs in one sitting. After he finished the last dog he felt nauseated and ill. Now 10 years later, Matt is still unable to eat hot dogs. This is an example of
   a. operant conditioning.
   b. a taste aversion.
   c. a reflex.
   d. stimulus generalization.

8. The process by which conditioned stimuli lose their ability to elicit conditioned responses because the conditioned stimuli are no longer associated with the unconditioned stimuli is better known as
   a. stimulus generalization.
   b. taste aversion.
   c. extinction.
   d. acquisition.

9. If, after a time of rest, an organism demonstrates a previously extinguished response, the organism is said to be showing
   a. stimulus generalization.
   b. extinction.
   c. spontaneous recovery.
   d. stimulus discrimination.

10. Kate has been conditioned to fear snow. She also experiences a fear response to fake "snow." Kate is demonstrating
    a. discrimination.
    b. extinction.
    c. generalization.
    d. spontaneous recovery.

11. When you approach a traffic light and see a red light, you stop. On the other hand, when you approach that same light and see a green light, you continue driving. This example illustrates
    a. discrimination.
    b. generalization.
    c. extinction.
    d. spontaneous recovery.

12. Carrie has been conditioned to fear Santa Claus. Santa Claus is repeatedly seen with a reindeer and now Carrie is also fearful of reindeer. This is an example of
    a. discrimination.
    b. generalization.
    c. extinction.
    d. higher order conditioning.

13. B.F. Skinner is best known for
    a. "Project Pigeon."
    b. development of programmed learning.
    c. authoring the novel Walden Two.
    d. all of the above.

14. A simple form of learning in which an organism learns to engage in certain behavior because of the effects of that behavior is known as
    a. classical conditioning.
    b. pavlovian conditioning.
    c. extinction learning.
    d. operant conditioning.

15. Every time Justin does the dishes his parents give him a dollar. This is an example of
    a. negative reinforcement.
    b. punishment.
    c. classical conditioning.
    d. positive reinforcement.

16. Nancy has a headache. She takes some aspirin and the headache goes away. Nancy's aspirin taking behavior has been
    a. negatively reinforced.
    b. positively reinforced.
    c. secondarily reinforced.
    d. punished.

17. Laurie studies hard and gets high grades in school, and as a result her parents and other adults continually praise her. She is always asked to represent her school at important functions. This is an example of
    a. a primary reinforcer.
    b. a secondary reinforcer.
    c. an immediate reinforcer.
    d. extinction.

18. Your employer gives merit wage increases the same time each year. This is an example of what type of reinforcement schedule?
    a. continuous reinforcement
    b. fixed-interval
    c. fixed-ratio
    d. variable-interval

19. You want to train your dog to bring you a soda. To do this you first reinforce the dog for picking up the soda can. Next you reinforce him only after he picks the can up and turns toward you. Then, finally, you only reinforce him for picking up the can and bringing it directly to you. This is an example of
    a. classical conditioning.
    b. partial reinforcement.
    c. shaping.
    d. imitation.

20. Sally watches her brother prepare and cook an omelet. A few days later Sally prepares herself an omelet for breakfast. Albert Bandura would say that Sally learned how to make the omelet via
    a. classical conditioning.
    b. reinforcement.
    c. observational learning.
    d. shaping.

Essay Questions:

1. What are taste aversions? Think of a taste aversion that you have acquired. In a brief essay to your instructor and using your own experience as an example, explain the concept of taste aversion and how you acquired the aversion you have. Be sure to use the proper terms to describe the learned behavior and its acquisition. Finally, in your essay answer the question, "Do you agree with the notion that the existence of taste aversions provides support for the evolutionary perspective in psychology? Why or why not?"

2. Briefly explain the difference between extinction and forgetting. Use concrete examples to illustrate each concept and be sure to use clear operational definitions for all terms.

3. You have decided to run for public office in your town. The local landfill is close to its capacity and the major issue in this year's election has to do with Trash. You feel that the solution to the town's problems is to encourage more recycling among the town's citizens. How would you encourage (shape) the town citizens to recycle? What type of incentives (rewards) might you offer?

4. Should children be punished for misbehavior? What are the effects of punishment? Does the research indicate that it works? If so, when is it most effective? Why do most psychologists disapprove of punishment?

CONNECT & EXPAND

1. **Advertising and Conditioning:** You and your study partners are an advertising team and you have been asked to develop an advertising strategy for a new brand of carbonated

beverage (soda). With your study group watch some current TV commercials for various brands of soda. What associations are the advertisers conditioning? How does this related to the way the soda companies want you to see their product?

With your study group develop an advertisement for this new brand of soda. Present your advertisement to the class and explain the conditioning principles that you used. What associations do you want to make with your brand? What rewards will you give consumers after they buy your product?

2. **Positive Reinforcement Tutorial:** Do you understand the concept of positive reinforcement? Take this tutorial and make sure you do!
   URL: http://server.bmod.athabascau.ca/html/prtut/reinpair.htm

3. **Negative Reinforcement U:** Understanding negative reinforcement is often one of the most difficult concepts for students to grasp. A visit to Negative Reinforcement University will assure that you have clear understanding of this difficult concept.
   URL: http://www.mcli.dist.maricopa.edu/proj/nru

4. **Train Fuzz:** Have you ever tried to train an animal using conditioning techniques? Here's an opportunity for you to train a virtual animal. While you are training Fuzz, pay attention to the various factors that influence whether Fuzz "learns" the desired behavior. Do you think that you also had to "learn" how to train Fuzz at the same time Fuzz had to learn what you wanted him to do? Do you think you could train Fuzz faster a second time? Why?
   URL: http://epsych.msstate.edu/adaptive/Fuzz/index.html

5. **Applications of Classical and Operant Conditioning:**
   Think of the last time you learned something new; for example a dance step, or how to play a new song on an instrument, or how to play a new game. How did you learn this new skill? Did you learn it through associative learning? What form of conditioning was used?

6. **Life Connections: Violence in the Media and Aggression:** In this section of your text your author talks about the need to educate and inform children about media violence to tone done its effects. Research the impact of watching violent media on children further and create a 10-20 minute oral presentation for parents of children between the ages of 4 and 10 years of age. If possible, give your presentation at a PTA meeting of a local elementary school.

Chapter Seven:
Memory: Remembrance of Things Past—and Future

PowerPreview: *Skim the major headings in this chapter in your textbook. Jot down anything that you are surprised or curious about. After this write down four or five questions that you have about the material in this chapter.*

Things that surprised me/I am curious about from Chapter 7:

Questions that I have about Memory:

-
-
-
-

QUESTION: *These are some questions that you should be able to answer after you finish studying this chapter:*

Five Challenges to Memory

Kinds of Memory: Looking Back, Looking Ahead

- ❖ *What is meant by explicit memory?*
- ❖ *What is meant by episodic memory?*
- ❖ *What is meant by semantic memory?*
- ❖ *What is meant by implicit memory?*
- ❖ *What is the difference between retrospective memory and prospective memory?*

Processes of Memory: Processing Information in Our Most Personal Computer

- ❖ *What is the role of encoding in memory?*
- ❖ *What is the role of storage in memory?*
- ❖ *What is the role of retrieval in memory?*

Stages of Memory: Making Sense of the *Short* and *Long* of It

- ❖ *What is the Atkinson-Shiffrin model of memory?*
- ❖ *How does sensory memory function?*
- ❖ *How does short-term memory function?*
- ❖ *Why are we most likely to remember the first and last items in a list?*
- ❖ *Is seven a magic number, or did the phone company get lucky?*
- ❖ *How does long-term memory function?*

- *Controversy in Psychology: Can we trust eyewitness testimony?*
- *What is the levels-of-processing model of memory?*
- *Why is it that some events, like the attack of September 11, 2001, can be etched in memory for a lifetime?*
- *How is knowledge organized in long-term memory?*
- *Why do we sometimes feel that the answer to a question is on the tip of our tongue?*
- *Why may it be useful to study in the room in which we will be tested?*

Forgetting: Will You Remember How We Forget?
- *What types of memory tasks are used in measuring forgetting?*
- *Why can learning Spanish make it harder to remember French?*
- *What is the Freudian concept of repression?*
- *Controversy in Psychology: Do people really recover repressed memories of sexual abuse at an early age, or are these "memories" implanted by interviewers?*
- *Can children remember events from the first couple of years of life?*
- *Why do people frequently have trouble recalling being in accidents?*

The Biology of Memory: The Brain as a Living Time Machine
- *What neural events are connected with memory?*
- *What structures in the brain are connected with memory?*

Life Connections: Using the Psychology of Memory to Enhance Your Memory

Reading for Understanding/Reflect: The *following section provides you with the opportunity to perform 2 of the R's of the PQ4R study method. In this section I will encourage you to check your understanding of your reading of the text by filling in the blanks in the brief paragraphs that relate to each of the preview questions. You will also be prompted to rehearse your understanding of the material with periodic Reflection breaks. Remember it is better to study in more frequent, short sessions then in one long "cram session." Be sure to reward yourself with short study breaks before each of the Rehearsal/Reflection exercises.*

Reading for Understanding about the "Kinds of Memory"
What is meant by explicit memory? There are various types of memories. Explicit memories, also referred to as (1)_____ memories, are memories for specific information. (2)_____ memories contain specific information that can be clearly stated or "declared." The information may be (3)_____ or refer to general knowledge. In contrast, (4)_____ memory is referred to as nondeclarative memory and is memory on how to do something, like perform a task. Psychologists have identified two types of explicit memories: (5)_____ and (6)_____.

What is meant by episodic memory? What is meant by semantic memory? An episodic memory, also referred to as (7)_____ memory, is a memory of a specific event that one has observed or participated in. (8)_____ memories are the memories of the things that have happened to us. (9)_____ memory is general knowledge memory, as in remembering that the United States has 50 states or that Shakespeare wrote *Hamlet*. We are more likely to say that we (10)_____ semantic memories and that we (11)_____ episodic memories.

What is meant by implicit memory? As we mentioned above, implicit memories are memories of (12)_____ . Implicit memories are suggested, or implied, but not plainly stated and are illustrated by the things we (13)_____ . (14)_____ memory means knowing how to do things, like write with a pencil or ride a bicycle. It is also called (15)_____ memory. Often implicit memories are repeated so frequently that the associations become relatively (16)_____, a phenomenon that psychologists refer to as (17)_____.

What is the difference between retrospective memory and prospective memory? (18)_____ memories concern events in the past that can be explicit or implicit. (19)_____ memories involve remembering to do things in the future. There are various types of prospective memory; these include (20)_____ tasks, like getting to class on time; (21)_____-based tasks, like remembering to brush your teeth after eating; and (22)_____-based tasks, like tuning into a favorite TV program at 8:00 PM. Prospective memory is affected by factors such as distraction, (23)_____, and age.

Reflection Break # 1:
Fill in the Blanks in the chart below on the relationships between the different types of memory:

```
            _____memories                              _____ memories
            (remembering things past)                        (remembering things to
             /               \                                do in the future)
  _____memories          _____memories
 (memories for specific  \      (memories of how to perform tasks)
  information)            \
      /              _____memories
  _____memories   (memories of general information)
 (memories of things you did)
```

Reading for Understanding about the "Processes of Memory: Processing Information in Our Most Personal Computers"
What is the role of encoding in memory? (24)_____ information means transforming information from the outside world so that we can place it in memory. We commonly use visual (pictures), auditory (sounds), and semantic (meanings) (25)_____ to convert physical and chemical stimulation into psychological formats that can be remembered.

What is the role of storage in memory? The second stage in the memory process is (26)_____. Storage means the (27)_____ information over time. The main methods of storing information are (28)_____, or rote repetition, in which you repeat information over and over again; and (29)_____, or relating it to things we already know. As we become more aware of the functioning of our memory, our (30)_____ becomes more sophisticated.

What is the role of retrieval in memory? (31)_____, the third memory process, means locating stored information and bringing it back into consciousness. Efficient retrieval requires use of the proper (32)_____ (just as to retrieve information stored on a hard drive, we need to know the file-name.) (33)_____ is defined as the processes by which information is encoded, stored, and retrieved.

Reading for Understanding about the "Stages of Memory: Making Sense of the *Short* and *Long* of It"

What is the Atkinson-Shiffrin model of memory? Atkinson and Shiffrin proposed that there are three stages of memory-(34)_____ memory, (35)_____ memory, and (36)_____ memory-and suggested that the progress of information through these stages determines whether and how long it is remembered.

How does sensory memory function? Each sense is believed to have a sensory (37)_____ that briefly holds the memory traces of stimuli in sensory memory. The traces then (38)_____. Visual sensory memory makes discrete visual sensations-produced by (39)_____ eye movements-seem continuous. To demonstrate that visual stimuli are maintained in sensory memory for only a fraction of a (40)_____, McDougall used the (41)_____ procedure in which he presented subjects 1 to 12 letters arranged in rows for a very brief amount of time and asked them to report every letter they saw. George Sperling modified McDougall's procedure and used the (42)_____ procedure to show that we can see more objects than we can report afterward. In (43)_____ procedure people were asked to report the contents of only one of the three rows, rather than all. Sperling also found that the amount of (44)_____ that elapsed before he indicated the row to report was crucial and thus he concluded that the memory trace of (45)_____ stimuli decay within a second.

(46)_____ are mental representations of visual stimuli. The sensory memory that holds icons is called (47)_____ memory. Iconic memory appears to be (48)_____, photographic memories, but are very brief. Some people, usually (49)_____, can maintain icons over long periods of time and are said to have (50)_____, or the extraordinary ability to "see" the memory trace of a visual stimulus in the sensory register long after the trace would have decayed in most people.

Echoes are representations of (51)_____ stimuli (sounds). The sensory register that holds echoes is referred to as (52)_____ memory. Echoes can be held in sensory memory for several (53)_____. It has been suggested that the differences in the lasting duration of visual and auditory traces has to do with (54)_____ differences in the ear and eye. None the less, both echoes and icons do (55)_____ with time, if they are to be retained, they must be attended to. Through the use of (56)_____ we sort certain stimuli out from background noise.

How does short-term memory function? (57)_____ memory is the second stage of memory processing. Focusing on a stimulus allows us to maintain it in short-term memory--also called (58)_____ memory--for a minute or so after the trace decays. In short-term memory the image tends to fade significantly after 10 to 12 seconds if it is not repeated or (59)_____. Rehearsal allows us to maintain information (60)_____. Once information is in our (61)_____ memory we can "work" on it, but it is not necessarily saved.

Why are we most likely to remember the first and last items in a list? This phenomenon is referred to as the (62)_____. It has been suggested that this effect may occur because we pay more (63)_____ to the first and last stimuli in a series since they serve as the boundaries for the other stimuli. However, it may be that we tend to remember the initial items in a list because they are rehearsed most often (the (64)_____effect) and that we tend to remember the final items in a list because they are least likely to have been displaced by the appearance of new information (the (65)_____effect).

Is seven a magic number, or did the phone company get lucky? The discrete elements to be kept in short-term memory are referred to as (66)_____. Miller showed that the average person can hold (67)_____ chunks of information (plus or minus (68)_____) in short-term memory. When we want to put information that consists of more then 7 chunks into short-term memory we tend to (69)_____ pieces into one larger chunk of information, for example the area code in a telephone will usually be coded as (70)_____ chunk—not (71)_____. Psychologists say that the appearance of new information beyond seven (72)_____ the old information.

How does long-term memory function? The third stage of information processing is (73)_____ memory. You can think of your long-term memory as a vast (74)_____ of information. However, long-term memories have not been shown to be perfectly (75)_____. We might not be able to (76)_____ all of them, some may be lost because of improper (77)_____, or they might be kept unconscious by forces of (78)_____. Elizabeth (79)_____ notes that our long-term memories are frequently distorted and biased because they are reconstructed according to our (80)_____-that is, our ways of mentally organizing our experiences. Loftus and Palmer also showed that the memories of (81)_____ can also be distorted by leading questions.

Controversy in Psychology: Can We Trust Eyewitness Testimony? Legal professionals are concerned about the (82)_____ of our long-term memories as reflected in eyewitness testimony. Misidentification of suspects creates a double horror—the wrong person is (83)_____ and the real (84)_____ is still on the streets. One problem with eyewitness testimony is that the (85)_____ used by the questioner have been shown to influence the reconstruction of the memory. Another problem is that (86)_____ tend to be more suggestible witnesses than (87)_____. Identification of criminals by eyewitnesses is also a problem since witnesses tend to pay more attention to the suspect's (88)_____ than to (89)_____ features, height and weight.

There is no known limit to the amount of information that can be (90)_____ in long-term memory, and memories can be stored for a (91)_____. Information is usually transferred from (92)_____ to (93)_____ memory by one of two paths: (94)_____ rehearsal (rote repetition) and (95)_____ rehearsal (relating information to things that are already known). The more often chunks of information are (96)_____, the more likely they are to be transferred to long-term memory, however (97)_____ rehearsal is the more effective method. In this type of rehearsal we make information more (98)_____ by purposefully relating the new information to things already well known. It has been suggested that people who use elaborative rehearsal to remember things are processing at a (99)_____ level than people who use maintenance rehearsal.

What is the levels-of-processing model of memory? This model, proposed by Fergus (100)_____ and Robert (101)_____ proposes that memories tend to endure when information is processed deeply and related to things we already know. The model views memory in terms of a single (102)_____-not three stages. It is hypothesized that we encode, store, and retrieve information more (103)_____ when we have processed it more deeply. Craik also argues that the reason older adults show memory loss is that they tend not to process information as deeply due to an inability to focus their (104)_____.

Why is it that some events, like the attack of September 11, 2001, can be etched in memory for a lifetime? It appears that we tend to remember events that are (105)_____, important and (106)_____ stirring more clearly. So-called (107)_____ memories, like the attack of September 11, 2001, the death of a public figure like Princess Diana or JFK, Jr., tend to occur within a web of unusual and (108)_____ arousing circumstances and to preserve experiences in detail. It is suggested that the reason why the memory is "etched" is the (109)_____ of the memory; in other words the events stand out because they are striking in an of themselves. Another suggestion may be that we may (110)_____ the experience more extensively, or elaboratively rehearse them.

How is knowledge organized in long-term memory? Memories in long-term memory are generally well (111)_____. We tend to organize information according to a (112)_____ structure. That is, we classify or arrange chunks of information into (113)_____ or classes according to common features. We are more likely to accurately (114)_____ information when information in long-term memory is correctly organized.

Why do we sometimes feel that the answer to a question is on the tip of our tongue? The (115)_____ (TOT) phenomenon, or feeling-of-knowing experience, refers to the frustrating experience of knowing that you know something, but not being able to remember it. Research suggests that the TOT phenomenon often reflects (116)_____ learning.

Why may it be useful to study in the room in which we will be tested? This is because memories are frequently dependent on the (117)_____ in which they were formed. Being in the proper context can dramatically enhance (118)_____. Context dependence refers to the finding that we often retrieve information more (119)_____ when we are in the same context we were in when we acquired it. One of the more eerie psychological experiences associated with context-dependent memory is (120)_____ in which we find our selves in a new place, but have the feeling we have been there before. The déjà vu experience seems to occur when we are in a context similar to one we have been in before and the (121)_____ seems to lead us to think "I've been here before." (122)_____ memory is an expansion of context-dependent memory and refers to the finding that we often retrieve information better when we are in the same state of consciousness or mood we were in when we learned it.

Reflection Break # 2:

Fill in the blanks to review your understanding of the various types of memory and memory processes.

Memory Processes:

❖ Process by which information is modified from one sensory modality so that it can be placed in memory _____	❖ Process of maintaining information over time. ❖ Can be done via maintenance or elaborative rehearsal _____	❖ Process of finding stored information and bringing it to conscious awareness ❖ Dependent on Cues _____

Stages of Memory:

❖ First stage in memory processing ❖ Type or stage of memory that is first encountered by a stimulus and briefly holds an impression of it. _____ Memory	❖ Second stage in memory processing ❖ Type or stage of memory that can hold information for up to a minute ❖ Also referred to a working memory ❖ Limited to 7 ± 2 chunks _____ Memory	❖ Third stage in memory processing ❖ Type or stage of memory that is capable of relatively permanent storage _____ Memory

Reading for Understanding about "Forgetting"

What types of memory tasks are used in measuring forgetting? (123)_____ syllables were developed by Ebbinghaus in the 19" century as a way of studying memory and forgetting. Since nonsense syllables are intended to be (124)_____ remembering them depends on (125)_____ rehearsal rather than elaborative rehearsal and thus makes them well suited for use in measurement of (126)_____.

(127)_____ is often tested through three types of memory tasks: recognition, recall, and relearning and nonsense syllables have been used to study each of them. (128)_____ is the easiest type of memory task used to measure forgetting and is demonstrated by a failure to recognize a previously read syllable. (129)_____ is tested by asking the subject to produce syllables from memory or through a (130)_____ task in which subjects are shown pairs of syllables and then asked to recall one item of the pair when shown the other item. (131)_____ is the third assessment method. Ebbinghaus devised the (132)_____ to study the efficiency of relearning in which he measured the number of repetitions required to initially learn, then relearn a list of nonsense syllables. The difference between the first and second sessions is the "(133)_____."

103

Why can learning Spanish make it harder to remember French? This is an example of (134)_____ interference, in which new learning interferes with old learning. In (135)_____ interference, on the other hand, old learning interferes with new learning. According to (136)_____ theory, people can forget because learning can cause cues (such as English words) to be connected with the wrong information (perhaps a Spanish word when a French word is sought).

What is the Freudian concept of repression? Repression according to (137)_____ is the automatic ejection of painful memories and acceptable urges from conscious awareness. Freud suggested that we are (138)_____ to forget threatening or unacceptable material. Psychoanalysts believe that (139)_____ is at the heart of disorders such as dissociative amnesia. Research on the recovery of repressed memories is quite (140)_____.

Controversy in Psychology: Do people recover repressed memories of sexual abuse at an early age, or are these "memories" implanted by interviewers? There is little doubt that the memory of traumatic events can be (141)_____. However, there is also little doubt that many so-called (142)_____ memories are sometimes induced by a therapist. Questions should be raised about the (143)_____of a recovered memory if the corroborating evidence is lacking, and when the details of the event are preposterous. Elizabeth Loftus has shown in numerous studies that it is very (144)_____ to implant a false memory.

Can children remember events from the first couple of years of life? Probably not. This phenomenon is referred to as (145)_____. Freud believed that infantile amnesia is due to (146)_____, but modern psychologists believe that infantile amnesia reflects factors such as immaturity of the (147)_____ and failure to use acoustic and semantic (148)_____ to help remember information. (149)_____ explanations also include the arguments that 1) infants are not particularly interested in remembering the past; 2) infants tend not to weave episodes together into (150)_____ stories and 3) infants do not make reliable use of (151)_____ to symbolize or classify events.

Why do people frequently have trouble recalling being in accidents? This is because the physical (152)_____ can interfere with memory formation. Two kinds of (153)_____ are caused by physical trauma. In (154)_____ amnesia, a traumatic event such as damage to the hippocampus prevents the formation of new memories. In (155)_____ amnesia, shock or other trauma prevents previously known information from being retrieved.

Reading for Understanding about "The Biology of Memory: The Brain as a Living Time Machine"

What neural events are connected with memory? Early in the century many psychologists used the concepts of the (156)_____ in their study of memory. Engrams were viewed as (157)_____ circuits in the brain that corresponded to memory traces—neurological processes that paralleled experiences. (158)_____ is apparently connected with the proliferation of dendrites and synapses in the brain. Learning and memory are also connected with the release of the (159)_____ serotonin and acetylcholine and the (160)_____ adrenaline and vasopressin. As a consequence of the neurotransmitter release transmission at these synapses becomes more efficient as learning progresses and this increased efficiency is termed

(161)_____.

What brain structures are connected with memory? Memory does not reside at a single point in the brain; the ability to recall appears to rely on large-scale (162)_____ that draw on the functions of various parts of the brain. The (163)_____ relays sensory information to the cortex and is therefore vital in formation of new memories. Visual memories appear to be stored in the visual (164)_____, auditory memories in the auditory cortex, and so on. The (165)_____ is connected with the formation of visual memories.

Reading for Understanding about "Life Connections: Using the Psychology of Memory to Enhance Your Memory"

How can people improve their memory? People can improve their memory through use of (166)_____ rehearsal, as in drill and practice, or (167)_____ rehearsal, as in relating new information to what is already known; forming unusual and (168)_____ associations; using the (169)_____, by selecting a series of related images from locations and relating things you want to remember to them; using mediation to form a (170)_____ bridge, or using (171)_____ devices or ancronyms.

Reflection Break # 3
Matching:

a.	hippocampus	i.	vasopressin	s.	infantile amnesia
b.	proactive interference	j.	paired associates	t.	acetylcholine
c.	adrenaline & noradrenaline	k.	repression	u.	retrograde amnesia
		l.	nonsense syllables	v.	estrogen & testosterone
d.	recall	m.	anterograde amnesia		
e.	glutamate	n.	recognition	w.	thalamus
f.	relearning	o.	method of loci	x.	interference theory
g.	method of savings	p.	mnemonic devices	y.	serotonin
h.	retroactive interference	q.	engram		
		r.	long-term potentiation		

_____1. Method of measuring retention of learned material by examining whether it is relearned more rapidly when presented a second time.

_____2. Electrical circuits in the brain that correspond to hypothetical memory traces.

_____3. Brain structure involved in visual memories.

_____4. In Freud's theory this is the ejection of anxiety producing ideas from conscious awareness.

_____5. Memory lapses for the period of time that follows a trauma, blow to the head or an operation.

_____6. Sex steroids; these hormones facilitate the functioning of working memory.

_____7. Method of memory enhancement that involves forming unusual associations with location.

_____8. Inability to remember memories due to older learning interfering with the capacity to retrieve more recently learned material.

_____9. Method of testing memory in which a subject is asked to indicate whether or not the nonsense syllable presented was presented before.

_____10. Memory device that organizes chunks of information into an acronym, jingle or phrase.

_____11. Also known as antidiuretic hormone; use of this hormone in the form of a nasal spray has shown beneficial effects on memory.

_____12. Pairs of nonsense syllables in which memory is tested by presenting the first member of the pair and asking the subject to recall the second.

_____13. Failure to remember events that took place before an accident.

_____14. Ebbinghaus's method of studying the efficiency of relearning in which he measured the differences in the number of repetitions required to learn a list of nonsense syllables.

_____15. Method of testing memory used by Ebbinghaus in which he would ask the subject to recite back a list of nonsense syllables.

_____16. These hormones work together to heighten memories for stressful events.

_____17. The term used to refer to the greater efficiency in neural transmission at synapses as learning progresses.

_____18. Increases in this chemical in the brain promote conditioning in mice.

_____19. The inability to retrieve old memories due to the interference from new learning.

_____20. Neurotransmitter that increases the efficiency of conditioning in sea snails.

_____21. Low levels of this neurotransmitter have been connected with Alzheimer's disease.

_____22. The inability to remember episodes or events that occurred prior to the age of three.

_____23. The view of memory that argues that we forget material in short-term and long-term memory due to interference from other memories.

_____24. Sets of meaningless groups of consonants with a vowel sandwiched between then to make a syllable.

_____25. Part of the Limbic system, brain structure believed to be responsible for storage of memories.

REVIEW: Key Terms and Concepts

FINAL CHAPTER REVIEW

Recite:

Go to the Recite section for this chapter on pages 287-289 in your textbook. Use the tear-off card provided at the back of the book to cover the answers of the Recite section. Read the questions aloud and recite the answers. This will help you cement your knowledge of key concepts.

Multiple Choice Questions

1. You remember that July 4 is Independence Day and that January 1 is New Year's Day. These are examples of _____ memory.
   a. implicit
   b. explicit
   c. short term
   d. episodic

2. Your memory of your 10th birthday party and the red bike that you were given is an example of _____ memory.
   a. implict
   b. semantic
   c. episodic
   d. sensory

3. General knowledge is to _____ memory as autobiographical information is to _____ memory.
   a. semantic; episodic
   b. implict; semantic
   c. episodic; semantic
   d. semantic; implicit

4. Kevin has not ridden a bike in 3 years. Yesterday he and his girlfriend went bike riding and he was able to successfully ride the bike. Kevin used his _____ memory when he remembered how to ride the bike.
   a. explicit
   b. semantic
   c. episodic
   d. implicit

5. Linda must remember to pay her college tuition next week. Sal remembers having already paid his tuition. Linda is using her _____ memory and Sal is used his _____ memory.
   a. retrospective; introspective
   b. prospective; introspective
   c. introspective; retrospective
   d. prospective; retrospective

6. The process of changing information so that we can place it in memory is termed
   a. storage.
   b. encoding.
   c. retrieval.
   d. visual coding.

7. Tricia is trying to memorize the different types of memories. To accomplish her task she creates a picture or mental image of the words. Tricia is using
   a. an acoustic code.
   b. a visual code.
   c. a semantic code.
   d. a paired associate task.

8. According to your textbook, the second memory process is
   a. encoding.
   b. retrieval.
   c. storage.
   d. forgetting.

9. Ken wants to remember his grocery list long enough to finish his shopping so he keeps repeating the items on the list over and over. Ken is engaging in
   a. maintenance rehearsal.
   b. elaborative rehearsal.
   c. semantic coding.
   d. none of the above.

10. According to psychologists, the awareness of the functioning of our memory is
    a. maintenance rehearsal.
    b. metamemory.
    c. elaborative rehearsal.
    d. semantic memory.

11. Which stage, according to the Atkinson-Shiffrin model of memory, is the first stage of memory processing?
    a. short-term memory
    b. sensory memory
    c. saccadic eye movements
    d. eidetic imagery

12. Sarah creates brief, accurate photographic memories of the environmental stimuli she sees. Sarah is using
    a. iconic memory.
    b. echoic memory.
    c. eidetic imagery.
    d. semantic coding.

13. What type of memory, according to Goldman-Rakic, is the "mental glue that links a thought through time from beginning to end"?
    a. Long-term memory
    b. Short term memory
    c. Sensory memory
    d. Iconic memory

14. Ken wants to remember his grocery list long enough to finish his shopping, so he tries to keep repeating the items on the list over and over. However, by the time he gets to the store he can only remember the first six items on his list. This is known as the
    a. chunking.
    b. recency effect.
    c. encoding specificity effect.
    d. primacy effect.

15. Psychologist Elizabeth Loftus argues that our memories are distorted by the way we conceptualize the world. These representations are called
    a. "procrustean beds."
    b. schemas.
    c. the serial position effect.
    d. eye witness testimonies.

16. Which of the following processing should you use when you want to transfer information from short-term memory into long term memory?
    a. Rote repetition
    b. Maintenance rehearsal
    c. Elaborative rehearsal
    d. Superficial processing

17. You probably have vivid memories of where you were and what you were doing at the time you found out about the loss of the space shuttle Columbia on February 1, 2003. This is an example of a (n)
    a. repressed memory.
    b. eidetic imagery.
    c. flashbulb memory.
    d. feeling of knowing experience.

18. Students who study in the same room that they will be tested in find that their recall for test material is better—that is, they do better on the exam. Psychologists attribute this to
    a. encoding specificity.
    b. flashbulb memories.
    c. content dependent memory.
    d. déjà vu.

19. Multiple choice tests like this one use which of the following memory tasks?
    a. Recall
    b. Recognition
    c. Relearning
    d. Paired associates

20. Joan was in a car accident in which she hit her head on the steering column. Since the accident Joan has been unable to remember the events before the accident. Most likely Joan is experiencing
    a. infantile amnesia.
    b. anterograde amnesia.
    c. retroactive interference.
    d. retrograde amnesia.

Essay Questions:
1. In a two-page essay define short-term memory and describe it in terms of its temporal duration and capacity. What suggestions would you give to a friend who wanted to improve her short-term memory capacity?

2. Do you know anyone with an extraordinary or photographic memory? In a brief essay to your instructor describe the behaviors that suggested to you that this person might have such a memory? How did you account for your friend's abilities before you began this chapter? How do psychologists account for it?

3. Imagine that one week ago you moved into a new city. You now have a new address and phone number to remember. For the first few weeks when someone asks for your phone number you will probably have a hard time remembering it. However, in six months, you will probably have difficulty remembering your old address and phone number. In a three-paragraph essay name and detail the processes responsible for your failure to remember both the new and eventually old phone number.

4. Describe when police interviews of eyewitnesses to a crime should take place and how they should be structured in order to minimize the possibility that a witness would recall inaccurate information.

5. List and give examples of at least five ways you can apply your new knowledge about memory to improve your study skills and, therefore, your performance on your next psychology exam. Which study aid/method mentioned in your textbook do you find most useful for you in studying psychology? Why? Do you think that this method will work as well in other disciplines? Why or why not? What methods do you find more beneficial for studying for your humanities classes? Your biology classes? Your math classes? Why?

CONNECT & EXPAND:

1. **The Biology of Memory: From Engram to Adrenaline**: In recent years the claims for the benefits of so called "smart drugs" have increased dramatically. Websites like the one below have sprung up all over the Internet. Gingko, Vinpocetine and MemRx are just a few herbal or food supplements that have been suggested to enhance your mental sharpness. Examine the various websites advertising these products and using your critical thinking skills evaluate the claims made. What do you think? Is there enough evidence to convince you that these products work? Why or why not? Discuss your findings with your study group.

2. **Controversy in Psychology: False Memory**. Have you ever been convinced that you were remembering something accurately only to discover later that your memory was not as accurate as you thought? How did you account for the distorted memory? Why do you think that you were so convinced that your memory was accurate? What position do psychologists take as to the accuracy of eyewitness reports? Research the articles on the websites below and present a summary of the various viewpoints. Which viewpoint do you feel presents the strongest argument?
   URL: http://faculty.washington.edu/eloftus
   URL: http://www.vcu.edu/hasweb/psy/psy101/forsyth/loftus.htm
   URL: http://www.apa.org/pubinfo/mem.html
   URL: http://www.skeptic.com/02.3.hochman-fms.html
   URL: http://www.jimhopper.com/memory/

3. **Stages of Memory: Gender Differences**. Are girls more likely then boys to remember dolls and teddy bears? Your text cites a study done by Renninger & Wozniak in 1985 that suggests that 2 year old girls are more likely to remember dolls the cars and puzzles in photographs. Is there more evidence to support this claim? Using your favorite web search engine search for support for stereotypical gender patterns in memory. Present your findings to your class in a format specified by your instructor.
   URL: http://www.yahoo.com
   URL: http://www.google.com
   URL: http://www.dogpile.com

4. **Processes and Stages of Memory:**
   Memory and Cognition Demos and Tutorials from Southwest Missouri State.
   Visit this site and explore the wide variety of demonstrations of memory phenomenon. The files are executable files that will run on Window 95, 98 or NT so you can download them and explore them off line. Included are demonstrations of Sperling's iconic memory, levels of processing and encoding specificity, proactive and retroactive interference, serial position effect, short term memory decay, and memory span. Download as many as you can and experience the different concepts.
   URL: http://courses.smsu.edu/tab293f/mem/mydemos.html

5. **Life Connections: Using the Psychology of Memory to Improve Your Memory.** Your textbook author suggests that the design (PQ4R) of the textbook is set up using the memory principles to enhance/encourage the ability of the student to better remember the material presented. Do you think that this approach has been successful? Has the PQ4R set up of the textbook helped you improve your retention of the course material? Which aspect of the method have you found most beneficial? Why? Which aspect of memory does this target?

Chapter Eight:
Thinking, Language And Intelligence

PowerPreview: *Skim the major headings in this chapter in your textbook. Jot down anything that you are surprised or curious about. After this write down four or five questions that you have about the material in this chapter.*

Things that surprised me/I am curious about from Chapter 8:

Questions that I have about Thinking, Language and Intelligence:

- •
- •
- •
- •

QUESTION: *These are some questions that you should be able to answer after you finish studying this chapter:*

Thinking: The Most Human Aspect of Our Psychology
- ❖ *What is thinking?*
- ❖ *How do concepts function as building blocks of cognition?*
- ❖ *How do people go about solving problems?*
- ❖ *It is best to use a tried and true formula to solve a problem?*
- ❖ *What factors make it easier or harder to solve a problem?*
- ❖ *How do people go about making judgments and decisions?*
- ❖ *How do people frame information in order to persuade others?*
- ❖ *Why do people tend to be convinced that they are right, even when they are dead wrong?*

Language: "Of Shoes and Ships and Sealing Wax,...and Whether Pigs Have Wings"
- ❖ *How do we define language?*
- ❖ *What are the properties of a "true" language as opposed to an inborn communication system?*
- ❖ *How does language develop?*
- ❖ *What are the roles of nature and nurture in language development?*
- ❖ *What are the relationships between language and thinking?*
- ❖ *Is it possible for English speakers to share the thoughts experienced by people who speak other languages?*

Intelligence: The Most Controversial Concept in Psychology?
- ❖ *Just what is intelligence?*
- ❖ *What are the various theories of intelligence?*

- *What is meant by multiple intelligences?*
- *What is Sternberg's triarchic model of intelligence?*
- *Just what is "emotional intelligence"?*
- *What is creativity? What are the relationships among creativity and intelligence?*
- *What is the Stanford Binet Intelligence Scale?*
- *What is different about the Wechsler scales of intelligence?*
- *What is mental retardation?*
- *What does it mean to be gifted?*
- *Do intelligence tests contain cultural biases against ethnic minority groups and immigrants?*
- *What are the genetic influences on intelligence?*
- *What are the environmental influences on intelligence?*
- *Controversy in Psychology: The Mozart Effect—Will music provide children with the sweet sounds of success?*

Life Connections: Bilingualism and Bilingual Education—Making Connections or Building Walls?
- *What does research reveal about the advantages and disadvantages of bilingualism?*

Reading for Understanding/Reflect: *The following section provides you with the opportunity to perform 2 of the R's of the PQ4R study method. In this section I will encourage you to check your understanding of your reading of the text by filling in the blanks in the brief paragraphs that relate to each of the preview questions. You will also be prompted to rehearse your understanding of the material with periodic Reflection breaks. Remember it is better to study in more frequent, short sessions then in one long "cram session." Be sure to reward yourself with short study breaks before each of the Reflection exercises.*

Reading for Understanding about "Thinking: The Most Human Aspect of Our Psychology"
What is thinking? (1)_____ is defined as mental activity that is involved in the understanding, processing, and communicating of information. Thinking also entails (2)_____ information, representing it (3)_____, reasoning about it, and making judgments and (4)_____. (5)_____ generally refers to conscious, planned attempts to make sense of the world.

How do concepts function as building blocks of cognition? Concepts are crucial to thinking and can (6)_____ objects, events and activities. (7)_____ provide mental categories that allow for the grouping together of objects, events, or ideas with common properties. We tend to organize concepts in (8)_____. (9)_____ are good examples of particular concepts. Simple prototypes are usually taught by means of (10)_____, or positive and negative instances of the concept.

How do people go about solving problems? People first attempt to (11)_____ the problem. Successful understanding of a (12)_____ requires three features: the parts of our mental representation of the problem must (13)_____ to one another in a meaningful way; the elements of our mental representation must (14)_____ to the elements of the problem in the outer world; and we must have a (15)_____ of background knowledge that we can apply to the problem.

Once problem solvers (16)_____ the problem successfully they use various strategies for attacking the problem, including algorithms, (17)_____ devices, and (18)_____. (19)_____ are specific procedures for solving problems (such as formulas) that invariably work as long as they are applied correctly. An example of a useful algorithm is the (20)_____ algorithm in which you would examine every possible combination of problem elements.

It is best to use a tried and true formula to solve a problem? Not necessarily. (21)_____ devices often help us "jump" to correct conclusions. Heuristics are rules of thumb that help us (22)_____ and solve problems. Heuristics are less (23)_____ than algorithms, but when they are effective, they allow us to solve problems more (24)_____. One commonly used heuristic device is the (25)_____ analysis, in which we assess the difference between our current situation and our goals and do what we can to reduce the discrepancy. An (26)_____ is partial similarity among things that are different in other ways. The (27)_____ heuristic applies the solution of an earlier problem to the solution of a new, similar problem.

What factors make it easier or harder to solve a problem? Three internal factors make problem solving easier or harder. These include your level of (28)_____ -- experts solve problems more efficiently and rapidly than novices; whether you fall prey to a (29)_____ -- mental sets can make our work easier but may (30)_____ us when the similarity between the problems is illusory; and whether you develop (31)_____, or that "Aha!" experience, into the problem. Often we may need to stand back from a problem and allow for the (32)_____ of insight. Other factors influencing the ease of problem solving include (33)_____, the extent to which the elements of the problem are fixed in function and the way the problem is (34)_____.

How do people go about making judgments and decisions? People sometimes make (35)_____ by carefully weighing the pluses and minuses, but most make decisions on the basis of limited information. Decision makers, like problem solvers, frequently use rules of thumb or (36)_____, which are shortcuts that are correct (or correct enough) most of the time. According to the (37)_____ heuristic, people make judgments about events according to the populations of events that they appear to represent. According to the (38)_____ heuristic, people's estimates of frequency or probability are based on how easy it is to find examples of relevant events. According to the (39)_____ and (40)_____ heuristic, we adjust our initial estimates as we receive additional information-but we often do so unwillingly.

How do people frame information in order to persuade others? People frequently phrase or frame arguments in ways to (41)_____ others. The (42)_____ effect refers to the way in which wording, or the context in which information is presented, can influence decision-making. For example, people on both sides of the abortion issue present themselves as being in (43)_____ of an important value either pro-life or pro-choice.

114

Why do people tend to be convinced that they are right, even when they are dead wrong? People tend to be (44)_____ about their decisions, whether they are right or wrong. People tend to (45)_____ their convictions, even when proven false, for several reasons. These include they tend to be unaware of the flimsiness of their (46)_____, they tend to focus on events that (47)_____ their judgments, they tend to (48)_____ things that run counter to our judgments and they work to bring about results (49)_____with their judgments.

Reflection Break # 1:
1. What are the steps that you would go through to solve the problem of finding the best Chinese restaurant in your new town?

2. Why do people often find some problems difficult to solve?

3. Match the term with its proper description.

Terms:
a. deductive reasoning
b. framing effect
c. availability heuristic
d. inductive reasoning

e. heuristic devices
f. representativeness heuristic
g. anchoring and adjustment heuristic

Descriptions:
_____1. Wording or presenting information in such a way as to influence decisions or judgments.
_____2. Heuristic in which we base our decisions on initial views or presumptions.
_____3. Rules of thumb used in decision-making.
_____4. Decision making rule based on how easy it is to find examples of relevant events.
_____5. Reasoning in which general decisions or conclusions are made based on individual cases.
_____6. Decision-making based on the population of events that a sample represents.
_____7. Reasoning that reaches conclusions based on an initial premise.

Reading for Understanding about "Language: "Of Shoes and Ships and Sealing Wax,…and Whether Pigs Have Wings""
How do we define language? What are the properties of a "true" language as opposed to an inborn communication system? (50)_____ is the communication of thoughts and feelings by means of symbols that are arranged according to rules of grammar. True language is distinguished from the communication systems of lower animals by properties such as semanticity, infinite creativity, and (51)_____. (52)_____ means that the symbols of a language have meaning. Infinite creativity is the capacity to combine words into (53)_____, never been spoken before, sentences. To produce these original sentences we must have a basic understanding of (54)_____, or the structure of grammar. (55)_____ is the ability to communicate information about events and objects from another time or place.

How does language develop? Language develops in a specific (56)_____ of steps world-wide. Children make the (57)_____ sounds of crying, cooing, and babbling before true language develops. The prelinguistic sounds are not (58)_____, and are therefore not considered language. During the second month babies begin (59)_____ which appears to be linked to feelings of pleasure". They begin to (60)_____ by the 5th or 6th month. In babbling babies frequently combine (61)_____ and (62)_____ sounds. The growth of language is (63)_____ at first. Single-word utterances that can express complex meanings, or (64)_____, occur at about 1 year of age and are the first linguistic utterances. Two-word utterances, known as (65)_____ are characteristic of children by the age of 2. Early language is characterized by (66)_____ of verbs ("She *sitted* down"). As time passes, (67)_____ grows larger, and sentence structure grows more (68)_____.

What are the roles of nature and nurture in language development? Language development, like other areas of development, reflects the interactions between the influences of (69)_____ (nature) and (70)_____ (nurture). (71)_____ theorists, who take a nurture perspective, see language as developing according to the laws of learning and usually refer to the concepts of (72)_____ and (73)_____. Social Cognitive theorists argue that parents serve as (74)_____ and that children learn language via (75)_____ and (76)_____. Learning theory cannot, however, account for the unchanging (77)_____ of language development and acquisition; and modeling and imitative learning do not explain why children tend to (78)_____ irregular verb forms or how they come to say sentences that they have not observed. The (79)_____ theory of language development argues that innate, or inborn factors cause children to attend to and acquire language in certain ways. According to (80)_____ theory language acquisition involves the interaction of environmental influences, like exposure to parental speech and reinforcement, and an inborn tendency top acquire language. Nom (81)_____ refers to this inborn tendency as a language acquisition device or (LAD) that prepares the nervous system to learn grammar.

What are the relationships between language and thinking? The relationship between language and thinking is complex. Piaget believed that language reflects (82)_____ of the world but that much knowledge can be (83)_____ with out language. (84)_____ is not necessary for thinking, but makes possible (85)_____ activity that involves use of symbols arranged according to rules of grammar.

Is it possible for English speakers to share the thoughts experienced by people who speak other languages? Perhaps it is. According to the (86)_____ hypothesis proposed by Benjamin Whorf language structures the way we perceive the world. Therefore, speakers of various languages would (87)_____ about the world in different ways. However, modern cognitive scientists suggest that the (88)_____ of a language suggests the range of concepts that the users have traditionally found to be useful, not their (89)_____ limits.

Reflection Break # 2:
1.   What are the characteristics of language? How do psychologists distinguish true language from the communication systems of lower animals?

2.   Briefly describe the typical sequence of language development in children. What differentiates prelinguistic sounds from the first true linguistic sounds?

3.   Describe the positions of the following theorists on the development of language:
Learning Theorists:

Social Cognitive Theorists:

Nativist Theorists:

Psycholinguistic Theorists:

4.   Compare and Contrast Piaget's view on the relationship between language and thinking
with Whorf's linguistic relativity hypothesis. What position do modern cognitive
scientists take?

**Reading for Understanding about "Intelligence: The Most Controversial Concept in
Psychology?"**

Just what is intelligence? The concept of intelligence is closely related to the concept of
(90)_____; but is thought of more broadly as the underlying ability to understand the world
and cope with its challenges. (91)_____ underlies (provides the cognitive basis for) thinking
and academic achievement. Intelligence allows people to (92)_____ complex ideas, reason
and solve problems, learn from (93)_____ and adapt effectively to the environment.

What are the various theories of intelligence? (94)_____ theories of intelligence argue that
intelligence is made up of a number of mental abilities. Spearman and (95)_____ are two
early psychologists that believed that intelligence is composed of a number of factors. Spearman
believed that a common factor, "(96)_____," underlies all intelligent behavior but that people
also have specific abilities, or (97)_____ factors. To test his views Spearman developed factor
analysis, a (98)_____ technique that allows researchers to determine which items on tests
seem to be measuring the same things. Thurstone also used factor analysis but suggested that
there are nine specific factors, which he labeled (99)_____. These included word fluency,
visual and (100)_____ abilities, perceptual (101)_____ and numerical ability.

More recently J.P. (102)_____ has expanded the number of factors found in intellectual
functioning to hundreds. The most significant critique of the (103)_____ theory approach to
intelligence is that it seems that the more factors identified the more (104)_____ there is
among them.

What is meant by multiple intelligences? Howard (105)_____ believes that people have
several intelligences, not one, and that each is based in a different area of the (106)_____. Two
such "intelligences" are language ability and logical-(107)_____ ability, but Gardner also
includes bodily –kinesthetic intelligence, (108)_____ intelligence and inter- and intra-
(109)_____ intelligences and has recently added a (110)_____ intelligence to refer to
scientific insight. Critics of Gardner's approach agree that people function more intelligently in
some aspects of life than in others but question whether special (111)_____ like body-
kinesthetic and musical abilities are really "intelligences."

What is Sternberg's triarchic model of intelligence? Robert Sternberg's (112)_____ theory proposes three kinds of intelligence: analytical, (113)_____, and practical. (114)_____ intelligence is equated with what we generally think of as academic ability and enables us to solve problems and acquire new knowledge. Analytic intelligence is surprisingly not necessarily the best predictor of (115)_____. (116)_____ intelligence is defined by the ability to cope with novel situations and to profit from experience. Practical intelligence, or "(117)_____," refers to the ability to adapt to the demands of the environment.

Controversy in Psychology: Is Emotional Intelligence a form of intelligence? Should it be taught in school? The theory of (118)_____ intelligence was proposed by psychologists Peter Salovey and John Mayer and popularized by Daniel Goleman. It holds that social and emotional skills are a form of (119)_____ that helps children avert violence and depression. The theory suggests that emotional skills like self-and social (120)_____ are best learned during childhood. They argue that it is important for schools to teach skills related to emotional intelligence along with academic ability since failure to develop emotional intelligence can lead to childhood (121)_____ and (122)_____.

Critics of the theory of emotional intelligence do not deny that emotional coping skills like self-awareness, self control, empathy, and cooperation are important; they do however question whether they represent a kind of (123)_____. Ulric Neisser claims that emotional intelligence skills are important for determining life outcomes but that (124)_____ is gained by calling them forms of intelligence.

Unfortunately, there is not an (125)_____ as to the nature of intelligence. David (126)_____, the originator of the most widely used intelligence tests, defines intelligence as "the capacity of the individual to understand the world [and the] resourcefulness to cope with its challenges." To Wechsler. Intelligence involves accurate (127)_____ of the world, and effective (128)_____, but leaves room for others to consider the kinds of (129)_____ that are to be considered intelligent.

What is creativity? What are the connections between creativity and intelligence? (130)_____ is the ability to do things that are novel and useful. Psychologists see creativity as the ability to make unusual (131)_____ to the elements of a problem to generate new (132)_____. An essential aspect of a creative response is the (133)_____ from the elements of the problem to a novel solution. Creative problem solving demands (134)_____ rather than convergent thinking. In (135)_____ thinking thought is limited to present facts and the problem solver narrows their thinking to find the best solution. In (136)_____ thinking the problem solver freely associates to the elements of the problem.

In his (137)_____ theory Robert Sternberg viewed creativity as one aspect of intelligence. However, most psychologists view creativity as distinct from the kind of (138)_____ ability measured by intelligence tests and research shows that here is only a (139)_____ relationship between creativity and academic ability.

What is the Stanford-Binet Intelligence Scale? Although there is disagreement as to exactly what intelligence is, lay people and psychologists are concerned with "(140)_____" intelligence people have so thousands of intelligence (141)_____ are administered every day. The (142)_____ Intelligence scale (SBIS) is the test originated by Alfred Binet and Theodore Simon in France and further developed by Louis Terman at Stanford University. (143)_____ assumed that intelligence increased with age so the scale includes a series of age-graded questions. The original Binet-Simon scale yielded a score called (144)_____, or MA, which showed the intellectual level at which a child was functioning. The current SBIS derives an IQ, or (145)_____, by dividing a child's (146)_____ age score by the child's (147)_____ age and then multiplying by (148)_____.

What is different about the Wechsler scales of intelligence? The (149)_____ intelligence scales, developed by David Wechsler, contain (150)_____ subtests, which require knowledge of verbal concepts, and (151)_____ subtests that measure spatial relations concepts. In this way the Wechsler scales highlight children's relative strengths and (152)_____ in addition to measuring overall intellectual functioning. The Wechsler tests also use (153)_____ IQ's, an idea introduced by Wechsler, which are derived by comparing a person's performance with that of age-mates.

Both the SBIS and Wechsler scales are (154)_____ tests in that they are administered to one person at a time. This one-to-one ratio is considered (155)_____. But shortage of trained examiners and the need to test large numbers of individuals lead to the development of (156)_____ tests that could be administered to large groups. At first these tests were viewed as remarkable instruments, but as the years passed group tests have come under increasing attack.

What is mental retardation? The average IQ score in the United Staes is very close to (157)_____. Mental retardation is defined as (158)_____ limitation in functioning that is characterized by an IQ score of no more than (159)_____ and problems in (160)_____ skills including communication, self-care, home-living social skills or functional academics. Most people who are retarded are (161)_____ retarded; they are capable of adjusting to the demands of educational institutions and eventually to society at large. Children with Down syndrome are most likely to be (162)_____ retarded. Severely and profoundly retarded children may not acquire (163)_____ and self-help skills and are likely to remain (164)_____ on others throughout their lives. Causes of retardation range from (165)_____ abnormalities to other genetic disorders, or (166)_____ damage. (167)_____ alcohol abuse, malnutrition or diseases during pregnancy can all lead to mental retardation.

What does it mean to be gifted? (168)_____ involves high scores on intelligence tests along with high performance in a specific academic area, creativity, leadership, or talent in physical activities. Louis (169)_____ longitudinal studies of genius found that gifted children generally turned out to be successful as adults.

Do intelligence tests contain cultural biases against ethnic minority groups and immigrants? (170)_____ tests were used historically to prevent many Europeans and others from immigrating to the United States. They were administered in (171)_____ to people who did not know English. It is now recognized that intelligence tests cannot be considered (172)_____ if used with people who do not understand the language, but most psychologists still consider intelligences tests (173)_____ against African Americans and members of lower socioeconomic classes. Intelligence tests measure traits that are required in (174)_____, high tech societies and reflect familiarity with cultural concepts associated with (175)_____ culture.

What are the genetic influences on intelligence? Research on the (176)_____ influences on human intelligence is generally based on kinship studies, twin studies, and adoption studies. (177)_____ studies compare the IQ scores of closely and distantly related people. If heratibility is a factor in intelligence then (178)_____ related people should have IQ scores more similar than (179)_____ related individuals. (180)_____ studies examine the correlation between MZ (identical) and DZ (fraternal) twins reared apart or together. Studies generally suggest that the (181)_____ of intelligence is between 40% and 60%. This means that about half of the (182)_____ between your IQ score and the IQ score of others can be explained in terms of genetic factors, not that half of your IQ comes from genetics.

What are the environmental influences on intelligence? Research on (183)_____ influences on intelligence employs a variety of research strategies including manipulation of the (184)_____ situation, observation of the role of the (185)_____ environment and evaluation of the effects of (186)_____ programs. Research studies support the view that children's early (187)_____ is linked to IQ scores and academic achievement.

Controversy in Psychology: The Mozart Effect—Will music provide children with the sweet sounds of success?
Research by Rauscher, Shaw and Ky suggests that listening to and studying (188)____may enhance at least one aspect of intellectual functioning—(189)_____ reasoning. The researchers suggest that musical training may develop (190)_____patterns used in spatial reasoning, but it remains unclear exactly what aspects of the treatment may have influenced the outcome. However, they caution that their results should be considered (191)_____ and attempts to replicate the Rauscher studies have met with (192)_____ success.

Although intelligence is viewed as permitting people to (193)_____ from education, (194)_____ also apparently contributes to intelligence as well. Preschool intervention programs like Head Start have lead to measurable intellectual (195)_____ and can have long-term (196)_____ effects on children. Additionally, schooling at later ages also contributes to intelligence test scores in that children who have been in school longer show (197)_____ IQ scores.

(198)_____ studies compare the IQ scores of adopted children and their biological and adoptive parents. The (199)____ adoption studies by Scarr & Weinberg suggest a genetic influence on intelligence. But the same studies also suggest a role for (200)_____ influences. In these studies (201)____ American children who were adopted during their first year by (202)_____ American parents with above average income and education obtained IQ scores 15 to 25 points higher than African American children reared by their (203)_____ parents. Caution should be used when interpreting these results, however since the adopted children's IQ's remained (204)_____ those of their adoptive parents, and follow-up studies of the children at age 17 suggested that the mean IQ score of the adopted children had (205)_____ by

9 points.

The majority of psychologists and educators believe that intelligence reflects a complex interaction of (206)_____ factors, (207)_____ experiences, (208)_____ factors and expectations and even the (209)_____ in which intelligence tests are conducted.

Reflection Break # 3:
1. Compare and contrast the factor theory, the theory of multiple intelligence, the triarchic theory of intelligence and the theory of emotional intelligence as to their definitions of intelligence. What are the similarities among the views of intelligence? What are the differences?

2. What is the connection between creativity and intelligence? Is creativity a necessary aspect of intelligent behavior?

3. What are the similarities and differences in the three types of Intelligences testing (SBIS, Wechsler and group tests)? Do you think that any of these assessments actually measure intelligence? Why or why not?

4. Briefly summarize the findings of research on the Mozart effect? What kind of conclusions can be drawn from this research?

5. What is meant by a culturally biased intelligence test? What types of items do you believe ought to be on intelligence tests? Do you think that the SBIS and Wechsler tests seem to be culturally biased? Do these tests include the types of things that you consider important for measurement of intelligence? Why or why not?

6. Compare the three approaches to researching the genetic influences on Intelligence:

Kinship studies	**Twin studies**	**Adoptee Studies**

How do the results obtained from each of these studies compare? What are the similarities? Differences?

Reading for Understanding about "Life Connections: Bilingualism and Bilingual Education—Making Connections or Building Walls?"
Most people throughout the world are (210)_____. A century ago it was thought that, due to limited (211)_____ capacity, children reared in bilingual homes were retarded in their (212)_____ and language development. Today, most linguists consider it (213)_____ for children to be bilingual. Contemporary research reveals that bilingualism (214)_____ people's perspectives and often helps them better learn their first language.

Educational approaches to bilingual education have varied over time. A (215)_____ ago the standard approach was to teach totally in English. This method is known as the (216)_____ or the sink or swim method.

Today, bilingual education (217)_____ requires that non-English speaking children be given the chance to study in their own language. This approach is accomplished in many different ways. So called (218)_____ programs put students into English speaking classrooms as quickly as possible; in (219)_____ programs students continue to study their own culture and language which mastering English. A third approach is (220)_____ in which native born American students are encouraged to achieve fluency in a foreign language at the same time immigrant children are learning English.

The critics of bilingual education contend that it is often more (221)_____ than educational. In recent years there has been a backlash (222)_____ bilingual education because of the concern that many children do not seem to benefit from it. Unfortunately the research in this field is (223)_____ done and thus there is not (224)_____ evidence as to the benefits or disadvantages of bilingual education.

Reflection Break # 4:
1. What special opportunities or problems were connected with bilingualism?

2. Based on what you have learned about bilingual education, thinking, language and intelligence, what do you think, should children who do not speak English in the home be taught in their native language in US schools? Why or why not?

REVIEW: Key Terms and Concepts

Thinking	292	*Language*	303	*Emotional intelligence*	312
Concept	292	*Semanticity*	304	*Creativity*	313
Hierarchies	293	*Infinite creativity*	304	*Convergent thinking*	314
Prototype	293	*Displacement*	304	*Divergent thinking*	314
Exemplars	293	*Linguistic-relativity*		*Intelligence Scale*	315
Algorithm	296	*hypothesis*	305	*Stanford-Binet*	
Systematic Random Search	296	*holophrases*	306	*Intelligence Scale*	315
Heuristics	296	*overregularization*	306	*SBIS*	315
Means-end analysis	296	*Psycholinguistic Theory*	308	*Alfred Binet*	315
Analogy	296	*Language Acquistion*		*Mental Age*	317
Mental set	298	*Device (LAD)*	308	*Intelligence Quotient (IQ)*	317
Insight	298	*Intelligence*	308	*Wechsler Scales of*	
incubation	299	*g*	310	*Intelligence*	317
Functional fixedness	299	*s*	310	*verbal tasks*	317
Representativeness heuristic	300	*Factor Analysis*	310	*Performance tasks*	318
Availability heuristic	300	*Primary Mental Abilities*	310	*mental retardation*	319
Anchoring and		*Analytical intelligence*	311	*giftedness*	322
adjustment heuristic	300	*Creative intelligence*	311	*Cultural Bias*	322
Framing effect	301	*Practical intelligence*	311	*Heritability*	324

FINAL CHAPTER REVIEW
Recite:

Go to the Recite section for this chapter on pages 331-333 in your textbook. Use the tear-off card provided at the back of the book to cover the answers of the Recite section. Read the questions aloud and recite the answers. This will help you cement your knowledge of key concepts.

Multiple Choice Questions:

1. Thinking is defined by psychologists as the mental activity involved in
   a. understanding, processing and communicating information.
   b. attending to information, representing it, mentally reasoning about it, and making decisions about it.
   c. our conscious planned attempts to make sense of our world.
   d. All of the above.

2. Mental categories used to group together objects, relations, events or abstractions that have common properties are
   a. prototypes.
   b. concepts.
   c. problems.
   d. schemas.

3. Kathy is trying to solve a geometry problem, Her first step in problem solving will be to
   a. evaluate the effectiveness of the rules by checking the solutions against the answers.
   b. understand what the problem is asking.
   c. use a heuristic to reach a conclusion.
   d. none of the above.

4. Algorithms are to _____ as heuristics are to _____.
   a. specific procedures; short cuts
   b. rules of thumb; specific procedures
   c. means-end analysis; systematic random searches
   d. means-end analysis; rules of thumb

5. Sam plays chess very well, he has a good memory for the elements of the game, and can form mental representations of the chess board that allow him to efficiently identify the best move. Psychologists would say that Sam is
   a. using an algorithm.
   b. an expert.
   c. Both a and b
   d. None of the above.

6. The tendency to respond to a new problem with the same approach that helped solve an earlier problem is
   a. an algorithm.
   b. Insight.
   c. functional fixedness.
   d. a mental set.

7. Kevin needs to tighten a screw in his desk chair. He has looked everywhere for a screwdriver and cannot find one. He totally ignores the knife on his desk. This is an example of
   a. an algorithm.
   b. insight.
   c. functional fixedness.
   d. a heuristic.

8. Kevin must make a decision about whether he should ask Elissa out for a date. He first decides to ask her out based on his presumption that she will say "yes". However, a friend of his tells him that he thinks she is dating someone else. Ultimately, Kevin grudgingly decides not to ask Elissa out. Kevin has used
   a. a representativeness heuristic.
   b. a availability heuristic
   c. an anchoring and adjustment heuristic
   d. none of the above.

9. When advertisers present their product positively and the competition negatively, they are using
   a. an availability heuristic.
   b. the framing effect.
   c. representativeness heuristic.
   d. a means–ends analysis.

10. True language is distinguished from the communication systems of lower animals by which of the following characteristics?
    a. Semanticity
    b. Infinite creativity
    c. Displacement
    d. All of the above.

11. Humans have the capacity to communicate information about events and objects in another time or place, which makes it possible for us to transmit knowledge and information from one generation to another. This describes the _____ property of language.
    a. infinite creativity
    b. displacement
    c. semanticity
    d. syntax

12. Adam is six months old and has begun to combine consonants and vowels to create sounds like "ba", "da" and "ga." These sounds are used randomly and do not represent objects or events. Psychologists would say that Adam has begun
    a. cooing.
    b. speaking.
    c. babbling.
    d. using holophrases.

13. The first linguistic utterances of children are one-word sayings called _____ and may be used to signify many meanings.
    a. coos
    b. babbles
    c. holophrases
    d. telegraphic speech.

14. When Gabby was three years old, she told you that "The childs goed to the park." This is an example of
    a. syntax errors.
    b. telegraphic speech.
    c. overregulation.
    d. infinite creativity.

15. You are in a discussion with a classmate on the development of language. Your classmate tells you that she believes that children learn language through the interaction of an inborn tendency to acquire language and exposure to parental speech and reinforcement. Which theoretical perspective is your classmate promoting?
    a. Learning
    b. Nativist
    c. Psycholinguistic
    d. Linguistic relativity

16. Dr. Parrish tells his students that he believes that language structures the way we perceive the world. Which of the following theorists would agree with Dr. Parrish?
    a. Jean Piaget
    b. Noam Chomsky
    c. Benjamin Whorf
    d. Sigmund Freud

17. The cognitive process that allows people to understand complex ideas, reason, solve problems and learn from experiences is the definition of what?
    a. creativity
    b. intelligence
    c. thinking
    d. language

18. A friend asks you to explain intelligence. You tell him that there are a number of different kinds of intelligence and that each kind has a neurological basis in different areas of the brain. Whose ideas are you describing?
    a. Robert Sternberg
    b. Howard Gardner
    c. David Weschler
    d. J. P. Guilford

19. Stan has the ability to do things that are novel and useful, he refuses to accept limitations and often tries to do the impossible. He appreciates art and music, often takes unpopular stands and challenges social norms. Psychologists would say that Stan's behavior demonstrates
    a. divergent thinking.
    b. intelligence.
    c. creativity.
    d. convergent thinking.

20. Your nine-year-old sister just took an intelligence test and she tells you that she took the test alone and that the test consisted of a number of separate sections. In some of the sections she was asked to verbally tell the person her answer and in some she was asked to do things—like arrange blocks into a design. Which IQ test is she most likely to have taken?
    a. The Stanford-Binet Intelligence Scale
    b. The Binet-Simon Scale
    c. The Wechsler Scale
    d. The Wechsler-Simon Scale

Essay Questions:

1. Have you ever thought about a problem for a long time and them had the solution just "come to you in a flash?" Why do you think that it happened like that? What was the experience like? What do you think happens within us when we stand back from a problem and allow insight to "incubate"? How do psychologists explain the occurrence of insight?

2. Do you know some brilliant people who aren't very creative? Do you know some creative people who are not necessarily brilliant? What do you think is the connection between creativity and intelligence? What does the psychological evidence suggest?

3. How do *you* define intelligence? Which of the theories of intelligence discussed in your text is most similar to yours? What are the similarities/differences among the view of intelligence described in the text? Are there any that you would not consider to be intelligence? Why? Write a two-page essay describing your definition of intelligence and comparing it to current psychological theory. In your essay be sure to clearly explain your ideas.

4. Just what do IQ tests measure? Do you agree or disagree with this statement: "The times on the SBIS and Wechsler scales actually measure achievement rather than intelligence?" Why? Be sure to clearly justify your position in your essay and make sure that you clearly define achievement and intelligence.

5. In a two-page essay respond to the question "How should society respond to people with exceptional intelligence?" In your essay be sure to compare the educational experiences of the mentally retarded and gifted. What kind of educational or training experiences do mentally retarded individuals receive? What about gifted individuals? Do these experiences seem appropriate? Are the current programs adequate? Why or why not?

6. As you look back on your own childhood can you point to any kinds of family or educational experiences that seem to have had an impact on your intellectual development or do you attribute your intelligence level more to genetics? Would you say that your background overall was deprived or enriched?

CONNECT & EXPAND

1. **Thinking:** Participate in one of the cognitive psychology experiments on-line at the Cognitive Psychology Experiments @ Purdue University or the Experimental Psych Lab links. How did participation in this study help expand your understanding of cognitive science? Describe your experience to the members of your study group and compare your experience to those of the other members of the group.
Cognitive Psychology Experiments @ Purdue University
URL: http://coglab.psych.purdue.edu
Experimental Psych Lab
URL: http://www.psych.unuzh.ch/genpsy/ulf/lab/webexppsylab.html

2. **21ˢᵗ Century Problem Solving:** This site claims that You have the opportunity to learn to solve problems easily and reliably. You only need to take the time to understand how problems are solved. This site shows you how to do this. Problem solving will no longer be an uphill battle. Visit the 21ˢᵗ Century Problem Solving site and try some of the recommendations. Did you find that your problem solving abilities improved? Do you find the claims of this site justified? Why or Why not? Compare your experience with those of the other members of your study group.
URL: http://www2.hawaii.edu/suremath/howTo.html

3. **Creativity:** Do you consider yourself to be creative? Why or Why not? Justify your answer by describing the characteristics of creativity. Do you think that you could become more creative? **Visit the Creativity Web** and the information presented to help you become more creative. Resources are numerous and include books, software, and techniques. Additional resources are included to stimulate your thinking: quotations, affirmations and humor. After examining these resources, did you change your mind? Which resources did you find helpful? Present a report to your study group in how they might improve their creativity based on your findings.
URL: http://www.ozemail.com.au/~caveman/Creative/

4. **Language:** Have you ever known anyone to claim that a pet could "speak" or understand English of another language? Did the pet really "speak"? Did the pet really understand language? What was the nature of the evidence presented to convince you? What was your conclusion?

   Do you believe that non-human animals are capable of true language? How do psychologists distinguish true language from the communication system of "lower" animals? Visit the WebLinks on animal language listed below. Did your view on animal language change after your visits to these websites? Report your findings in a one-page position paper.
   URL: http://pubpages.unh.edu/~jel/apelang.html
   URL: http://www.santafe.edu/~johnson/articles.chimp.html

5. **The Measurement of Intelligence:** You have probably taken a number of intelligence tests—most of which were group tests. What were the experiences like? Were you informed as to how well you did? Do you believe that the test assessed you fairly or arrived at an accurate estimate of your intelligence? Take two of the online IQ tests at the links below. Are the score the same? How accurate do you think these are?
   Cyberia Shrink
   URL: http://www.queendom.com/tests/iq/classical_iq_r2_access.html
   "Uncommonly Difficult IQ Tests"
   URL: http://www.eskimo.com/~miyaguch/
   Q-Tests
   URL: http://iqtests.fabiand.net/
   Wizard Realm
   URL: http://www.wizardrealm.com/tests
   Self Discovery Workshop
   URL: http://www.iqtest.com/
   The Intelligence Testing center
   URL: http://www.tjhsst.edu/Psych/iq/

6. **Determinants of Intelligence: Where Does Intelligence Come From?**
   Visit the following websites and read the reviews of *The Bell Curve*. Prepare a two-page essay that briefly summarizes and evaluates the major points of each article. In your conclusion provide a your final evaluation of the controversy.
   APA's view
   URL: http://www.apa.org/releases/intell.html
   Howard Gardner On The Bell Curve:
   URL: http://www.prospect.org/print/V6/20/gardner-h.html
   Robert Sternberg's Views on The Bell Curve in Skeptic magazine.
   URL: http://www.skeptic.com/03.3.fm-sternberg-interview.html

7. **Controversy in Psychology—The Mozart Effect:** Use your favorite web search engine (http://www.dogpile.com http://www.google.com or http://www.ask.com) to conduct a websearch using the term "Mozart Effect" as the key word to research this issue. What do you think, does the data suggest that early music exposure will provide children with the

sweet sounds of success? Prepare a report (in a format specified by your instructor) for your class on your findings.

8. **Life Connections: Bilingualism and Bilingual Education--Making Connections or Building Walls?** Interview someone whose first language was not English as to their educational experiences. Which method of Bilingual education were they exposed to? Was it effective? Were they successful in their education—in other words did they graduate? How fluent is their English? Compare your findings with those of others in your class. What do your findings suggest about bilingual education.

Chapter Nine: Motivation and Emotion

PowerPreview: *Skim the major headings in this chapter in your textbook. Jot down anything that you are surprised or curious about. After this write down four or five questions that you have about the material in this chapter.*

Things that surprised me/I am curious about from Chapter 9:

Questions that I have about Motivation and Emotion:

-
-
-
-

QUESTION: *These are some questions that you should be able to answer after you finish studying this chapter:*

The Psychology of Motivation: The *Whys* of Why
- ❖ *What is the psychology of motivation? What are motives, needs, drives and incentives?*

Theories of Motivation: Which Why Is Which?
- ❖ *What is meant by species-specific behaviors?*
- ❖ *What is drive-reduction theory?*
- ❖ *Are all motives aimed at the reduction of tension?*
- ❖ *How does humanistic theory differ from other theories of motivation?*
- ❖ *What is Maslow's hierarchy of needs?*
- ❖ *Why are people motivated to eliminate inconsistencies in their worldviews?*
- ❖ *Why are people who go unrewarded more likely then those who are rewarded to think or say that what they are doing is worthwhile for its own sake?*

Hunger: Do You Go by "Tummy-Time"?
- ❖ *What bodily mechanisms regulate the hunger drive? What psychological processes are at work?*

Sexual Motivation: The Battle Between Culture and Nature
- ❖ *What do we know about the sex lives of people in the United States?*
- ❖ *What are the effects of sex hormones on sexual motivation?*
- ❖ *Controversy in Psychology: Is the human sex drive affected by pheromones?*
- ❖ *What is meant by sexual orientation?*
- ❖ *What do we know about the origins of gay male and lesbian sexual orientation?*
- ❖ *What is the sexual response cycle?*

Aggression: Of Australopithecines, Humans, Robins and Testosterone

❖ *What have psychologists and other scientists learned about the roles of genetics and environmental influences on aggressive behavior?*

Achievement Motivation: "Just Do It"
   ❖ *Why do some people strive to get ahead?*

Emotion: Adding Color to Life
   ❖ *Just what is an emotion?*
   ❖ *How can we tell when other people are happy or sad?*
   ❖ *Can smiling give rise to feelings of good will? Can frowning produce anger?*
   ❖ *How do the physiological, situational, and cognitive components of emotions interact to produce feelings and behavior??*

Life Connections: Obesity and Eating Disorders: This Meal Is Too Big; This Meal Is Too Little—Can You Ever Get It Just Right?
   ❖ *If obesity is connected with health problems and unhappiness with the image in the mirror, why are so many people overweight?*
   ❖ *So what can people do to shed a few pounds?*

Reading for Understanding/Reflect: *The following section provides you with the opportunity to perform 2 of the R's of the PQ4R study method. In this section I will encourage you to check your understanding of your reading of the text by filling in the blanks in the brief paragraphs that relate to each of the preview questions. You will also be prompted to rehearse your understanding of the material with periodic Reflection breaks. Remember it is better to study in more frequent, short session then in one long "cram session." Be sure to reward yourself with short study breaks before each of the Reflection exercises.*

Reading for Understanding about "The Psychology of Motivation: The Whys of Why" and "Theories of Motivation: Which Why Is Which?"

What is the psychology of motivation? The psychology of motivation concerns (1)_____ people do certain things. Motives are hypothetical states within an organism that (2)_____ behavior and propel the organism toward (3)_____. Motives are inferred from (4)_____ Psychologists assume that motives can take the form of (5)_____, drives and (6)_____. Psychologists speak of (7)_____ *needs,* such as those for oxygen and food, and of (8)_____ needs, such as those for achievement and self-esteem. Needs give rise to (9)_____; for example, depletion of food gives rise to the hunger drive. Drives (10)_____ us to action and tend to be (11)_____ when we have been deprived longer. An (12)_____ is an object, person, or situation that can satisfy a need or is desirable for its own sake.

Although psychologists agree that it is important to understand why humans and animals do things, they do not agree about the precise nature of (13)_____. The chapter examines four theoretical perspectives on motivation: the (14)_____ perspective, Hull's (15)_____ theory; Maslow's (16)_____ theory; and Festinger's (17)_____ theory.

What is meant by species-specific behaviors? The evolutionary perspective considers the role of (18)_____ behaviors, or instincts. According to (19)_____ theory, organisms are born with preprogrammed tendencies to behave in certain ways in certain situations. These pre-programmed tendencies are called instincts, or species-specific behaviors, or (20)_____ (FAPs). Psychologists (21)_____ whether humans have instincts, and if so, what they are.

What is drive-reduction theory? According to (22)_____ theory, we are motivated to engage in behavior that reduces drives. (23)_____ drives such as hunger and pain are based on the biological makeup of the organism. (24)_____ drives such as the drive for money are learned. Drives trigger (25)_____ (tension) and (26)_____ behavior. We learn to do what (27)_____ tension. The body has a tendency called (28)_____ to maintain a steady state; therefore, food deprivation leads to the hunger drive and eating, which reduces the hunger drive.

Are all motives aimed at the reduction of tension? Apparently not. Stimulus motives, like physiological motives, are innate, but they involve motives to (29)_____ rather than (30)_____ "tension" or the amount of stimulation acting on the organism. Sensory-deprivation studies suggest that inactivity and lack of stimulation are (31)_____ in humans. People and many lower animals appear to be motivated to seek (32)_____ stimulation and activity. Psychologists suggest that (33)_____ motives provide an evolutionary advantage since animals that are active and motivated to learn about their environment are more likely to (34)_____.

How does humanistic theory differ from other theories of motivation? Whereas instincts and drives are mainly (35)_____ and aimed at survival, Abraham (36)_____ believed that people are motivated by the conscious desire for personal growth. He argued that people are motivated to strive for (37)_____, or our self-initiated striving to become whatever we believe we are capable of being.

What is Maslow's hierarchy of needs? Maslow hypothesized that people have a (38)_____ of needs. Once lower-level needs such as (39)_____ and (40)_____ needs are satisfied, people strive to meet higher-level needs such as those for love, (41)_____ and self-actualization. Critics of Maslow's theory argue that there is too much (42)_____ for the hierarchy to apply to everyone.

Why are people motivated to eliminate inconsistencies in their worldviews? According to cognitive-dissonance theory, people are thinking beings who seek (43)_____ in their behaviors and attitudes. According to the theory, people are motivated to (44)_____ and (45)_____ events. People must (46)_____ the world accurately in order to accomplish these goals, and therefore their cognitions need to be (47)_____, or consistent with one another.

Why are people who go unrewarded more likely than those who are rewarded to think or say that what they are doing is worthwhile for its own sake? In one of the first studies done on (48)_____ one group of participants received $1 for telling someone else that a boring task was interesting and members of a second group were given $20. Both groups were asked to engage in (49)_____ behavior, that is behavior that was the opposite of what they really thought. The subjects were then asked to rate their own (50)_____ of the task. Subjects paid (51)_____ rated the task as more interesting then those paid (52)_____. Cognitive-dissonance theory hypothesizes that people dislike situations in which their attitudes and behavior are (53)_____. Such situations apparently induce (54)_____, which people can reduce by changing their attitudes. For example, people engage in (55)_____; that is, they tend to justify boring or fruitless behavior to themselves by concluding that their efforts are worthwhile, even when they go unrewarded.

Reflection Break # 1:
Compare each of the theories of motivation by filling in the chart below.

	Evolutionary	Drive-Reduction	Humanistic	Cognitive-Dissonance
Beliefs	✓	✓	✓	✓
	✓	✓	✓	✓
	✓	✓	✓	
	✓	✓	✓	

Reading for Understanding about "Hunger: Do You Go by "Tummy-Time"?"
What bodily mechanisms regulate the hunger drive? What psychological processes are at work?
Hunger is regulated by several (56)_____ mechanisms, including stomach contractions, blood sugar level, receptors in the mouth and liver, and the responses of the hypothalamus. Chewing and swallowing provide some sensations of (57)_____, or satisfaction with the amount eaten. Stomach contractions, or (58)_____, correspond with hunger but do not fully regulate it. When we are deprived of food the level of sugar in the (59)_____ drops and this is communicated to the (60)_____. The (61)_____ of the hypothalamus functions as a stop-eating center. Damage to the VMN leads to (62)_____ in rats; that is, the animals grow to several times their normal body weight. The (63)_____ may function as a start-eating center; if you destroy this area in rats they become (64)_____--that is they stop eating all together. The (65)_____ mechanisms are only a part of the regulation of hunger, however. (66)_____ factors also play an important role.

Reflection Break # 2:
1. Briefly summarize the biological mechanisms that appear to regulate the hunger drive.
   Biological:
   -
   -
   -
   -

Reading for Understanding about "Sexual Motivation: The Battle Between Culture and Nature"
What do we know about the sex lives of people in the United States? There are many difficulties in gathering data on sexual behavior, including the (67)_____ of people to participate in research, and the fact that people who do respond are (68)_____ willing to disclose intimate information and may be more (69)_____ in their sexual behavior than those who do not. The well-known (70)_____ reports, collected between 1938-1949, interviewed US males and females about their sexual experiences with masturbation, oral and premarital sex. The results of the survey were surprising, in that a majority of (71)_____ reported engaging in masturbation and premarital sex and a minority of (72)_____. However, Kinsey had not obtained a

132

(73)_____ sample of the population due to a high refusal rate. His sample (74)_____ the poor, people of color, people from rural areas, older people and Catholics and Jews. A more recent study-the (75)_____ Survey-may be more representative of the population and thus is considered to be more accurate. The NHSLS considered the (76)_____ factors of gender, level of education, religion and race/ethnicity in many aspects of sexual behavior. The results indicated that (77)_____ report having more sex partners then (78)_____, and that people with some college report having had (79)_____ sex partners. The results also suggest that both (80)_____ upbringing and (81)_____ are also connected with sexual behavior. (82)_____ religious beliefs appear to limit number of sexual partners while European and African Americans have the (83)_____ numbers of sex partners and Asian Americans the (84)_____.

What are the effects of sex hormones on sexual motivation? Sex hormones are clearly connected with sexual (85)_____ in both men and women. Research with men who produce little (86)_____ shows that sex drive is increased when they receive replacement therapy, and lack of sexual desire in (87)_____ is also connected with testosterone levels. Sex hormones promote the (88)_____ of male and female sex organs, (89)_____ the menstrual cycle and have activating and organizing effects on sexual behavior.

Controversy in Psychology: In the human sex drive affected by pheromones? What are pheromones? Some scientists suggest that love potions exist in the form of chemical secretions known as (90)_____. It has been suggested that responses to pheromones are (91)_____- they release certain fixed action patterns. Research has suggested that pheromones are odorless chemicals detected through the (92)_____ organ (VNO) located in the mucous lining of the nose. The VNO acts as a pathway for sex hormones in the brain during (93)_____ development, but it shrinks prior to birth and there is debate as to whether is continues to work or not. Preliminary studies suggest that certain substances may enhance the (94)_____ of women and make them more (95)_____ to sexual advances, but none tested appear to directly (96)_____ behavior in humans like they do in animals.

What is meant by sexual orientation? In addition to activating effects, sex hormones also have (97)_____, or organizing effects, in that they predispose lower animals toward masculine or feminine mating patterns. The great majority of people have a (98)_____ orientation in that they are sexually attracted to and interested in forming romantic relationships with people of the opposite sex. Some people, on the other hand have a (99)_____ orientation, in that they are attracted to and interested in forming romantic relationships with people of their own sex. Homosexual males are referred to as (100)_____ and homosexual women are referred to as (101)_____. (102)_____ people are sexually attracted to, and interested in forming romantic relationships with, both men and women. The concept of (103)_____, which should not be confused with sexual activity, refers to the direction of one's erotic interests. Engaging in sexual activity with people of one's own sex (104)_____ mean that one has a homosexual orientation.

What do we know about the origins of gay male and lesbian sexual orientations? Theories of the origins of sexual orientation look at both (105)_____ (biological make-up) and (106)_____ (environmental influences). (107)_____ theory connects sexual orientation with improper resolution of the Oedipus and Electra complexes. Learning theorists focus on the role of (108)_____ of early patterns of sexual behavior. Evidence of a (109)_____ contribution to sexual orientation is accumulating. Sex hormones may play a role in determining sexual orientation during (110)_____ development. In sum, the determinants of sexual orientation are mysterious and complex and the precise (111)_____ among biological and social factors is not yet understood.

What is the sexual response cycle? The sexual response-cycle describes the changes in the body response as men and women become sexually (112)_____. The sexual response cycle is characterized by (113)_____, the swelling of the genital tissues with blood, and (114)_____, or muscle tension. The cycle consists of (115)_____ phases: excitement, plateau, orgasm, and resolution. (116)_____ is characterized by erection in the male and lubrication in the female. During the (117)_____ phase the level of sexual arousal remains somewhat stable, breathing may become rapid and heart rate my increase to 100 to 160 beats per minute. (118)_____ is characterized by muscle contractions and release of sexual tension. In the male there are two stages of muscle contractions, in the first (119)_____ fluid collects at the base of the penis, and in the second the (120)_____ is propelled out of the body. In the female, (121)_____ is manifested by 3 to 15 contractions of the pelvic muscles. During the (122)_____ phase, and following orgasm, males enter a refractory period during which they are temporarily unresponsive to sexual stimulation.

Reflection Break # 3:
1. Briefly summarize the research findings on human sexual behavior described in the text.

2. Clearly differentiate between sexual orientation and sexual activity and describe the different types of sexual orientation?

3. Matching:
   Review your understanding of the sexual response cycle by matching the term with its correct description.

   a. refractory   d. excitement phase   g. vasocongestion
   b. orgasm   e. resolution phase
   c. mytonia   f. plateau phase period

   _____1. The phase of the sexual response cycle in which the level of sexual arousal remains somewhat stable.
   _____2. The swelling of the genital tissues with blood.
   _____3. The term used for muscle tension.
   _____4. The phase of the sexual response cycle in which vasocongestion causes erection in men and the vaginal wall lubricates in females.
   _____5. The phase of the sexual response cycle in which the female experiences 3 to 15 contractions of the pelvic muscles that surround the vaginal barrel.
   _____6. The period immediately following orgasm in which men cannot experience another orgasm or ejaculate.

_____7. Phase of the sexual response cycle in which the testes return to their normal size and the clitoris and vaginal barrel shrink to their normal size.

Reading for Understanding about "Aggression: Of Australopithecines, Humans, Robins, and Testosterone"
What have psychologists and other scientists learned about the roles of genetics and environmental influences on aggressive behavior? There are those that argue that social deprivation and inequity lay at the root of human (123)_____ and that if we were to remove poverty, inequity and social injustice there would be an end to crime. Robert (124)_____, in his book *African Genesis*, called this view the romantic fallacy. He believed that humans had (125)_____ a number of instincts, including aggression and territoriality. However, critical thinking tells us that this reasoning is (126)_____.

Numerous biological (127)_____ and (128)_____ appear to be involved in aggression. The (129)_____ appears to be involved in inborn reactions patterns since electrical (130)_____ of it triggers stereotypical aggressive behavior in lower animals. Chemically, (131)_____ appears to affect the tendencies to dominate and control other people.

(132)_____ views on aggression have considered the role of the unconscious and frustration. (133)_____ theory views aggression as stemming from inevitable frustrations of daily life. According to (134)_____ theory the best way to prevent harmful aggression may be to encourage less harmful aggression. Psychoanalysts refer to the venting of aggressive impulses as (135)_____. (136)_____ perspectives, on the other hand, assert that our behavior is influenced by our values and that it is natural for people to attempt to understand their environment and make decisions. That is, people (137)_____ their situation and decide to whether to act aggressively depending on the outcome of that appraisal. (138)_____ theories view aggression as stemming from experience and reinforcement of aggressive skills. Social-cognitive theorists believe that (139)_____ and (140)_____ play key roles in aggressive behavior among humans, that is we are not likely to act aggressively unless we believe that aggression is (141)_____ under the circumstances and likely to be (142)_____.

(143)_____ and environmental factors can also contribute to aggression. When people act as (144)_____, fear of consequences and awareness of their moral values tend to prevent them from hurting others. In a mob however, people may experience (145)_____, a state of reduced self-awareness in which they behave more aggressively than they would as individuals. Factors that contribute to deindividuation include (146)_____; diffusion, or sharing of (147)_____; a high level of emotional (148)_____ and a focus on group norms. Bad-smelling pollutants, extremes of noise, and extreme heat are all (149)_____ factors that can increase aggression.

Reading for Understanding about "Achievement Motivation: "Just Do It""
Why do some people strive to get ahead? One reason may be that they have more (150)_____ motivation than other people. David McClelland studied achievement motivation by means of people's responses to (151)_____ cards. He found that college graduates with (152)_____ achievement motivation found jobs in occupations characterized by risk, decision-making and the chance for great success. Research also shows

that people with high achievement motivation attain higher (153)_____ and earn more (154)_____ than people of comparable ability with lower achievement motivation. People may be motivated to achieve in school by performance or learning (155)_____. (156)_____ goals are tangible rewards, such as money or getting into graduate school. (157)_____ goals involve the enhancement of knowledge or skills.

Reflection Break # 4:
Match the proper motive with its description:
1. Briefly summarize the biological and chemical influences on aggressive behavior.
   - Biological:
   - Chemical:

2. Compare and contrast the various psychological influences on aggressive behavior.
   - Psychodynamic:
   - Cognitive:
   - Behavioral:
   - Social Cognitive:

3. Compare performance and learning goals. Which of the two are you "driven" by in your schoolwork?

Reading for Understanding about "Emotion: Adding Color to Life"
Just what is an emotion? Emotions add (158)_____ to our lives. An (159)_____ is a state of feeling with physiological, cognitive, and behavioral components. Emotions (160)_____ behavior and also serve as goals. Fear, for example, is connected with arousal of the (161)_____ division of the autonomic nervous system, (162)_____ that one is in danger, and (163)_____ tendencies to escape.

How can we tell when other people are happy or despondent? The expression of many emotions may be (164)_____. (165)_____ are one factor in the expression of emotion. Darwin believed that the universal recognition of facial expressions had (166)_____ value. According to Paul (167)_____, there are several basic emotions whose expression is recognized in cultures around the world. However, there is no perfect one-to-one relationship between expressions and emotions.

Can smiling give rise to feelings of good will? Can frowning produce anger? It does appear that facial expressions can influence one's experience of emotion. The (168)_____ argues that facial expressions can also affect our emotional state. Psychological research suggests that the contraction of facial muscles may be influential in (169)_____ states.

How do the physiological, situational, and cognitive components of emotions interact to produce feelings and behavior? (170)_____ theory suggests that something happens that is interpreted by the person and the emotion follows. According to the (171)_____ theory, emotions are associated with specific patterns of arousal and action that are triggered by certain external events. The emotion (172)_____ the behavioral response. The (173)_____ theory proposes that processing of events by the brain gives rise simultaneously to feelings and bodily responses.

According to this view, feelings (174)_____ bodily responses. According to Schachter and Singer's theory of (175)_____, emotions are associated with similar patterns of arousal, but the level of arousal can differ. The emotion a person experiences in response to an external stimulus reflects that person's (176)_____ of the stimulus. Research evidence suggests that emotions are not as distinct as the (177)_____ theory would suggest, but that patterns of arousal are more specific than suggested by the theory of (178)_____ and that cognitive appraisal does play a role in determining our responses to events.

Reflection Break # 5:
Compare the four theories of Emotion by completing the following:

Theory	Proposes
Commonsense Theory	
James-Lange Theory	
Cannon-Bard Theory	
Cognitive Appraisal Theory	

Reading For Understanding About: "Life Connections: Obesity and Eating Disorders: This Meal Is Too Big; This Meal Is Too Little—Can You Ever Get It Just Right?"
More than half of adult Americans are (179)_____. Biological factors in obesity include (180)_____, (181)_____ tissue (body fat), and the (182)_____ rate (the rate at which the individual converts calories to energy). (183)_____ factors such as stress, observational learning and emotional states can also contribute to overeating.

Sound weight control programs involve improving (184)_____ knowledge (e.g., eating more fruits and vegetable and fewer fatty foods), (185)_____ calorie intake, exercising, and changing eating habits. (186)_____ helps people construct healthful diets and cope with temptations.

The (187)_____ disorders, anorexia nervosa and bulimia nervosa, are characterized by persistent, gross disturbances in eating patterns. (188)_____ is a life threatening disorder characterized by an extreme fear of being too heavy, dramatic weight loss, a distorted body image and resistance to eating enough to reach or maintain a healthful weight. The typical person with anorexia is a young, European American (189)_____ of higher (190)_____ status. (191)_____, a companion disorder to anorexia nervosa is characterized by recurrent cycles of binge eating and purging. Like anorexia it tends to afflict women during (192)_____ and young adulthood.

Health professionals have done a great deal of research into the (193)_____ of eating disorders, yet many questions remain unanswered. Psychologists suggest that (194)_____ may symbolize the young woman's efforts to cope with sexual fears, or her attempt to regress to her lifestyle prior to puberty. Others suggest that they may result from a response to a negative

(195)_____ environment. Still others point to a history of (196)_____ as a risk factor for eating disorders. (197)_____ and (198)_____ factors have also been suggested.

(199)_____ of eating disorders is a challenge. The disorders are connected with serious health problems, yet (200)_____ is a key feature of anorexia nervosa and many do not admit they have a problem. When the individual with anorexia nervosa does not adequately eat through the mouth a (201)_____ tube feeding may be used. (202)_____ often accompanies eating disorders and antidepressant medication is frequently used in treatment with success. Antidepressants increase the activity of the neurotransmitter (203)_____, which in turn increases food intake in anorexic individuals and decreases binge eating inn bulimic people. Because family problems are commonly connected with eating disorders (204)_____ is often used. (205)_____ therapy is used to help challenge the perfectionism and body image problems.

REVIEW: Key Terms and Concepts

FINAL CHAPTER REVIEW
Recite:
Go to the Recite section for this chapter on pages 373-375 in your textbook. Use the tear-off card provided at the back of the book to cover the answers of the Recite section. Read the questions aloud and recite the answers. This will help you cement your knowledge of key concepts.

Multiple Choice Questions:

1. Psychologists define hypothetical states that activate behavior and propel one towards goals as
    a. needs.
    b. motives.
    c. drives.
    d. incentives.

2. According to the drive-reduction theory, _____ trigger arousal and activate behavior to reduce the tension.
    a. instincts
    b. homeostasis
    c. drives
    d. stimulus motives

3. According to humanistic theory, people are separated from lower animals by our capacity for _____.
    a. instinctual behavior
    b. stimulus needs
    c. self-actualization
    d. cognitive dissonance

4. According to cognitive dissonance theory, when people experience cognitive dissonance the discomfort motives them to engage in
    a. attitude –discrepant behavior.
    b. self-actualization.
    c. effort justification.
    d. homeostasis.

5. When the ventromedial nucleus of a rat's hypothalamus is surgically distroyed the rat will
    a. become hyperphagic.
    b. stop eating.
    c. become aphagic.
    d. not experience any stomach contractions.

6. Biological factors in hunger include
    a. stomach contractions.
    b. blood sugar level.
    c. the hypothalamus.
    d. all of the above.

7. According to the NHSLS
    a. males report having less sexual partners than females.
    b. those who have some college, or who have graduated from college have more liberal views on sex.
    c. Methodists, Lutherans and Presbyterians report lower numbers of sex partners then Catholics.
    d. all of the above

8. Sex drive in males is to _____ as sex drive in women is to _____.
    a. testosterone, testosterone
    b. estrogen, estrogen
    c. progesterone, testosterone
    d. testosterone, estrogen

9. Your roommate has been approached by a friend of his about an investment opportunity –selling colognes and perfumes containing human sex pheromones—and asks you for your advice. You tell him that in a recent study
    a. pheromones decreased mating behaviors in insects.
    b. men who used pheromones increased their frequency of sexual intercourse.
    c. men who used pheromones increased their frequency of masturbation, but not their frequency of sexual intercourse with female partners.
    d. Steroid pheromones enhanced the moods of men, but not women.

10. Mitch is attracted to, and interested in forming romantic relationships with other males. Psychologists would say that Mitch is a _____ and he has a _____ sexual orientation.
    a. lesbian; heterosexual
    b. gay male; bisexual
    c. gay male; homosexual
    d. lesbian; bisexual

11. According to _____ theory an individuals sexual orientation is the result of the outcomes of the Oedipus or Electra complex and identification with male or female figures.
    a. biological
    b. learning
    c. socio-cultural
    d. psychodynamic

12. Tom and Rob are twins. Tom is gay. According to heritability studies, Rob is more likely to be gay if they are _____ twins.
    a. fraternal
    b. identical
    c. it does not matter, there appears to be no role for genes in sexual orientation.
    d. dizygotic

13. Sarah is sexually aroused. Her breathing is rapid and her heart rate has increased to between 100 and 160 beats per minute. She is also experiencing vasocongestion of the outer part of the vagina. Sarah is most likely in which phase of the sexual response cycle?
    a. Excitement
    b. Orgasmic
    c. Plateau
    d. Resolution

14. _____psychologists assert that people decide whether or not they will be aggressive based on their previous experience with aggression and their interpretation of the other person's motives.
    a. Psychodynamic
    b. Freudian
    c. Cognitive
    d. Behavioral

15. A state of reduced self awareness and focusing on ones' own values is known as
    a. deindividuation.
    b. cognitive dissonance.
    c. diffusion of responsibility.
    d. none of the above.

16. Tangible rewards are to _____ goals, as enhancing knowledge is to _____ goals.
    a. performance, learning
    b. secondary; primary
    c. learning; performance
    d. primary; secondary

17. Brian is depressed. The arousal of his parasympathetic nervous system represents the _____ component of the emotion while his thoughts of helplessness represent the _____ component.
    a. behavioral; cognitive
    b. physiological; behavioral
    c. cognitive; physiological
    d. physiological; cognitive

18. The song "Put on a Happy Face" presents the view that facial expressions can influence our emotional state. This claim is similar to that made in the
    a. soci-cultural theory.
    b. facial-feedback hypothesis.
    c. cognitive dissonance theory.
    d. psychoanalytic theory of emotion.

19. You and your girlfriend are discussing the experience of an emotion. You argue that certain external stimuli will instinctively trigger specific patterns of arousal and action that you know as a specific emotion. Your girlfriend argues that emotions do not differ greatly in their physiological arousal and that how you label the emotion you are experiencing will depend on your assessment of the arousal. You are presenting the arguments of the _____ theory while your girlfriend is arguing the _____.
    a. Cannon-Bard; Theory of Cognitive appraisal
    b. James-Lange; Cannon-Bard
    c. James-Lange; Theory of Cognitive appraisal
    d. Theory of Cognitive Appraisal; Cannon-Bard

20. Shauna is extremely concerned about her weight. Although she weighs less then 85 % of her desirable body weight and has lost 25 % of her weight within the last year she is still convinced that she is "fat". Most likely Shauna has
    a. bulimia nervosa.
    b. anorexia nervosa.
    c. either a or b, there is not enough information given to tell.
    d. neither a nor b.

Essay Questions:

1. College students frequently <u>like</u> humanistic theory more than they like instinct theory or drive reductionism. Who do you think this is so? Now that you have studied all of the theories of motivation, which one do you feel is the strongest? Why? Answer these questions in a three-paragraph essay for your instructor. Be sure to use the format that he/she specifies.

2. Were you ever subjected to difficult hazing upon joining a sorority, fraternity or other kind of group? Did the experience affect your feelings about being a member of the group? How? Connect your experience to the concept of effort justification in a one-page essay. Be sure to clearly describe your experience and justify your answer.

3. Why do some people seem satisfied to just get by, whereas other people are driven to work and improve despite their achievements? Do you seem to be driven mainly by performance goals or learning goals? Explain your answer in a one-page essay for your instructor.

4. Have you ever been able to change the way you <u>feel</u> by doing <u>something</u>? Have you tried to "keep a stiff upper lip" when you were under stress, or have you preferred to "let it all hang out"? What do the facial-feedback hypothesis and various theories of emotional expression suggest about the effects of one approach or the other? Prepare a brief essay comparing the various theories of emotional expression and the suggestions they make.

CONNECT & EXPAND:

1. **Theories of Motivation: Which Why is Which?** Survey 20 friends from your other classes as to why they decided to attend college. Keep track of the various answers and the number of times that they occur. Create a summary of the different types of answers that you obtained. Categorize them as to the different motivational theories they represent. Bring your summary to class and compare your findings with those of the other members in your study group. Combine your findings with those of your study group and share them with the rest of the class.

2. **Hunger: Do You Go by "Tummy Time"?** Compare the information presented in the advertising of some of the major weight loss programs. (Jenny Craig, Weight Watchers, etc.) How do healthy weight control programs make use of knowledge of the hunger drive? Summaries the information to share with your classmates in a format specified by your instructor.
   URL: http://www.weightwatchers.com
   URL: http://www.jennycraig.com

3. **Controversy in Psychology: Do People Respond Instinctively to Pheromones?** What do you now think about the impact of pheromones on behavior? Do we respond instinctively to pheromones? Are pheromones involved in human mate selection? Explain your answer. As always be sure to support your comments with good supporting evidence.
   URL: http://www.cf.ac.uk/biosi/staff/jacob/teaching/sensory/pherom.html
   Society For Neuroscience Brain Briefings On Pheromones
   URL: http://www.sfn.org/briefings/pheromones.html
- **Pheromones: An On-Line Resource**.
   URL: http://www.pheromones.com

4. **Aggression: of Australopithecines, Humans, Robins and Testosterone:** Using your favorite search engines research further the ways in which gender, ethnicity and cultural factors may be related to aggression.
   URL: http://www.google.com
   URL: http://www.dogpile.com
   URL: http://www.ask.com

5. **Emotion: Adding Color to Life:** Your study group has been appointed to a state taskforce on the use of lie detectors in legal proceedings. It is your taskforce's responsibility to prepare a report that summarizes the research on the reliability and validity of lie detectors in identifying lies. Do lie detectors work? Do they accurately tell when people are lying? How reliable do you think these are? Just what do lie detectors detect? What does your taskforce recommend? Should lie detectors be used as absolute evidence of truthfulness? Present your "taskforce's" findings and position to "congress" (your class).

6. **Life Connections: Obesity and Eating Disorders: This Meal Is Too Big; This Meal Is Too Little—Can You Ever Get It Just Right?"** Examine your own eating patterns. Do you need to lose/gain weight? Are you *sure*? What standard are you using in making this

judgment? Do you have difficulty controlling your weight? If so, which of the behavior patterns discussed in the text seem to be contributing to the problem? What does food mean to you? Is food more than a way of satisfying the hunger drive? If so, how? How do you know when you are hungry? What do you experience? Have you ever eaten because you were anxious or bored or because something just "looked good"? Prepare a two-page essay that describes your eating patterns and the effects they have on your health. In your conclusions be sure to discuss the things that can you do to change your unhealthy eating patterns to healthy ones. Which of the strategies mentioned in the text are likely to work for you? Why?

Chapter Ten: Stress, Health & Adjustment

PowerPreview: *Skim the major headings in this chapter in your textbook. Jot down anything that you are surprised or curious about. After this write down four or five questions that you have about the material in this chapter.*

Things that surprised me/I am curious about from Chapter 10:

Questions that I have about Stress, Health and Adjustment:

-
-
-
-

QUESTION: *These are some questions that you should be able to answer after you finish studying this chapter:*

Health Psychology
- ❖ *What is health psychology?*

Stress: Presses, Pushes, and Pulls
- ❖ *What is stress?*

Sources of Stress: Don't Hassle Me? (Right)
- ❖ *What are daily hassles?*
- ❖ *How is it that too much of a good thing can make you ill?*
- ❖ *Controversy in Psychology: Just how are daily hassles and life changes connected with health problems?*
- ❖ *What is conflict?*
- ❖ *How do irrational beliefs create or compound stress?*
- ❖ *What is the Type A behavior pattern?*

Psychological Moderators of Stress
- ❖ *How do our self-efficacy expectations affect our ability to withstand stress?*
- ❖ *What characteristics are connected with psychological hardiness?*
- ❖ *Is there any evidence that "A merry heart doeth good like a medicine"?*
- ❖ *How do predictability and control help us cope with stress?*
- ❖ *Is there evidence that social support helps people cope with stress?*

Stress and the Body: The War Within
- ❖ *What is the general adaptation syndrome?*
- ❖ *How does the immune system work?*
- ❖ *How does stress affect the functioning of the immune system?*

Psychology and Health: Headaches, Cardiovascular Disorders, Cancer and Sexually

Transmitted Infections

- ❖ *What is the Multifactorial Approach to Health?*
- ❖ *How has psychology contributed to our understanding of the origins and treatment of headaches?*
- ❖ *How has psychology contributed to our understanding of origins and treatment of coronary heart disease?*
- ❖ *How has psychology contributed to our understanding of the origins and treatment of cancer?*
- ❖ *What kinds of sexually transmitted infections are there? What are their effects?*

Life Connections: Preventing and Coping with Health Problems-Stress, Headaches, Heart Disease, Cancer and Sexually Transmitted Infections

Reading for Understanding/Reflect: The *following section provides you with the opportunity to perform 2 of the R's of the PQ4R study method. In this section I will encourage you to check your understanding of your reading of the text by filling in the blanks in the brief paragraphs that relate to each of the preview questions. You will also be prompted to rehearse your understanding of the material with periodic Reflection breaks. Remember it is better to study in more frequent, short session then in one long "cram session." Be sure to reward yourself with short study breaks before each of the Reflection exercises.*

Reading for Understanding about "Health Psychology"
What is health psychology? (1)_____ psychology studies the relationships between psychological factors and the prevention and treatment of physical health problems. Health psychologists study the ways in which: (2)_____ factors such as stress, behavior patterns and attitudes can lead or aggravate (3)_____; people can cope with (4)_____; the way that stress and pathogens interact to influence the (5)_____ system; people decide whether to seek (6)_____; and psychological forms of (7)_____ like health education and behavior modification can contribute to physical health.

Reading for Understanding about "Stress: Presses, Pushes, and Pulls"
What is stress? In psychology, (8)_____ is the demand made on an organism to adapt, cope or adjust. Whereas some stress-called (9)_____-is desirable to keep us alert and occupied, too much stress can tax our adjustive capacities and contribute to (10)_____ health problems.

Reading for Understanding about "Sources of Stress: Don't Hassle Me? (Right)"
There are many sources of (11)_____ including: daily hassles, life changes, conflict, irrational beliefs and type A behavior.

What are daily hassles? (12)_____ are regularly occurring experiences that threaten or harm our well-being. The opposite of daily hassles are called (13)_____. There are several kinds of hassles, including (14)_____, health, (15)_____, inner concern, environmental, (16)_____ responsibility, work, and future security hassles. Daily hassles are linked to psychological variables such as nervousness, (17)_____, inability to get started, and feelings of sadness and (18)_____.

How is it that too much of a good thing can make you ill? Too many positive life changes can affect one's (19)_____ because life changes require adjustment, whether they are positive or negative. In contrast to daily hassles, (20)_____ are positive and desirable and occur irregularly. Research shows that hassles and life changes are connected with health problems such as (21)_____ and (22)_____.

Controversy in Psychology: Just how are daily hassles and life changes connected with health problems? The links between daily hassles, life changes and health problems are supported by research—but what leads to what? It appears obvious that hassles and life changes should cause (23)_____ problems, however, there are a number of (24)_____ to the research and, as a result, the (25)_____ connections between the two may not be as clear as researchers would like. These limitations include: the studies that have demonstrated the connection between life changes and health have mostly been (26)_____; positive life changes may be (27)_____ disturbing then hassles and negative life changes; people with different (28)_____ respond to stress differently; and the stress of an event depends on how we (29)_____ the hassles, and life experiences.

What is conflict? (30)_____ is the stressful feeling of being pulled in two or more directions by opposing motives. Conflict is (31)_____. There are four kinds of conflict: (32)_____, in which each of the two goals is desirable; (33)_____, in which you are motivated to avoid both goals; (34)_____ (in the case of a single goal), and (35)_____, when each alternative has its pluses and minuses. Approach-approach conflicts are the (36)_____ stressful since each of the two goals is desirable. Avoidance-avoidance conflicts are (37)_____ stressful since avoiding one goal requires approaching the other. Approach-avoidance conflicts produce mixed motives and may seem more (38)_____ from a distance, but (39)_____ up close. The most (40)_____ conflict is the multiple approach-avoidance since each of several alternative courses of action have pluses and minuses.

How do irrational beliefs create or compound stress? Albert Ellis notes that our (41)_____ about events, as well as the events themselves, can be stressors. He shows that negative (42)_____ events (A) can be made more aversive (C) when (43)_____ (B) compound their effects. People often (44)_____ negative events. Two common irrational beliefs are excessive needs for (45)_____ and (46)_____. Both set the stage for (47)_____ and increased stress.

What is the Type A behavior pattern? Some people create stress for themselves through the (48)_____ behavior pattern. Type A behavior is connected with a sense of (49)_____ and characterized by competitiveness, (50)_____, and aggressiveness. Type A people find it difficult to just do things for fun; they often watch their form, perfect their technique and demand continual (51)_____. (52)_____ people relax more readily and focus more on the quality of life. Type B people are less (53)_____ and less impatient and pace themselves.

Reflection Break # 1:
1. What is Health Psychology?

2. Briefly explain how your cognitions (beliefs & attitudes) affect how external stressors like daily hassles and conflict have on your well being.

Reading for Understanding about "Psychological Moderators of Stress"
There is no (54)_____ relationship between stress and physical or psychological health problems. But, none-the-less, psychological factors do play a role in influencing, or (55)_____ the effects of stress. (56)_____ moderators of stress include: self-efficacy expectations, psychological hardiness, a sense of humor, predictability, and social support.

How do our self-efficacy expectations affect our ability to withstand stress? People who are (57)_____ are less prone to be disturbed by adverse events. (58)_____ encourage us to persist in difficult tasks and to endure discomfort. Self-efficacy expectations are also connected with (59)_____ levels of adrenaline and noradrenaline, thus have a braking effect on bodily (60)_____.

What characteristics are connected with psychological hardiness? Kobasa found that psychological hardiness among business executives is characterized by (61)_____, they involved themselves rather then feeling alienated; (62)_____, they believe that change, rather than stability is normal in life; and (63)_____, they felt and behaved as though they were influential and demonstrated, what Julian Rotter termed, an internal (64)_____. Kosbasa argues that (65)_____ people are more resistant to stress because they choose to face it and interpret stress as making life more interesting.

Is there any evidence that "A merry heart doeth good like a medicine"? Yes. Another psychological moderator of stress appears to be a (66)_____. Research evidence shows that students who produce humor under adversity experience (67)_____ stress. Moreover, watching humorous videos apparently enhances the functioning of the (68)_____ system. How exactly humor helps people (69)_____ with stress is uncertain. One possibility is that laughter stimulates the output of (70)_____, which could benefit the functioning of the immune system.

How do predictability and control help us cope with stress? (71)_____ allows us to brace ourselves, and (72)_____ permits us to plan ways of coping with it. Control, even the (73)_____ of being in control, helps people cope with stress. Predictability is of greater benefit to (74)_____, or those who wish to exercise control over their situations, than to (75)_____.

Is there evidence that social support helps people cope with stress? (76)_____ has been shown to help people resist infectious diseases such as colds. (77)_____, people who lack social skill and live by themselves, seem more prone to developing infectious diseases. Social support also helps people cope with the stress of (78)_____ and other health problems. Kinds of social support include expression of (79)_____ concern, instrumental aid, information, appraisal, and simple (80)_____.

Reading for Understanding about "Stress and the Body"
What is the general adaptation syndrome? The GAS, or (81)_____, is a cluster of bodily changes triggered by stressors labeled by Hans Selye. The GAS consists of (82)_____ stages: alarm, resistance, and exhaustion. During the (83)_____ reaction stage the body prepares it self for defense. This reaction involves a number of body changes that are initiated

by the (84)_____ and further regulated by the (85)_____ system and the (86)_____ division of the autonomic nervous system (ANS). The (87)_____ secretes corticotrophin releasing hormone, which causes the (88)_____ gland to secrete adrenocorticotrophic hormone which then causes the (89)_____ to secrete cortisol and other corticosteroids. (90)_____ help resist stress by fighting inflammation and allergic reactions. The (91)_____ also releases two other hormones that play an important role in the alarm reaction, adrenaline and noradrenaline. The mixture of adrenaline and noreadrenaline (92)_____ the body by accelerating the heart rate and causing the liver to release glucose. In the (93)_____ stage of the GAS levels of endocrine and sympathetic activity are higher than normal, but lower than in the alarm reaction phase. The (94)_____ division of the ANS predominates during the exhaustion stage of the GAS and is connected with depression and inactivity. Prolonged stress is (95)_____ and may lead to what Selye terms "diseases of adaptation".

How does the immune system work? Research shows that stress (96)_____ the immune system. The (97)_____ system has several functions that combat disease. One of these is the production of (98)_____, or white blood cells, that engulf and kill pathogens, worn-out body cells, and cancerous cells. The immune system also "remembers" how to battle (99)_____ by maintaining their antibodies in the bloodstream. The immune system also facilitates (100)_____, which increases the number of white blood cells that are transported to a damaged area. (101)_____ is a sub-specialty of biology, psychology and medicine in which the relationships between psychological factors, the nervous system, the endocrine system, the immune system and disease are examined. One of the major areas of concern in psychoneuroimmunology is the effect of (102)_____ on the immune system.

How does stress affect the functioning of the immune system? Stress (103)_____ the functioning of the immune system by stimulating the production of steroids. (104)_____ counter inflammation and interfere with the formation of antibodies; they also suppress the functioning of the immune system.

Reflection Break # 2:
1.   What psychological factors can you use to moderate the effect that stress has on your health?

2.   Briefly summarize the physical effects of prolonged stress on the body.

Reading for Understanding about "Psychology and Health: Headaches, Cardiovascular Disorders, Cancer and Sexually Transmitted Infections"

What is the Multifactorial Approach to Health? The (105)_____ approach to health recognizes that many factors, including biological, psychological, sociocultural, and environmental factors, affect our health. This approach to health recognizes that the likelihood of contracting a disease can reflect the (106)_____ of many factors—one of these is genetic factors. Of all the biological factors, (107)_____ factors tend to tempt people to take a fatalistic approach and to assume there is little they can do about their health. However, in many cases genes only create (108)_____ towards health problems. Jane (109)_____ notes that predispositions need a conducive environment in which to express themselves and that a bad

148

family environment should not be considered a certainty of a bad outcome. Many health problems are also affected by sociocultural, environmental, and (110)_____ factors, such as attitudes, emotions and behavior.

How has psychology contributed to our understanding of the origins and treatment of headaches? Psychologists participate in research concerning the origins of (111)_____, including stress and tension. The most frequent kind of headache, the (112)_____ headache, comes on gradually and is characterized by feelings of tightness and a dull steady pain on both sides of the head. Persistent (113)_____ can lead to constant contraction of the muscles in the shoulders, neck and forehead, causing muscle tension headaches. Psychological factors such as the tendency to (114)_____, or blow things out of proportion, negative events can bring on a tension headache.

In contrast, the (115)_____ headache has a sudden onset and is identified by severe throbbing on one side of the head. Triggers for migraine headaches include: a (116)_____ behavior pattern, barametric pressure, pollen, certain drugs, (117)_____--a flavor enhancer, chocolate, aged cheese, beer, champagne, red wine and (118)_____ changes connected with menstruation.

How has psychology contributed to our understanding of origins and treatment of coronary heart disease? Psychologists have participated in research that shows that the risk factors for (119)_____ disease include family history; physiological conditions such as hypertension and high levels of serum (120)_____; behavior patterns such as heavy drinking, smoking, eating (121)_____ foods, and Type A behavior; work overload; chronic (122)_____ and fatigue; and physical (123)_____.

How has psychology contributed to our understanding of the origins and treatment of cancer? (124)_____ is characterized by the development of abnormal, or mutant cells that may take root any where in the body. If their spread is not controlled early the cancerous cells may (125)_____, or establish colonies elsewhere in the body. Psychologists have participated in research that shows that the risk factors for (126)_____ include family history, smoking, drinking alcohol, eating animal fats, sunbathing, and stress. (127)_____ Americans, possibly because of genetic and socioeconomic factors, are more likely then (128)_____Americans to contract most forms of cancer. The following measures can be helpful in (129)_____ and (130)_____ cancer: controlling exposure to behavioral risk factors for cancer, having regular medical checkups, regulating exposure to stress, and vigorously fighting cancer if it develops.

What kinds of sexually transmitted infections are there? What are their effects? Sexual relationships can be sources of pleasure and personal fulfillment, however they also carry (131)_____. The most significant risk is that of contracting AIDS or other (132)_____. (133)_____ experience the effects of most STI's disproportionally since they are more likely to develop infertility if an STI spreads through the reproductive system. (134)_____ risk factors for STI's include both cognitive and behavioral factors. Cognitively most people tend to (135)_____, or underestimate, their risk of infection; and despite their knowledge of the effects of infection, many people do not change their (136)_____ in an effort to prevent an infection.

Reading for Understanding about "Life Connections: Preventing and Coping with Health Problems-Stress, Headaches, Heart Disease, Cancer and Sexually Transmitted Infections"

(137)_____ takes many forms and can harm our psychological well-being and physical health. Three ways for coping with stress include: controlling (138)_____, lowering arousal and (139)_____.

People often feel pressure from their own (140)_____. In order to keep irrational thoughts from producing stress we must (141)_____ them. (142)_____ psychologists have outlined a multi-step process for doing so. It involves becoming (143)_____ of the thoughts, evaluating the (144)_____ of the thoughts, preparing and practicing (145)_____ thoughts, and (146)_____ one self for changing.

Stress tends to trigger (147)_____. Arousal serves as a sign that something may be (148)_____. However, once we are aware that a (149)_____ is acting on us, high levels of (150)_____ are not helpful. Psychologists have developed many methods for teaching people to (151)_____ arousal including meditation, biofeedback training, and progressive relaxation. In (152)_____, people purposefully tense and then relax muscle groups to develop awareness of muscle tensions and learn how to let the tensions go.

(153)_____ enhances our psychological well-being and also strengthens the (154)_____ system, our fitness, or "condition" so that we can better (155)_____ the bodily effects of stress.

Since headaches are related to stress, one way to lessen them is to decrease (156)_____. All of the methods of stress reduction discussed in the text: challenging (157)_____ beliefs, lowering (158)_____ and (159)_____ may be of help in headache control. Risks for CHD can be controlled by help people achieve healthier cardiovascular systems by stopping (160)_____, controlling (161)_____, reducing (162)_____, lowering (163)_____ levels, changing Type (164)_____ behavior, reducing (165)_____, and exercising. Similarly cancer can be fought by (166)_____exposure to behavioral risk factors for cancer, having regular medical checkups, regulating exposure to (167)_____, and vigorously fighting cancer if it develops.

(168)_____ is the primary weapon against STI's. People need to learn about the (169)_____, symptoms, (170)_____ of STI's and safer sex (171)_____. However, (172)_____ is not enough because of what psychologists call the A—B problem, that is that people do not always (173)_____(B) according to their (174)_____(A). A number of things can be done to Nprevent the transmission of HIV and other STI's and the best include: not (175)_____ the treatment of STI's, remaining (176)_____, and engaging in a (177)_____ relationship with an uninfected person.

Reflection Break # 3:

1. How can an understanding of Health Psychology help a person remain healthy?

2. After reading this chapter what can you do to cope with the stresses of your life?

Review: Key Terms and Concepts

FINAL CHAPTER REVIEW

Recite:

Go to the Recite section for this chapter on pages 409-410 in your textbook. Use the tear-off card provided at the back of the book to cover the answers of the Recite section. Read the questions aloud and recite the answers. This will help you cement your knowledge of key concepts.

Multiple Choice Questions:

1. The branch of psychology that studies the relationships between psychological factors and the prevention and treatment of physical health problems is
   a. Psychopathology.
   b. Neuropsychology.
   c. Psychoanalysis.
   d. Health Psychology.

2. Lisa is a single parent of three children. During the course of each week she prepares meals, shops for food and takes care of the household. She also works out side the home in a demanding job that she does not like yet is concerned about meeting her everyday expenses. Psychologists call these stresses
   a. daily hassles.
   b. uplifts.
   c. pathogens.
   d. environmental hassles.

3. Hans Selye termed stress that is healthful
   a. stress.
   b. daily hassles.
   c. eustress.
   d. conflict.

4. Sam wants to be a clinical psychologist. He has been accepted at two different graduate schools. Both schools are equally prestigious and would provide him with an outstanding education. He must choose to attend one of the schools. Psychologists would call this type of conflict an
   a. avoidance-avoidance conflict.
   b. approach-avoidance conflict.
   c. approach-approach conflict.
   d. multiple approach-avoidance conflict.

5. Irrational events can create or compound stress by
   a. making negative events more aversive.
   b. causing stressed individuals to catastrophize the negative events.
   c. both a and b.
   d. neither of the above.

6. Karen is a highly driven person. She is competitive, impatient and often aggressive. She walks eats, walks and talks rapidly and constantly feels rushed and under pressure. Psychologists would say that Karen's behavior is typical of a person
   a. with eustress.
   b. with a Type B personality.
   c. with a Type A personality.
   d. who tends to catastrophize.

7. Eugene believes that he can bring about positive changes in his life through his own efforts. Psychologists would say that Eugene has high
   a. eustress.
   b. daily hassles.
   c. Type A personality traits.
   d. self-efficacy expectations.

8. People with high self-efficacy expectations
   a. are able to withstand stress.
   b. have higher levels of adrenaline and noradrenaline in the bloodstream.
   c. are more prone to be disturbed by adverse events.
   d. all of the above.

9. Carole seems to be incredibly healthy; she is able to resist illness no matter how much stress she is under. She tends to fully involve herself in whatever she is doing, she believes that change is normal and that she has control over the course of her life. Psychologists would say that Carole has
   a. an external locus of control.
   b. high psychological hardiness.
   c. moderate self-efficacy expectations.
   d. Type A behavior.

10. Your friend Suki's grandmother has always told her that happier people experience less stress. Since she knows that you are taking a psychology course, she asks you whether or not psychologists would agree with her grandmother . Which of the following would you be most likely to tell her?
    a. Yes, Grandma was correct, research has shown that humor can moderate the effects of stress.
    b. No, Grandma does not know what she is talking about. There is no good evidence to support the claim that a sense of humor allows you to lead a less stressful life.
    c. Grandma could be correct, but psychologists are uncertain since the research has been inconsistent.
    d. Grandma is mistaken; humor can help us cope with painful illnesses, but not stress.

11. Psychological factors that can moderate the way an individual handles stress include
    a. self-efficacy expectations.
    b. psychological hardiness.
    c. a sense of humor.
    d. all of the above.

12. Susan is in the first stage of Selye's General Adaptation Syndrome; which of the following is most likely to be occurring?
    a. Her heart and respiration rates have slowed down and her muscles have become fatigued. She has developed hives all over her upper torso.
    b. Her endocrine and sympathetic activity is above normal, but lower than in the alarm.
    c. Her hypothalamus is secreting corticotrophin-releasing hormones, which in turn cause her pituitary gland to secrete cortisol.
    d. Her body has been activated and she is experiencing a fight or flight reaction.

13. Kevin is in the final stage of Selye's General Adaptation Syndrome; which of the following is most likely to be occurring?
    a. His heart and respiration rates have slowed down and his muscles have become fatigued. He has developed hives all over his upper torso.
    b. His endocrine and sympathetic activity is above normal, but lower than in the alarm.
    c. His hypothalamus is secreting corticotrophin-releasing hormones, which in turn causes his pituitary gland to secrete cortisol.
    d. His body has been activated and he is experiencing a fight or flight reaction.

14. The immune system combats disease
    a. by having leukocytes destroy foreign agents and unhealthy cells.
    b. by having antibodies attach themselves to foreign substances, deactivating them.
    c. when inflammation occurs.
    d. All of the above.

15. Dr. Caldwell studies the relationships among psychological factors, the nervous system, the endocrine system, the immune system and disease. Most likely Dr. Caldwell is a
    a. neuropsychologist.
    b. health psychologist.
    c. psychoneuroimmunologist.
    d. psychopathologist.

16. The view that recognizes that many factors, including biological, psychological, sociocultural and environmental factors affect our health is known as
    a. the psychodynamic view.
    b. an eclectic view.
    c. the multifactorial approach.
    d. Health psychology.

17. John has a headache. The pain is a dull, steady pain on both sides of his head that came on gradually. Most likely John's headache
    a. is a migraine.
    b. results from psychological factors.
    c. is a tension headache.
    d. both b and c.

18. The leading cause of death in the United States is
    a. diabetes.
    b. migraine headaches.
    c. coronary heart disease.
    d. obesity.

19. Which of the following are not risk factors for Coronary heart disease?
    a. A family history of CHD.
    b. High serum cholesterol levels and hypertension.
    c. A physically active life style.
    d. Heavy drinking, smoking, overeating and a high-fat diet.

20. Human papilloma virus (HPV) is to _____ as chlamydia is to _____.
   a. pelvic inflammatory disease; AIDS
   b. genital herpes; pelvic inflammatory disease
   c. genital warts; AIDS
   d. genital warts; pelvic inflammatory disease

Essay Questions:

1. What is stress? In a three-paragraph essay describe the definition of stress you had before reading the chapter, and compare it with the psychological definition provided in your textbook.

2. Controversy in Psychology: Just how are daily hassles and life changes connected with health problems? How many daily hassles do you experience? Are they temporary or permanent? How many are connected with your role as a student? Can you think of any positive life changes in your own life that caused your stress? Make a list of your hassles and hang-ups that you must cope with in your daily life and group them in the following categories:

   Household/ hassles   Work hassles
   Time pressure hassles   School hassles
   Health hassles   Future/security hassles
   Family hassles   Social hassles
   Financial responsibility hassles   Other

   After you complete your list rank your hassles on a scale of 1 to 10 with 1 representing the least important; 10 the most important. Which category of daily hassles are the most pressing for you? How can you decrease the stress they produce? Present your information to your classmates on a poster board in a format specified by your instructor and compare your profile to those of your classmates. Are you more or less stressed than your peers?

3. How do your attitudes and beliefs affect the impact that external stressors have? In a two-page essay explain how our cognitions--our attitudes and beliefs-- affect the impact that external stressors have on us, and how we can moderate these effects through psychological mechanisms. In your essay be sure to address the role of irrational beliefs in our interpretation of events and how we can use changes in self-efficacy expectations, a sense of humor and social support. Format your essay as specified by your instructor.

4. Does your behavior pattern influence your risk of CHD and can you reduce your risk? In a short report differentiate between Type A and Type B behavior patterns, and discuss the link between Type A behavior and coronary heart disease (CHD). Conclude your report with recommendations for reducing the risk of CHD. Format your report as specified your instructor.

5. Does your behavior pattern influence your risk of contracting HIV and STI's and can you reduce your risk? In a short report summarize the risk factors for contracting an STI.

Conclude your report with recommendations for reducing the risk of STI. Present this report as an oral present to a group of preteens.

CONNECT & EXPAND:

1. **Health Psychology:** *What is Health Psychology? What type of career opportunities is available in Health psychology?* Read about careers in health psychology on the "Careers in Health Psychology" page from West Chester University @ http://www.wcupa.edu/_ACADEMICS/sch_cas.psy/Career_Paths/Health/Career02.htm. Pick one of the sub-fields presented and prepare a three-minute oral report on it. Be sure to describe the specialization's emphasis and the types of job responsibilities that someone might have if they chose this career.

2. **Sources of Stress: Don't Hassle Me? (Right):** *Controversy in Psychology: Just how are daily hassles and life changes connected with health problems?* Do you find that the more life hassles you have, the more likely you are to get sick? How often do you find that you get sick during, or right after exam week? Or spring break? Have each member of your study group interview 20-college students with the above questions. Tabulate the results. Do the data suggest that stressful times tend to be correlated with illness? Prepare a report for your class that describes your findings and outlines the different ways that college students can try to prevent becoming ill during peak stress periods.

3. **Psychological Moderators of Stress:** *How Resilient Are You?* Your textbook discussed the role of psychological factors in our experience of stress. Factors such as self-efficacy expectations, psychological hardiness and a sense of humor are all important in determining how stressful life events are. How Resilient Are You? Take the quiz by Al Siebert @ http://www.thrivenet.com/articles/resilien.html. How do you react to unexpected difficulties? Healthy, resilient people have stress-resistant personalities and learn valuable lessons from rough experiences, are you one of these? If not how can you become more resilient? Report your findings to your classmates in a format specified by your instructor.

4. **Stress and the Body:** *What are the biological consequences of stress?* What do you experience happening in your body when you are under stress? How do those sensations fit the description of the general adaptation syndrome? After reading the textbook's description you might want to start your search at the "Medical Basis of Stress, Depression, Anxiety, Sleep Problems, and Drug Use" page @ http://www.teachhealth.com. Summarize the effects of stress on brain chemistry and the physical symptoms of over stress. Why do people often turn to caffeine, alcohol and other drugs when they get stressed? Report back to your classmates on your findings in a format specified by your instructor.

5. **Life Connections: Life Connections: Preventing and Coping with Health problems-Stress, Headaches, Heart Disease, Cancer and Sexually Transmitted Infections:** *How can you help yourself to better cope with stress?* Visit the following websites on Stress and Stress management, and with your study group prepare an informational brochure for your class that outlines the various Stress management techniques suggested
Mind Tools Website--Stress @ http://www.demon.co.uk/mindtool/smpage.html.

Stress Management Site (by Wesley E. Sime, Ph.D./MPH./Ph.D.)
http://www.unl.edu/stress/mgmt/
How To Fight & Conquer Stress (Rose Medical Center in Denver CO.)
http://www.coolware.com/health/medical_reporter/stress.html

Chapter Eleven: Personality: Theory and Measurement

PowerPreview: *Skim the major headings in this chapter in your textbook. Jot down anything that you are surprised or curious about. After this write down four or five questions that you have about the material in this chapter.*

Things that surprised me/I am curious about from Chapter 11:

Questions that I have about Personality: Theory and Measurement

-
-
-
-

QUESTION: *These are some questions that you should be able to answer after you finish studying this chapter:*

Introduction to Personality: "Why Are They Sad and Glad and Bad?"
- ❖ *Just what is personality?*

The Psychodynamic Perspective: Excavating the Iceberg
- ❖ *What is Freud's theory of psychosexual development?*
- ❖ *Who are some other psychodynamic theorists? What are their views on personality?*
- ❖ *What are the strengths and weaknesses of the psychodynamic perspective?*

The Trait Perspective: The Five-Dimensional Universe
- ❖ *What are traits?*
- ❖ *What is the history of the trait perspective?*
- ❖ *How have contemporary researchers used factor analysis to reduce the universe of traits to smaller lists of traits that show common features?*
- ❖ *What are the strengths and weaknesses of trait theory?*

Learning Theory Perspective: All the Things You Do
- ❖ *What does learning theory have to contribute to our understanding of personality?*
- ❖ *What is Watson's contribution to personality theory?*
- ❖ *How did Skinner develop Watson's views?*
- ❖ *How does social-cognitive theory differ from the behaviorist view?*
- ❖ *What are the strengths and weaknesses of learning theories as they apply to personality?*

The Humanistic-Existential Perspective: How Becoming?
- ❖ *What is humanism? What is existentialism?*

- ❖ *How do humanistic psychologists differ from psychodynamic theorists?*
- ❖ *Just what is your self? What is self-theory?*
- ❖ *What are the strengths and weaknesses of humanistic-existential theory?*

The Socio-cultural Perspective: Personality in Context
- ❖ *Why is the Socio-cultural perspective important to the understanding of personality?*
- ❖ *What does it mean to be individualistic? What is meant by individualism and collectivism?*
- ❖ *How does acculturation affect the psychological well-being of immigrants and their families?*
- ❖ *Controversy in Psychology: Just how much acculturation is enough?*

Measurement of Personality
- ❖ *How are personality measures used?*
- ❖ *What are objective personality tests?*
- ❖ *How do projective tests differ from objective tests? What are some of the more widely used projective tests?*

Life Connections: Gender Typing—On Becoming a Woman or a Man

Reading for Understanding/Reflect: The *following section provides you with the opportunity to perform 2 of the R's of the PQ4R study method. In this section I will encourage you to check your understanding of your reading of the text by filling in the blanks in the brief paragraphs that relate to each of the preview questions. You will also be prompted to rehearse your understanding of the material with periodic Reflection breaks. Remember it is better to study in more frequent, short session then in one long "cram session." Be sure to reward yourself with short study breaks before each of the Reflection exercises.*

Reading for Understanding about "Introduction to Personality: "Why Are They Sad and Glad and Bad?"
Just what is personality? (1)_____ is defined as the reasonably stable patterns of behavior, including thoughts and emotions that distinguish one person from another. Psychologists seek to explain how personality (2)_____ and to (3)_____ how people with certain personality traits respond to life's demands. This chapter discusses five (4)_____ on personality: the psychodynamic, trait, learning, humanistic-existential and socio-cultural.

Reading for Understanding about "The Psychodynamic Perspective: Excavating the Iceberg"
There are several psychodynamic theories of personality, each of which owes its origin to the thinking of Sigmund (5)_____; all teach that personality is characterized by a dynamic struggle, or (6)_____.

What is Freud's theory of psychosexual development? Freud's theory is termed (7)_____ because it assumes that we are driven largely by unconscious motives and by the movement of unconscious forces within our minds. Freud concluded that the human mind was like an (8)_____and labeled the region that pokes through into awareness the (9)_____. The (10)_____ mind contains elements of the mind that are out of awareness, but can be made conscious by focusing on them and the (11)_____ contains biological instincts such as sex and aggression and cannot be experienced consciously. According to Psychodynamic theory, people experience (12)_____ as basic instincts of hunger, sex, and aggression come up against social pressures to follow laws, rules, and moral codes. At first this conflict is (13)_____, but as we develop, it is (14)_____. In the unconscious mind primitive drives seek (15)_____, while internalized values try to keep them in check; this (16)_____ can lead to emotional outbursts and psychological problems. To explore the unconscious mind Freud engaged in (17)_____, a form of therapy in which people are prodded to talk about anything that pops in to their mind.

Freud believed that there were three mental, or (18)_____ structures that described the clashing forces of the personality. The unconscious (19)_____ is present at birth and represents psychological drives and seeks instant gratification. The (20)_____, or the sense of self or "I," is governed by the reality principle and develops through experience. The ego takes into account what is (21)_____ and possible in gratifying the impulses of the (22)_____. Defense mechanisms such as repression protect the ego from (23)_____ by repressing unacceptable ideas or distorting reality. The (24)_____, which develops throughout early childhood, is the conscience and develops largely through the Oedipus complex and identification with others. Freud believed that the super-ego functioned according to the (25)_____ principle, holding forth shining examples of the ideal self.

Freud created controversy by stating that (26)_____impulses are a central factor in personality development. He believed that a major instinct, (27)_____, was aimed at preserving and perpetuating life and it was fueled by a psychological energy that he termed (28)_____. People undergo psychosexual development as libidinal energy, is transferred from one (29)_____ zone to another during childhood. There are (30)_____ stages of development: oral, anal, phallic, latency, and genital. Freud believed that children encounter (31)_____ during each stage of psychosexual stage of development. (32)_____ in a stage leads to development of traits associated with the stage.

Who are some other psychodynamic theorists? What are their views on personality? Carl Jung's theory, (33)_____ psychology, features a (34)_____ unconscious and numerous (35)_____, both of which reflect the history of our species. Alfred Adler's theory, (36)_____ psychology, features the (37)_____ self, inferiority complex and the compensating drive for (38)_____. Karen Horney's theory focuses on (39)_____ relationships. She asserted that genuine and consistent (40)_____ can alleviate the effects of even the most traumatic childhood. Erik Erikson's theory of (41)_____ development highlights the importance of early social relationships rather than the gratification of childhood (42)_____ impulses. Erikson extended (43)_____'s five developmental stages to eight, including stages that occur in adulthood.

What are the strengths and weaknesses of the psychodynamic perspective? Freud fought for the idea that personality is subject to (44)_____ analysis at a time when many people still viewed psychological problems as signs of (45)_____. He also focused attention on the importance of (46)_____, the effects of child rearing, and the fact that people (47)_____ perceptions according to their needs. On the other hand, there is no evidence for the existence of (48)_____, and his theory is fraught with (49)_____ about child development. Additionally Freud's (50)_____ of gathering evidence from clinical sessions are also suspect.

Reflection Break # 1

Part I. *Match the terms with their correct descriptions.*

a.	Pleasure principle	m.	Libido	y.	Genital stage
b.	Identification	n.	Unconscious	z.	Incest taboo
c.	Preconscious	o.	Erogenous zones	aa.	Analytical psychology
d.	Repression	p.	Oral stage	bb.	Collective unconscious
e.	Psychoanalysis	q.	Fixation	cc.	archetypes
f.	Resistance	r.	Anal stage	dd.	Eros
g.	Psychic structures	s.	Conscious	ee.	Inferiority complex
h.	Id	t.	Phallic stage	ff.	Creative self
i.	Reality principle	u.	Oedipus complex	gg.	Individual psychology
j.	Defense mechanism	v.	Electra complex	hh.	ego
k.	Superego	w.	Displacement		
l.	Moral principle	x.	Latency		

_____1. The portion of the mind that enters into awareness.

_____2. Principle that guides the superego; sets moral standards and holds examples of an ideal self.

_____3. The portion of the mind that is beneath awareness but can be made conscious by focusing on them.

_____4. The portion of the mind that contains biological instincts such as sex and aggression and is shrouded in mystery.

_____5. The automatic ejection of anxiety evoking ideas from awareness.

_____6. The cultural prohibition against marrying, or having sexual relations with a close blood relative.

_____7. A conflict of the phallic stage in which a boy wishes to have sexual relations with his mother, and perceives his father as a rival.

_____8. The mature stage of psychosexual development characterized by preferred expression of libido through intercourse with an adult of the opposite sex.

_____9. Psychic structure that develops throughout early childhood usually incorporating the moral standards and values of the parents.

_____10. The stage of psychosexual development in which sexual gratification is obtained through contraction and relaxation of the muscles that control elimination of bodily waste.

_____11. The conflict of the phallic stage of development in which a female child longs for her father and resents her mother.

_____12. Jung's psychodynamic theory which emphasizes the collective unconscious and archetypes.

_____13. The unconscious assumption of the behavior of another person.

_____14. Adler's psychodynamic theory which emphasizes feelings of inferiority and the creative self.

_____15. The transfer of emotions or feelings to more socially appropriate objects.

_____16. Freud's term for the energy of the Eros or sexual instinct.

_____17. The desire to avoid thinking about or discussing anxiety-evoking ideas.

_____18. Freud's method of exploring the conscious mind.

_____19. An area of the body that is sensitive to sexual sensations.

_____20. Freud's term for the mental structures used to describe the clashing forces of the personality.

_____21. Psychic structure present at birth, represents physiological drives; is entirely unconscious.

_____22. The stage of psychosexual development characterized by the development of a sexual attachment to the parent of the opposite gender.

_____23. An unconscious function of the ego that protects it from anxiety–evoking material by preventing accurate recognition of this material.

_____24. Basic primitive images that reflect the history of our species.

_____25. The stage of psychosexual development in which sexual feelings remain unconscious.

_____26. The principle used by the id to give its desires; it demands instant gratification with out consideration of law, social custom or the needs of others.

_____27. The stage of psychosexual development in which gratification is hypothesized to be obtained through activities such as sucking and biting.

_____28. Jung's hypothesized storehouse of primitive images that reflect the history of our species.

_____29. Arrested development; failure to move onward to the next stage of psychosexual development.

_____30. Freud's term for the basic instinct to preserve life and perpetuate life.

_____31. Psychic structure that begins to develop in the first year of life and stands for reason and good sense.

_____32. Feelings of inadequacy hypothesized by Adler to serve as a central motivating force.

_____33. Principle that guides the desires of the ego; takes into account what is practical.

_____34. Self-aware aspect of personality that strives to overcome obstacles and develop the individual's potential.

2. _Match the psychodynamic theorist with the proper description of their view._
a.   Erik Erickson   c.   Alfred Adler
b.   Karen Horney   d.   Carl Jung

_____1. Argued that little girls do not feel inferior to boys; that these views were based on Western cultural prejudice.

_____2. Became a member of Freud's inner circle, but fell into disfavor over the importance of sexual instinct; believed in a collective unconscious.

_____3. Asserted that social relationships were more crucial determinants of personality than sexual urges; proposed eight stages of psychosocial development throughout the lifespan.

_____4. Believed that people are motivated by an inferiority complex and the need to compensate for these feelings; self-awareness plays a key role; spoke of a creative self.

Reading for Understanding about "The Trait Perspective: The Five-Dimensional Universe"
What are traits? What is the history of the trait perspective? (51)_____ are reasonably stable personality elements that are inferred from behavior and that account for behavioral consistency. Trait theory dates back to (52)_____ , the ancient Greek physician, who believed that personality reflects the balance of liquids or "(53)_____" in the body. Sir Francis

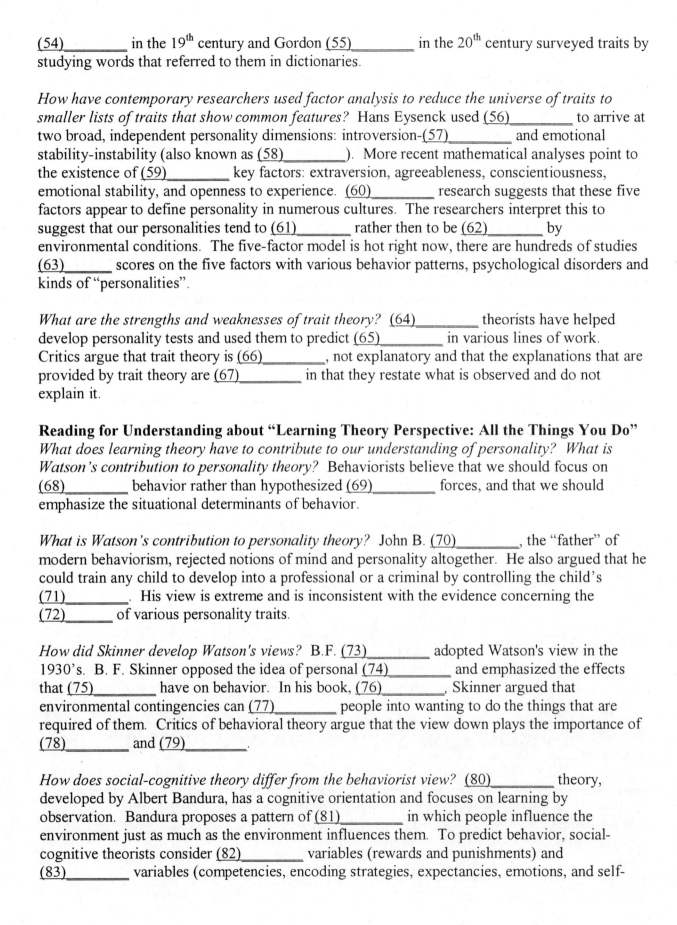

(54)_____ in the 19th century and Gordon (55)_____ in the 20th century surveyed traits by studying words that referred to them in dictionaries.

How have contemporary researchers used factor analysis to reduce the universe of traits to smaller lists of traits that show common features? Hans Eysenck used (56)_____ to arrive at two broad, independent personality dimensions: introversion-(57)_____ and emotional stability-instability (also known as (58)_____). More recent mathematical analyses point to the existence of (59)_____ key factors: extraversion, agreeableness, conscientiousness, emotional stability, and openness to experience. (60)_____ research suggests that these five factors appear to define personality in numerous cultures. The researchers interpret this to suggest that our personalities tend to (61)_____ rather then to be (62)_____ by environmental conditions. The five-factor model is hot right now, there are hundreds of studies (63)_____ scores on the five factors with various behavior patterns, psychological disorders and kinds of "personalities".

What are the strengths and weaknesses of trait theory? (64)_____ theorists have helped develop personality tests and used them to predict (65)_____ in various lines of work. Critics argue that trait theory is (66)_____, not explanatory and that the explanations that are provided by trait theory are (67)_____ in that they restate what is observed and do not explain it.

Reading for Understanding about "Learning Theory Perspective: All the Things You Do"
What does learning theory have to contribute to our understanding of personality? What is Watson's contribution to personality theory? Behaviorists believe that we should focus on (68)_____ behavior rather than hypothesized (69)_____ forces, and that we should emphasize the situational determinants of behavior.

What is Watson's contribution to personality theory? John B. (70)_____, the "father" of modern behaviorism, rejected notions of mind and personality altogether. He also argued that he could train any child to develop into a professional or a criminal by controlling the child's (71)_____. His view is extreme and is inconsistent with the evidence concerning the (72)_____ of various personality traits.

How did Skinner develop Watson's views? B.F. (73)_____ adopted Watson's view in the 1930's. B. F. Skinner opposed the idea of personal (74)_____ and emphasized the effects that (75)_____ have on behavior. In his book, (76)_____, Skinner argued that environmental contingencies can (77)_____ people into wanting to do the things that are required of them. Critics of behavioral theory argue that the view down plays the importance of (78)_____ and (79)_____.

How does social-cognitive theory differ from the behaviorist view? (80)_____ theory, developed by Albert Bandura, has a cognitive orientation and focuses on learning by observation. Bandura proposes a pattern of (81)_____ in which people influence the environment just as much as the environment influences them. To predict behavior, social-cognitive theorists consider (82)_____ variables (rewards and punishments) and (83)_____ variables (competencies, encoding strategies, expectancies, emotions, and self-regulatory systems and plans).

(84)_____ include knowledge of rules that guide conduct, concepts about ourselves and other people, and skills. Our ability to use (85)_____ to make plans depends on our competences. Competencies influence (86)_____which in turn influence motivation to perform. (87)_____ expectations are beliefs that we can accomplish certain things. We tend to regulate our own behavior, even in the absence of (88)_____ constraints. (89)_____ helps us influence our environment; depending on our expectations we (90)_____ the situations to which we expose our selves and the arena in which we will compete.

What are the strengths and weaknesses of learning theories as they apply to personality?
(91)_____ theorists have highlighted the importance of referring to publicly observable behaviors in theorizing. They have elaborated on the (92)_____ that foster learning and have shown that we can learn to do things because of (93)_____ and that many behavior patterns are acquired by (94)_____ others. However, behaviorism does not describe, explain, or suggest the richness of (95)_____ human experience. Critics of social-cognitive theory note that it does not address (96)_____ or adequately account for the development of (97)_____. It may also not pay enough attention to (98)_____ variation in explaining individual differences in behavior.

Reflection Break # 2:
Compare and contrasts the Trait, Learning and Social Cognitive Theories of personality in the chart below:

	Premise	Critique
Trait		
Behavioral		
Social Cognitive		

Reading for Understanding about "The Humanistic-Existential Perspective: How Becoming?"
What is humanism? What is existentialism? (99)_____ puts people and self-awareness at the center and argues that we are capable of free choice, self-fulfillment, and ethical behavior. (100)_____ argue that our lives have meaning when we give them meaning. Psychological salvation, according to the existentialist, requires giving (101)_____ to things and making personal choices.

How do humanistic psychologists differ from psychodynamic theorists? Whereas Freud wrote that people are motivated to gratify (102)_____ drives, humanistic psychologists believe that people have a conscious need for (103)_____, or to become all that they can be. Abraham (104)_____ argues that people are not at the mercy of unconscious primitive impulses; instead, the main threat to an individual's personality development is control by other people. He claims that people must be free to get in touch with and actualize our (105)_____.

Just what is your self? What is self-theory? According to Carl Rogers, the (106)_____ is your ongoing sense of who and what you are, your sense of how and why you react to the environment and how you choose to act on the environment. Self-theory begins by assuming the existence of the self and each person's unique (107)_____, or our own way of looking at ourselves.. The self attempts to (108)_____ (develop its unique potential) and best does so when the person receives (109)_____, or acceptance based on intrinsic merit regardless of their behavior at the moment. Rogers also argues that (110)_____, the belief that you may only have merit if you behave in a specific way, may lead to a distorted self-concept, to disowning of parts of the self, and to anxiety. According to Rogers the path to self-actualization requires getting in touch with our (111)_____ feelings, accepting them, and acting on them.

What are the strengths and weaknesses of humanistic-existential theory? Humanistic-existential theory is appealing because of its focus on the importance of (112)_____. But critics argue that concepts such as conscious experience and self-actualization are (113)_____. Self-actualization, like trait theories yields (114)_____ explanations for behavior; and like (115)_____ theories, humanistic-existential theories have very little to say about the development of different personality traits or types.

Reading for Understanding about "The Socio-cultural Perspective: Personality in Context"
Why is the Socio-cultural perspective important to the understanding of personality? One cannot fully understand the personality of an individual without understanding the (116)_____ beliefs and (117)_____ conditions that have affected that individual. The Socio-cultural perspective encourages us to consider the roles of ethnicity, (118)_____, culture, and socioeconomic status in personality formation, behavior, and mental processes.

What does it mean to be individualistic? What is meant by individualism and collectivism? (119)_____ define themselves in terms of their personal identities and to give priority to their personal goals. (120)_____ define themselves in terms of the groups to which they belong and to give priority to the group's goals. Cross-cultural studies suggest that many (121)_____ societies are individualistic and foster individualism in personality while many (122)_____ societies are collectivist and foster collectivism in personality.

How does acculturation affect the psychological well-being of immigrants and their families? (123)_____ refers to the process of adaptation in which immigrant and native groups identify with a new, dominant culture by learning about that culture and making behavioral and attitudinal change.

Controversy in Psychology: Just how much acculturation is enough? Patterns of acculturation take various forms. Some immigrants are completely (124)_____ by the dominate culture; they (125)_____ the language and customs of their country of origin and become like the dominant culture in the new host country. Others do the opposite, they maintain almost complete (126)_____ and retain the language and customs of the country of origin and never acclimate to the new country. Others become (127)_____, they remain fluent in the language of their native country but also become fluent in the language of their new country. Research suggests that immigrants who (128)_____ the customs and values of their country of origin but who also (129)_____ those of their new host country, and blend the two, tend to have (130)_____ self-esteem than immigrants who either become completely assimilated or who maintain complete separation from the new dominant culture.

The (131)_____ perspective provides valuable insight into the roles of ethnicity, gender, culture and socioeconomic status in personality formation. The perspective enhances our sensitivity to (132)_____ differences and (133)_____ and allows us to appreciate the richness of human behavior and mental processes.

Reflection Break # 3:
Compare and contrast the Humanistic–Existential and Socio-cultural perspectives on personality in the chart below.

	Premise	Critique
Humanistic-Exisitential		
Socio-Cultural		

Reading for Understanding about "Measurement of Personality"
Methods of personality assessment take a sample of behavior to (134)_____ future behavior. Standardized interviews, (135)_____, in which trained observers check off each occurrence of a specific behavior within a specified time frame, and objective and projective tests are all used in personality assessment.

How are personality measures used? Personality measures are used in many ways, including (136)_____ psychological disorders, predicting the likelihood of (137)_____ in various lines of work, measuring (138)_____, and determining academic placement.

What are objective personality tests? (139)_____ tests present test takers with a standardized set of test items to which they must respond in specific, limited ways (as in (140)_____ or true-false tests). A (141)_____ format asks respondents to indicate which of two or more statements is true for them or which of several activities they prefer. The Minnesota Multiphasic Personality Inventory (MMPI) is presented in a true-false format and is widely used in the assessment of psychological (142)_____. The MMPI is usually scored for 4 (143)_____ scales, which suggest whether the answers actually represent the person's thoughts, and 10 (144)_____ scales. The validity scales assess different (145)_____, or biases, in answering the questions. The MMPI scales were constructed (146)_____, that is, on the basis of actual clinical data rather than on the basis of psychological theory.

How do projective tests differ from objective tests? What are some of the more widely used projective tests? (147)_____ tests do not have specific correct answers. They present (148)_____ stimuli and allow the test taker to give range of responses that reflect individual differences. Examples include the (149)_____ inkblot test, developed by Hermann Rorschach, and the (150)_____ Test. The Rorschach is thought to provide insight into a person's intelligence, interests, cultural background and many other variables; while the (151)_____ is widely used in clinical practice and research on motivation.

Reflection Break # 4:
Match the personality assessment technique with its correct description.

a. Behavior-rating scales	d. MMPI	g. Rorschach Inkblot test
b. objective tests	e. projective tests	h. Thematic Apperception Test
c. forced-choice format	f. standardized test	

_____1. A true-false formatted test that contains hundreds of items; is used in clinical and counseling psychology to help diagnose psychological disorders.

_____2. A psychological test that presents ambiguous stimuli onto which the test taker projects their own personality.

_____3. A method of presenting test questions that requires the test taker to select one of a number of possible answers.

_____4. A projective test that contains 10 cards of ambiguous images; five of which are in color.

_____5. A test that is given to a large number of test-takers so that data concerning the typical responses can be accumulated and analyzed.

_____6. Tests whose items that have concrete answers that are considered correct.

_____7. A systematic method for recording the frequency with which a target behavior occurs.

_____8. Projective test that presents drawings that are open to interpretations.

Reading for Understanding about "Life Connections: Gender Typing—On Becoming a Woman or a Man"
Throughout history and in many cultures it has been assumed that women and men must be (152)_____ in personality in order to fulfill different roles in the family and society. (153)_____ theorists have a relatively easy time describing and interpreting the physical gender differences they study. Gender differences in (154)_____, however, are not as obvious as biological gender differences and, in most cases, the differences that do exist are (155)_____. In fact, in many ways men and women are more psychologically (156)_____.

Research into gender differences suggests that girls are somewhat superior to boys in (157)_____ abilities, and girls seem to develop (158)_____ somewhat faster than boys do. (159)_____seem to be somewhat superior in the ability to manipulate visual images in working memory and seem to excel in visual-spatial abilities of the sort used in math, science and map reading. Males also tend top obtain higher scores on (160)_____ tests; however females tend to excel in (161)_____ abilities in elementary school.

Personality differences have also been observed in sociability, happiness, anxiety, trust and nurturance with (162)_____ exceeding (163)_____. Men are perceived as exceeding women in social (164)_____ and tough mindedness. Additionally, male friendships with other men appear to be (165)_____ and less (166)_____ than women's friendships with other women. Sexually, (167)_____ tend to want to combine sex with a romantic relationship while (168)_____ report being more interested in casual sex and multiple sex partners. Males generally act more (169)_____ then women; however, research by Ann (170)_____ suggests that females will behave as aggressively as males if they believe the aggression is (171)_____.

Gender differences in mate selection have been examined in cross-cultural studies and findings indicate that (172)_____ tend to place more emphasis on traits such as professional status, dependability, kindness and fondness for children. Males, on the other hand, tend to place greater emphasis on (173)_____.

The process by which psychological gender differences develop is termed (174)_____. (175)_____ views of gender-typing focus on the roles of evolution, genetics, and prenatal influences in predisposing men and women to gender-linked behavior patterns. According to evolutionary psychologists, gender differences were fashioned by (176)_____ in response to problems in adaptation that were repeatedly encountered by humans over thousands of generations. This (177)_____ process is expressed through structural differences between males and females. For example, research has suggested that although males and females have the same (178)_____ in the brain, but they seem to use them somewhat differently. Gender differences in brain (179)_____ might explain, in part, why women excel in verbal skills and men excel in specialized spatial-relations. Sex (180)_____ are responsible for prenatal differentiation of sex organs. (181)_____ in the brains of male fetuses spurs greater growth of the right hemisphere of the brain, which may be connected with the ability to manage spatial relations tasks. Testosterone is also connected with (182)_____.

What are some psychological views of gender-typing? Psychologists have attempted to explain (183)_____ in terms of psychodynamic, social-cognitive, and gender-schema theories. Freud explained gender-typing in terms of (184)_____ with the parent of the same gender through resolution of the (185)_____ and (186)_____ complexes. (187)_____ theorists explain gender-typing in terms of the ways in which experience helps the individual create concepts of gender-appropriate behavior, and how the individual is motivated to engage in such behavior. Social-cognitive theorists use terms such as observational learning, (188)_____, or the continuous learning process in which children are influenced by rewards to imitate the behavior of same sex adults, and (189)_____, in which parents and other adults inform children about how they are expected to behave. Research shows that women can behave as (190)_____ as men when they are provoked, have the means, and believe that the social climate will tolerate their aggression. (191)_____ theory proposes that once children learn the gender schema of their culture, their self-esteem becomes tied up in how well they express the traits considered relevant to their gender. Sandra Bem argues that people look at the social world through "(192)_____." She argues that our (193)_____ polarizes females and males by organizing social life around mutually exclusive (194)_____. No pressure is required, once children understand the (195)_____ boy and girl, they have a basis for blending their self-concepts with the gender (196)_____ of their culture.

Finally, most researchers would agree that both (197)_____ and (198)_____ factors effect most areas of behavior and mental processes—including the complex processes involved in gender typing.

REVIEW: Key Terms and Concepts

FINAL CHAPTER REVIEW

Recite:

Go to the Recite section for this chapter on pages 449-451 in your textbook. Use the tear-off card provided at the back of the book to cover the answers of the Recite section. Read the questions aloud and recite the answers. This will help you cement your knowledge of key concepts.

Multiple Choice Questions:

1. Priscilla is a psychologist. When she says that someone has a "personality", what is she referring to?
   a. The person's lively and bubbly demeanor.
   b. The person tendency to act shyly in some situations and gregariously in other situations.
   c. The person's stable pattern of emotions, motives and behavior.
   d. The person's behavioral characteristics that make them similar to their family members.

2. According to the _____ theory, the personality is characterized by a dynamic struggle or conflict.
   a. trait
   b. learning
   c. psychodynamic
   d. humanistic

3. Freud's concept of the conscious is to _____ as the unconscious is to _____.
   a. mystery; instincts
   b. instincts; awareness
   c. awareness; non-awareness
   d. fears; awareness

4. The automatic ejection of anxiety-evoking ideas from awareness is
   a. resistance.
   b. psychoanalysis.
   c. repression.
   d. preconscious.

5. Karissa meets with her therapist on a regular basis. During the sessions she is prodded to talk about anything that pops into her mind while she remains comfortable and relaxed. Karissa is most likely experiencing
   a. repression.
   b. resistance.
   c. psychoanalysis.
   d. pleasure.

6. The id is to _____; as the ego is to _____.
   a. defense mechanisms; reality principle
   b. pleasure principle; moral principle
   c. moral principle; pleasure principle
   d. pleasure principle; reality principle

7. The psychic structure that incorporates the moral standards and values of parents and develops throughout early childhood is known as the
   a. id.
   b. superego.
   c. reality principle.
   d. ego.

8. Fred is overweight and continually over eats. He abuses alcohol, smokes and bites his nails. Freud would theorize that these behaviors are likely the result of
   a. an anal fixation.
   b. regression to the phallic stage.
   c. an oral fixation.
   d. a failure to resolve the Oedipus conflict.

9. Which of the following represents the correct developmental sequence of Sigmund Freud's psychosexual stages of development?
   a. oral, phallic, anal, genital, latency
   b. anal, oral, phallic, latency, genital
   c. phallic, oral, genital, latency, anal
   d. oral, anal, phallic, latency, genital

10. Carl Jung is to _____ as Alfred Adler is to _____.
   a. collective unconscious; inferiority complex
   b. creative self; archetypes
   c. individual psychology; collective unconscious
   d. archetypes; analytical psychology

11. Your psychology professor argues that the nature of the mother-infant relationship and social relationships are more crucial determinants of personality than sexual urges. She additionally argues that we are conscious architects of our own personality. Your professor's views are closest to those of
   a. Karen Horney.
   b. Carl Jung.
   c. Alfred Adler.
   d. Erik Erikson.

12. Aaron is intelligent, reliable, outgoing, and honest. This description of Aaron's personality would most likely be given by
   a. a trait theorist.
   b. a learning theorist.
   c. a psychodynamic theorist.
   d. cognitive theorist.

13. According to the _____ perspective, our personality is largely the result of environmental influences and situational variables.
   a. trait
   b. learning
   c. psychodynamic
   d. sociocultural

14. Learning theory perspective is to _____ ; as social cognitive theory is to _____.
   a. reinforcement histories; expectancies
   b. expectancies; reciprocal determinism
   c. reciprocal determinism; situational variables
   d. situational variables; reinforcements

15. Which of the following would not be considered person variables according to social-cognitive theorists?
   a. competencies
   b. encoding strategies
   c. reinforcement histories
   d. self efficacy expectations

16. You hear a classmate tell a friend of his that we are free to do what we choose with our lives and that the meaning of our lives is the meaning we give to it. He further explains that we all have unique ways of looking at the world, known as our frame of reference. Your classmate is describing the views of
   a. Abraham Maslow.
   b. John Watson.
   c. Carl Rogers.
   d. Hans Eysenck.

17. The old advertisement for the U.S. Army that encouraged us to "Be all that you can be" by joining the armed forces illustrates which of the following psychological concepts?
   a. repression
   b. regression
   c. self-efficacy expectation
   d. self-actualization

18. You attend a parenting lecture where the speaker argues that parents need to accept children as they are regardless of their behavior at the moment. The speaker is advocating Carl Rogers' notion of
   a. conditions of worth.
   b. frames of reference.
   c. unconditional positive regard.
   d. self.

19. The process by which immigrants become acclimated to the customs and behavior patterns of their new host culture is known as
   a. collectivists.
   b. individualists.
   c. acculturation.
   d. bilingualism.

20. Steve has just completed taking a personality assessment in which he was shown a series of cards one at a time and asked to make up stories about them. Which of the following is he most likely to have taken?
   a. The Rorschach Inkblot test
   b. The MMPI
   c. The Thematic Apperception Test
   d. An Objective test

Essay Questions:
1. How do you describe personality? Think of a friend who is single. How did you describe their personality the last time you were trying to fix him or her up on a date and you were asked what kind of "personality" he or she had? What would your answer be now? Has your response changed now that you have a more through understanding of personality and personality theory? How? Compose a brief essay that compares the two descriptions of your friend. Explain which personality concepts prompted you change your description.

2. Write a short story about a person with an overdeveloped superego. Include a depiction or description of that person's personality, the problems that the person's personality creates, and how the person copes with the difficulties of daily living. Use psychodynamic concepts to explain why your character acts or behaves in the way they do.

3. How would you describe yourself in terms of traits? Where would you place yourself on the dimensions of introversion-extroversion and emotional stability? Are you conscientious? Are you open to experience? Is there such a thing as being *too* conscientious? As being *too* open to experience? Explain your descriptions in a two-page essay for your instructor. In your essay be sure to provide the evidence for your list of traits.

4. In a brief paper explain the concept of self-esteem. You will want to visit the home page of the National Association for self-esteem at http://www.self-esteem-nase.org/ and follow some of their links. After visiting the site, address the following questions in your essay: Do you think that self-esteem is constant or variable? Do you have higher self-esteem in some situations than in others? How do different environments and conditions affect you? How does your self concept affect how you think, feel, and behave when you try on a bathing suit, go for a job interview, or have dinner with your boss for the first time? Why?
   URL: http://www.self-esteem-nase.org/links.shtml

5. Should employers use personality tests in employee screening? Read the following report:
   - ❖ Which traits predict job performance from APA @
     http://helping.apa.org/work/personal.html

Based on your understanding of this article and your text readings on personality testing, would you recommend the use of personality testing in hiring employees? Why or why not? In a format specified by your instructor, prepare a report with your recommendations and the reasoning behind them.

CONNECT & EXPAND:

1. **Introduction to Personality: "Why Are They Sad and Glad and Bad"?** Is personality stable? Before you answer this question read the following articles, then report your findings to your classmates in a format specified by your instructor.
   - ❖ *How do parents matter? Let us count the ways, APA Monitor* @
     URL: http://www.apa.org/monitor/julaug00/parents.html
   - ❖ *Elderly people not as 'set in their ways' as is popularly believed, studies show, APA Monitor*
     URL: http://www.apa.org/monitor/feb99/set.html
   - ❖ *Study on working moms gets widespread press, APA Monitor*
     URL: http://www.apa.org/monitor/apr99/mom.html

2. **The Trait Perspective:** Visit the Great Ideas in Personality site @ http://www.personalityresearch.org/ and look up further information on the trait theory. Based on your reading do you think that traits exist? What are the advantages and disadvantages of trait theory? Prepare a report of your findings for your classmates in a format specified by your instructor.
   URL: http://www.personalityresearch.org/

3. **The Humanistic-Existential & The Socio-Cultural Perspective:** Visit the Great Ideas in Personality site @ http://www.personalityresearch.org/ and look up further information on the humanistic and socio-cultural theories. Prepare an essay that compares the two approaches. Can you "believe in" more than one theory of personality?

4. **Searching For the Self On-line:** Have you created a "fake" identity for on-line chat? Do you find that the Internet allows you to let your guard down and say things that you might not say "in person"? Why do you think that people do this? Do you think this is "healthy"? Interview 20 college students and ask them the above question; then ask 20 middle aged adults the same question. Are there age related differences? Compare and discuss your results with your study group.

5. **Measurement of Personality: On-line Personality Tests:** Take the *Keirsey Temperament Sorter* personality test at http://www.advisorteam.com/user/kts.asp or http://www.keirsey.com/. (The Keirsey Temperament Sorter scores results according to the Myers-Briggs system and will provide a personality profile similar to one obtained using the Myers Briggs.)

- What was the test designed to measure?
- Briefly describe the elements of personality that are being measured and how appropriate you think the test is for measuring those personality characteristics.
- Were the descriptions of personality offered specific or very general?
- Do you agree with the test's assessment of your personality?

Now take another personality test at one of the following websites. How do the two assessments compare? Report your findings to your class.

URL: http://www.wizardrealm.com/tests
URL: http://www.2h.com/Tests/personality.phtml
URL: http://www.queendom.com/tests/index.html
URL: http://test3.thespark.com/person/
URL: http://www.personalitypage.com/
URL: http://www.davideck.com/online-tests.html

6. **Life Connections: Gender Typing—On Becoming a Woman or a Man":** Your textbook describes numerous gender differences in personality, yet it suggests that many of these differences are small. The text also points out that there may be a greater variation in these skills within the gender groups then between males and females. Research gender differences in personality characteristics using your favorite research engine. What do your research findings suggest? Present and discuss your findings with your study group.

Chapter Twelve: Psychological Disorders

PowerPreview: *Skim the major headings in this chapter in your textbook. Jot down anything that you are surprised or curious about. After this write down four or five questions that you have about the material in this chapter.*

Things that surprised me/I am curious about from Chapter 12:

Questions that I have about Psychological Disorders:

-
-
-
-

QUESTION: *These are some questions that you should be able to answer after you finish studying this chapter.*

Historic Views of Psychological Disorders: "The Devil Made Me Do It"?
- ❖ *How have people historically explained psychological disorders?*

What are Psychological Disorders?
- ❖ *How, then, do we define psychological disorders?*

Classifying Psychological Disorders
- ❖ *How are psychological disorders grouped or classified?*
- ❖ *Controversy in Psychology: Is a Gay male or Lesbian Sexual Orientation a Psychological Disorder?*

Anxiety Disorders
- ❖ *What kinds of anxiety disorders are there?*
- ❖ *What is known about the origins of anxiety disorders?*

Dissociative Disorders
- ❖ *What kinds of Dissociative disorders are there?*
- ❖ *What is known about the origins of Dissociative disorders?*

Somatoform Disorders
- ❖ *What kinds of Somatoform disorders are there?*
- ❖ *What is known about the origins of Somatoform disorders?*
- ❖ *Contorversy in Psychology: Are Somatoform Disorders the Special Province of Women?*

Mood Disorders
- ❖ *What kinds of mood disorders are there?*
- ❖ *Controversy in Psychology: Is there a Thin Line between Genius and Madness?*
- ❖ *What is known about the origins of mood disorders?*

Schizophrenia
- ❖ *What is schizophrenia?*
- ❖ *What kinds of schizophrenia are there?*
- ❖ *What is known about the origins of schizophrenia?*
- ❖ *Controversy in Psychology: Should we Ban the Insanity Plea?*

Personality Disorders
- ❖ *What kinds of Personality disorders are there?*
- ❖ *What is known about the origins of personality disorders?*

Life Connections: Understanding and Preventing Suicide
- ❖ *Why do people commit suicide?*
- ❖ *What socio-cultural factors are connected with suicide?*
- ❖ *What are some of the myths and realities about suicide?*

Reading for Understanding/Reflect: The *following section provides you with the opportunity to perform 2 of the R's of the PQ4R study method. In this section I will encourage you to check your understanding of your reading of the text by filling in the blanks in the brief paragraphs that relate to each of the preview questions. You will also be prompted to rehearse your understanding of the material with periodic Reflection breaks. Remember it is better to study in more frequent, short session then in one long "cram session." Be sure to reward yourself with short study breaks before each of the Reflection exercises.*

Reading for Understanding about "Historic Views of Psychological Disorders: "The Devil Made Me Do It"?"

How have people historically explained psychological disorders? People throughout history have attributed psychological disorders to some sort of (1)_____. The ancient (2)_____ believed that people with such disorders were being punished by the gods. Since the Middle Ages, Europeans mainly attributed these disorders to possession by the (3)_____. We still see remnants of this history in our phraseology; for example, we often hear the expressions "Something got into me" or "The Devil made me do it."

Reading for Understanding about "What are Psychological Disorders and Classifying Psychological Disorders."

How do we define psychological disorders? Psychological disorders are behaviors, or mental processes, that are connected with various kinds of (4)_____. Psychological (5)_____ are characterized by unusual behavior, socially unacceptable behavior, faulty perception of reality, personal distress, dangerous behavior, or self-defeating behavior.

How are psychological disorders grouped or classified? The most widely used (6)_____ scheme is found in the *Diagnostic and Statistical Manual (DSM)* of the American Psychiatric Association. The current edition of the DSM, the *DSM-IV*, groups disorders on the basis of (7)_____ and no longer uses the category of neuroses. The DSM uses a (8)_____ system of assessment. There are five axes, Axis (9)_____ presents the primary clinical syndrome, Axis (10)_____ presents developmental and personality disorder, Axis (11)_____ provides information on the general medical conditions, Axis (12)_____ examines the psychosocial and environmental problems and Axis (13)_____ examines the global assessment of functioning. People may receive an Axis I or Axis II (14)_____ or a combination of the two.

Controversy in Psychology: Is a Gay male or Lesbian Sexual Orientation a Psychological Disorder? The superficial answer today is (15)_____. Until 1973 a gay male or lesbian sexual orientation (16)_____ considered to be a psychological disorder by the American Psychiatric Association. The decision to drop homosexuality as a disorder was made through a (17)_____. Many members of the association objected to the vote on the grounds that the vote was (18)_____ motivated, and thus they continued to believe that homosexuality was a disorder. Thus the question still remained.

Recent carefully controlled studies have examined the psychological (19)_____ of gay males and lesbian women. These studies found that gay males and lesbians are (20)_____ likely then heterosexuals to experience feelings of anxiety and depression. This however does not mean that homosexuality is itself a (21)_____. Psychologist J. Michael (22)_____ has carefully reviewed the issues surrounding homosexuality and proposes four possible interpretations of the research, these include: Societal (23)_____ may cause the higher incidence of depression and suicidality found in gay males and lesbians; the possibility that homosexuality reflects a (24)_____ from typical development and could be associated with other differences; the possibility that sexual orientation reflects unusual balances in (25)_____ sex hormones that make gay males more prone to typically female psychological disorders; or that psychological health problems among homosexual people could reflect differences in (26)_____.

Reflection Break # 1:
Match the DSM Axis with its proper description.

I.   Axis I
II. Axis II
III. Axis III

IV. Axis IV
V.   Axis V

_____ 1. Presents developmental and personality disorders; includes deeply ingrained, maladaptive ways of perceiving others.

_____ 2. An overall judgment of the current functioning and the highest level of functioning the past year according to social, psychological and occupational criteria.

_____ 3. Includes psychological disorders that impair functioning and are stressful to the individual.

_____ 4. Includes chronic and acute illnesses, injuries, allergies that affect functioning and treatment.

_____ 5. Describes stressors that occurred during the last year that may have contributed to the development of a new mental disorder.

Reading for Understanding about "Anxiety Disorders"
What kinds of anxiety disorders are there? (27)_____ disorders are characterized by motor tension, feelings of dread, and overarousal of the sympathetic branch of the autonomic nervous system. These disorders include irrational, excessive fears, or (28)_____, or persistent (29)_____ of specific objects; (30)_____ disorder, characterized by sudden attacks in which people typically fear that they may be losing control or going crazy; generalized or

pervasive anxiety, in which the central feature is (31)_____; obsessive-compulsive disorder, in which people are troubled by intrusive thoughts or (32)_____ and impulses to repeat some activity, (33)_____; and (34)_____ disorders, in which a stressful event is followed by persistent fears and intrusive thoughts about the event. (35)_____ stress disorder can occur 6 months or more after the event, whereas (36)_____ stress disorder occurs within a month.

What is known about the origins of anxiety disorders? The (37)_____ perspective tends to view anxiety disorders as conflicts originating in childhood. Generalized Anxiety disorder is explained as difficulty in (38)_____ primitive impulses and obsessions are explained as leakage of (39)_____. Many (40)_____ theorists view phobias as conditioned fears. Social Cognitive learning theorists note that (41)_____ plays a role in acquisition of fears. (42)_____ theorists focus on ways in which people interpret threats. (43)_____ factors also playa role in anxiety disorders. Some people may be (44)_____ to acquire certain kinds of fears. (45)_____ disorders tend to run in families. Twin studies find a higher (46)_____ rate for anxiety disorders among identical twins than among fraternal twins. Some psychologists suggest that (47)_____ factors-which could be inherited-may create a predisposition toward anxiety disorders. One such factor is faulty regulation of (48)_____.

Reading for Understanding about "Dissociative Disorders"
What kinds of Dissociative disorders are there? (49)_____ disorders are characterized by sudden, temporary changes in consciousness or self-identity. They include; Dissociative (50)_____ in which the individual forgets their past; Dissociative (51)_____, which involves forgetting plus fleeing and adopting a new identity; Dissociative (52)_____ disorder, otherwise known as multiple personality disorder, in which a person behaves as if more than one personality occupies his or her body; and (53)_____ disorder, characterized by feelings that one is not real or that one is standing outside oneself.

What is known about the origins of Dissociative disorders? Dissociative disorders are some of the (54)_____ psychological disorders and there is some (55)_____ about their existence. In any event the different theoretical perspectives have offered suggestions as to the origins of Dissociative disorder. (56)_____ theory proposes that people with Dissociative disorders use massive repression to keep disturbing memories or ideas out of mind. (57)_____ theories propose that people with Dissociative disorders have learned not to think about bad memories or disturbing impulses to avoid feelings of guilt and (58)_____. Surveys find that the memories being avoided may involve episodes of childhood (59)_____ or physical abuse.

Reading for Understanding about "Somatoform Disorders"
What kinds of Somatoform disorders are there? People with (60)_____ disorders exhibit or complain of physical problems, although no medical evidence of such problems can be found. The Somatoform disorders include conversion disorder and hypochondriasis. In (61)_____ disorder, stress is converted into a physical symptom, and the individual may show "(62)_____," or an indifference to the symptom. In (63)_____ people insist that they are suffering from a serious physical illness, even though no medical evidence of illness can be found.

What is known about the origins of Somatoform disorders? Controversy in Psychology: Are

Somatoform Disorders the Special Province of Women? These disorders were once called "(64)_____" and expected to be found more often among women. However, they are also found among men and may reflect the relative benefits of focusing on (65)_____ symptoms rather than fears and conflicts. (66)_____ theory proposes that symptoms of Somatoform disorders protect the individual from feelings of shame and guilt, or another source of stress.

Reflection Break # 2:
Compare and contrast the Anxiety, Dissociative and Somatoform Disorders by completing the following chart.

	Characteristic Symptoms	**Theoretical Origins**
Anxiety Disorders		
Dissociative Disorders		
Somatoform Disorders		

Reading for Understanding about " Mood Disorders"
What kinds of mood disorders are there? (67)_____ disorders involve disturbances in expressed emotions. (68)_____ is the most common of the psychological disorders. (69)_____ depression is characterized by persistent feelings of sadness, loss of interest, feelings of worthlessness or guilt, and inability to concentrate. Feelings of unworthiness and guilt may be so excessive that they are considered (70)_____. (71)_____ disorder, formerly known as manic-depressive disorder, is characterized by dramatic swings in mood between elation and depression; (72)_____ episodes include pressured speech and rapid flight of ideas.

Controversy In Psychology: Is There a Thin Line Between Genius And Madness? Researchers have found links between (73)_____ and the psychological disorders of (74)_____ and (75)_____. Although there is no clear understand about the relationship between creativity, mania and depression, many writers, painters and composers were at their most (76)_____ during manic period or found (77)_____ in the despair of depression. Kay Redfield (78)_____ found that artists are 18 times more likely to commit suicide than the general population, 2 to 10 times more likely to be depressed and 10 to 20 times as likely to have bipolar disorder and medicines that are used to treat mood disorders tend to limit (79)_____.

What is known about the origins of mood disorders? Research emphasizes possible roles for

(80)_____, (81)_____ styles, and under utilization of (82)_____ in depression. From the (83)_____ perspective, bipolar disorder may be seen as alternating states in which the personality is dominated by the superego and ego. (84)_____ theorists, on the other hand, suggest that depressed people behave as though they cannot obtain reinforcement and point to links between depression and learned helplessness. (85)_____ theorists note that people who tend to ruminate about feelings of depression are more likely to prolong them. And Seligman notes that people who are depressed are more likely than other people to make internal, or (86)_____, stable, and (87)_____ (large) attributions for failures; factors that they are relatively powerless to change. Researchers are also searching for (88)_____ factors in mood disorders. (89)_____ factors involving regulation of neurotransmitters may also be involved in mood disorders. For example, people with severe depression often respond to drugs that heighten the action of (90)_____.

Reading for Understanding about "Schizophrenia"
What is schizophrenia? (91)_____ is a most severe psychological disorder that is characterized by disturbances in thought and language, such as loosening of associations and (92)_____; in perception and attention, as found in (93)_____; in motor activity, as shown by a (94)_____ or by excited behavior; in (95)_____, as in flat or inappropriate emotional responses; and in (96)_____, as in social withdrawal and absorption in daydreams or fantasy.

What kinds of schizophrenia are there? The major types of (97)_____ are paranoid, disorganized, and catatonic. (98)_____ schizophrenia is characterized largely by systematized delusions and frequently related auditory hallucinations. They often have (99)_____ of grandeur and persecution. (100)_____ schizophrenia is characterized by incoherence, loosening of associations, disorganized behavior, delusions and flat or highly inappropriate emotional responses. Extreme (101)_____ is common with schizophrenia. (102)_____ schizophrenia is characterized by a striking motor impairment; often it is a slowing of activity into a stupor that may suddenly change into an agitated phase. Catatonic schizophrenic may also show a (103)_____ in which the person maintains positions into which they have been manipulated by others and mutism.

What is known about the origins of schizophrenia? The (104)_____ view argues that schizophrenia occurs because the ego is overwhelmed by sexual or aggressive impulses from the id and the person regresses to an early phase of the oral stage. (105)_____ theorists explain schizophrenia in terms of conditioning and observational learning. (106)_____, schizophrenia is connected with smaller brains, especially fewer synapses in the prefrontal region, and larger ventricles in the brain. According to the (107)_____ theory of schizophrenia, people with schizophrenia use more dopamine than other people do, perhaps because they have more dopamine in the brain along with more dopamine receptors than other people. According to the (108)_____ model, genetic vulnerability to schizophrenia may interact with other factors, such as stress, complications during pregnancy and childbirth, and quality of parenting, to cause the disorder to develop.

Controversy in Psychology: Should We Ban the Insanity Plea? Many people would like to (109)_____ the insanity plea due to the perception that people are literally getting away with murder because of it. In pleading the insanity defense lawyers use the (110)_____ rule, named after Daniel M'Naghten who tried to assassinate Sir Robert Peel, the British Prime Minister. The rule states that the accused did not (111)_____ what she or she was doing at the time of the act, did not realize it was (112)_____ or was succumbing to an (113)_____ impulse. The insanity defense in (114)_____ of felony cases and people who are found not guilty by reason of insanity are (115)_____ for indefinite terms, typically (116)_____ then the prison sentence they would have served if found guilty.

Reading for Understanding about "Personality Disorders"
What kinds of Personality disorders are there? (117)_____ disorders are inflexible, maladaptive behavior patterns that impair personal or social functioning and cause distress for the individual or others. There are a number of (118)_____ disorders including paranoid, schizotypal, schizoid, antisocial and avoidant personality disorders. The defining trait of (119)_____ personality disorder is suspiciousness. People with (120)_____ personality disorders show oddities of thought, perception, and behavior but the bizarre behaviors of schizophrenia are absent. (121)_____, indifference to relationships and flat emotional response are the major characteristic of schizoid personality disorder. People with (122)_____ personality disorders persistently violate the rights of others and are in conflict with the law. They show little or no guilt, or (123)_____ over their misdeeds and are largely undeterred by punishment. People with (124)_____ personality disorder tend to avoid entering relationships for fear of rejection and criticism.

What is known about the origins of personality disorders? (125)_____ theory connected many personality disorders with hypothesized Oedipal problems. (126)_____ theorists suggest that childhood experiences can contribute to maladaptive ways of relating to others. (127)_____ psychologists find that antisocial adolescents encode social information in ways that bolster their misdeeds. (128)_____ factors may be involved in some personality disorders. (129)_____ personality disorder tends to run in families and may develop from some combination of genetic vulnerability (less gray matter in the prefrontal cortex of the brain, which may provide lower--than--normal levels of arousal), inconsistent discipline, and cynical processing of social information.

Reflection Break # 3:
Compare and contrast the Mood, Schizophrenic and Personality Disorders by completing the following chart.

	Characteristic Symptoms	**Theoretical Origins**
Mood Disorders		
Schizophrenic Disorders		
Personality Disorders		

Reading for Understanding about "Life Connections: Understanding and Preventing Suicide"

According to the National Center for Health Statistics (130)_____ is the third or fourth leading cause of death among older teenagers. Suicide usually reflects feelings of helplessness and (131)_____. Jill (132)_____ and her colleagues have found that suicidal adolescents experience four areas of psychological problems: confusion about the self, impulsiveness, emotional instability and interpersonal problems. Suicide attempts are more common after (133)_____ life events, and especially events that involve loss of (134)_____. Other contributors to suicidal behavior among adolescents include concerns about (135)_____, pressures to (136)_____ at school, problems at home and (137)_____. Lack of (138)_____ ability is also connected with suicide. Additionally, suicide tends to run in families, but it is unclear whether the reasons are (139)_____ or (140)_____.

It is mythical that people who truly intend to kill themselves do it without (141)_____, and that those who fail at the attempt are just seeking attention. Many people who commit (142)_____ had issued warnings, and many had made prior attempts. It is also (143)_____ that only insane people take their own lives and suicidal thinking is not necessarily a sign a sign (144)_____.

The great majority of people who commit suicide send out a variety of (145)_____ about their impending act. These include: changes in eating and (146)_____ patterns, difficulty (147)_____ on school work, or a sharp (148)_____ in school performance and attendance, loss of interest in previously enjoyed activities, giving away prized possessions and withdrawal from (149)_____, personality or (150)_____ changes and threatening to commit suicide.

If some one you know tell you they are considering suicide there are many things you can do. Your first objective should be to encourage them to consult a (151)_____, but if they refuse to do so keep them talking to you or another trusted person, be a good (152)_____, suggest alternative (153)_____ to their problems, and let them know you (154)_____.

REVIEW: Key Terms and Concepts

Dissociative identity disorder 454	Panic disorder 459	Dissociative fugue 463
Multiple personality disorder 454	Generalized anxiety disorder 459	Somatoform disorders 464
Insanity 454	Obsession 459	Conversion disorder 465
Schizophrenia 454	Compulsion 459	La belle indifference 465
Psychological disorders 454	Posttraumatic stress disorder 460	Hypochondriasis 465
Hallucination 455	Acute stress disorder 461	Major depression 466
Ideas of persecution 455	Concordance 462	Psychomotor retardation 466
Specific phobias 458	Gamma-aminobutyric acid 462	Bipolar disorder 466
Claustrophobia 458	Benzodiazepines 462	Manic 466
Acrophobia 458	Dissociative disorders 463	Rapid flight of ideas 466
Social phobias 459	Dissociative amnesia 463	Learned helplessness 468
Agoraphobia 459		Attributional style 468
		Neuroticism 469
		Delusions 470

FINAL CHAPTER REVIEW
Recite:
Go to the Recite section for this chapter on pages 483-484 in your textbook. Use the tear-off card provided at the back of the book to cover the answers of the Recite section. Read the questions aloud and recite the answers. This will help you cement your knowledge of key concepts.

Multiple Choice Questions:

1. Which of the following is not a characteristic of psychological disorders?
   a. A faulty perception or interpretation of reality.
   b. Personal distress.
   c. Socially appropriate behavior.
   d. Self-defeating behavior.

2. The DSM-IV-TR,
   a. is the most widely used classification system for psychological disorders.
   b. is multiaxial.
   c. groups mental disorders on the basis of observable behaviors or symptoms.
   d. All of the above

3. Katie is excessively fearful of doing something that will be humiliating or embarrassing when in public. Psychologists would likely diagnose Katie with a
   a. social phobia.
   b. acrophobia.
   c. Claustrophobia.
   d. both a and c.

4. An abrupt attack of acute anxiety in which the individual may experience shortness of breath, heavy sweating and pounding of the heart that is not triggered by a specific object or situation, is known as
   a. a specific phobia.
   b. a compulsion.
   c. an obsession.
   d. a panic disorder.

5. Lloyd experiences persistent feelings of dread, motor tension, and dry mouth, along with a racing heart, light-headedness, and a tendency to be easily distracted. Lloyd is likely to be diagnosed with
   a. a panic disorder.
   b. a generalized anxiety disorder.
   c. an obsessive-compulsive disorder.
   d. a phobia.

6. Naomi has recurrent anxiety provoking thoughts that are irrational and beyond her control. These thoughts are so compelling that they disrupt her daily life. Naomi is experiencing
   a. compulsions.
   b. panic.
   c. obsessions.
   d. depression.

7. Gulf War veterans are at risk for feelings of anxiety and helplessness caused by the traumatic experience of the war. They will be at risk for which of the following anxiety disorders?
   a. An obsessive-compulsive disorder
   b. A generalized anxiety disorder
   c. Post-traumatic stress disorder
   d. A panic disorder

8. When it comes to explaining anxiety disorders, Biological theorists' views are to _____; as Learning theorists' views are to _____.
   a. genetic concordance; thinking
   b. thinking; conditioning
   c. conditioning; genetics
   d. GABA; conditioning

9. Your boss knows that you are enrolled in a psychology class. He tells you that his mother-in-law has suddenly left home and traveled to another state. When the police found her she had been living in the new town for 6 months. She had invented a totally false past and had no memory of her real past life. He wants to know what psychological disorder you think she is likely to be diagnosed with?
   a. Dissociative amnesia
   b. Dissociative identity disorder
   c. Depersonalization disorder
   d. Dissociative fugue disorder

10. A separation of thoughts, emotions, identity, and memory is to _____ disorders; as worrying, fear of the worst, nervousness and an inability to relax is to _____ disorders.
    a. dissociative; anxiety
    b. schizophrenic; anxiety
    c. anxiety; mood
    d. mood; dissociative

11. Sonya's psychologist tells her that she believes that patients with dissociative disorders use massive repression to prevent them from recognizing improper impulses or remembering unpleasant events. Sonya's psychologist ascribes to which theoretical view?
    a. Biological
    b. Psychodynamic
    c. Learning
    d. Cognitive

12. Somatoform disorders are characterized by
    a. a disturbance in expression of emotions.
    b. a complaint of physical problems such as paralysis, pain, or a persistent belief that they have a serious disease when one does not exist.
    c. the separation of mental processes such as thoughts, emotions, identity, memory or consciousness.
    d. disturbances in thought and language, perception and attention, motor activity, and mood, and withdrawal and absorption in daydreams and fantasy.

13. Twanna has all of sudden developed an inability to see at night. Doctors cannot identify a medical reason for her blindness. Although her family is very concerned about her loss of night vision, she appears to have accepted her limitations and shows little concern. Psychologists would label this indifference feature of Twanna's behavior as
    a. a conversion disorder.
    b. hypochondriasis.
    c. la belle indifference.
    d. hysteria.

14. Kim has a poor appetite, and has experienced a serious weight loss. He is unable to concentrate and make decisions. He often expresses feelings of unworth and guilt for things he has not done. He says he no longer cares about life and has talked about death and how he would welcome it. Psychologists would likely diagnose Kim with which of the following disorders?
    a. Schizophrenia
    b. Conversion disorder
    c. Major depression
    d. Bipolar disorder

15. The disorder characterized by extreme mood swings from ecstatic elation to deep depression is know by psychologists today as
    a. mania.
    b. bipolar disorder.
    c. minor depressive disorder.
    d. manic-depression.

16. You recently interviewed for a new job but did not get the job. When you attribute the rejection to the fact that you "messed up" in the interview what kind of attributional style are you using?
    a. internal
    b. external
    c. specific
    d. global

17. Grant believes that he has been sent to earth to save mankind. He believes that women are evil and that any male who speaks to, or associates with, a female is doomed to a life as a servant to the female's wishes. He often tells you of his grand plan to save males from the influences of the female. Nothing you say or do will convince him that his ideas are untrue. Grant is demonstrating
    a. hallucinations.
    b. stupor.
    c. delusions.
    d. waxy flexibility.

18. Grant believes that he has been sent to earth to save mankind. He believes that women are evil and that any male who speaks to, or associates with a female is doomed to a life as a servant to the female's wishes. Recently he has told you that the females on campus want to silence him and he has become agitated and fearful. Nothing you say or do will convince him that his ideas are untrue. With what disorder would Grant most likely be diagnosed?
    a. Disorganized schizophrenia
    b. Paranoid schizophrenia
    c. Catatonic schizophrenia
    d. Schizotypal personality disorder

19. Jenna has few close friends outside her immediate family. Although she is interested in others and shows warmth towards them, she is unwilling to enter into any relationships without an assurance of full acceptance. Jenna would likely be diagnosed with a
    a. an antisocial personality disorder.
    b. an avoidant personality disorder.
    c. a paranoid personality disorder.
    d. a schizotypal personality disorder.

20. Mr. Feeny lives at the end of your street. He has never married and lives alone. He does not seem to have any friends and often says odd things. His behavior is often peculiar. Psychologists would say that Mr. Feeny's behavior matches the description of
    a. an antisocial personality disorder.
    b. a paranoid personality disorder.
    c. paranoid schizophrenia.
    d. schizotypal personality disorder.

Essay Questions:

1. How do we diagnose psychological disorders? What is the DSM-IV? When was it published? What is its goal? Why does the DSM group disorders on the basis of observation features or symptoms? In a brief report describe the five axes of the DSM-IV system. What do you see as the strengths and weaknesses of the current diagnostic system? In your report suggest an alternative system, or any changes to the current system that you feel would address its weaknesses and make diagnosis more effective. Be sure to explain your rationale.

2. Is anxiety normal? Do you ever find your self "in a panic" or know people who repeatedly check that the doors are locked or the gas jets are turned off before they leave home? Or people who refuse to step on the cracks in the sidewalk? What is the difference between "being in a panic" and having a panic disorder? Between being concerned and thorough and having an obsessive-compulsive disorder? How are anxiety disorders abnormal? Prepare a brief (one-to-two-page) essay comparing normal anxiety to an anxiety disorder.

3. Controversy in Psychology: Are Somatoform disorders the special province of women? Somatoform disorders were once referred to as "hysterical neuroses" and were once considered the special disorder of women. Why? In a brief essay characterize the history of Somatoform disorders. What does the word "hysterical" mean when used to describe Somatoform disorders? What are the social problems in labeling these disorders as hysterical? What kinds of problems do you think are involved in trying to determine whether someone has a true physical health problem or a conversion disorder? How would you distinguish between "normal" depression or "normal" enthusiasm and a mood disorder? Do you ever feel depressed? What kind of experiences make you feel depressed? Do you find it easy or difficult to admit to having feelings of sadness or depression? How are your feelings of depression differ from a major depressive disorder? Explain.

4. How have advances in biological psychology and brain imaging advanced the study of schizophrenia? In a brief report discuss the evidence for a biological and genetic role in schizophrenia. What would you tell the son or daughter of a person with schizophrenia? What would you tell the son or daughter of a person with schizophrenia about the likelihood of his or her developing schizophrenia? Explain.

5. What is the difference between people with "bad personalities" and people with personality disorders? Do you know people that you consider to have a "bad personality? How does the term "bad personality differ from the diagnosis of a personality disorder? In a three-paragraph essay describe the different types of personality disorders and how they differ from people with "bad personalities."

CONNECT & EXPAND:

1. **Controversy in Psychology: Should We Ban the Insanity Plea?** How does insanity differ from abnormality? Conduct a Web search using your favorite search engine (Google, Dogpile, Ask Jeeves) to examine the Insanity defense. What is Insanity? Who determines whether someone is "insane"? How often does the insanity defense lead to an acquittal? Also, what happens to an individual after they are found "Not Guilty by reason of insanity"? Present your findings to your classmates in a format specified by your instructor.

2. **Controversy in Psychology: Is a Gay Male or Lesbian Sexual Orientation a Psychological Disorder?** Your textbook discusses the position of the American Psychiatric Association and the controversy that remains. What do your friends think? Interview your classmates and friends as to their opinions. Do they consider the behavior of homosexual individuals indicative of a psychological disorder? Why or why not? Tally your results and share them with your study group.

3. **What Are Psychological Disorders?** Behavior that may be considered appropriate or "normal" in one culture may be considered as abnormal in another culture. After reading the information presented @ http://www.stlcc.cc.mo.us/mc/users/vritts/psypath.htm choose one culture and in a two page report compare the perceptions and views of abnormality to those of the United States.

4. **Anxiety Disorders.** Pick one of the anxiety disorders and look up the major characteristics, using your favorite Internet search engine. How does the disorder differ from normal behavior? Compare what you find with the information found on the Mental Help Net @ http://mentalhelp.net/. Share your findings with your classmates.

5. **Dissociative Disorders on the Screen.** Have you seen a film or a TV show in which a character was supposed to have Dissociative identity disorder (perhaps it was called "multiple personality")? In brief essay describe the behavior of a movie character portraying the characteristics of a Dissociative identity disorder. In your essay be sure to identify what movie and which character you are discussing. What kind of behavior did the character display? In the film or TV show, what were the supposed origins of the disorder? Does the behavior seem consistent with the description of the disorder in the text?

6. **Somatoform Disorders.** Visit the online mental health resources listed below and take the quizzes. What disorders do you show symptoms of? Do the results of the two quizzes compare? What disorder do the quizzes indicate that you may show symptoms of? What differentiates your behavior from that of a mentally ill person?
   Diseaseworld.com @ http://www.diseaseworld.com
   NIMH page @ http://www.nimh.nih.gov/publicat/index.cfm

7. **Mood Disorders-Alleviating Depression.** Visit the American Psychiatric Association's public information page on depression. @ http://www.psych.org/public_info/depression.cfm. It contains numerous links for coping with depression. Prepare a brief promotional piece for

your college's counseling department on methods of coping with depression. Use the format provided by your instructor to present your information.

8. **Schizophrenia.** Have you ever heard the expression "split personality"? Does the expression seem to apply more to dissociative identity disorder or schizophrenia? Look up the major characteristics of Schizophrenic disorders on the Mental Help Net @ http://mentalhelp.net/. Or using your favorite Internet search engine (Google, Dogpile, ask Jeeves). Compare and contrast the characteristics of schizophrenia to those of Dissociative identity disorder on a poster board. Share your poster with your study group and discuss why people often confuse these two disorders.

9. **Personality Disorders.** Pick two different types of Personality disorders and, using the advanced search on Mental Help Net @ http://mentalhelp.net/, look up their major characteristics. How does each disorder differ from normal behavior? How do they compare to each other? Prepare a report for your class in a format specified by your instructor.

10. **Life Connections: Suicide and Diversity: Who Commits Suicide?** Your textbook discusses factors that are connected with suicide in adolescents. Using your favorite search engine research cultural differences in suicide and in a two-page report summarize age, gender, educational and ethnic differences in suicide attempts. Why do you think that the differences exist? Be sure to fully explain your ideas in your report.

Chapter Thirteen: Methods of Therapy

PowerPreview: *Skim the major headings in this chapter in your textbook. Jot down anything that you are surprised or curious about. After this write down four or five questions that you have about the material in this chapter.*

Things that surprised me/I am curious about from Chapter 13:

Questions that I have about Methods of Therapy:

-
-
-
-

QUESTION: *These are some questions that you should be able to answer after you finish studying this chapter:*

What Is Therapy? The Search for a "Sweet Oblivious Antidote"
- ❖ *What is psychotherapy?*
- ❖ *How have people with psychological problems and disorders been treated throughout the ages?*

Psychodynamic Therapies: Digging Deep Within
- ❖ *How, then, do psychoanalysts conduct a traditional Freudian psychoanalysis?*
- ❖ *How do modern psychodynamic approaches differ from traditional psychoanalysis?*

Humanistic-Existential Therapies: Strengthening the Self
- ❖ *What is Carl Rogers's method of client-centered therapy?*
- ❖ *What is Fritz Perls method of Gestalt therapy?*

Behavior Therapy: Adjustment Is What You Do
- ❖ *What is behavior therapy?*
- ❖ *What are some behavior therapy methods for reducing fears?*
- ❖ *How do behavior therapists use aversive conditioning to help people break bad habits?*
- ❖ *How do behavior therapists apply principles of operant conditioning in behavior modification?*
- ❖ *How can you use behavior therapy to deal with temptation and enhance your self-control?*

Cognitive Therapies: Adjustment I What Your Think (and Do)
- ❖ *What is cognitive therapy?*
- ❖ *What is Aaron Beck's method of cognitive therapy?*
- ❖ *What is Albert Ellis's method of rational emotive behavior therapy?*

Group Therapies

- *What are the advantages and disadvantages of group therapy?*
- *What are encounter groups? What are their effects?*
- *What is family therapy?*

Controversy in Psychology: Does Psychotherapy Work?
- *What kinds of problems do researchers encounter when they conduct research on psychotherapy?*
- *What do we know about the effectiveness of psychotherapy?*
- *What kinds of issues develop when people from different ethnic groups, women, and gay males and lesbians could profit from psychotherapy?*

Biological Therapies
- *What kinds of drug therapy are available for psychological disorders?*
- *What is electroconvulsive therapy (ECT)?*
- *Controversy in Psychology: Should Health professionals Use Electroconvulsive Therapy*
- *What is psychosurgery? How is it used to treat psychological disorders?*
- *What do we know about the effectiveness of biological therapies?*

Life Connections: Alleviating Depression (Getting Out of the Dumps)

Reading for Understanding/Reflect: The *following section provides you with the opportunity to perform 2 of the R's of the PQ4R study method. In this section I will encourage you to check your understanding of your reading of the text by filling in the blanks in the brief paragraphs that relate to each of the preview questions. You will also be prompted to rehearse your understanding of the material with periodic Reflection breaks. Remember it is better to study in more frequent, short session then in one long "cram session." Be sure to reward yourself with short study breaks before each of the Reflection exercises.*

Reading for Understanding about "What Is Therapy? The Search for a "Sweet Oblivious Antidote"

What is psychotherapy? (1)_____ is a systematic interaction between a therapist and a client that uses psychological principles to help the client overcome psychological disorders or adjust to problems in living.

How, then, have people with psychological problems and disorders been treated throughout the ages? Mostly (2)_____. It has been generally assumed that psychological disorders represented (3)_____ due to witchcraft or divine retribution, and cruel methods such as (4)_____ were used to try to rid the person of evil spirits. (5)_____ were the first institutions for people with psychological disorders, and eventually, as a result of (6)_____ reform movements, mental hospitals, whose function is (7)_____, not (8)_____ and the community mental health movement came into being.

Read for Understanding about "Psychodynamic Therapies: Digging Deep Within"
Psychodynamic therapies are based on the thinking of Sigmund (9)_____. They assume that psychological problems reflect early (10)_____ experiences and internal (11)_____ involving the shifting of psychic, or (12)_____, energy among the three psychic structures. The goals of (13)_____ are to provide self-insight in to those conflicts that are believed to be the roots of a person's problems; encourage the spilling forth, or (14)_____ of psychic energy; and replace defensive behavior with coping behavior.

How, then, do psychoanalysts conduct a traditional Freudian psychoanalysis? The main method is (15)_____, in which the client is asked to talk about any topic that comes to mind; but (16)_____ analysis and interpretations are used as well. Freud felt that although repressed impulses clamor for release, the ego persists in trying to (17)_____ unacceptable urges and shows (18)_____, or the tendency to block the free expression of impulses and primitive ideas. The job of the therapist is to occasionally offer an (19)_____ of an utterance showing how it suggests resistance or deep-seated feelings and conflicts. Additionally they must help the client work through any (20)_____, or the translating of one's feelings and attitudes towards another. For example, a psychoanalyst may help clients gain insight into the ways in which they are transferring feelings toward their (21)_____ onto a spouse or even onto the analyst.

Freud considered (22)_____ the "royal road to the unconscious" and believed that the content of dreams is determined by (23)_____ processes as well as by the events of the day. In his theory the perceived content of the dream is its visible, or (24)_____ content and its presumed hidden or symbolic content is its (25)_____ content. Unconscious impulses tend to be expressed in dreams as a form of (26)_____ and unacceptable sexual urges and aggressive impulses are likely to represented by (27)_____.

How do modern psychodynamic approaches differ from traditional psychoanalysis? Traditional Psychoanalysis can extend for months or even (28)_____. Modern approaches are briefer, less (29)_____, and more (30)_____, and the therapist and client usually sit face to face. Additionally, the focus tends to be on the (31)_____ rather than the (32)_____.

Reading for Understanding about "Humanistic-Existential Therapies: Strengthening the Self"

What is Carl Rogers's method of client-centered therapy? Whereas psychodynamic therapies focus on internal (33)_____ and (34)_____ processes, (35)_____ therapies focus on the quality of the clients' subjective, conscious experience. (36)_____ therapy uses nondirective methods to help clients overcome obstacles to self-actualization. Rogers's method is intended to help people get in touch with their (37)_____ feelings and pursue their own interests, regardless of other people's wishes. In client-centered therapy the therapist shows (38)_____, or a respect for clients as human beings with unique values and goals, (39)_____, or a recognition of the client's experiences and feelings, and (40)_____, or an openness in responding to the client. Client–centered therapy is (41)_____ on college campuses. Client centered therapy is (42)_____ in that the therapists do not tell others what to do; they help clients arrive at their own decisions.

What is Fritz Perls method of Gestalt therapy? Like client-centered therapy, (43)_____ therapy assumes that people disown parts of themselves that might meet with social disapproval. Fritz Perls argues that people put on "(44)_____" and pretend to be things they are not. Perls's highly (45)_____ method aims to help people integrate these conflicting parts of their personality. He aimed to make clients (46)_____ of conflict, (47)_____ its reality, and make (48)_____ despite fear. There are a number of Gestalt exercises and games including: the (49)_____, in which the client undertakes verbal confrontations between opposing wished and ideas to heighten awareness of internal conflict; the ending of statements with phrases like

"(50)_____," and playing the (51)_____ in which clients role play people with whom they are in conflict.

Reflection Break # 1:
Compare and contrast Psychodynamic, Client-centered, and Gestalt therapy by completing the table below.

Type of Therapy	Characteristics
Psychodynamic Therapy	
Client-Centered Therapy	
Gestalt Therapy	

Reading for Understanding about "Behavior Therapy: Adjustment Is What You Do"

What is behavior therapy? Behavior therapists focus on what people (52)_____. Behavior therapy, also called (53)_____, relies on psychological (54)_____ principles (for example, conditioning and observational learning) to help clients develop adaptive behavior patterns and discontinue maladaptive ones.

What are some behavior-therapy methods for reducing fears? (55)_____ therapy methods include flooding, systematic desensitization, and modeling. (56)_____ exposes a person to fear-evoking stimuli without aversive consequences until fear is extinguished *(Did you remember this from Chapter 5? I hope so!)*. (57)_____ counterconditions fears by gradually exposing clients to a hierarchy of fear-evoking stimuli while they remain relaxed. Rothbaum and her colleagues are conducting desensitization by the means of (58)_____ where clients wear goggles and head phones such that they perceive them selves in the fearful setting. (59)_____ encourages clients to imitate another person (the model) in approaching fear-evoking stimuli.

How do behavior therapists use aversive conditioning to help people break bad habits? (60)_____ is a controversial form of behavior-therapy method used for discouraging undesirable behaviors by repeatedly pairing clients' self-defeating behaviors or impulses (for example, alcohol, cigarette smoke, deviant sex objects) with aversive stimuli so that the behavior becomes aversive rather than tempting. Aversive conditioning has been used successfully with problems as diverse as (61)_____, sexual abuse, retarded children's (62)_____ behavior and (63)_____.

How do behavior therapists apply principles of operant conditioning in behavior modification? In the operant conditioning section of the learning chapter we learned that behavior that is not reinforced tends to become (64)_____. Behavior therapists also use the principles of

(65)_____ conditioning to change behavior. Operant conditioning behavior methods are behavior therapy methods that foster adaptive behavior through principles of (66)_____. Examples of operant conditioning based behavior methods include token (67)_____, successive (68)_____, social skills training, and (69)_____ training. In a (70)_____ a controlled environment is created in which people are reinforced for desired behaviors with tokens that may be exchanged for privileges. (71)_____ is often used to help people build good habits by successively reinforcing a series of behaviors that become progressively more similar to the target behavior. In social skills training behavior therapists attempt to (72)_____ social anxiety and build social (73)_____ by encouraging the client to (74)_____, or keep a record of their own behavior and record successes; practice and provide feedback. (75)_____ training helps clients become more aware of and gain control over various body functions by attaching devices that measure the body function and signal desired changes.

How can you—yes you—use behavior therapy to deal with temptation and enhance your self-control? Behavior-therapy methods for adopting desirable behavior patterns and breaking bad habits begin with a (76)_____ to determine the antecedents and consequences of the problem behavior, along with the details of the behavior itself. They then focus on modifying the (77)_____(stimuli that act as triggers) and (78)_____ (reinforcers) of behavior and on modifying the behavior itself.

Reading for Understanding about "Cognitive Therapies: Adjustment Is What You Think (and Do)"

What is cognitive therapy? (79)_____ therapies aim to give clients insight into irrational beliefs and cognitive distortions and replace these cognitive errors with rational beliefs and accurate perceptions.

What is Aaron Beck's method of cognitive therapy? Aaron (80)_____'s therapy method focuses on the client's cognitive distortions and notes that clients develop emotional problems such as depression because of cognitive errors that lead them to minimize accomplishments and catastrophize failures. The (81)_____ that contribute to the client's misery include a selective perception of the world, overgeneralization and magnification of events and absolutist thinking, or seeing the world in shades of black and white. He found that depressed people experience cognitive distortions such as the (82)_____; that is, they expect the worst of themselves, the world at large, and the future. Beck teaches clients how to (83)_____ cognitive errors.

What is Albert Ellis's method of Rational-Emotive Behavior Therapy? Albert (84)_____ originated Rational Emotive Behavior Therapy (REBT), which holds that people's (85)_____ about events, not only the events themselves, shape people's responses to them. Ellis points out how (86)_____ beliefs, such as the belief that we must have social approval, can worsen problems. Ellis methods are active and (87)_____, he literally (88)_____ clients out of irrational beliefs.

Reflection Break # 2:
Compare and contrast behavior therapy, Beck's cognitive therapy, and Ellis's rational-emotive behavior therapy by completing the table below.

Behavior Therapy	
Beck's Cognitive Therapy	
Ellis's Rational Emotive Behavior Therapy	

Reading for Understanding about "Group Therapies"

What are the advantages and disadvantages of group therapy? Group therapy has many advantages; first, it is more (89)_____ than individual therapy. Moreover, group members benefit from the (90)_____ and experiences of other members and appropriate behavior receives support. Also, in (91)_____ therapy it is easy to imagine that we are different from others; affiliating with others with similar problems minimizes this. However, (92)_____ is not for everyone; some clients cannot disclose their problems in the group setting; they need individual attention.

What are encounter groups? What are their effects? (93)_____ groups attempt to foster personal growth by heightening awareness of people's needs and feelings through intense confrontations between strangers. Encounter groups can be (94)_____ when they urge too rapid disclosure of personal matters or when several members attack an individual. (95)_____ therapy helps couples enhance their relationship by improving communication skills and helping them mange conflict. Today the main approach to couple therapy is (96)_____, it teaches communication skills and ways of solving problems.

What is family therapy? In (97)_____ therapy, one or more families make up the group. Family therapy undertaken from the "(98)_____" modifies family interactions to enhance the growth of individuals in the family and the family as a whole. The family therapist attempts to teach the family to (99)_____ more effectively and encourage growth and (100)_____ in each family member.

Reading for Understanding about "Controversy in Psychology: Does Psychotherapy Work?"

In 1952 Hans (101)_____ published a review of psychotherapy that shocked the psychotherapeutic community. On the basis of his review of the research Eysenck concluded that the rate of improvement among people in psychotherapy was not greater than the rate of (102)_____, or the rate of improvement that would be shown with no treatment at all. Since that time sophisticated research studies -- many of them using a statistical averaging method called (103)_____-- have strongly suggested that psychotherapy is (104)_____.

What kinds of problems do researchers encounter when they conduct research on psychotherapy? The ideal method for evaluating the effectiveness of treatment is the (105)_____. However, experiments are difficult to arrange and (106)_____. It is difficult and perhaps impossible to (107)_____ assign clients to therapy methods such as traditional psychoanalysis. Moreover, clients cannot be kept (108)_____ as to the treatment they are receiving. Further, it can be difficult to sort out the effects of (109)_____ factors, such as instillation of hope, from the effects of specific methods of therapy.

What do we know about the effectiveness of psychotherapy? Despite the problems in evaluating the (110)_____ of therapy, research has been on going. Statistical analyses such as (111)_____, which combines and averages the results of individual studies, show that people who obtain most forms of psychotherapy fare (112)_____ than people who do not. (113)_____ and (114)_____ approaches are particularly helpful with well-educated, highly verbal and motivated individuals. Cognitive and behavior therapies are often integrated into (115)_____ therapy and are probably most effective in treatment of anxiety disorders, social skills deficits and problems in self control. It is, however, not enough to ask which (116)_____of therapy is most effective. We must also ask which type is most effective for a (117)_____problem and patient.

Reflection Break # 3:

1.   Under what circumstances would you recommend that someone go for group therapy rather then individual therapy? Why?

2.   Briefly summarize the difficulties that arise when psychologists try to access the effectiveness of therapy.

Reading for Understanding about "Biological Therapies"
Psychotherapies apply (118)_____ principles to treatment, where as (119)_____ therapies apply knowledge of biological structures and processes to the treatment of psychological disorders. Biological, or (120)_____ approaches to treating psychological disorders include: drug therapy, electroconvulsive therapy and psychosurgery.

What kinds of drug therapy are available for psychological disorders? (121)_____ drugs belong to the chemical class known as the benzodiaepines and act by depressing the activity of the central nervous system, which in turn decreases sympathetic activity. (122)_____, or the feeling of being tired or drowsy, is the most common side effect of antianxiety medication. The use of antianxiety drugs for daily tensions and anxieties is not recommended because people who use them rapidly build (123)_____, for the drugs and withdrawal may lead to (124)_____ in which the patients anxiety may become worse than it was initially.

Antipsychotic drugs help many people with schizophrenia by blocking the action of (125)_____ receptors. (126)_____ drugs reduce agitation, delusions and hallucinations.

Antidepressants often help people with severe (127)_____, apparently by raising levels of (128)_____ available to the brain. There are several different types of (129)_____ drugs. (130)_____ inhibitors block the activity of an enzyme that breaks down noradrenaline and serotonin. (131)_____ prevent the reuptake of noradrenaline and serotonin and selective serotonin-uptake inhibitors block the reuptake of (132)_____. (133)_____ inhibitors appear to be more effective than (134)_____. (135)_____ often helps people with bipolar disorder, apparently by regulating levels of glutamate and can be used to strengthen the effects of antidepressant medication.

What is electroconvulsive therapy (ECT)? In (136)_____ an electrical current is passed through the temples, inducing a seizure and frequently relieving severe depression. ECT was originally used for a variety of psychological disorders, but because of the advent of (137)_____ drugs, it is now mainly used for people with (138)_____ who do not respond to antidepressants.

Controversy in Psychology: Should Health Professionals Use Electroconvulsive Therapy? ECT is (139)_____ for many reasons, including side effects such as loss of (140)_____ and because nobody knows why it works.

What is psychosurgery? How is it used to treat psychological disorders? (141)_____ is a controversial method for alleviating agitation by severing nerve pathways in the brain. The best-known psychosurgery technique, (142)_____, was used with people with severe disorders but has been largely discontinued because of side effects.

What do we know about the effectiveness of biological therapies? There is little question that (143)_____ has helped many people with severe psychological disorders. However there is controversy as to whether (144)_____ or drug therapy should be used with people with anxiety disorders or depression. Drugs do not teach people how to (145)_____ and build relationships. Having said that, (146)_____ are apparently advisable when psychotherapy does not help people with depression; furthermore, (147)_____ appears to be helpful in some cases when neither psychotherapy nor drug therapy (antidepressants) is of help. (148)_____ is all but discontinued because of questions about whether it is effective and because of side effects. Most health professionals agree that antipsychotic drugs are of benefit to large numbers of people with (149)_____.

Reflection Break # 4:
Compare the different types of biological therapy by completing the following table

	Description
Drug Therapy	
Electroconvulsive Shock Therapy	
Psychosurgery	

Read for Understanding about "Life Connections: Alleviating Depression (Getting Out of the Dumps)"

(150)_____ is characterized by inactivity, feelings of sadness and cognitive distortions. (151)_____therapies point out that there are many things we can do to cope with milder feelings of depression. These include: engaging in (152)_____ thoughts, thinking (153)_____, exercising and (154)_____ourselves.

There is a (155)_____ between our moods and what we do, so engaging in pleasant thoughts can, and will, generate (156)_____ of happiness and joy. Thinking rationally can help you to pinpoint your irrational, depressing, (157)_____ and construct rational alternatives. (158)_____ is activity, which is the opposite of depression and inactivity and it enhances physical and psychological well-being. Finally (159)_____ our selves and learning to express our feelings and relate to others has been shown to alleviate feelings of depression. Assertive behavior permits more (160)_____ interactions with others and thus removes sources of (161)_____ while at the same time expanding our social support.

REVIEW: Key Terms and Concepts

Psychotherapy	488	Frame of reference	495	Rational emotive behavior	
Asylum	489	Genuineness	495	therapy	504
Psychoanalysis	490	Gestalt therapy	495	Encounter group	508
Catharsis	491	Behavior therapy	497	Family therapy	509
Free association	491	Systematic desensitization		Meta-analysis	509
Resistance	491		498	Rebound anxiety	515
Interpretation	492	Hierarchy	498	Antidepressant	515
Transference	492	Modeling	499	Monoamine oxidase	
Wish fulfillment	493	Aversive conditioning	499	inhibitors	515
Phallic symbol	493	Rapid smoking	499	Tricyclic antidepressants	
Manifest content	493	Token economy	500		515
Latent content	493	Successive approximations		Serotonin-uptake	
Ego analyst	493		500	inhibitors	515
Client-centered therapy		Self-monitoring	500	Electroconvulsvie therapy	
	494	Behavior rehearsal	500		516
Unconditional positive		Feedback	500	Sedative	516
regard	494	Biofeedback training	501	Psychosurgery	517
Empathic understanding		Functional analysis	501	Prefrontal lobotomy	517
	495	Cognitive therapy	502		

FINAL CHAPTER REVIEW

Recite:

Go to the Recite section for this chapter on pages 523-525 in your textbook. Use the tear-off card provided at the back of the book to cover the answers of the Recite section. Read the questions aloud and recite the answers. This will help you cement your knowledge of key concepts.

Multiple Choice Questions

1. The systematic interaction between a therapist and a client that applies psychological principles to affect the client's thoughts, feelings or behavior is
   a. medical therapy.
   b. psychotherapy.
   c. operant conditioning.
   d. extinction.

2. Asylums are to _____ as a mental hospital is to _____.
   a. St Mary's; Bedlam
   b. warehousing; treatment
   c. Bedlam; St. Mary's
   d. treatment; warehousing

3. Your psychology instructor claims that psychological problems reflect early childhood experiences and internal conflicts involving the shifting of psychic energy among the psychic structures. Your instructor is voicing claims similar to
   a. Carl Rogers.
   b. Abraham Maslow.
   c. Sigmund Freud.
   d. John Watson.

4. You go to your therapist for the first time and he tells you to lie on a couch in a slightly darkened room. He then asks you to talk about anything that comes to your mind, no matter how trivial it may be. What kind of psychotherapy are you undergoing?
   a. systematic desensitization
   b. traditional psychoanalysis
   c. flooding
   d. person centered therapy

5. You go to your therapist for the first time and he tells you to lie on a couch in a slightly darkened room. He then asks you to talk about anything that comes to your mind, no matter how trivial it may be. The technique being used by your therapist is known as?
   a. catharsis
   b. repression
   c. free association
   d. resistance

6. Freud believed that clients do not only respond to the analyst as an individual, they also respond in ways that reflect their attitudes and feelings towards other people in their lives. He called this process
   _____.
   a. resistance
   b. free association
   c. repression
   d. transference

7. Justin has had a dream that he was flying over his school and could see all the interactions among the people. Freud would label Justin's recollection of the dream sequence as the _____ content and the hidden, or symbolic content would be labeled the _____ content.
   a. phallic, manifest
   b. manifest; latent
   c. latent; phallic
   d. manifest; phallic

8. You meet with your therapist for the first time, and she tells you that she believes that we have a natural tendency toward health and growth and that we are free to make choices and control our destinies. She also tells you that she feels that therapy is intended to help people get in touch with their genuine feelings. What kind of therapy is she likely to practice?
    a. psychoanalysis
    b. behavioral
    c. client-centered
    d. gestalt

9. Which of the following according to Carl Rogers, is not a quality of client-centered therapy?
    a. genuineness
    b. sympathetic understanding
    c. unconditional positive regard
    d. non-direction

10. Shauna is a psychotherapist. She assumes that people don social masks and disown parts of themselves that might meet with social disapproval or rejection. She says that the goal of therapy should be to help the client integrate the conflicting parts of their personality. Shauna will most likely practice
    a. gestalt therapy.
    b. psychoanalytic psychotherapy.
    c. psychoanalysis.
    d. client-center therapy.

11. Frank applied the principles of learning to directly promote desired behavioral changes in his clients. Frank is practicing
    a. gestalt therapy.
    b. rational-emotive behavior therapy.
    c. behavior therapy.
    d. functional analysis.

12. The method for reducing phobic responses in which the client gradually learns to handle increasingly disturbing stimuli is known as
    a. counter conditioning.
    b. systematic desensitization.
    c. modeling.
    d. virtual reality training.

13. Katherine wants to quit smoking. The first therapist she visits suggests that she can help her quit by using a Rapid smoking technique. If she agrees to this technique what will happen to Katherine?
    a. She will be shown increasingly more disgusting pictures of the lungs of smokers.
    b. She will smoke a pipe with flavored tobacco
    c. Smoke will be blown into her face as she smokes a cigarette.
    d. She will be given tokens for every cigarette she smokes.

14. Johnny is given a sticker every time he completes an assignment. When he has accrued 5 stickers, Johnny is allowed to visit the class treasure box. Which behavior therapy method is Johnny's teacher is using?
    a. aversive conditioning
    b. successive approximation
    c. token economy
    d. modeling

15. Cognitive Therapy tends to focus on _____ whereas behavior therapy focuses on _____.
    a. cognitive distortions; behavior modification
    b. the unconscious; the conscious
    c. the conscious; the unconscious
    d. flooding; challenging beliefs

16. Rational-emotive behavior therapy is to _____ as client-centered therapy is to _____.
   a. conscious; unconscious
   b. direction; nondirection
   c. passivity; activity
   d. all of the above

17. Group therapy that is intended to promote personal growth of the group members by heightening the awareness of one's own needs and feelings and those of others through intense confrontations is known as
   a. couple therapy.
   b. family therapy.
   c. encounter group.
   d. transcendental meditation sessions.

18. Your mother wants to know what you have learned about the usefulness of psychotherapy. Which of the following would you be most likely to tell her?
   a. Recent research has shown that the rate of improvement among people in psychotherapy was not greater than the rate of "spontaneous remission."
   b. Meta–analytic research have shown that psychotherapy is effective.
   c. It is difficult to conduct research into the effectiveness of psychotherapy.
   d. Both b and c.

19. Steve's physician has prescribed a medication that belongs to a class of chemicals known as the benzodiazepines. Most likely Steve is being treated for
   a. depression.
   b. bipolar disorder.
   c. schizophrenia.
   d. anxiety.

20. In what controversial method of biological therapy is an electrical current passed through the temples inducing a seizure?
   a. A prefrontal lobotomy
   b. Electroconvulsive therapy
   c. Biofeedback therapy
   d. None of the above.

Essay Questions:
1. How has psychology's approach to therapy changed over the last 100 years? In a three-page essay trace the evolution of thinking about psychological disorders in Western Culture and the various approaches to treatment. What reforms have taken place in treatment? What changes do you foresee occurring in the next decade? Why?

2. What do the humanistic therapies of Carl Rogers and Fritz Perls have in common? How are they different? Compare and contrast the two approaches to therapy in a three-paragraph essay.

3. Imagine that you are a psychologist and that a woman comes into your office complaining that he washes her hands over 100 times a day. In a two-page report describe how you would approach therapy with your patient if you were to use cognitive therapy. Explain how, as a cognitive therapist, you would explain this woman's problem and what methods would you

use to help her overcome this problem. How would your approach to treatment be different if you used behavioral therapy? Why?

4. Approaches to psychotherapy differ in the degree to which the client is directed by the therapist. Compare and contrast the directiveness of the following therapies: psychoanalysis, client-centered, and behavior.

5. Why do many health care professionals prefer the use of psychotherapy to prescribing medicine? Prepare a one-page essay that provides your view in a format specified by your instructor.

CONNECT & EXPAND:

1. **What is Therapy? The Search for a "Sweet Oblivious Antidote".** What is psychotherapy and who can provide therapy? Visit the APA's website on therapy @ *http://helping.apa.org/.* Research information the information there concerning what psychotherapy is and is not and the type of credentials that a therapist must have? What are the APA's licensing requirements? Are there any special requirements for licensing of psychotherapists in your state? (Hint you should be able to find this information on the Internet by looking up your state professional regulations. Prepare an informational pamphlet for aspiring therapists in a format specified by your instructor.

2. **Psychodynamic Therapies: Digging Deep Within.** With your study group create a hypothetical transcript of a session of traditional Freudian psychoanalysis. Create a second transcript of an exchange between the same patient and a more current day psychoanalyst. Present your "sessions" to your class and lead a discussion on the differences between traditional Freudian psychoanalysis and modern psychoanalysis.

3. **Humanistic-Existential Therapies: Strengthening the Self.** Can An AI-Based Humanistic Therapist Help You Solve Your Problems? Talk to Eliza @ *http://www-ai.ijs.si/eliza/eliza.htm* about a problem you have been experiencing. Does the interaction seem real? Do you think that Eliza could help you solve a problem? Why or why not? Compare your experiences to those of your study partners.

4. **Virtual Reality as an Aid in Therapy.** Can "online counseling" help? Visit the websites of any of the "Cyberpsychologists" listed below and examine the information provided. Using your critical thinking skills evaluate these "on-line counseling" centers. Would you use an on line counselor? Why or why not? What might be the advantages and disadvantages of an Internet based counselor?
    Cyberpsychologist @ http://www.cyberpsych.com/ The site claims belongs to Dr. Rob Sarmiento a licensed psychologist in practice for twenty years in Houston, Texas."

    Cyber-Psych @ http://www.cyber-psych.com/ This site claims that "Cyber-Psych is committed to bringing high quality, professional psychological information to the on-line community."

Psychology.com's Advice Center @ http://www.psychology.com/Advice/
This site claims to provide someone to offer personal direction, and personal on-line consultation with a licensed clinical therapist.

Metanoria by Martha Ainsworth @ http://www.metanoia.org/imhs/ Claims to be the original and only independent consumer guide to therapists and counselors who provide services over the Internet - compiled by consumers, for consumers.

5. **Controversy in Psychology: Does Psychotherapy Work? Psychotherapy and Human Diversity.** Are there cultural differences in acceptance of psychotherapy? Consider your part of the country and your socio-cultural background. Do people in your area and from your background frequently go for "therapy"? Is psychotherapy considered a normal option for people having problems in your area, or is it stigmatized? What about people in other countries and cultures? Visit the Infusing Culture into Psychopathology website @ *http://www.stlcc.cc.mo.us/mc/users/vritts/psypath.htm* and research the cultural views on psychopathology and therapy in two different countries. Prepare a brief oral report comparing the differences in cultural traditions pertaining to therapy. Present your report to your classmates at a time specified by your instructor.

6. **Biological Therapies.** Research the use of antidepressant medication. How prevalent is it? Conduct a survey of 25 college students as to their usage of antidepressant medication. What percentage of your sample is currently taking antidepressants? How many have ever taken them? Which type of antidepressant seems to be the most frequently prescribed? Report your findings to your classmates and lead a discussion as to the benefits that have been demonstrated by antidepressant drugs? What concerns are being raised regarding the widespread use of Prozac and other antidepressants?

7. **Life Connections: Alleviating Depression (getting Out of the Dumps).** Create a flyer or other form of handout for college students on the various methods of coping with depression. Be sure to include all the suggestions discussed in your text as well as any other that you may find.

Chapter Fourteen: Social Psychology

PowerPreview: *Skim the major headings in this chapter in your textbook. Jot down anything that you are surprised or curious about. After this write down four or five questions that you have about the material in this chapter.*

Things that surprised me/I am curious about from Chapter 14:

Questions that I have about Social Psychology:

-
-
-
-

QUESTION: *These are some questions that you should be able to answer after you finish studying this chapter:*

Social Psychology: Individuals Among Others
- ❖ *What is social psychology?*

Attitudes–"The Good, the Bad and the Ugly"
- ❖ *What are attitudes?*
- ❖ *Do people do as they think? (For example, do people really vote their consciences?)*
- ❖ *Where do attitudes come from?*
- ❖ *Can you really change people?-their attitudes and behavior, that is?*

Social Perception: Looking Out, Looking Within
- ❖ *Do first impressions really matter? What are the primacy and recency effects?*
- ❖ *What is attribution theory? Why do we assume that other people intend the mischief that they do?*
- ❖ *What is body language?*

Interpersonal Attraction: On Liking and Loving
- ❖ *What factors contribute to attraction in our culture?*
- ❖ *Just what is love? What is romantic love?*

Social Influence: Are You an Individual or One of the Crowd?
- ❖ *Why will so many people commit crimes against humanity if they are ordered to do so? (Why don't they refuse?)*
- ❖ *Why do so many people tend to follow the crowd?*

Group Behavior
- ❖ *Do we run faster when we are in a group?*
- ❖ *How do groups make decisions?*

- *Are group decisions more risky or more conservative than those of the individual members of the group? Why?*
- *What is groupthink?*
- *Do mobs bring out the beast in us? How is it that mild-mannered people commit mayhem when they are part of a mob?*
- *Why do people sometimes sacrifice themselves for others and, at other times, ignore people who are in trouble?*

Life Connections: Understanding and Combating Prejudice
- *What is prejudice? Why are people prejudiced?*

Reading for Understanding/Reflect: The *following section provides you with the opportunity to perform 2 of the R's of the PQ4R study method. In this section I will encourage you to check your understanding of your reading of the text by filling in the blanks in the brief paragraphs that relate to each of the preview questions. You will also be prompted to rehearse your understanding of the material with periodic Reflection breaks. Remember it is better to study in more frequent, short session then in one long "cram session." Be sure to reward yourself with short study breaks before each of the Reflection exercises.*

Reading for Understanding about "Social Psychology: Individuals Among Others"
What is social psychology? (1)_____ psychology is the field of psychology that studies the factors that influence people's thoughts, feelings, and behaviors in social situations. Areas of interest include: attitudes, social (2)_____, interpersonal (3)_____, social (4)_____, and group behavior.

Reading for Understanding about "Attitudes-The Good, the Bad and the Ugly"
What are attitudes? (5)_____ are behavioral and cognitive tendencies expressed by evaluating particular people, places, or things with favor or disfavor. Attitudes are (6)_____ and they affect behavior. Attitudes can be (7)_____, but not easily.

Do people do as they think? (For example, do people really vote their consciences?)
When we are free to act as we wish, our behavior is often (8)_____ with our beliefs and feelings. But as indicated by the term A-B problem, the links between (9)_____ (A) and (10)_____ (B) are often weak to moderate. The following factors strengthen the (11)_____ connection: specificity of attitudes, strength of attitudes, whether people have a vested interest in the outcome of their behavior, and the accessibility of the attitudes. People are more likely to behave in accordance with their attitudes when the attitude is (12)_____, strong, (13)_____, and when they have a (14)_____ in the outcome.

Where do attitudes come from? Attitudes are (15)_____ (not inborn). They can be learned somewhat mechanically by means of (16)_____ or learning by (17)_____. Attitudes formed through (18)_____ may be stronger and easier to recall. However, people also appraise and (19)_____situations and often form their own judgments based on new information.

Can you really change people?-their attitudes and behavior-that is? People attempt to change other people's attitudes and behavior by means of (20)_____. According to the (21)_____ model, persuasion occurs through both central and peripheral routes. Change occurs through the (22)_____ route by means of consideration of arguments and evidence. (23)_____ routes involve associating the objects of attitudes with positive or negative cues, such as attractive or unattractive communicators. (24)_____ messages generally "sell" better than messages delivered only (25)_____. People tend to show greater response to (26)_____ than to purely factual presentations. Persuasive communicators tend to show (27)_____, trustworthiness, (28)_____, or similarity to the audience.

People, however, (29)_____ always just absorb what information is feed to them. If the information discredits their own (30)_____ and prejudices they often show selective (31)_____ and selective (32)_____. That is, they will seek out communicators whose outlook (33)_____ with their own and (34)_____ those whose does not. Aspects of the immediate (35)_____, such as music and mood, also increase the likelihood of persuasion. Research also shows that people who have lower (36)_____ are less likely to resist social pressure. Additionally, the (37)_____ technique, suggests that people are more likely to comply with requests with larger requests if they already have complied with smaller ones.

Reflection Break # 1:
Match the term with its proper description.

a. central route
b. Attitudes
c. selective exposure
d. stereotypes
e. fear appeal

f. elaboration likelihood model
g. peripheral route
h. selective avoidance
i. foot-in-the-door technique

_____1. The diversion of one's attention from information that is inconsistent with your attitudes.
_____2. Behavioral and cognitive tendencies that are expressed by evaluating people, places or things positively or negatively.
_____3. Describes the ways in which people respond to persuasive messages.
_____4. The deliberate attention to information that is consistent with your attitudes.
_____5. Route of persuasion that inspires thoughtful consideration of arguments and evidence.
_____6. A type of persuasive communication that influences behavior on the basis of arousing fear instead of a rational analysis of the issues.
_____7. A method for inducing compliance in which a small request is followed by a larger request.
_____8. Route of persuasion the relies on the association of the product with appealing images or attractive communicators.
_____9. Prejudices about certain groups that lead people to view members of those groups in a biased fashion.

Reading for Understanding about "Social Perception: Looking Out, Looking Within"
Do first impressions really matter? What are the primacy and recency effects? An important area of concern in social psychology is (38)_____, or the ways in which we perceive other people. First impressions can last ((39)_____) because we tend to label or describe people in terms of the behavior we see initially. The (40)_____ appears to be based on the fact

that-other things being equal-recently learned information is easier to remember.

What is attribution theory? Why do we assume that other people intend the mischief that they do? An (41)_____ is an assumption about why people do things. The tendency to infer the motives and traits of others through observation of their behavior is referred to as the (42)_____. (43)_____ psychologists describe two types of attributions: dispositional and situational. In (44)_____ attributions, we attribute people's behavior to internal factors such as their personality traits and decisions. In (45)_____ attributions, we attribute people's behavior to their circumstances or external forces such as social influence or socialization. In cultures that view the self as (46)_____ people tend to attribute other people's behavior to internal factors; this error, or bias in the attribution process, is known as the (47)_____ error. This is not the case in cultures that stress (48)_____, such as Asian culture, where people are more likely to attribute other people's behavior to that person's social roles and obligations.

According to the (49)_____ effect, we tend to attribute the behavior of others to internal, (50)_____ factors and our own behavior to external, (51)_____ factors. The (52)_____ bias refers to the finding that we tend to attribute our successes to internal, stable factors and our failures to external, unstable factors.

The attribution of behavior to internal or external causes is influenced by three factors: (53)_____, or the number of people responding in a certain way; (54)_____, or the degree to which the person responds the same on other situations; and (55)_____, or the extent to which the person responds differently in different situations. For example, when few people act in a certain way that is, when the consensus is low-we are likely to attribute behavior to (56)_____ factors.

What is body language? (57)_____ refers to the tendency to infer people's thoughts and feelings from their postures and gestures. For example, people who feel positively toward one another position themselves (58)_____ together and are more likely to touch. Touching results in a (59)_____ reaction when it suggests more intimacy than is desired. (60)_____ into another's eyes can be a sign of love, but a hard stare is an aversive challenge.

Reading for Understanding about "Interpersonal Attraction: On Liking and Loving"
What factors contribute to attraction in our culture? Sexual interactions usually take place within (61)_____. Feelings of (62)_____, or an attitude of liking or disliking, can lead to liking and perhaps to love, and to a more lasting relationship. Attraction is influenced by factors such as physical (63)_____ and attitudes. Many aspects of beauty appear to be (64)_____. Physically, (65)_____ seem to find large eyes and narrows jaws to be attractive in women. In our culture, (66)_____ is considered attractive in both men and women, and (67)_____ is valued in men. Women tend to see themselves as being heavier than the (68)_____. We are more attracted to (69)_____ people. Similarity in (70)_____ and (71)_____ factors (ethnicity, education, and so on), and (72)_____ in feelings of admiration, also enhance attraction. According to the (73)_____, we tend to seek dates and mates at our own level of attractiveness, largely because of fear of rejection. (74)_____ is a powerful determinant of attraction; we tend to return feelings of admiration.

Just what is love? What is romantic love? Sternberg's (75)_____ theory of love suggests that love has three components: intimacy, passion, and commitment. (76)_____ refers to a couple's closeness, (77)_____ means romance and sexual feelings, and (78)_____ means deciding to enhance and maintain the relationship. Different kinds of (79)_____ combine these components in different ways. (80)_____ love is characterized by the combination of passion and intimacy. (81)_____ is most critical in short-term relationships. (82)_____ love has all three factors.

Men are generally more reluctant than women to make (83)_____ in their romantic relationships. The (84)_____ hypothesis, developed by David Buss attempts to explain this. Buss's research shows that women tend to experience a (85)_____ affective shift, or greater feelings of love and commitment, after first-time sex then men and that men with high numbers of sex partners tend to experience a (86)_____ affective shift following first-time sex. This negative shift motivates them to (87)_____ the relationship. Evolutionary psychologists also suggests that men may be naturally more (88)_____ than women because they are the genetic heirs of ancestors who reproductive success was connected with the (89)_____ of women they could impregnate. Women on the other hand can produce relatively few children in their life time, thus must be more (90)_____ in their mating partners.

Reflection Break # 2:

1. Why do we tend to hold others accountable for their misbehavior and excuse our selves for the same behavior?

2. Briefly describe the factors that contribute to attraction in our culture.

3. Describe Sternberg's three components of love and compare the level of each component in short-term relationship, romantic love and consummate love.

Reading for Understanding about "Social Influence: Are You an Individual or One of the Crowd?"

Why will so many people commit crimes against humanity if they are ordered to do so? (Why don't they refuse?) (91)_____ is the area of social psychology that studies the ways in which people alter the thoughts, feelings and behavior of others. Classic studies by Stanley (92)_____ examined one aspect of social influence, obedience to an authority. The majority of subjects in the Milgram studies (93)_____ with the demands of authority figures, even when the demands required that they (94)_____ innocent people by means of electric shock. Factors contributing to (95)_____ include socialization, lack of social comparison, perception of legitimate authority figures, the foot-in-the-door technique, inaccessibility of values, and buffers between the perpetrator and the victim.

Why do so many people tend to follow the crowd? Another area of interest in the study of social influence is (96)_____, or the changing of our behavior in order to adhere to social (97)_____, or widely accepted expectations concerning social behavior. Social norms can be (98)_____, as in rules and laws that are directly spoken to us; and (99)_____, or unspoken. Solomon (100)_____'s research in which subjects judged the lengths of lines suggests that the majority of people will follow the crowd, or (101)_____, even when the crowd is wrong.

Personal factors such as desire to be (102)_____ by group members, low (103)_____, high (104)_____ , and shyness contribute to conformity. Belonging to a (105)_____ society and group size also contribute to conformity.

Reading for Understanding about "Group Behavior"
Do we run faster when we are in a group? The concept of social (106)_____ refers to the effects on performance that result from the presence of other people. The presence of others may (107)_____ performance for reasons such as increased arousal and (108)_____, or the concern that others are evaluating our performance. The presence of others can also (109)_____ performance. When we are anonymous group members, we may experience (110)_____ in which each person feels less obligation to help because others are present, and task performance may fall off. This phenomenon is termed social (111)_____.

How do groups make decisions? Social psychologists have identified several rules, or social (112)_____, that govern group decision-making. These include the (113)_____ scheme, in which the group's decision is the one that was initially supported by the majority; the (114)_____ scheme, in which the group comes to recognize that one approach is objectively correct; the (115)_____ scheme, in which a two thirds vote makes the decision and the (116)_____ rule, in which the group tends to adopt the decision that reflects the first shift in opinion expressed by any group member.

Are group decisions more risky or more conservative than those of the individual members of the group? Why? Group decisions tend to be more (117)_____ and (118)_____ than individual decisions, largely because groups diffuse responsibility. Group (119)_____ refers to the tendency of groups to take a more extreme position than the individuals in the group would individually. Polarization tends to lead groups make riskier decisions, or show a "(120)_____".

What is groupthink? (121)_____ is an unrealistic kind of decision-making that is fueled by group cohesiveness and the perception of external threats to the group, or to those whom the group wishes to protect. It is facilitated by a dynamic group (122)_____; feelings of (123)_____; the group's belief in its rightness; the (124)_____ of information that contradicts the group's decision; conformity, and the stereotyping of members of the (125)_____. In groupthink group members tend to be more influenced by the group (126)_____ and a dynamic leader than by the realities of the situation. (127)_____ decisions are frequently made as a result of groupthink. Groupthink can however, be avoided if the leaders encourage members to remain (128)_____ about options and feel free to ask questions and disagree with one another.

Do mobs bring out the beast in us? How is it that mild-mannered people commit mayhem when they are part of a mob? Highly emotional crowds may induce attitude-discrepant behavior through the process of (129)_____, which is a state of reduced self-awareness and lowered concern for social evaluation. Many factors lead to deindividuation; these include: (130)_____, diffusion of (131)_____, and arousal due to noise and (132)_____. (133)_____ behavior can be averted by dispersing small groups that could gather into a large crowd and having individuals remind themselves to stop and think when ever they begin to feel aroused in a group.

Why do people sometimes sacrifice themselves for others and, at other times, ignore people who are in trouble? (134)_____, or the selfless concern for the welfare of others is connected with heroic behavior. A number of factors contribute to altruism. Among them are (135)_____, being in a good mood, feelings of (136)_____, knowledge of how to help, and acquaintance with-and similarity to-the person in need of help. According to the (137)_____ effect, or the failure to come to the aid of someone in need, we are unlikely to aid people in distress when we are members of crowds. (138)_____ tend to diffuse responsibility.

Reflection Break # 3:
1. What is conformity, how is it different from obedience, and what makes us conform to group norms?

2. Why does group membership sometimes enhance performance and sometimes lessen performance?

3. What factors affect decisions to help (or not to help) other people?

Reading for Understanding about "Life Connections: Understanding and Combating Prejudice"
What is prejudice? Why are people prejudiced? (139)_____ is an attitude toward a group that leads people to evaluate members of that group negatively. (140)_____ is a form of negative behavior that results from prejudice; discrimination takes forms such as (141)_____ of access to jobs, housing, and the voting booth. Prejudices are typically based on (142)_____, which are fixed, conventional ideas about groups of people that lead people to view members of those groups in a biased fashion.

Sources of prejudice include dissimilarity, social (143)_____, social learning, the relative ease of processing information according to stereotypes, and social categorization. Prejudice can be combated by: encouraging (144)_____ contact and co-operation; attacking (145)_____ behavior; holding discussion forums and examining your own beliefs.

REVIEW: Key Terms and Concepts

Social psychology	529	*foot-in-the-door technique*		*attraction*	540
Attitude	529		534	*matching hypothesis*	542
a-b problem	529	*primacy effect*	535	*reciprocity*	543
stereotype	529	*recency effect*	535	*triangular model of love*	543
elaboration likelihood model		*dispositional attribution*	536	*intimacy*	543
	531	*situational attribution*	536	*passion*	543
fear appeal	532	*fundamental attribution error*		*consummate love*	544
selective avoidance	533		536	*romantic love*	544
selective exposure	533	*actor-observer effect*	536	*affective shift hypothesis*	544
social perception	534	*self-serving bias*	537	*social influence*	545
		consensus	537	*conform*	548

FINAL CHAPTER REVIEW

Recite:

Go to the Recite section for this chapter on pages 561-563 in your textbook. Use the tear-off card provided at the back of the book to cover the answers of the Recite section. Read the questions aloud and recite the answers. This will help you cement your knowledge of key concepts.

Multiple Choice Questions:

1. The subfield of psychology that studies attitudes, social perceptions, interpersonal attraction, social influence and group behavior is known as
   a. environmental psychology.
   b. neuropsychology.
   c. sociocultural psychology.
   d. social psychology.

2. Behavioral and cognitive tendencies that are learned and expressed by evaluating particular people places or things with favor or disfavor are known as
   a. elaborations.
   b. attitudes.
   c. eustress.
   d. values.

3. According to the elaboration likelihood model, TV advertisements for Excedrin that describe the effectiveness of the product on combating headache pain are using
   a. a peripheral route.
   b. central route.
   c. fear appeal.
   d. foot-in-the-door technique.

4. Advertisements that present a "doomsday" approach to getting the attention of the consumer are using which of the following techniques of persuasion?
   a. foot-in-the-door technique
   b. fear appeal
   c. selective exposure
   d. selective avoidance

5. You need someone to help you with the office holiday party. You know that if you just ask Sherry to help she will say that she is too busy, so, you first ask her to chair the committee. Once she says "no" to chairing the committee you ask her to "just help a little." According to research on the _____ she is more likely to say yes to the second request.
   a. foot-in-the-door technique
   b. fear appeal
   c. selective exposure
   d. selective avoidance

6. The area of social psychology concerned with first impressions, attribution theory, body language and ways in which we perceive other people is
   a. social attitude formation
   b. social perception
   c. social persuasion
   d. social obedience

7. Keisha takes care to look especially good for her job interview. This demonstrates that Keisha recognizes that _____ are important in impression formation.
   a. recency effects
   b. first impressions
   c. attributions
   d. body language

8. When we make assumptions about why people do the things they do we are making _____.
   a. an attribution.
   b. a first impression.
   c. a stereotype.
   d. an actor observer bias.

9. When you see a classmate in class or at a study session, they are always very friendly towards you. However, when you run into them at an upscale party, they act as if they do not know you. Since you know they are really a friendly person, you are most likely to attribute your classmate's behavior to
   a. a fundamental attribution error.
   b. a stereotype.
   c. situational attributions.
   d. a dispositional attribution.

10. The tendency to attribute other people's behavior to dispositional factors and our own behavior to situational influences is known as
    a. the fundamental attribution error.
    b. a stereotype.
    c. the actor-observer effect.
    d. the foot in the door technique.

11. Jim feels that he has worked very hard to get his promotion. However when his last sales pitch did not end up in a sale he attributed the failure to the fact that the company he was "pitching to" was having financial difficulties. Jim's behavior is an illustration of _____.
    a. the actor-observer effect.
    b. the foot-in-the-door technique.
    c. the self-serving bias.
    d. a fundamental attribution error.

12. Which of the following is not a factor that contributes to the attribution process?
    a. distinctiveness
    b. consensus
    c. consistency
    d. clarity

13. Body language is
    a. the tendency to infer the motives and traits of others through observation of their behavior.
    b. the tendency to infer people's thoughts and feelings from their postures and gestures.
    c. The tendency to express behavioral and cognitive tendencies by evaluating people and places with favor or disfavor.
    d. The tendency for a person's performance to be affected by the presence of others.

14. According to the _____ we tend to date people who are similar to ourselves in physical attractiveness.
    a. foot-in-the-door techniques
    b. primacy effect
    c. matching hypothesis
    d. reciprocity

15. Intimacy and passion are to
_____ as intimacy, passion
and commitment are to

_____
   a. consumate love ; sexual arousal
   b. romantic love; consumate love
   c. attachment; short-term love
   d. long-term love; romantic love

16. The area of social psychology that studies
the ways in which people alter the
thoughts, feelings and behaviors of others
is known as
   a. social influence.
   b. social perception.
   c. attitude formation.
   d. social cognition.

17. Your boss tells you to report to work at
3:00 am. You are not happy at reporting to
work at such an unusal hour, yet you report
as requested. Your behavior is an example
of
   a. obedience.
   b. conformity.
   c. groupthink.
   d. deindividuation.

18. Lisa has been invited to a party
Immediately after receiving the invitation
she meets with a group of friends to
discuss what they plan to wear to the party.
Lisa then makes the decision on what she
will wear. Lisa's party dressing behavior
demonstrates
   a. obedience to an authority.
   b. conformity.
   c. a social decision scheme.
   d. groupthink.

19. Sarah can recite her speech for her oral
communications class perfectly when she
is all-alone. However, when she is in front
of the group she often loses her "train of
thought" because of her concern that the
audience is judging her performance.
Sarah's performance has been influenced
by
   a. a diffusion of responsibility.
   b. a risky shift.
   c. evaluation apprehension.
   d. altruism.

20. The selfless concern for the welfare of
others is known as
   a. deindividuation.
   b. altruism.
   c. prejudice.
   d. social facilitation.

Essay Questions:
1. Prepare a one-page essay that briefly describes the field of Social Psychology. What type of
topics are social psychologists interested in? What career opportunities are available for
Social Psychologists?

2. Is what you say and do always consistent with your attitudes? How did you develop these
attitudes? (Are you sure?) Have you ever-encountered information that disconfirmed an
attitude, stereotype, or prejudice that you held? Did you change you attitude? Why or why
not? In a two-page essay explain how attitudes are formed and maintained and the
relationship between attitudes and behavior.

3. Do people hold any stereotypes of your sociocultural group? Are these stereotypes positive
or negative? How do you treat people of different religions or races? Do you treat them as
individuals or are your expectations based on stereotypes? What are the effects of the

stereotypes? In a brief essay explain the difference between prejudice, discrimination and stereotypes using examples from your own behavior.

4. In a brief essay compare the features that males tend to find most attractive to those of females. How might the features found attractive by males and females provide humans with an evolutionary advantage?

5. Do you ever do anything that is wrong? (Be honest!) How do you explain your misdeeds to yourself? Do you try to excuse your behavior by making a situational or dispositional attribution? Describe an example of a time when you tried to excuse your behavior and the type of attribution that you used. Now think about a friend's behavior. What type of attribution do you usually make about their behavior? Why? Using the key concepts of attribution theory explain the differences in your attribution process in the two situations.

6. You are eating out at a restaurant with a group of people. All of the others in your party have ordered and now it is your turn to order. Using the research on conformity, what factors will influence whether you are likely to conform? In a brief essay describe the conditions that will influence the likelihood of conformity and how.

7. In a brief essay explain the effect that groups have on individual behavior. Why do we sometimes go along with others—even when we don't want to? What factors encourage/hinder bystanders to help during emergencies? Why does group membership sometimes enhance performance and some times lessen performance?

CONNECT & EXPAND:

1. **Social Psychology:** *Social Psychology Research on the Web.* Go to The Social Psychology Network @ http://www.socialpsychology.org/expts.htm and participate in one of the Social Psychology studies taking place on-line. Report your experience to your classmates in a format specified by your instructor.

2. **Attitudes---"The Good, the Bad and the Ugly":** Using the information about persuasion, attitude formation, and prejudice create a persuasive advertisement for a product or event. Share your advertisement with your study group and discuss the effectiveness of the various principles used. What could you change to make the ad more persuasive?

3. **Social Perception: Looking Out, Looking Within:** Participate in a Social Perception study on the Internet @ *http://cogweb.iig.uni-freiburg.de/IF/new-index.html* or *http://www.socialpsychology.org/expts.htm*
Report your experience to your classmates in a format specified by your instructor.

4. **Interpersonal Attraction: On Liking and Loving:** Participate in one of the on-line studies on Interpersonal Attraction at http://www.socialpsychology.org/expts.htm or http://cogweb.iig.uni-freiburg.de/IF/new-index.html and report your experience to your classmates in a format specified by your instructor. Are the characteristics that you find

attractive the same or different from those of others? Do you think that there are components of "beauty" that are universal? Why or Why not?

5. **Group Behavior.** How does being a member of a group influence your behavior? Have you ever done something as a member of a group that you would not have done as an individual? What motivated you? How do you feel about it? What psychological factors were at work that affected the behavior of the individuals in the group? Interview 15 individuals by asking them the above questions. Prepare a brief report that describes and summarizes the answers you obtained. In your report be sure to also address the various kinds of behaviors that you found were mostly prone to group influences? In the conclusion to your report be sure to discuss importance of understanding group behavior and group dynamics and the benefits this knowledge provides.

6. **Life Connections: Combating Prejudice:** The internet article *"What to tell Your Children about Prejudice and Discrimination from the Anti-defamation league"* at: http://www.adl.org/what_to_tell/whattotell_intro.asp introduces the concepts of prejudice and discrimination with the goal of preparing all children to live and work harmoniously and productively alongside others who represent various and many racial and cultural groups, backgrounds and abilities in our society. After reading this article and discussing it with your study group create a children's game that would apply the principles discussed to teach children ages 4-10 years of age about prejudice and discrimination. Share your game with your class.

Appendix A: Statistics

PowerPreview: *Skim the major headings in this appendix in your textbook. Jot down anything that you are surprised or curious about. After this, write down four or five questions that you have about the material in this appendix.*

Things that surprised me/I am curious about from Appendix A:

Questions that I have about Statistics:

-
-
-
-

QUESTION: *These are some questions that you should be able to answer after you finish studying Appendix A:*

Statistics
- ❖ *What is statistics?*
- ❖ *What are samples and populations?*

Descriptive Statistics
- ❖ *What is descriptive statistics? (Why isn't it always good to be a "10"?)*
- ❖ *What is a frequency distribution?*
- ❖ *What are measures of central tendency?*
- ❖ *What are measures of variability?*

The Normal Curve
- ❖ *What is a normal distribution?*

The Correlation Coefficient
- ❖ *What is the correlation coefficient?*

Inferential Statistics
- ❖ *What are inferential statistics?*
- ❖ *What are "statistically significant" differences?*

Reading For Understanding/Reflect: *The following section provides you with the opportunity to perform 2 of the R's of the PQ4R study method. In this section, you are encouraged to check your understanding of your reading of the text by filling in the blanks in the brief paragraphs that relate to each of the Preview questions. You will also be prompted to rehearse your understanding of the material with periodic Reflection breaks. Remember, it is better to study in more frequent, short sessions than in one long "cram session." Be sure to reward yourself with short study breaks before each Reflection exercises.*

Reading for Understanding About "Statistics"

What is statistics? (1)_____ is the science concerned with obtaining and organizing numerical information or measurements. Statistics assembles (2)_____ in such a way that they provide useful information about measures or scores. Such measures or scores include people's height, weight, and scores on (3)_____ such as IQ tests.

What are samples and populations? A (4)_____ is part of a population. A (5)_____ is a complete group from which a sample is drawn. The example with basketball players shows that a sample must (6)_____ population if it is to provide accurate information about the population. Psychologists are careful in their attempts to select a (7)_____ that accurately represents the entire (8)_____.

Reading for Understanding About "Descriptive Statistics"

What is descriptive statistics? (Why isn't it always good to be a "10"?) (9)_____ statistics is the branch of statistics that provides information about distribution of scores. Descriptive statistics can be used to clarify our understanding of a (10)_____ of scores such as heights, test grades, IQs, or anything else.

What is a frequency distribution? A (11)_____ organizes a set of data, usually from low scores to high scores, and indicates how frequently a score appears. (12)_____ may be used on large sets of data to provide a quick impression of how the data tends to cluster. The histogram and frequency polygon are two ways of (13)_____ data to help people visualize the way in which the data are distributed. In both these types of graphs, the class intervals are drawn on the (14)_____ line, or x-axis, and the frequency is drawn on the (15)_____ line, or Y-axis. In a (16)_____ the number of scores in each class interval is represented by a bar so that the graph looks like a series of steps. In a (17)_____ the number of sores in each class interval is plotted as a point and the points are connected to create a many sided geometric figure.

What are measures of central tendency? Measures of (18)_____ are "averages" that show the center or balancing points of a frequency distribution. There are (19)_____ commonly used types of measures of central tendency: mean, median, and mode. The (20)_____, which is what most people consider the average, is obtained by adding up the scores in a distribution and dividing by the number of scores. The (21)_____ is the score in the middle, or the central case in a distribution. The (22)_____ is the most common score in a distribution. Distributions can be (23)_____ (having two modes) or multimodal. When there are a few extreme scores in a distribution, the (24)_____ is a better indicator of central tendency.

What are measures of variability? Measures of (25)_____ provide information about the spread of scores in a distribution. Two commonly used measures of variability are the range and the (26)_____. The (27)_____ is defined as the difference between the highest and lowest scores. The range is an imperfect measure of variability because it is highly influenced by (28)_____ scores. The standard deviation is a statistic that shows how scores cluster around the (29)_____. The (30)_____ does a better job of showing how the scores in a distribution are spread because it considers every score in the distribution, not just the extreme scores. The standard deviation is calculated by taking the sum of the squared deviations from the mean, dividing this sum by the number of scores, and then taking the (31)_____. Distributions with higher standard deviations are (32)_____ spread out.

Reading for Understanding About "The Normal Curve"

What is a normal distribution? Many human characteristics examined by psychologists appear to be distributed in a pattern known as a (33)_____ distribution. The normal, or (34)_____ curve is hypothesized to occur when the scores in a distribution occur by chance. The normal curve has one (35)_____, its mean, median, and mode fall at the (36)_____ and approximately two of the three scores (68%) are found within one (37)_____ of the mean. Fewer than 5 % of cases are found beyond (38)_____ standard deviations from the mean.

Reflection Break 1:
Match the term with its proper description.

a. mode
b. statistics
c. sample
d. range
e. descriptive statistics
f. frequency distribution
g. median
h. frequency polygon
i. mean
j. population
k. bimodal
l. standard deviation
m. frequency histogram
n. normal curve

_____ 1. Numerical facts assembled so that they provide useful information scores.
_____ 2 A graphic representation of the frequency of occurrence of scores that connects points to represent the frequency with which scores occur.
_____ 3. A complete group that is of interest.
_____ 4 In a frequency distribution, the most frequently occurring score.
_____ 5. The central score in a frequency distribution, beneath which *50%* of the cases fall.
_____ 6. A portion of the group of interest; the group that is actually tested.
_____ 7. A measure of variability found by summing the squared deviations from the mean, dividing by the number of scores, and taking the square root.
_____ 8. Graphic representation of a symmetrical distribution that is assumed to reflect chance fluctuations.
_____ 9. A measure of variability calculated by subtracting the lowest score from the highest score.
_____ 10. A type of average calculated by adding all scores and then dividing by the number of scores.
_____ 11. Branch of statistics concerned with providing description information about a distribution of scores.
_____ 12. Refers to a distribution that has two modes.
_____ 13. A graphic representation of the frequency of occurrence of scores that uses bars to represent the frequency with which scores occur.
_____ 14. A set of data that indicates how often the scores appears.

Reading for Understanding About "The Correlation Coefficient"

What is the correlation coefficient? The (39)_____ is a statistic that describes how variables such as IQ and grade point average are related. Correlational research is used to

216

examine (40)_____ between variables that cannot be manipulated. Correlation research shows that variables are related, but cannot reveal information about (41)_____. Correlation coefficients vary from +1.00 to (42)_____. When correlations between two variables are (43)_____, it means that one variable (such as school grades) tends to rise as the other variable (such as IQ) rises. (44)_____ correlations indicate that as one variable tends to rise, the other tends to fall. A numerical value of 1.00 (whether it is positive or negative) indicates a (45)_____ correlation, and a correlation of (46)_____ reveals no relationship between the variables.

Reading for Understanding About "Inferential Statistics"
What are inferential statistics? (47)_____ statistics is the branch of statistics that indicates whether researchers can extend their findings with samples to the populations from which they were drawn. In other words, inferential statistics help researchers (48)_____, or determine whether their results are "real" or "chance" occurrences.

What are "statistically significant" differences? Instead of speaking of "real" or "actual differences," researchers use the term "(49)_____." Statistically significant differences are believed to represent (50)_____ differences between groups, and not (51)_____ fluctuation.

Reflection Break 2:
1. Briefly explain the limitations of correlational methods.

2. What does it mean when a researcher says that the differences in scores between the two groups is statistically significant?

REVIEW: Key Terms And Concepts

statistics	566	frequency histogram	569	normal distribution	574
sample	566	frequency polygon	569	normal curve	574
population	566	mean	570	correlation coefficient	575
range	566	median	570	inferential statistics	577
average	566	mode	570	infer	577
descriptive statistics	567	bimodal	570		
frequency distribution	567	standard deviation	571		

FINAL CHAPTER REVIEW
Recite
Go to the Recite section for this chapter on page 580 in your textbook. Use the tear-off card provided at the back of the book to cover the answers of the Recite section. Read the questions aloud, and recite the answers. This will help you cement your knowledge of key concepts.

Multiple Choice Questions:

1. The science concerned with obtaining and organizing numerical information or measurements is known as
   a. Sociology.
   b. Psychology.
   c. Statistics.
   d. Calculus.

2. Professor West is interested in researching the impact of a new video game technology in the treatment of attention deficit disorder. He selects 20 boys diagnosed with attention deficit disorder from each of 8 cities in the U.S. and has them use his video game technology for 6 weeks. Their levels of attention are compared to control subjects who have not used the technology. The population of interest in this study is
   a. boys with attention deficit disorder.
   b. the 20 boys tested on the video game technology.
   c. the 160 boys tested on the video game technology.
   d. all people with attention deficit disorder.

3. Professor West is interested in researching the impact of a new video game technology in the treatment of attention deficit disorder. He selects 20 boys diagnosed with attention deficit disorder from each of 8 cities in the U.S. and has them use his video game technology for 6 weeks. Their levels of attention are compared to control subjects who have not used the technology. The sample in this study is
   a. all boys with attention deficit disorder.
   b. the 20 boys tested on the video game technology.
   c. the 160 boys tested on the video game technology.
   d. all people with attention deficit disorder.

4. Information about distributions of scores is to _____ statistics, as generalizing differences among samples to the population is to _____ statistics.
   a. correlational; descriptive
   b. experimental; inferential
   c. descriptive; inferential
   d. experimental; correlational

5. Professor West is interested in researching the impact of a new video game technology in the treatment of attention deficit disorder. He selects 20 boys diagnosed with attention deficit disorder from each of 8 cities in the U.S. and has them use his video game technology for 6 weeks. Their levels of attention are compared to control subjects who have not used the technology. Professor West will use _____ statistics to provide information about the distribution of scores in the sample.
   a. correlational
   b. descriptive
   c. experimental
   d. inferential

6. When Lucy takes scores, or raw data, puts them into order from the lowest to the highest and indicates how often a score appears, she is creating
   a. a sample.
   b. a median.
   c. a frequency distribution.
   d. a standard deviation.

7. A graphic representation of a frequency distribution that uses bars to represent the frequency with which scores appear is known as a
   a. a frequency polygon.
   b. a frequency histogram.
   c. an inferential statistic.
   d. a frequency distribution.

8. The scores on Professor Chandler's first quiz were 2, 7, 8, 6, 4, 8, 7, 8, 7, 6. What is the mean of this distribution?
   a. 6.3
   b. 63
   c. 7 and 8
   d. 10

9. The scores on Professor Chandler's first quiz were 2, 7, 8, 6, 4, 8, 7, 8, 7, 6. What is the mode of this distribution?
   a. 7
   b. 8
   c. 2
   d. both a and b

10. The median is to the _____ as the mode is to _____.
   a. middle; most frequent
   b. most frequent; middle
   c. middle; average
   d. average; most frequent

11. Measures of variability are
   a. measures that inform us about the spreads of scores.
   b. the middle of a distribution of scores.
   c. measures that show the center, or balancing points of a frequency distribution.
   d. scores that assist us in determining whether we can generalize differences among samples to the population.

12. The scores on Professor Chandler's first quiz were 2, 7, 8, 6, 4, 8, 7, 8, 7, 6. What is the range of the scores of the distribution?
   a. 6
   b. 10
   c. 8
   d. 1.9

13. The bell shaped curve is another name for
   a. a statistic used to calculate IQ
   b. the normal distribution.
   c. a symmetrical distribution in which the mean, median and mode all fall at the same point.
   d. Both b and c.

14. You are interested in examining whether there is a relationship between educational level and number of sexual partners. Which statistic should you use?
   a. The standard deviation
   b. The mean
   c. The correlation coefficient
   d. The median

15. If the number of sexual partners increases as the educational level increases, the correlation coefficient will be
   a. negative
   b. zero
   c. positive
   d. cannot be determined.

16. Which of the following does not represent a perfect correlation?
   a. + 1.00
   b. −0.00
   c. −1.00
   d. both a and c

17. Which of the following does <u>not</u> represent a perfect correlation?
    a. + 1.00
    b. −0.00
    c. −1.00
    d. both a and c

18. Which type of statistics assist researchers in determining whether they can generalize among samples to the population?
    a. Descriptive
    b. Central tendency
    c. Inferential
    d. Variability

19. In a research study differences between groups that are unlikely to be due to chance fluctuation are called
    a. real differences.
    b. actual differences.
    c. statistically significant differences.
    d. variations.

20. When Professor West says there is a statistically significant difference in attention between the boys trained on the video game technology and the control subjects, what does he mean?
    a. The differences are likely to be due to chance fluctuation.
    b. The standard deviation is smaller in the control group.
    c. The differences are unlikely to be due to chance fluctuations.
    d. The treatment group has the smaller standard deviation.

Essay Questions:
1. The following scores represent the amount of weight loss that each member of a weight loss class had over the previous month. Draw a frequency histogram and frequency polygon for the distribution using two different class intervals. Which class interval presents the data best?

Dieter	Weight Loss (in lbs.)
1	10
2	12
3	25
4	31
5	22
6	8
7	6
8	17
9	9
10	28
11	7

12	16
13	8
14	2
15	1
16	20
17	11
18	9
19	10
20	15

2. Calculate the three measures of central tendency (mean, median, mode) and the range and standard deviation for the data in question 1.

3. A research study indicated a negative correlation between the amount of Lucky Charms eaten as a child and cancer rate. (In other words, Lucky Charms eaters were less likely to develop cancer.) Another study found a positive correlation between eating oatmeal as a child and the development of cancer. Can the authors of these correlational studies conclude that Lucky Charms prevents cancer while oatmeal causes it? Why or why not? (Hint: What kind of conclusions can be drawn from correlations?)

CONNECT & EXPAND:

1. **Statistics.** Visit David Stockburger's Online Statistics textbook at http://www.psychstat.smsu.edu/introbook/sbk02.htm and read his introduction to descriptive statistics entitled A Mayoral Fantasy to gain a better understanding of the need for statistics.

2. **Descriptive Statistics.** Visit Descriptive Statistics Online at http://www.mste.uiuc.edu/hill/dstat/dstat.html for further insights into and practice calculating the mean, median, mode, standard deviation, and range. Once you have a firm grasp of these concepts, with the help of your study group take a survey of your classmates. Ask them to tell you how many siblings they have, the age at which they first got their drivers license, the age at which they graduated from high school, and how many cups of coffee they drink per day. Draw a frequency histogram and frequency polygon for each frequency distribution. Calculate each of the measures of descriptive statistics for each measurement. Report your findings to your classmates in a format specified by your instructor.

3. **The Correlation Coefficient.** Read the section on correlation in David Stockburger's Online Statistics text at http://www.psychstat.smsu.edu/introbook/sbk17.htm and then complete the Correlation Estimation for Scatter plots exercises at http://www.psychstat.smsu.edu/introbook/exercises/scattermain.htm.
    In the Learning Mode, these exercises will allow you to view many different scatter plots and the corresponding correlation coefficients. Clicking the "Generate" button will cause the program to generate a new set of paired data values. The data pairs are displayed in a scatter

plot, and the correlation coefficient is given in a text box. The "Exit" button will return to the main selection screen. In the Test Mode you are required to click on an estimated correlation before the actual correlation is presented. The selected button will turn yellow and the correct button will turn red if the estimated correlation coefficient is incorrect. The selected button will turn green if it is correct. The program will keep track of the number of correct estimates in a row you have made without making an error.

ANSWER

KEYS

Answers to Chapter 1:

Answers to the Reading for Understanding on "What is Psychology?"

1. scientific
2. behavior
3. mental
4. nervous
5. memory
6. social
7. describe
8. predict
9. explain
10. control
11. theories

Reflection Break # 1:

Goals of Psychology:
1. Description
2. Prediction
3. Control
4. Prediction
5. Description
6. Control
7. Explanation
8. Explanation

Answers to the Reading for Understanding on "What Psychologists Do?"

12. research
13. practice
14. basic
15. applied
16. Practicing
17. Clinical
18. depression
19. Psychiatrists
20. Counseling
21. clinical
22. School
23. educational
24. placement
25. planning
26. Developmental
27. cognitive
28. personality
29. causes
30. social
31. experimental
32. organizational
33. industrial
34. Human Factors
35. consumer
36. Health
37. sports

Reflection Break # 2:

Types of Psychologists:
1.o, 2. j, 3. f, 4. g, 5. d, 6. e, 7. i, 8. a, 9. k, 10. b, 11. n; 12. l, 13. c, 14. h, 15. m

Answers to the Reading for Understanding on "Psychology's History"

38. Aristotle
39. mind
40. empiricism
41. rules
42. Democritus
43. Socrates
44. introspection
45. 1879
46. Wundt
47. mind
48. objective
49. subjective
50. structuralism
51. James
52. introspection
53. Functionalism
54. structuralists
55. functionalists
56. Watson
57. behavior
58. Behaviorism.
59. Watson
60. Skinner
61. reinforced
62. conditioned
63. Gestalt
64. perception
65. whole
66. insight
67. psychoanalysis
68. unconscious
69. physician
70. mind
71. impulses
72. psychodynamic

Reflection Break # 3:

Key Figures in the History of Psychology:
1. a, 2. h, 3. d, 4. c, 5. e, 6. g, 7. i, 8. b, 9. j, 10. f, 11. q, 12. o, 13. r, 14. p, 15. n, 16. k, 17. m, 18. l, 19. t, 20. s

Answers to the Reading for Understanding on "Psychology Today"

13.	evolutionary	80.	self-fulfillment	87.	behaviorist
74.	hereditary	81.	Humanistic	88.	conscious
75.	biological	82.	Existentialism	89.	reinforcement
76.	brain	83.	psychodynamic	90.	social-cognitive
77.	hormones	84.	neoanalysts	91.	observing
78.	cognitive	85.	experience	92.	socio-cultural
79.	mind	86.	learning	93.	ethnic

Reflection Break # 4:

Psychology Today:
1. Socio-Cultural
2. Biological
3. Cognitive
4. Psychodynamic
5. Humanistic–Existential
6. Learning

Answers to the Reading for Understanding about "How Psychologists Study Behavior and Mental Processes"

94.	measurement	117.	male	140.	+ 1.00
95.	correlational	118.	minority	141.	positively
96.	empirical	119.	generalizing	142.	negatively
97.	evidence	120.	random	143.	effect
98.	arguments	121.	stratified	144.	experiment
99.	good	122.	volunteer	145.	treatment
100.	scientific	123.	sampling	146.	observed
101.	testing	124.	anecdotes	147.	control
102.	question	125.	observing	148.	cause
103.	theory	126.	Case	149.	independent
104.	hypothesis	127.	inaccuracy	150.	dependent
105.	test	128.	distort	151.	dependent
106.	conclusion	129.	expectations	152.	independent
107.	critical	130.	surveys	153.	experimental
108.	skeptical	131.	thousands	154.	control
109.	correlation	132.	misrepresent	155.	variables
110.	replicate	133.	socially	156.	chance
111.	publish	134.	falsify	157.	expectations
112.	sample	135.	naturalistic observation	158.	unaware
113.	population	136.	observe	159.	placebo
114.	represent	137.	unobtrusive	160.	blind
115.	generalize	138.	correlational	161.	double-blind
116.	representative	139.	coefficient		

Reflection Break # 5:

Briefly list and describe the basic principles (procedures) of the scientific method followed by psychologists.

* *Formulate a research question and hypothesis*
* *Test the hypothesis using controlled methods*
* *Draw conclusions based on the outcome of the testing*
* *Replicate the outcome of the study*
* *Publish the results of the study in a scientific journal*

Answers to the Reading for Understanding on "Ethics in Psychology"

162. dignity
163. integrity.
164. harmful
165. ethics review
166. ethical

167. informed
168. confidential
169. privacy
170. deceiving
171. debriefed

172. animals
173. ethical
174. harm

Answers to the Reading for Understanding on "Life Connections: Critical Thinking, Science and Pseudoscience"

175. scientists
176. skeptical
177. analyzing
178. definitions
179. assumptions

180. cautious
181. alternative
182. oversimplify
183. evidence
184. pseudosciences

185. Astrology
186. empirical
187. authority

Reflection Break # 6:

1. *A skeptical thinker is one who is willing to believe claims, however they require good evidence in support of claims. They might ask: What am I being asked to believe? What type of evidence is being given? Is there empirical evidence given? Does the author attempt to oversimplify or overgeneralize? Does the evidence fully support the claim?*

Answers to the Final Review Multiple Choice Questions

1.   c (p. 4)
2.   b (p. 5)
3.   c (p. 5)
4.   b (p. 5)
5.   c (p. 6)
6.   d (p. 6)
7.   b (p. 8)
8.   c (p. 18)
9.   c (p. 9)
10. c (p. 8-17)
11. c (p. 11)
12. c (p. 14)
13. a (p. 15)
14. d (p. 21)
15. d (p. 21)
16. b (p. 24)
17. d (p. 23)
18. b (p. 21)
19. a (p. 26)
20. d (p. 27)

Answers to Chapter 2:
Answers to the Reading for Understanding on "Evolution And Evolutionary Psychology"

1. Galton
2. classifying
3. Cambridge
4. Beagle
5. Galapagos
6. evolved
7. scorn
8. Wallace
9. humans
10. evolution
11. mutations
12. adaptive
13. increase
14. extinct
15. adaptation
16. natural selection
17. behavior
18. instinctive
19. instinct

Reflection Break # 1:
Evolution and Evolutionary Psychology

According to Darwin's theory of evolution, there is a struggle for survival as various species and individuals compete for the same territories. Small random genetic variations called mutations lead to differences in physical traits within organisms. Species that are adaptive manage to survive, or are naturally selected, and their numbers increase and they transmit their traits to future generations. Species that do not adapt dwindle in numbers and may become extinct.

Answers to the Reading for Understanding on "Heredity: The Nature of Nature"

20. genes
21. Heredity
22. Psychology
23. behaviors
24. genetics
25. Molecular
26. Genes
27. chromosome
28. 46
29. pairs
30. rungs
31. nature
32. nurture
33. genes
34. more
35. Kinship
36. twin
37. adoption
38. identical
39. fraternal
40. genetic
41. environments
42. natural
43. breeding

Reflection Break # 2:
"Heredity: The Nature of Nature"

1. *Heredity refers to the biological transmission of traits from generation to generation by means of chromosomes and genes. Behavioral geneticists study the genetic transmission of traits that give rise to patterns of behavior.*

2. *Kinship studies like those that compare identical (monozygotic) twins allow scientists to hold the biological make up of the individual constant and compare the effects of different environments. Disadvantages include the inability to totally control differences in environment and the fact that family members will have both similar genetics and similar environments, thus making it difficult to separate the effects of one over the other.*

Answers to the Reading for Understanding on "The Nervous System: On Being Wired":

44. cells
45. receive
46. neurons
47. neurotransmitters
48. chemical
49. impulse
50. glial
51. nourish
52. insulate
53. Neurons
54. dendrites
55. axon
56. terminals
57. one
58. dendrite
59. axon
60. terminals
61. myelin
62. electrical
63. efficiently
64. afferent
65. efferent
66. electro-chemical
67. chemical
68. ions
69. positively
70. depolarized
71. pumped
72. resting
73. resting
74. action
75. electro
76. neurotransmitters.
77. fired
78. neurotransmitters
79. all-or-none

80. large	101. emotional	122. sensory
81. thousandths	102. Parkinson's	123. motor
82. refractory	103. noradrenaline	124. skin
83. synapses	104. inhibitory	125. central
84. transmitting	105. eating	126. skeletal
85. dendrite	106. depression	127. autonomic
86. synaptic cleft	107. endorphins	128. digestion
87. electrical	108. axons	129. sympathetic
88. neurotransmitters	109. dendrites	130. parasympathetic
89. axon terminal	110. thought	131. sympathetic
90. chemical	111. emotional	132. build
91. receptor site	112. brain	133. central
92. reuptake	113. nerves	134. spinal
93. excite	114. spinal	135. brain
94. inhibit	115. central	136. nerves
95. contraction	116. sensory	137. receptors
96. emotions	117. efferent	138. glands
97. deficiencies	118. peripheral	139. reflexes
98. depression	119. peripheral	140. brain
99. acetylcholine	120. somatic	141. gray
100. learning	121. autonomic	142. white

Reflection Break # 3:
"The Nervous System: On Being Wired"
I. Neurons: Into the Fabulous Forest
1. dendrites
2. nucelus
3. nodes of ranvier
4. axon
5. myelin sheath
6. cell body or soma

II. Neurotransmitters: The Chemical Keys to Communication:
1. Acetylcholine
2. Endorphins
3. Dopamine
4. Noradrenaline
5. Serotonin
6. Noradrenaline
7. Acetylcholine
8. Serotonin
9. Dopamine

III. The Parts of the Nervous System:
1. Central
2. Peripheral
3. Brain
4. Spinal Cord
5. Somatic
6. Autonomic
7. Parasympathetic
8. Sympathetic

Answers to the Reading for Understanding on "The Brain: The Star of the Human Nervous System"

143. accidents
144. Gage
145. damage
146. stimulation
147. scans
148. lesion
149. limbic system
150. eating
151. Penfield
152. electroencephalogram
153. brain
154. tumors
155. Computer
156. computerized axial tomograph
157. positron emission tomography
158. magnetic resonance imaging
159. x-ray
160. three
161. glucose
162. active
163. magnetic
164. radio
165. hindbrain
166. medulla
167. pons
168. cerebellum
169. reticular activating
170. thalamus
171. hypothalamus
172. emotion
173. cerebrum
174. amygdala
175. hippocampus
176. cerebrum
177. cognitive
178. convoluted
179. fissures
180. hemispheres
181. corpus callosum
182. lobes
183. frontal
184. parietal
185. temporal
186. occipital
187. visual
188. auditory
189. somatosensory
190. prefrontal
191. motor
192. hemispheres
193. differ
194. left
195. Broca's
196. Wernicke's
197. Aphasia
198. produce
199. understanding
200. *Dyslexia*
201. hemispheres
202. left
203. logical
204. problem
205. Right
206. aesthetic
207. reasoning
208. exaggerated
209. independently
210. handwriting
211. left-handed
212. language
213. stuttering
214. migrane
215. creativity
216. genetic
217. gene
218. corpus callosum
219. normal
220. verbally
221. language
222. cannot

Reflection Break # 4:
The "Brain and Cerebral Cortex"

1. n; 2. x; 3. w; 4. aa; 5. z; 6. t; 7. v; 8. y; 9. u; 10. s; 11. a; 12. b; 13. o; 14. q; 15. r; 16. p; 17. c; 18. l; 19. bb; 20. d; 21. m; 22. e; 23. k; 24. j; 25. cc; 26. g; 27. i; 28. h; 29. f

Answers to the Reading for Understanding on "The Endocrine System"

223. glands
224. passageways
225. ductless
226. endocrine
227. hormones
228. neurotransmitters
229. hypothalamus
230. pituitary
231. hormonal
232. master
233. hypothalamus
234. growth
235. prolactin
236. antidiuretic hormone
237. oxytocin
238. pineal
239. sleep/wake
240. puberty
241. thyroxin
242. hypothyroidism
243. cretinism
244. hyperthyroidism
245. cortex
246. stress
247. glucose
248. medulla
249. Adrenaline
250. emotions
251. anxiety
252. Noreadrenaline
253. testosterone
254. muscle
255. sex
256. female
257. ovaries
258. Estrogen
259. progesterone
260. cognitive
261. well-being

Reflection Break # 5:
"Hormones and the Endocrine System"

1. e; 2. j; 3. a; 4. k; 5. f; 6. c; 7. b; 8. i; 9. d; 10. l; 11. h; 12. g

Answers for Read for Understanding on Life Connections: "Raging Hormones"

262.	Women	272.	without	282.	Exercise
263.	menstruation	273.	hormone replacement	283.	controversial
264.	premenstrual	274.	men's	284.	sheep
265.	decade	275.	women's	285.	testosterone
266.	biological	276.	Andropause	286.	antidepressant
267.	exercise	277.	Viropause	287.	testosterone
268.	hormone	278.	manopause	288.	prostate
269.	neurotransmitters	279.	gradual	289.	cardiovascular
270.	Menopause	280.	physical		
271.	climacteric	281.	erection		

Reflection Break # 6:
"Life Connections: Raging Hormones"

1. *HRT may reduce hot flashes and other symptoms. Research has shown that HRT raises levels of HDL (good cholesterol) and lowers levels of LDL and it may reduce the risk of heart disease in women. Estrogen replacement appears to lower the risk of osteoporosis, colon cancer and age related cognitive declines. HRT also is associated with increase risk of breast and endometrial cancer and stroke and heart attacks.*
2. *The decline in the production of male sex hormones is much more gradual and problems related to low levels of sex hormones in men do not even have an agreed upon name. However, although men can continue to father children into their 70's, many men do experience problems in maintaining and achieving erections. Irritable Male syndrome has been identified in animals, but researchers are skeptical if it exists in humans. Without more research into age-related decline in sex hormones in males, controversy will still exist.*

Answers to the Final Review Multiple Choice Questions

1. c (p. 41)
2. c (p. 41)
3. d (p. 45)
4. c (p. 47)
5. a (p. 51)
6. d (p. 52)
7. b (p. 56)
8. c (p. 57)
9. a (p. 58)
10. c (p. 59)
11. a (p. 60)
12. b (p. 63)
13. b (p. 64)
14. d (p. 69)
15. a (p. 69)
16. b (p. 69)
17. b (p. 74)
18. a (p. 70)
19. d (p. 75)
20. c (p. 76)

Answers to Chapter 3
Answers to the Reading for Understanding about "Prenatal Development: The Beginning of Our Life Story"

1.	months	5.	week	9.	fetal	
2.	neonate	6.	second	10.	size	
3.	germinal	7.	amniotic	11.	movements	
4.	embryonic	8.	placenta			

Reflection Break 1:
Prenatal Development:

	Time Period	Major Characteristics
Germinal	*Conception until implantation*	*The zygote, the single cell formed by the union of the sperm and egg, divides as it travels through the fallopian tube and becomes implanted in the uterine wall.*
Embryonic	*Implantation to eighth week*	*The major organ systems are formed. By the end of the second month, the nervous system begins to transmit messages and the sex organs begin to differentiate. The embryo is suspended in the amniotic sac and exchanges nutrients and wastes with the mother through the placenta.*
Fetal	*Eighth week until birth*	*Characterized by maturation and gains in size. It is during the fetal period that the mother will detect the first fetal movements.*

Answers to the Reading for Understanding about "Childhood: Physical, Cognitive, and Social Development"

12.	birth	30.	Maturational	48.	reversibility
13.	Physical	31.	discontinuous	49.	Kohlberg
14.	infancy	32.	cognitive	50.	preconventional
15.	five	33.	cognitive	51.	conventional
16.	triple	34.	Piaget	52.	postconventional
17.	Reflexes	35.	stages	53.	postconventional
18.	see	36.	assimilation	54.	Social
19.	face	37.	accommodation	55.	Erikson
20.	depth	38.	Schemes	56.	crisis
21.	hear	39.	sensorimotor	57.	trust versus mistrust
22.	mother	40.	object permanence	58.	autonomy
23.	pleasant	41.	preoperational	59.	shame
24.	sweet	42.	dimensional	60.	guilt
25.	touch	43.	egocentrism	61.	industriousness
26.	continuously	44.	animism	62.	Ainsworth
27.	discontinuously	45.	artificialism	63.	Attachment
28.	behavioral	46.	conservation	64.	strange situation
29.	continuous	47.	concrete operational	65.	securely

66.	avoidantly	76.	critical	86.	strictness
67.	Ambivalently	77.	imprinted	87.	authoritative
68.	indiscriminate	78.	parenting	88.	underreported
69.	familiar	79.	instrumental competence	89.	stress
70.	primary caregiver	80.	parental	90.	rigid
71.	Behaviorists	81.	Authoritative	91.	does
72.	Harlow	82.	Authoritarian	92.	abused
73.	contact comfort	83.	Permissive		
74.	ethologist	84.	uninvolved		
75.	instinctual	85.	warmth		

Reflection Break # 2:

Childhood: Physical, Cognitive and Social Development

Part I:

Sense	Capabilities
Vision	*Newborn babies can see quite well and show greater interest in complex visual stimuli than in simple ones. Infants are capable of depth perception by the time they can crawl.*
Hearing	*Newborns can normally hear and show a preference for their mother's voice.*
Taste & Smell	*Newborns show preferences for pleasant odors and sweet foods.*
Touch	*Newborns are sensitive to touch but are relatively insensitive to pain.*

Part II. Matching:

1. c; 2. d; 3. w; 4. n; 5. m; 6. i; 7. p; 8. s; 9. j; 10. l; 11. r; 12. t; 13. u; 14. o; 15. y; 16. z; 17. a; 18. g; 19. b; 20. f; 21. e; 22. h; 23. bb; 24. aa; 25. q; 26. x; 27 v; 28. k

Answers to the Reading for Understanding about "Adolescence: Physical, Cognitive and Social Development"

93.	adolescence	107.	stages	121.	caring
94.	growth spurt	108.	capable	122.	turbulence
95.	Puberty	109.	continuously	123.	biological
96.	testosterone	110.	sequence	124.	sociocultural
97.	ovaries	111.	rejected	125.	conflict
98.	Estrogen	112.	moral reasoning	126.	independence
99.	menarche	113.	conventionally	127.	parents
100.	Formal operational	114.	post conventional	128.	ego identity
101.	abstract	115.	standards	129.	role diffusion
102.	egocentrism	116.	personal values	130.	puberty
103.	personal fable	117.	support	131.	hormone
104.	imaginary audience	118.	higher	132.	contraceptives
105.	personal fable	119.	Gilligan	133.	decline
106.	accuracy	120.	justice		

Reflection Break # 3:
Adolescence: Physical, Cognitive and Social Development:
Part I. Matching:
1. o; 2. a; 3. b; 4. n; 5. c; 6. g; 7. h; 8. i; 9. m; 10. d; 11. j; 12. e; 13. l; 14. f; 15. k

Part II:
Biologically, cognitively and socially the adolescent is undergoing change. Physically, they begin to look like an adult. Their sex hormones surge and stimulate a new interest in sexuality. Cognitively, their thinking is expanding and they can think about new possibilities. Socially, they are striving to be independent, but are cognitively aware of their limitations. Since different systems in the body grow at different rates, their co-ordination and body control may be awkward. This may lead them to question themselves; impacting the formation of their self-concept and self-esteem; thus impacting their social interactions.

Answers to the Reading for Understanding about "Adulthood: Physical, Cognitive, and Social Development"

134. lifespan
135. physical
136. peak
137. decline
138. Menopause
139. difficulty
140. acuity
141. lengthens
142. immune
143. Heredity
144. programmed senescence
145. wear-and-tear theory
146. Lifestyle
147. cognitive
148. creative
149. Memory
150. verbal
151. Crystallized

152. fluid
153. familiarity
154. Alzheimer's
155. acetylcholine
156. plaque
157. declines
158. social
159. personality
160. healthier
161. Young
162. intimacy versus isolation
163. age- 30 transition
164. settling down
165. crisis
166. Generativity
167. Stagnation
168. midlife crisis
169. discrepancies

170. gender
171. earlier
172. women
173. optimistic
174. empty-nest
175. ego integrity versus despair
176. physical deterioration
177. wisdom
178. challenges
179. biological
180. social
181. stereotypes
182. satisfied
183. successful aging

Reflection Break # 4:
Adulthood: Physical, Cognitive and Social Development:
Briefly describe the physical and cognitive changes that occur during these adulthood by filling in the chart below:

	Physical	Cognitive	Psychosocial
Early adulthood	*People are usually at the height of their physical powers during young adulthood. Sexually, most young adults become easily aroused and men are more likely to think about ejaculating too quickly than whether or not he will be able to maintain an erection.*	*People are usually at the height of their cognitive powers during early adulthood, but people can be creative for a lifetime. Some developmental theorists have proposed the existence of post formal thought, a stage of cognitive development after formal operational thought that is characterized by creative thinking, the ability to solve complex problems and the posing of new questions.*	*Young adulthood is generally characterized by efforts to advance in the business world and the development of intimate ties. Many young adults reassess the directions of their lives during the "age- 30 transition." Emerging adulthood is a hypothesized period that exists in wealthy societies. It roughly spans the ages of 18 through 25 and affords young people extended periods of role exploration. The concept dovetails with Erikson's concept of a prolonged adolescence we find in industrialized societies, one that permits a period of moratorium during*

			which the individual searches for personal identity. *Sheehy proposes that the 20's are a period in which people basically strive to advance their careers and establish their pathway in life. During this time many young adults adopt what Daniel Levinson call the dream, or the drive to "become "someone and to leave a mark on history, this then serves as a tentative blueprint for their life.* *Erikson characterizes young adulthood as the stage of intimacy versus isolation, or the time for the establishment of intimate relationships. The ages of 28 to 33 have been labeled by Levinson as the age-30 transition and by Sheehy as the catch 30's because of the tendency for reassessment. Often we find that the lifestyles that we adopted during our 20's do not fit as comfortably as we had expected and the later thirties are characterized by settling down.*
Middle adulthood	*Middle adulthood is characterized by a gradual decline in strength. Menopause, or the cessation of menstruation, usually occurs in the late 40's or early 50's and has been thought to depress many women, but research suggests that most women go through this passage without great difficulty. Menopause is the final stage of the climacteric, a falling off in the secretion of the hormones estrogen and progesterone that women experience.*	*Memory functioning declines with age, but the declines are not usually as large as people assume. People tend to retain verbal ability, as shown by vocabulary and general knowledge, into advanced old age. Crystallized intelligence, or one's vocabulary and accumulated knowledge, generally increases with age; while fluid intelligence, the ability to process information rapidly, declines more rapidly.*	*Erikson labeled the life crisis of middle age as generativity vs. stagnation. Generativity involves doing things that we believe are worthwhile and enhances and maintains self-esteem. Stagnation means treading water, or moving backwards and has powerful destructive effects on self-esteem. Many theorists view middle adulthood as a time of crisis (the "midlife crisis") and further reassessment. Many adults try to come to terms with the discrepancies between their achievements and the dreams of their youth during middle adulthood. Some middle-aged adults become depressed when their youngest child leaves home (the so-called empty-nest syndrome), but many report increased satisfaction, stability, and self-confidence. On a more positive note, many people in middle adulthood experience "middlescence"-a phase during which they redefine themselves and their goals for the 30 to 40 healthy years they expect lie ahead of them. Marriage remains the most popular lifestyle in the United States, and people still think of marriage as permanent.*

Later adulthood	Older people show less sensory acuity, and their reaction time lengthens. Older people develop wrinkles and gray hair due to the decline in melanin and collagen and elastin. Although people are capable of enjoying sexual experiences throughout their lifetime, changes do occur. Older men and women experience less interest in sex and men may have difficulty reaching and maintaining an erection. Women may experience less vaginal lubrication. The immune system weakens and changes occur that eventually result in death.	Alzheimer's disease is characterized by a general, gradual cognitive deterioration in memory, language, and problem solving. On a biological level, it is connected with reduced levels of acetylcholine in the brain and with the build-up of plaque in the brain. Alzheimer's disease does not reflect the normal aging process. There are, however, normal, more gradual declines in intellectual functioning and memory among older people.	Erikson characterizes late adulthood as the stage of ego integrity versus despair. He saw the basic challenge as maintaining the belief that life is worthwhile in the face of physical deterioration. Ego integrity derives from wisdom, which can be defined as expert knowledge about the meaning of life, balancing one's own needs and those of others and striving for excellence in one's behavior and achievements. Other views of late adulthood stress the importance of creating new challenges; however biological and social realities my require older people to become more selective in their pursuits. Many stereotypes about aging are growing less prevalent. Most older Americans report being generally satisfied with their lives. Those who experience "successful aging" reshape their lives to focus on what they find to be important, maintain a positive outlook, and find new challenges.

Answers to the Reading for Understanding about "On Death and Dying"

184. Kubler-Ross
185. bargaining
186. death

Answers to the Reading for Understanding about "Life Connections: Day Care—Blessing, Headache, or Both?"

187. attachment
188. more
189. small
190. securely
191. mixed
192. peer
193. higher
194. Day care
195. better
196. low
197. high
198. no different
199. out scored
200. language
201. cognitive
202. mothers
203. caution
204. small

Answers to the Final Review Multiple Choice Questions

1. d (p. 88)
2. d (p. 89)
3. a (p. 89)
4. b (p. 91)
5. d (p. 95)
6. c (p. 96)
7. b (p. 98)
8. b (p. 101)
9. d (p. 103)
10. c (p. 106)
11. b (p. 106)
12. d (p. 110)
13. b (p. 111)
14. c (p. 112)
15. c (p. 116)
16. a (p. 119)
17. b (p. 119)
18. c (p. 112)
19. c (p. 112)
20. c (p. 128-9)

Answers to Chapter 4:

Answers to the Reading for Understanding about "Sensation and Perception: Your Tickets of Admission to the World Outside"

1. sensation
2. central
3. sense
4. energy
5. perception
6. learning
7. psychophysics
8. transduction
9. fechner
10. weakest
11. psychophysicists
12. sensitive
13. weber
14. minimum
15. weber's
16. just
17. noticeable
18. detection
19. characteristics
20. psychological
21. hubel
22. wiesel
23. features
24. angles
25. auditory
26. sensitive
27. adaptation
28. sensitization
29. desensitization

Reflection Break # 1:

1. *Sensation is a mechanical process that involves the stimulation of sensory receptors and transmission of the sensory information to the brain. Perception is an active process in which sensations are organized and interpreted to form a representation of the world.*

2. *According to signal-detection theory the intensity of a stimulus is one factor in determining whether people will perceive sensory stimuli, another is the degree to which the signal can be distinguished from background noise and still another is the attention that you pay to the stimulus. Your city slicker friend will be more apt to hear the quiet sounds of nature due to the lack of the normal noise they are used to hearing. The intensity and novelty of the new city sounds will cause you to hear them until you learn to block them out.*

Answers to the Reading for Understanding about "Vision: Letting The Sun Shine In"

30. electromagnetic
31. waves
32. wavelengths
33. hue
34. shortest
35. longest
36. prism
37. occipital
38. cornea
39. pupil
40. iris
41. lens
42. retina
43. photoreceptors
44. cones
45. rods
46. optic
47. ganglion
48. fovea
49. blind
50. acuity
51. shape
52. presbyopia
53. cones
54. fovea
55. dark
56. rods
57. value
58. wavelength
59. value
60. saturation
61. psychological
62. circle
63. cool
64. warm
65. complementary
66. green
67. yellow
68. gray
69. afterimages
70. color
71. wavelengths
72. two
73. trichromatic
74. red
75. green
76. blue-violet
77. cones
78. opponent process
79. red
80. blue
81. dark
82. afterimages
83. both
84. trichromats
85. monochromats
86. dichromats
87. total
88. partial
89. males

Reflection Break # 2:

1.v; 2.d; 3.r; 4.w; 5. j; 6. s; 7. g; 8. z; 9. e; 10. x; 11. q; 12. a; 13. f; 14. p; 15. m; 16. u; 17. i; 18. h; 19. c; 20. t; 21. l; 22. o; 23. y; 24. k; 25. n; 26. b

Answers to the Reading for Understanding about "Visual Perception: How Perceptive!"

90. recognizing
91. relationships
92. mechanical
93. perception
94. perceptual organization
95. closure
96. figure-ground
97. ambiguous
98. rubin
99. necker
100. proximity
101. similarity
102. continuity
103. common fate
104. top-down
105. bottom-up
106. position
107. apparent
108. autokinetic
109. stroboscopic
110. frames
111. phi phenomenon
112. depth
113. monocular
114. pictorial
115. motion
116. smaller
117. perspective
118. relative size
119. clearness
120. interposition
121. shadowing
122. texture gradients
123. monocular
124. motion parallax
125. binocular
126. retinal disparity
127. difference
128. closer
129. convergence
130. constancies
131. learn
132. distance
133. lighting
134. illusions

Reflection Break # 3:

Gestalt Laws of Perceptual Organization:

1. Similarity
2. Proximity
3. Continuity
4. Common fate

Perceptual Organization, Movement, Depth, Constancies and Illusions:

1. u; 2. r; 3. d; 4. i; 5. c; 6. p; 7. k; 8. l; 9. a; 10. m; 11. t; 12. e; 13. s; 14. b; 15. n; 16. o; 17. j; 18. q; 19. v; 20. g; 21. f; 22; h

---

Answers to the Reading for Understanding about "Hearing: Making Sense of Sound"

135. auditory
136. waves
137. vibrations
138. frequency
139. loudness
140. pitch
141. frequency
142. one
143. higher
144. amplitude
145. decibels
146. zero
147. loss
148. ear
149. outer
150. middle
151. inner
152. eardrum
153. amplifier
154. bones
155. vibrating
156. oval
157. cochlea
158. chambers
159. basilar
160. corti
161. hair
162. basilar
163. auditory
164. louder
165. front
166. turn
167. loudness
168. corti
169. louder
170. pitch
171. place
172. frequency
173. volley
174. deafness
175. conductive
176. hearing aids
177. sensorineural
178. cochlear

Reflection Break # 4:

1. *Vibrating air molecules are funneled via the outer ear to the eardrum, which in turn vibrates and transmits the sounds to the middle and inner ears. The three bones in the middle ear (the hammer, anvil and stirrup) vibrate which amplifies the sound by increasing the pressure of the air in the ear. Attached to the stirrup is another vibrating membrane, the oval window. The round window of the inner ear pushes outward when the oval window pushes in and is pulled inward when the oval window vibrates outward. The vibrations are then transmitted to the cochlea, which is a bony tube that is divided into three fluid-filled chambers. The basilar membrane is one of these membranes. The organ of Corti is attached to the basilar membrane. It contains*

16,000 receptor hair cells that dance in response to the vibrations of the basilar membrane. The movements of these cells generate the neural impulses that travel via the auditory nerve to the temporal lobe of the brain.

2. *Place theory claims that the pitch of a sound is sensed according to the place along the basilar membrane that vibrates in response to it. This accounts for pitches greater than 4,000 HZ*
   Frequency theory claims that pitch perception depends on the stimulation of neural impulses that match the frequency of the sound waves. This appears to only account for perception of pitch between 20 and a few hundred cycles per second.

   Volley theory argues that groups of neurons take turns firing in response to sound waves of certain frequencies. This principle appears to account for pitch discrimination between a few hundred and 4,000 cycles per second.

Answers to the Reading for Understanding about "The Chemical Senses: Smell and Taste"

179. chemical	185. sour	191. blind
180. odors	186. bitter	192. genetic
181. gaseous	187. texture	193. taste
182. olfactory	188. tongue	194. smell
183. flavor	189. sweetness	
184. Taste	190. twice	

Answers to the Reading for Understanding about "The Skin Senses (Yes it Does)"

195. skin	198. pressure	201. skin
196. temperature	199. two-point	202. separate
197. Touches	200. more	

Answers to the Reading for Understanding about "Kinesthesis and The Vestibular Sense and Virtual Reality and ESP"

203. Kinesthesis
204. tendons
205. vestibular

Answers to the Reading for Understanding about " Extrasensory Perception: Is There Perception Without Sensation?"

206. psi communication	209. telepathy	212. telepathy
207. precognition	210. clairvoyance	213. file-drawer
208. psychokinesis	211. scientific	

Reflection Break # 5:

1. *The flavor of food involves its taste, but is more complex. The flavor of food depends on its odor, texture and temperature as well as its taste. It is our sense of smell that detects odors and since when we have a cold our sense of smell is disrupted, so will our sense of the flavor of food.*

2. *Some parts of the body have nerve endings that are more densely packed. Additionally more sensory cortex is devoted to the perception of sensations in these same areas.*

3. *Due to the difficulties in investigating "Psychic" phenomenon using scientific methods and the inability in replicating those studies that have been conducted, psychologists remain skeptical about ESP and psychic phenomena.*

Answers to the Read for Understanding about "Life Connections: Pain, Pain, Go Away-- Don't Come Again Another Day"

214. Pain	217. chemicals	220. aspirin
215. sharpest	218. Prostaglandins	221. neuromatrix
216. originates	219. inflammation	222. gate

223.	phantom	227.	hypothalamus	231.	successful
224.	decrease	228.	endorphins		
225.	spinal cord	229.	medical		
226.	acupuncturists	230.	information		

Answers to Final Review Multiple Choice.

1. c (p. 138)
2. d (p. 139)
3. c (p. 141)
4. a (p. 141)
5. a (p. 142-143)
6. b (p. 144)
7. d (p. 148-149)
8. a (p. 150)
9. d (p. 152)
10. c (p. 153)
11. a (p. 154)
12. d (p.154)
13. b (p. 156)
14. b (p.163)
15. a (p. 164)
16. c (p.165)
17. a (p. 168)
18. b (p. 169)
19. b (p. 170)
20. c (p. 170)

Answers to Chapter 5:

Answers to the Reading for Understanding about "What Is Consciousness?"

1. Consciousness
2. James
3. Watson
4. brain
5. construct
6. awareness
7. attention
8. self
9. waking
10. Consciousness
11. aware
12. unaware
13. selective attention
14. learn
15. cocktail party
16. inner awareness
17. scientifically
18. psychoanalysis
19. unconscious
20. preconscious
21. Freud
22. Repression
23. suppression

Reflection Break # 1:

1. *A psychological construct is a concept or a theory that is developed to help make sense or integrate the observations made of phenomenon.*

2. *The construct of Consciousness is defined as:*
- *Sensory awareness or our ability to sense the environment.*
- *Selective Attention, or our ability to choose what sensory stimuli in our environment to pay attention to and what to ignore.*
- *Direct Inner awareness refers to consciousness as our awareness of our own internal thoughts, emotions, images and memories.*
- *Personal Unity refers to consciousness as our sense of self as a different, independent person.*
- *Waking State refers to consciousness as the aroused alert state of a person.*

3. *Most contemporary psychologists would agree that consciousness is a proper area of study. However a student could present a view similar to John Watson's and argue that it is not. Good answers would support their answer with support from the text.*

Answers to the Reading for Understanding about "Sleep and Dreams"

24. circadian rhythm
25. hours
26. stages
27. electroencephalograph
28. wakefulness
29. four
30. REM
31. lightest
32. deepest
33. alpha
34. theta
35. eye
36. hypnagogic
37. one
38. amplitude
39. frequency
40. spindles
41. delta
42. deepest
43. rapid eye
44. paradoxical
45. five
46. restorative
47. deprived
48. attention
49. memory
50. deprivation
51. REM
52. development
53. neurons
54. rem rebound
55. dreams
56. REM
57. unconscious
58. awareness
59. consistent
60. activation-synthesis
61. memories
62. restorative
63. awakens
64. previous
65. Nightmares
66. Insomnia
67. apnea
68. sleepwalking
69. half
70. women
71. men
72. stress
73. noise
74. allergies
75. narcolepsy
76. minutes
77. paralysis
78. REM
79. Stimulants
80. antidepressant
81. Apnea
82. obstruction
83. obesity
84. snoring
85. stroke
86. deformities
87. weight-loss
88. sleep terrors
89. children
90. nightmares
91. never
92. Bed-wetting
93. adolescence
94. sleep walking
95. remember

Reflection Break # 2:

Stage One	Stage Two	Stage Three	Stage Four	REM Stage
<ul><li>**Type of Sleep?:** *Non Rapid eye movement sleep*</li><li>**Brain Waves?:** *Low amplitude Brain waves of 8 to 13 cycles (Alpha waves) shift, to waves of 6 to 8 cycles per second (theta)*</li><li>**Eye Movements?:** *Slow rolling eye movements*</li><li>**Dreams?:** *Hypnagogic state in which we experience brief dream-like images*</li></ul>	<ul><li>**Type of Sleep?:** *Non Rapid eye movement sleep*</li><li>**Brain Waves?:** *Brain waves shift from theta waves to waves medium in amplitude with a frequency of about 4 to 7 cycles per second*</li><li>*Waves are punctuated with sleep spindles, waves with a frequency of 12-16 cycles per second*</li><li>**Eye Movements?:** *None to speak of.*</li><li>**Dreams?:** *No reports of dreaming.*</li></ul>	<ul><li>**Type of Sleep?:** *Non Rapid eye movement sleep*</li><li>**Brain Waves?:** *Brain waves shift to a delta wave with a frequency of 1 to 3 cycles per second*</li><li>**Eye Movements?:** *None to speak of.*</li><li>**Dreams?:** *No reports of dreaming.*</li></ul>	<ul><li>**Type of Sleep?:** *Non Rapid eye movement sleep*</li><li>**Brain Waves?:** *Brain waves shift to a delta wave with a frequency of .5 to 2 cycles per second*</li><li>*Is the deepest stage of sleep most difficult to be awakened from.*</li><li>**Eye Movements?:** *None to speak of.*</li><li>**Dreams?:** *No reports of dreaming.*</li></ul>	<ul><li>**Type of Sleep?:** *Rapid Eye Movements*</li><li>**Brain Waves?:** *Brain waves are rapid, low amplitude brain waves that resemble those of stage one.*</li><li>**Eye Movements?:** *Rapid mvement of eyes under closed eyelids*</li><li>**Dreams?:** *Most sleepers' report that they have been dreaming.*</li><li>**Other?** *Also known as paradoxical sleep*</li><li>*When deprived of this we experience REM rebound.*</li></ul>

Sleep Disorders:
1. e; 2. b; 3. d; 4. c; 5. a; 6. f

Answers to the Reading for Understanding about "Altering Consciousness Through Hypnosis: On Being Entranced"

96. Hypnosis
97. Mesmer
98. anesthetic
99. anxiety
100. EEG
101. passivity
102. pseudomemories
103. hypermnesia
104. hallucinations
105. amnesia
106. state
107. role-play
108. response set
109. neodissociation

Answers to the Reading for Understanding about "Altering Consciousness Through Meditation: Letting Your World Fade Away"

110. mediation
111. mantra
112. consciousness
113. Transcendental
114. relaxation
115. words
116. sounds
117. benson
118. hypertensive
119. relaxation
120. alpha
121. melatonin
122. more

Answers to the Reading for Understanding about "Altering Consciousness Through BioFeedback: Getting in Touch with the Untouchable"

123. Bodily
124. biofeedback
125. involuntary
126. waves

Reflection Break # 3:

1. The state of consciousness is referred to as the hypnotic trance. Traditionally the subject is asked to narrow their attention to a small light, or an object held by the hypnotist. The hypnotist usually suggests that the person's limbs are becoming warm , heavy and relaxed. The subject may also be told that they are becoming sleepy. Hypnosis is however different from sleep as shown on EEG recordings. Hypnotized people are said to have hypnotic suggestibility, and are prone to fantasy, can compartmentalize unwanted memories and want to cooperate without the hypnotist. Subjects are passive, have narrowed attention, pseudomemories and hypermnesia; suggestibility; they play unusual roles and experience perceptual distortions, they apparently do not remember events that took place in the trance state and are prone to posthypnotic suggestions.

2. In mediation the individual purposely (actively) thinks of a mantra, or words or sounds that is designed to allow the person to achieve an altered state of consciousness. In mediation the individual demonstrates a relaxation response and the blood pressure of the individual may decrease; in hypnosis there does not appear to any change in blood pressure. In biofeedback, again, the individual purposely learns to change their body functions voluntarily.

Answers to the Reading for Understanding about "Altering Consciousness Through Drugs"

127. abuse	151. malnutrition	175. blood pressure
128. Dependence	152. cirrhosis	176. Overdoses
129. organizing	153. Cognitive-behavior	177. Nicotine
130. tolerance	154. Alcoholics Anonymous	178. adrenaline
131. withdrawal	155. narcotics	179. neurotransmitters
132. abstinence	156. opiods	180. cigarette
133. curiosity	157. depressants	181. hydrocarbons
134. rebellion	158. euphoric	182. withdrawal
135. excitement	159. Opiate	183. anxiety
136. reinforced	160. heroin	184. Heart
137. withdrawal	161. methadone	185. passive
138. genetic	162. narcotic	186. Hallucinogenic
139. slowing	163. methaqualone	187. psychedelic
140. depressant	164. pain management	188. Hallucinations
141. productivity	165. barbiturates	189. Marijuana
142. employment	166. stimulants	190. medical
143. alcohol	167. amphetamines	191. Grinspoon
144. stimulating	168. restlessness	192. LSD
145. sedative	169. withdrawal	193. flashbacks
146. intoxicating	170. Ritalin	194. mescaline
147. dependence	171. Tolerance	195. phencyclidine
148. excuse	172. methamphetamine	196. dependence
149. healthy	173. controversy	
150. reluctant	174. cocaine	

Reflection Break # 4:

Altering Consciousness Through Drugs

1. e; 2. b; 3. h; 4. j; 5. k; 6. l; 7. g; 8. i; 9. d; 10. m; 11. c; 12. f; 13. a; 14. n

Answers to the Reading for Understanding about "Life Connections: Getting to Sleep—and Elsewhere—Without Drugs"

197. pills
198. reducing
199. tolerance
200. Psychological

201. coping
202. Cognitive behavioral
203. commitment
204. self-relaxation

Answers to the Final Review Multiple Choice Questions

1. d (p. 180)
2. b (p. 182)
3. d (p. 183)
4. a (p. 183)
5. c (p. 183)
6. d (p. 183)
7. d (p. 187)
8. a (p. 187)
9. b (p. 188)
10. c (p. 188)
11. b (p. 190)
12. d (p. 190)
13. b (p. 192)
14. b (p. 193)
15. c (p. 194)
16. d (p. 196)
17. d (p. 198)
18. d (p. 201)
19. b (p. 202)
20. d (p. 204)

Answers to Chapter 6:

Answers to the Reading for Understanding about "Learning" and "Classical Conditioning: Learning What Cones After What"

1. Learning
2. cognitive
3. behavioral
4. physical
5. associative
6. anticipate
7. Pavlov
8. salivation
9. reflex
10. conditioned
11. conditional
12. stimulus
13. conditioned
14. differently
15. observable
16. contiguous
17. relationships
18. information
19. classical
20. US
21. conditioned
22. response
23. Taste aversions
24. classical
25. single
26. nausea
27. hours
28. evolutionary

Answers to the Reading for Understanding about "Factors in Classical Conditioning"

29. recovery
30. expectations
31. Extinction
32. representation
33. predictions
34. spontaneous recovery
35. inhibition
36. Evolutionary
37. adaptive
38. Generalization
39. discrimination
40. higher-order

Reflection Break # 1:

1. *Behavioral psychologists define learning in terms of a change in observable behavior. Cognitive psychologists define learning in terms of mental changes that may or may not be observable. To the cognitive psychologist, learning is demonstrated by changes in behavior; to the behaviorist the change in behavior is the learning.*

2. Fill in the Blanks:

   (US) *Tasha's parents leaving*   **(UR)** *Tasha crying when her parents leave*

   (CS) *Aleshia the babysitter*   **(CR)** *Tasha crying at the party*

3. Matching:
1. f; 2. d; 3. b; 4. e; 5. c; 6. a

Answers to the Reading for Understanding about "Operant Conditioning: Learning What Does What to What"

41. anticipations
42. Operant
43. Thorndike
44. repetition
45. Effect
46. Punishments
47. reinforcement
48. operant
49. cumulative
50. modification
51. missiles
52. effects
53. operants
54. reinforced
55. chamber
56. Skinner box
57. pressing
58. operant
59. probability
60. Reinforcers
61. increase
62. increase
63. Immediate
64. biological
65. Secondary
66. conditioned

Answers to the Reading for Understanding about "Factors in Operant Conditioning"

67. Extinction
68. extinguished
69. unreinforced
70. spontaneous recovery
71. increase
72. events
73. effects
74. rewards
75. punishments
76. Rewards
77. reinforcement
78. effects
79. Punishments
80. hurts
81. acceptable
82. hostility
83. specific
84. generalize
85. stress
86. rewarding
87. time out

88. Discriminative	94. expect	100. Ratio
89. cues	95. four	101. scallops
90. Continuous	96. fixed-interval	102. successive approximations
91. acquisition	97. variable-interval	103. Shaping
92. partial	98. fixed-ratio	
93. resistant	99. variable-ratio	

Reflection Break # 2:

1. *In classical conditioning we learn to associate stimuli so that a simple passive response that is made to one stimulus can also be made to another. In operant conditioning organisms learn to do, or not to do things based on the consequences of their behavior. In both types of conditioning associations are formed; classical conditioning focuses on how organisms form anticipations about their environments and operant conditioning focuses on what they do about them.*

2.

	Stimulus is desired (wanted, pleasant)	Stimulus is undesired (not wanted, unpleasant)
Stimulus is applied	**Example:** *Dog is given a treat when he obeys a command.* Does behavior increase or decrease? ___Increase___ Is this reinforcement or punishment? __Reinforcement__ If it is reinforcement, is it positive or negative? __Positive__	**Example:** *You cursed, so you must do extra chores.* Does behavior increase or decrease? __Decrease__ Is this reinforcement or punishment? __Punishment__ If it is reinforcement, is it positive or negative? ___N/A___
Stimulus is removed	**Example:** *A student gets an F on a test, so they cannot got to Friday nights party.* Does behavior increase or decrease? __Decrease__ Is this Reinforcement or punishment? __Punishment__ If it is reinforcement, is it positive or negative? __N/A__	**Example:***Your headache goes away when you take asprin* Does behavior increase or decrease? __Increase__ Is this Reinforcement or punishment? __Reinforcement__ If it is reinforcement, is it positive or negative? __Negative__

3. Matching:
1. e; 2. b; 3. a; 4. d; 5. h; 6. f; 7. c; 8. g; 9. i;

Answers to the Reading for Understanding on "Cognitive Factors in Learning"

104. information	110. reinforcement	116. rewarded
105. decisions	111. performance	117. Observational
106. schemas	112. rewarded	118. model
107. contingency	113. motivation	119. vicariously
108. information	114. Bandura	
109. latent	115. observed	

Answers to the Reading for Understanding about "Life Connections: Violence in the Media and Aggression"

120. models
121. aggressive
122. arousal

123. habituating
124. cognitive
125. informing

126. consequences

Reflection Break # 3:

1. *According to Rescorla's contiguity theory Tasha cried when Aleshia arrived at the party because Aleshia's arrival (CS) provided information that the US, her parents leaving, was likely to happen.*

2. *Research into cognitive factors in learning challenges the traditional behaviorist idea that you must engage in behavior to learn. Both Latent learning and observational learning suggest that organisms learn by watching; suggesting that an organisms mental representations of the environment may be important for areas of study for psychologists.*

Answers to the Final Review Multiple Choice Questions
1. b (p. 218)
2. d (p. 218)
3. a (p. 219)
4. a (p. 219 ff.)
5. c (p. 221)
6. a (p. 221)
7. b (p. 222-223)
8. c (p. 224)
9. c (p. 225)
10. c (p. 226)
11. a (p. 226)
12. d (p. 226)
13. d (p. 226)
14. d (p. 227)
15. d (p. 227)
16. a (p. 233)
17. b (p. 233)
18. b (p. 237)
19. c (p. 239)
20. c (p. 243)

Answers to Chapter 7:

Answers to the Reading for Understanding about the "Kinds of Memory: Looking Back, Looking Ahead"

1. declarative
2. Explicit
3. autobiographical
4. implicit
5. episodic
6. semantic
7. autobiographical
8. Episodic
9. Semantic
10. know
11. remember
12. doing
13. do
14. Procedural
15. skill
16. automatic
17. priming
18. Retrospective
19. Prospective
20. habitual
21. event
22. time
23. mood

Reflection Break # 1:

Retrospective memories
(*remembering things past*)

/

Prospective memories
(*remembering things to
do in the future*)

\

Explict memories
(*memories for specific
information*)

\
\
/

Implicit memories
(*memories of how to
perform tasks*)

\
\
\

Episodic memories
(*memories of things you did*)

Semantic memories
(*memories of general information*)

Answers to the Reading for Understanding about the "Processes of Memory: Processing Information in Our Most Personal Computers"

24. Encoding
25. codes
26. storage
27. maintaining
28. maintenance rehearsal
29. elaborative rehearsal
30. metamemory
31. Retrieval
32. cues
33. Memory

Answers to the Reading for Understanding about the "Stages of Memory: Making Sense of the *Short* and *Long* of It"

34. sensory
35. short-term
36. long-term
37. register
38. decay
39. saccadic
40. second
41. whole-report
42. partial-report
43. Sperling's
44. time
45. visual
46. Icons
47. iconic
48. accurate
49. children
50. eidetic imagery
51. auditory
52. echoic
53. seconds
54. biological
55. fade
56. selective attention
57. Short-term
58. working
59. rehearsed
60. indefinitely
61. short-term
62. serial-position effect
63. attention
64. primacy
65. recency
66. chunks
67. seven
68. two
69. group
70. one
71. three
72. displaces
73. long term
74. storehouse
75. accurate
76. retrieve
77. cues
78. repression
79. Loftus
80. schemas
81. eyewitnesses
82. accuracy
83. accused
84. criminal
85. words
86. children
87. adults
88. clothing
89. facial
90. stored
91. lifetime
92. short-term
93. long-term
94. maintenance
95. elaborative
96. rehearsed

97. elaborative	106. emotionally	115. tip-of-the-tongue
98. meaningful	107. flashbulb	116. incomplete
99. deeper	108. emotionally	117. context
100. Craik	109. distinctiveness	118. recall
101. Lockhart	110. elaborate	119. efficiently
102. dimension	111. organized	120. déjà vu
103. efficiently	112. hierarchical	121. familiarity
104. attention	113. groups	122. State-dependence
105. surprising	114. recall	

Reflection Break # 2:
Memory Processes:

❖ Process by which information is modified from one sensory modality so that it can be placed in memory

❖ Process of maintaining information over time.
❖ Can be done via maintenance or elaborative rehearsal
STORAGE

❖ Process of finding stored information and bringing it to conscious awareness
❖ Dependent on Cues
RETRIEVAL

Stages of Memory:

❖ First stage in memory processing
❖ Type or stage of memory that is first encountered by a stimulus and briefly holds an impression of it.

SENSORY Memory

❖ Second stage in memory processing
❖ type or stage of memory that can hold information for up to a minute
❖ also referred to a working memory
❖ Limited to 7 ± 2 chunks
SHORT-TERM Memory

❖ Third stage in memory processing
❖ Type or stage of memory that is capable of relatively permanent storage

LONG-TERM Memory

Answers to the Reading for Understanding about "Forgetting"

123. Nonsense	135. proactive	147. hippocampus
124. meaningless	136. interference	148. codes
125. maintenance	137. Freud	149. Cognitive
126. forgetting	138. motivated	150. meaningful
127. Forgetting	139. repression	151. language
128. Recognition	140. controversial	152. trauma
129. Recall	141. repressed	153. amnesia
130. paired associates	142. recovered	154. anterograde
131. Relearning	143. accuracy	155. retrograde
132. method of savings	144. easy	
133. savings	145. infantile amnesia	
134. retroactive	146. repression	

Answers to the Reading for Understanding about "The Biology of Memory: The Brain as a Living Time Machine"

156. engram
157. electrical
158. Learning
159. neurotransmitters

160. hormones
161. long-term potentiation
162. networks
163. hippocampus

164. cortex
165. thalamus

Answers to the Reading for Understanding about "Life Connections: Using Psychology of Memory to Improve Your Memory"

166. maintenance
167. elaborative

168. exaggerated
169. method of loci

170. conceptual
171. mnemonic

Reflection Break # 3:

1. f; 2. q; 3. w; 4. k; 5. m; 6. v; 7. o; 8. b; 9. n; 10. p; 11. i; 12. j; 13. u; 14. g; 15. d; 16. c; 17. r; 18. e; 19. h; 20. y; 21. t; 22. s; 23. x; 24. l; 25. a

Answers to the Final Review Multiple Choice Questions

1.   b (p. 253)
2.   c (p. 253)
3.   a (p. 254)
4.   d (p. 254)
5.   d (p. 255)
6.   b (p. 257)
7.   b (p. 257)
8.   c (p. 257)
9.   a (p. 257)
10.   b (p. 257)
11.   b (p. 259)
12.   a (p. 261)
13.   b (p. 263)
14.   d (p. 264)
15.   b (p. 266)
16.   c (p. 258)
17.   c (p. 271)
18.   c (p. 273)
19.   b (p. 275)
20.   d (p. 280)

Answers to Chapter 8:

Answers to the Reading for Understanding about "Thinking":

1. Thinking
2. attending
3. mentally
4. decisions
5. Thinking
6. represent
7. Concepts
8. hierarchies
9. Prototypes
10. exemplars
11. understand
12. problem
13. relate
14. correspond
15. storehouse
16. represent
17. heuristic
18. analogies
19. Algorithms
20. systematic random search
21. Heuristic
22. simplify
23. reliable
24. rapidly
25. means-end
26. analogy
27. analogy
28. expertise
29. mental set
30. mislead
31. insight
32. incubation
33. functional fixedness
34. defined
35. decisions
36. heuristics
37. representativeness
38. availability
39. anchoring
40. adjustment
41. persuade
42. framing
43. favor
44. overconfident
45. retain
46. assumptions
47. confirm
48. forget
49. consistent

Reflection Break # 1:

1. *You would first attempt to understand the problem. Successful understanding of a problem requires three features: the parts of your mental representation of the problem must relate to one another in a meaningful way; the elements of your mental representation must correspond to the elements of the problem in the outer world; and you must have a storehouse of background knowledge that we can apply to the problem. Once you have represented the problem successfully you could use various strategies for attacking the problem, including algorithms, heuristic devices, and analogies.*

2. *Three internal factors make problem solving easier or harder. These include your level of expertise--experts solve problems more efficiently and rapidly than novices; whether you fall prey to a mental set--mental sets can make our work easier but may mislead us when the similarity between the problems is illusory; and whether you develop insight, or that "Aha!" experience, into the problem. Often we may need to stand back from a problem and allow for the incubation of insight. Other factors influencing the ease of problem solving include the extent to which the elements of the problem are fixed in function and the way the problem is defined. Functional fixedness or your tendency to think of objects in terms of its name or it familiar function.*

3. 1. b; 2. d; 3. e; 4. c; 5. f; 6. a; 7. a;

Answers to the Reading for Understanding about "Language: "Of Shoes and Ships and Sealing Wax,…and Whether Pigs Have Wings""

50. Language
51. displacement
52. Semanticity
53. original
54. syntax
55. Displacement
56. sequence
57. prelinguistic
58. symbolic
59. Cooing
60. babble
61. consonants
62. vowel
63. slow
64. holophrases
65. telegraphic speech
66. overregularization
67. vocabulary
68. complex
69. heredity
70. environment
71. Learning
72. imitation
73. reinforcement
74. models
75. imitation
76. observation
77. sequence
78. overregularize
79. nativist
80. psycholinguistic
81. Chomsky
82. knowledge
83. acquired
84. Language
85. cognitive
86. linguistic-relativity
87. think
88. vocabulary

89.   cognitive

Reflection Break # 2:

1. *Language is the communication of thoughts and feelings by means of symbols that are arranged according to rules of grammar. True language is distinguished from the communication systems of lower animals by properties such as semanticity, infinite creativity, and displacement. Semanticity means that the symbols of a language have meaning. Infinite creativity is the capacity to combine words into original, never been spoken before, sentences. Displacement is the ability to communicate information about events and objects from another time or place.*

2. *Language develops in a specific sequence of steps world-wide. Children make the prelinguistic sounds of crying, cooing, and babbling before true language develops. Prelinguistic sounds are not symbolic, and are therefore not considered language. During the second month babies begin cooing sounds that appear to be linked to feelings of pleasure. They begin to babble by the 5ᵗʰ or 6ᵗʰ month. In babbling babies frequently combine vowels and consonants. Single-word utterances that can express complex meanings, known as holophrases, occur at about 1 year of age and are the first linguistic utterances. Two-word utterances, known telegraphic speech are characteristic of children by the age of 2. Early language is characterized by overregualization of verbs ("She sitted down"). As time passes, their vocabulary grows larger, and sentence structure grows more complex.*

3. **Learning Theorists**: *These theorists take a nurture perspective and see language as developing according to the laws of learning. They usually refer to the concepts of imitation and reinforcement.*

    Social Cognitive Theorists: *These theorists argue that parents serve as models and that children learn language via imitation and observation.*

    Nativist Theorists: *These theorists argue that innate, or inborn factors cause children to attend to and acquire language in certain ways.*

    Psycholinguistic Theory: *According this theory language acquisition involves the interaction of environmental influences, like exposure to parental speech and reinforcement, and an inborn tendency top acquire language. Nom Chomsky calls this inborn tendency as a language acquisition device or (LAD) that prepares the nervous system to learn grammar.*

4. *The relationship between language and thinking is complex. Piaget believed that language reflects knowledge of the world but that much knowledge can be acquired with out language. He argued that language is not necessary for thinking, but makes possible cognitive activity that involves use of symbols arranged according to rules of grammar.*

    According to the linguistic relativity hypothesis proposed by Benjamin Whorf language structures the way we perceive the world. Therefore, speakers of different languages would think about the world in different ways.

    Modern cognitive scientists suggest that the vocabulary of a language suggests the range of concepts that the users have traditionally found to be useful, not their cognitive limits.

Answers to the Reading for Understanding about "Intelligence: The Most Controversial Concept in Psychology?"

90. thinking	97. s	104. overlap
91. Intelligence	98. statistical	105. Gardner
92. understand	99. primary mental abilities	106. brain
93. experience	100. spatial	107. mathematical
94. Factor	101. speed	108. musical
95. Thurstone	102. Guilford	109. personal
96. g	103. factor	110. naturalist

111.	talents	144.	mental age	177.	Kinship
112.	triarchic	145.	intelligence quotient	178.	closely
113.	creative	146.	mental	179.	distantly
114.	Analytical	147.	chronological	180.	Twin
115.	success	148.	100	181.	heritability
116.	Creative	149.	Wechsler	182.	difference
117.	street smarts	150.	verbal	183.	environmental
118.	emotional	151.	performance	184.	testing
119.	intelligence	152.	weaknesses	185.	home
120.	awareness	153.	deviation	186.	educational
121.	depression	154.	individual	187.	home environment
122.	aggression	155.	optimal	188.	music
123.	intelligence	156.	group	189.	spatial
124.	nothing	157.	100	190.	neural firing
125.	agreement	158.	substantial	191.	preliminary
126.	Wechsler	159.	70 to 75	192.	mixed
127.	representation	160.	adaptive	193.	profit
128.	problem solving	161.	mildly	194.	education
129.	resourcefulness	162.	moderately	195.	gains
130.	Creativity	163.	speech	196.	positive
131.	associations	164.	dependent	197.	higher
132.	combinations	165.	chromosomal	198.	Adoption
133.	leap	166.	brain	199.	Minnesota
134.	divergent	167.	Maternal	200.	environmental
135.	convergent	168.	Giftedness	201.	African
136.	divergent	169.	Terman's	202.	European
137.	triarchic	170.	Intelligence	203.	natural
138.	academic	171.	English	204.	below
139.	moderate	172.	valid	205.	decreased
140.	how much	173.	culturally biased	206.	heredity
141.	tests	174.	developed	207.	early childhood
142.	Stanford-Binet	175.	European American	208.	sociocultural
143.	Binet	176.	genetic	209.	atmosphere

Reflection Break # 3:

1. *Similarities and Differences include:*
   - *Factor Theory argues that intelligence is made up of a number of factors.*
   - *Both the Theory of Multiple Intelligence and the triarchic Theory propose the existence of several intelligences. They just disagree as to how many different kinds of intelligences exist.*
   - *All approaches to intelligence include some aspect of reasoning abilities.*
   - *Only the Triarchic theory argues that creative behavior is intelligent.*

2. *Creativity is the ability to make unusual and sometimes remote associations to or among the elements of a problem in order to generate new combinations. Creativity is characterized by divergent thinking. Creative people show traits such as flexibility, fluency, and independence. There is only a moderate relationship between creativity and performance on intelligence tests and academic ability. However, as you will see in the next chapter, at least one psychologist (Robert Sternberg) disagrees and argues that creativity and creative thinking is a very important aspect of intelligence.*

3. *Both the SBIS and Wechsler tests are individual tests that are administered to one person at a time. Both scales test skills like reasoning, memory and language. Only the Wechsler scales include a nonverbal "performance" scale. The Wechsler scale contains subtests that measure individual intellectual tasks and can highlight children's strengths and weaknesses. Both types of individual tests are scored by comparing the individuals performance to their age mates.*

4. *Numerous studies have shown that early environment is linked to IQ score and academic achievement. Recent research also suggests that listening to and studying music may enhance spatial reasoning in children. However, many psychologists caution that these results are preliminary and not all studies that have attempted to replicate the original studies have succeeded.*

5. *Culturally biased tests assume that the individual taking the test is familiar with the language and cultural concepts of the dominant culture in which the test is based. Most currently used intelligence tests reflect middle-class European American culture, thus may not demonstate an accurate representation of the intelligence of an individual unfamiliar with the cultural values. In the rest of your answer be sure to support your view with concrete references to theories of intelligence.*

6. *Kinship Studies compare the IQ scores of closely and distantly related people. If heritability is a factor in intelligence then closely related people should have IQ scores more similar than distantly related individuals. Results of these kinds of studies indicate moderate correlations between closely related individuals (twins, siblings, parents) and weak correlations between individuals of distant relationships (foster children and cousins).*

    Twin Studies examine the correlation between MZ (identical) and DZ (fraternal) twins reared apart or together. As expected the correlations between DZ twins is the same as those of other siblings. MZ twins on the other hand show that they are more similar than DZ twins in spatial memory and word comprehension. MZ twins reared together show higher correlations than those reared apart.

    Adoptee Studies compare the IQ scores of adopted children and their biological and adoptive parents. Several studies have found stronger relationships between the IQ scores of adopted children and their biological parents then with their adoptive parents.

Answers to the "Reading for Understanding about Life Connections: Bilingualism and Bilingual Education—Making Connections or Building Walls?"

210.	bilingual	215.	century	220.	two-way immersion
211.	cognitive	216.	total immersion	221.	political
212.	intellectual	217.	legislation	222.	against
213.	advantageous	218.	transitional	223.	poorly
214.	expands	219.	maintenance method	224.	clear-cut

Reflection Break # 4:

1. *Most people throughout the world are bilingual. Contemporary research reveals that bilingualism broadens people's perspectives and often helps them better learn their first language.*

2. *The research on the benefit of bilingual education is limited and the topic has become more of a political issue than a scientific one. In your answer you should cite research whenever possible to support your position.*

Answers to the Final Review Multiple Choice Questions

1. d (p. 292)	11. b (p. 304)
2. b (p. 292)	12. c (p. 306)
3. b (p. 295)	13. c (p. 306)
4. a (p. 296)	14. c (p. 306)
5. b (p. 297)	15. c (p. 308)
6. d (p. 298)	16. c (p. 305)
7. c (p. 299)	17. b (p. 309)
8. c (p. 300)	18. b (p. 310)
9. b (p. 301)	19. c (p. 313)
10. d (p. 304)	20. c (p. 317)

Answers to Chapter 9:

Answers to the Reading for Understanding about "The Psychology of Motivation: The Whys of Why" and "Theories of Motivation: Which Why Is Which?"

1. why
2. activate
3. goals
4. behavior
5. needs
6. incentives
7. physiological
8. psychological
9. *drives*
10. arouse
11. stronger
12. *incentive*
13. motivation
14. evolutionary
15. drive reduction
16. humanistic
17. cognitive-dissonance
18. species specific
19. evolutionary
20. fixed-action patterns
21. debate
22. drive-reduction
23. Primary
24. Acquired
25. arousal
26. activate
27. reduces
28. homeostasis
29. increase
30. decrease
31. aversive
32. novel
33. stimulus
34. survive
35. mechanical
36. Maslow
37. self-actualization
38. hierarchy
39. physiological
40. safety
41. esteem
42. individual variation
43. consistency
44. predict
45. control
46. represent
47. consistent
48. cognitive-dissonance
49. attitude-discrepant
50. liking
51. less
52. more
53. inconsistent
54. cognitive-dissonance
55. effort-justification

Reflection Break # 1:

	Evolutionary	Drive-Reduction	Humanistic	Cognitive-Dissonance
Beliefs	✓ Believes that, organisms are born with preprogrammed tendencies to behave in certain ways in certain situations. ✓ Pre-programmed tendencies are called instincts, or species-specific behaviors, or fixed-action patterns (FAPs). ✓ FAPs occur in the presence of stimuli called releasers.	✓ Argues that we are motivated to engage in behavior that reduces drives. ✓ Primary drives such as hunger and pain are based on the biological makeup of the organism. ✓ Acquired drives such as the drive for money are learned. ✓ Drives trigger arousal and activate behavior. ✓ We learn to do what reduces drives. ✓ The body has a tendency called homeostasis to maintain a steady state.	✓ Argues that people are self-aware and that behavior can be growth-oriented. ✓ Maslow believed that people are motivated by the conscious desire for personal growth, or self-actualization ✓ Self-actualization is our self-initiated striving to become whatever we believe we are capable of being. ✓ People have a hierarchy of needs. ✓ Once lower-level needs (physiological and safety) are satisfied, people strive to meet higher-level needs (love, esteem and self-actualization).	✓ According to cognitive-dissonance theory, people are motivated to understand and predict events. People must represent the world accurately in order to accomplish these goals, and therefore their cognitions need to be consistent with one another. ✓ When attitudes and behaviors are inconsistent people engage in effort justification, in that they explain their behavior to themselves in such a way that unpleasant tasks seem worth it.

Answers to the Reading for Understanding about "Hunger: Do You Go by "Tummy-Time"?

56. internal
57. satiety
58. hunger pangs
59. blood

60. hypothalamus
61. ventromedial nucleus (VMN)
62. hyperphagia

63. lateral hypothalamus
64. aphagic
65. body
66. Psychological

Reflection Break # 2:

1. **Biological:**

   - *Chewing and swallowing provide sensations of satiety or satisfaction.*
   - *Hunger pangs are stomach contractions that coincide with hunger.*
   - *The hypothalamus is a key brain structure that appears to regulate hunger. It receives information about blood sugar levels.*
   - *Two other brain structures are the ventromedial nucleus, which seems to function as a stop eating center and the lateral hypothalamus, which may function as a "start-eating center.*

Answers to the Reading for Understanding about "Sexual Motivation: The Battle Between Culture and Nature"

67. refusal
68. more
69. liberal
70. Kinsey
71. males
72. females
73. random
74. underrepresented
75. National Health and Social Life
76. sociocultural
77. males
78. females
79. more
80. religious
81. ethnicity
82. Conservative
83. highest
84. lowest

85. motivation
86. testosterone
87. women
88. development
89. regulate
90. pheromones
91. instinctive
92. vomeronasal
93. prenatal
94. moods
95. receptive
96. stimulate
97. directional
98. heterosexual
99. homosexual
100. gay males
101. lesbians
102. Bisexual
103. sexual orientation

104. does not
105. nature
106. nurture
107. Psychodynamic
108. reinforcement
109. genetic
110. prenatal
111. interaction
112. aroused
113. vasocongestion
114. myotonia
115. four
116. Excitement
117. plateau
118. Orgasm
119. seminal
120. ejaculate
121. orgasm
122. resolution

Reflection Break # 3:

1. *There are many difficulties in gathering data on sexual behavior, including the refusal of people to participate in research, and the fact that people who do respond are more willing to disclose intimate information and may be more liberal in their sexual behavior then those who do not. The results of the most recent study-the NHSLS-indicated that males report having more sex partners then women, and that people with some college report having had more sex partners. The results also suggest that both religious upbringing and ethnicity are also connected with sexual behavior. Conservative religious beliefs appear to limit number of sexual partners while European and African Americans have the highest numbers of sex partners and Asian Americans the lowest.*

2. *Engaging in sexual activity with people of one's own sex does not mean that one has a homosexual orientation. The concept of sexual orientation, which should not be confused with sexual activity, refers to the direction of one's erotic interests. The great majority of people have a heterosexual orientation in that they are sexually attracted to and interested in forming romantic relationships with people of the opposite sex. Some people, on the other hand have a homosexual orientation, in that they are attracted to and interested in forming romantic relationships with people of their own sex. Homosexual males are referred to as gay males and homosexual*

women are referred to as lesbians. Bisexual people are sexually attracted to, and interested in forming romantic relationships with, both men and women.

3. Matching:
   1. f; 2. g; 3. c; 4. d; 5. b; 6. a; 7. e

Answers to the Reading for Understanding about "Aggression: Of Australopithecines, Humans, Robins, and Testosterone"

123. aggression	133. Freudian	143. Situational
124. Ardrey	134. psychodymanic	144. individuals
125. inherited	135. catharsis	145. deindividuation
126. flawed	136. Cognitive	146. anonymity
127. structures	137. appraise	147. responsibility
128. chemicals	138. Behavioral	148. arousal
129. hypothalamus	139. consciousness	149. environmental
130. stimulation	140. choice	
131. testosterone	141. appropriate	
132. Psychological	142. reinforced	

Answers to the Reading for Understanding about "Achievement Motivation: "Just Do It""

150. achievement	153. grades	157. Learning
151. Thematic Apperception Test (TAT)	154. money	
152. high	155. goals	
	156. Performance	

Reflection Break # 4:

1. Briefly summarize the biological and chemical influences on aggressive behavior.
   - *Biological: Biological theories examine the role of the central nervous system in aggression. The hypothalamus appears to be involved in inborn reactions patterns since electrical stimulation of it triggers stereotypical aggressive behavior in lower animals.*
   - *Chemical: Chemically, hormones like testosterone appears to affect the tendencies to dominate and control other people.*

2. Compare and contrast the various psychological influences on aggressive behavior.
   - **Psychodynamic:** *Freudian theory views aggression as stemming from inevitable frustrations of daily life. According to psychodynamic theory the best way to prevent harmful aggression may be to encourage less harmful aggression. Psychoanalysts refer to the venting of aggressive impulses as catharsis.*
   - **Cognitive:** *Cognitive perspectives, assert that our behavior is influenced by our values and that it is natural for people to attempt to understand their environment and make decisions. That is, people appraise their situation and decide to whether to act aggressively depending on the outcome of that appraisal.*
   - **Behavioral:** *Behavioral theories view aggression as stemming from experience and reinforcement of aggressive skills.*
   - **Social Cognitive:** *Social-cognitive theorists believe that consciousness and choice play key roles in aggressive behavior among humans, that is we are not likely to act aggressively unless we believe that aggression is appropriate under the circumstances and likely to be reinforced.*

3. Compare performance and learning goals. Which of the two are you "driven" by in your schoolwork?
   Performance goals are tangible rewards, such as money or getting into graduate school.
   Learning goals involve the enhancement of knowledge or skills.
   The remaining parts of this answer will depend on individual differences.

Answers to the Reading for Understanding about "Emotion: Adding Color to Life"

158. color	160. motivate	162. cognitions
159. emotion	161. sympathetic	163. behavioral

164. universal
165. Facial expressions
166. survival
167. Ekman
168. facial-feedback hypothesis
169. emotional

170. Commonsense
171. James-Lange
172. follows
173. Cannon-Bard
174. accompany
175. cognitive appraisal

176. appraisal
177. James-Lange
178. cognitive appraisal

Reflection Break # 5:

Compare the four theories of Emotion by completing the following:

Theory	Proposes
Commonsense Theory	*Something happens that is interpreted and the emotion follows.*
James-Lange Theory	*Emotions follow our behavioral responses to events.* *Stimuli trigger specific instinctive patterns of arousal and action.*
Cannon-Bard Theory	*Events trigger bodily responses and the experience of an emotion simultaneously.* *Emotions accompany body responses but are no caused by the body responses.*
Cognitive Appraisal Theory	*The label given to an emotion depends on our cognitive appraisal.* *Emotions are associated with similar patterns of a body arousal.* *Social comparison is used to decide the appropriate emotional response.*

Answers to the Reading For Understanding About: "Life Connections: Obesity And Eating Disorders: This Meal Is Too Big; This Meal Is Too Little—Can You Ever Get It Just Right?"

179. overweight
180. heredity
181. adipose
182. metabolic
183. Psychological
184. nutritional
185. decreasing
186. Behavior modification
187. eating

188. Anorexia nervosa
189. female
190. socioeconomic
191. Bulimia nervosa
192. adolescence
193. origins
194. anorexia
195. family
196. child abuse

197. Sociocultural
198. genetic
199. Treatment
200. denial
201. nasogastric
202. Depression
203. serotonin
204. family therapy
205. Cognitive behavioral

Answers to the Final Review Multiple Choice Questions:

1. b (p. 337)
2. c (p. 337)
3. c (p. 339)
4. c (p. 340)
5. a (p. 342)
6. d (p. 342-3)
7. b (p. 344)
8. a (p. 346)
9. b (p. 346)
10. c (p. 347)

11. d (p. 348)
12. b (p. 349)
13. c (p. 350)
14. c (p. 354)
15. a (p. 354)
16. a (p. 357)
17. d (p. 358)
18. b (p. 361)
19. c (p. 363)
20. b (p. 367)

Answers to Chapter 10:

Answers to the Reading for Understanding about "Health Psychology"

1. Health
2. psychological
3. illness
4. stress
5. immune
6. health care
7. intervention

Answers to the Reading for Understanding about "Stress: Presses, Pushes, and Pulls"

8. stress
9. eustress
10. physical
11. stress
12. Daily hassles
13. uplifts
14. household
15. time-pressure
16. financial
17. worrying
18. loneliness
19. health
20. life changes
21. heart disease
22. cancer
23. health
24. limitations
25. causal
26. correlational
27. less
28. personalities
29. appraise
30. Conflict
31. frustrating
32. approach-approach
33. avoidance-avoidance
34. approach-avoidance
35. multiple approach-avoidance
36. least
37. more
38. attractive
39. undesirable
40. complex
41. beliefs
42. activating
43. irrational beliefs
44. catastrophize
45. social approval
46. perfectionism
47. disappointment
48. Type A
49. time urgency
50. impatience
51. self-improvement
52. Type B
53. ambitious

Reflection Break # 1:

1. What is Health Psychology?

   Health psychology studies the relationships between psychological factors and the prevention and treatment of physical health problems. Health psychologists study the ways in which: psychological factors such as stress, behavior patterns and attitudes can lead or aggravate illness; people can cope with stress; the way that stress and pathogens interact to influence the immune system; people decide whether to seek health care; and psychological forms of intervention like health education and behavior modification can contribute to physical health.

2. Briefly explain how your cognitions (beliefs & attitudes) affect how external stressors like daily hassles and conflict have on your well being.

   Stress is the demand made on an organism to adapt, cope or adjust. Whereas some stress-called eustress-is desirable to keep us alert and occupied, too much stress can tax our adjustive capacities and contribute to physical health problems. Albert Ellis argues that our beliefs about events, as well as the events themselves, can be stressors. He shows that negative activating events (A) can be made more aversive (C) when irrational beliefs (B) compound their effects. People often catastrophize negative events. Two common irrational beliefs are excessive needs for social approval and perfectionism. Both set the stage for disappointment and increased stress.

Answers to the Reading for Understanding about "Psychological Moderators of Stress"

54. one-to-one
55. moderating
56. Psychological
57. self-confident
58. Self-efficacy expectations
59. lower
60. arousal
61. commitment
62. challenge
63. control
64. locus of control
65. psychologically hardy
66. sense of humor
67. less
68. immune
69. cope
70. endorphins
71. Predictability
72. control
73. illusion
74. internals
75. externals
76. Social support
77. Introverts
78. cancer
79. emotional
80. socializing

Answers to the Reading for Understanding about "Stress and the Body"

81.	general adaptation syndrome	89.	adrenal cortex	98.	leukocytes
82.	three	90.	Corticosteroids	99.	antigens
83.	alarm	91.	adrenal medulla	100.	inflammation
84.	brain	92.	arouses	101.	Psychoneuroimmunology
85.	endocrine	93.	resistance	102.	stress
86.	sympathetic	94.	parasympathetic	103.	depresses
87.	hypothalamus	95.	dangerous	104.	Steroids
88.	pituitary	96.	suppresses		
		97.	immune		

Reflection Break # 2:

1. What psychological factors can you use to moderate the effect that stress has on your health?

    There is no one-to-one relationship between stress and physical or psychological health problems. But, none-the-less, psychological factors do play a role in influencing or moderating the effects of stress. Psychological moderators of stress include: self-efficacy expectations, psychological hardiness, a sense of humor, predictability and social support.

    - ***Self-efficacy expectations:*** *Self-efficacy expectations encourage us to persist in difficult tasks and to endure discomfort. Self-efficacy expectations are also connected with lower levels of adrenaline and noradrenaline, thus having a braking effect on bodily arousal.*
    - ***Psychological hardiness:*** *Psychological hardiness among business executives is characterized by commitment, they involved themselves rather then feeling alienated; challenge, they believe that change, rather than stability is normal in life; and control, they felt and behaved as though they were influential and demonstrated what Julian Rotter termed an internal locus of control. Kosbasa argues that psychological hardy people are more resistant to stress because they choose to face it and interpret stress as making life more interesting.*
    - ***A Sense of Humor:*** *Research evidence shows that students who produce humor under adversity experience less stress. Moreover, watching humorous videos apparently enhances the functioning of the immune system. How exactly humor helps people cope with stress is uncertain. One possibility is that laughter stimulates the output of endorphins, which could benefit the functioning of the immune system.*
    - ***Predictability:*** *Predictability allows us to brace ourselves, and control permits us to plan ways of coping with it. Control, even the illusion of being in control helps people cope with stress.*
    - ***Social Support:*** *Social support has been shown to help people resist infectious diseases such as colds. Introverts, people who lack social skill and live by themselves seem more prone to developing infectious diseases. It also helps people cope with the stress of cancer and other health problems. Kinds of social support include expression of emotional concern, instrumental aid, information, appraisal, and simple socializing.*

2. Briefly summarize the physical effects of prolonged stress on the body.

    Research shows that stress suppresses the immune system. The immune system has several functions that combat disease. The general adaptation syndrome (GAS), is a cluster of bodily changes triggered by stressors. The GAS consists of three stages: alarm, resistance, and exhaustion. During the alarm reaction stage the body prepares it self for defense. This reaction involves a number of body changes that are initiated by the brain and further regulated by the endocrine system and the sympathetic division of the autonomic nervous system. Corticosteroids help resist stress by fighting inflammation and allergic reactions. Adrenaline arouses the body by activating the sympathetic nervous system, which is highly active during the alarm and resistance stages of the GAS. Sympathetic activity is characterized by rapid heartbeat and respiration rate, release of stores of sugar, muscle tension, and other responses that deplete the body's supply of energy. The parasympathetic division of the ANS predominates during the exhaustion stage of the GAS and is connected with depression and inactivity. Prolonged stress is dangerous.

    Psychoneuroimmunology is a sub-specialty of biology, psychology and medicine in which the relationships between psychological factors, the nervous system, the endocrine system, the immune system and disease are examined. One of the major areas of concern in psychoneuroimmunology is the effect of stress on the immune

Answers to the Reading for Understanding about "Psychology and Health: Headaches, Cardiovascular Disorders, Cancer and Sexually Transmitted Infections"

105. multifactorial
106. interaction
107. genetic
108. predispositions
109. Brody
110. psychological
111. headaches
112. muscle tension
113. stress
114. catastrophize
115. migraine
116. Type A
117. monosodium glutamate (MSG)
118. hormonal
119. coronary heart
120. cholesterol
121. fatty
122. tension
123. inactivity
124. Cancer
125. metastasize
126. cancer
127. African
128. European
129. preventing
130. treating
131. risks
132. sexually transmitted infections (STI's)
133. Women
134. Psychological
135. deny
136. behavior

Answers to the Reading for Understanding about "Life Connections: Preventing and Coping with Health Problems-Stress, Headaches, Heart Disease, Cancer and Sexually Transmitted Infections"

137. Stress
138. irrational thoughts
139. exercising
140. thoughts
141. change
142. Cognitive-behavioral
143. aware
144. accuracy
145. incompatible
146. rewarding
147. arousal
148. wrong
149. stressor
150. arousal
151. reduce
152. progressive relaxation
153. Exercise
154. cardiovascular
155. resist
156. stress
157. irrational
158. arousal
159. exercising
160. smoking
161. weight
162. hypertension
163. low density lipoprotein
164. A
165. anger
166. limiting
167. stress
168. Prevention
169. transmission
170. consequences
171. techniques
172. knowledge
173. behave
174. attitudes
175. ignoring
176. abstinent
177. monogamous

Reflection Break # 3:

1. How can an understanding of Health Psychology help a person remain healthy?

    The Multifactorial Approach to health and coping with stress recognizes that many factors, including biological, psychological, sociocultural, and environmental factors, affect our health. Nearly 1 million preventable deaths occur each year in the United States. Measures such as quitting smoking, eating properly, exercising, and controlling alcohol intake would prevent nearly 80% of them.

    Health Psychologists participate in research concerning the origins of headaches, including stress and tension. Health Psychologists help people alleviate headaches by reducing tension. They have also developed biofeedback training methods for helping people cope with migraines.

    Health Psychologists have participated in research that shows that the risk factors for coronary heart disease include family history; physiological conditions such as hypertension and high levels of serum cholesterol; behavior patterns such as heavy drinking, smoking, eating fatty foods, and Type A behavior; work overload; chronic tension and fatigue; and physical inactivity. They help people achieve healthier cardiovascular systems by stopping smoking, controlling weight, reducing hypertension, lowering LDL levels, changing Type A behavior, reducing hostility, and exercising.

    Health. Research shows that stress suppresses the immune system. The immune system has several functions that combat disease. Psychologists have participated in research that shows that the risk factors for cancer include family history, smoking, drinking alcohol, eating animal fats, sunbathing, and stress. The following measures can be helpful in preventing and treating cancer: controlling exposure to behavioral risk factors for cancer, having regular medical checkups, regulating exposure to stress, and vigorously fighting cancer if it develops.

2. After reading this chapter what can you do to cope with the stresses of your life?
   Three ways for coping with stress include: controlling irrational thoughts, lowering arousal and exercising.

   a. ***Control Irrational Thinking:*** *People often feel pressure from their own thoughts. In order to keep them from producing stress we must change them. Cognitive –behavioral psychologists have outlined a three-step process for doing so. It involves becoming aware of the thoughts, preparing and practicing incompatible thoughts, and rewarding one self for changing.*

   b. ***Relax:*** *Stress tends to trigger arousal. Arousal serves as a sign that something may be wrong; however, once we are aware that a stressor is acting on us, high levels of arousal are not helpful. Psychologists have developed many methods for teaching people to reduce arousal including meditation, biofeedback training, and progressive relaxation. In progressive relaxation, people purposefully tense and then relax muscle groups to develop awareness of muscle tensions and learn how to let the tensions go.*

   c. ***Exercise:*** *Exercise enhances our psychological well-being and also strengthens the cardiovascular system, our fitness, or "condition" so that we can better resist the bodily effects of stress.*

Answers to the Final Review Multiple Choice Questions:

1. d (p. 378)
2. a (p. 379)
3. c (p. 379)
4. c (p. 383)
5. c (p. 384)
6. c (p. 385)
7. d (p. 386)
8. a (p. 386)
9. b (p. 386)
10. a (p. 387)
11. d (p. 386)
12. d (p. 389)
13. a (p. 384)
14. d (p. 392)
15. c (p. 393)
16. c (p. 394)
17. d (p. 396)
18. c (p. 397)
19. c (p. 397)
20. d (p. 401)

Answers to Chapter 11:

Answers to the Reading for Understanding about "Introduction to Personality: "Why Are You Sad and Glad and Bad?"

1. Personality
2. develops
3. predict
4. perspectives

Answers to the Reading for Understanding about "The Psychodynamic Perspective: Excavating the Iceberg"

5. Freud
6. conflict
7. psychodynamic
8. iceberg
9. conscious
10. preconscious
11. unconscious
12. conflict
13. external
14. internalized
15. expression
16. conflict
17. psychoanalysis
18. psychic
19. id
20. ego
21. practical
22. id
23. anxiety
24. superego
25. moral
26. sexual
27. eros
28. libido
29. erogenous
30. five
31. conflict
32. Fixation
33. analytical
34. collective
35. archetypes
36. individual
37. creative
38. superiority
39. parent-child
40. love
41. psychosocial
42. sexual
43. Freud
44. scientific
45. possession
46. sexuality
47. distort
48. psychic structures
49. inaccuracies
50. methods

Reflection Break # 1:
Part I.
1. s; 2. l; 3. c; 4. n; 5. d; 6. z; 7. u; 8. y; 9. k; 10. r; 11. v; 12. aa; 13. b; 14. gg; 15. w; 16. m; 17. f; 18. e; 19. o; 20. g; 21. h; 22. t; 23. j; 24. cc; 25. x; 26. a; 27. p; 28. bb; 29. q; 30. dd; 31. hh; 32. ee; 33. i; 34. ff

Part II.
1. b; 2. d; 3. a; 4. C

Answers to the Reading for Understanding about "The Trait Perspective: The Five Dimensional Universe""

51. Traits
52. Hippocrates
53. humors
54. Galton
55. Allport
56. factor analysis
57. extraversion
58. neuroticism
59. five
60. Cross cultural
61. mature
62. shaped
63. correlating
64. Trait
65. adjustment
66. descriptive
67. circular

Answers to the Reading for Understanding about "Learning Theory Perspective: All the Things You Do"

68. observable
69. unconscious
70. Watson
71. environment
72. heritability
73. Skinner
74. freedom
75. reinforcements
76. *Walden Two*
77. shape
78. consciousness
79. choice
80. Social-cognitive
81. reciprocal determinism
82. situational
83. person
84. Competencies
85. information
86. expectancies
87. Self-efficacy
88. external
89. Self-regulation
90. select
91. Learning

92. conditions	95. inner	98. genetic
93. reinforcements	96. self-awareness	
94. observing	97. traits	

Reflection Break # 2:

Compare and contrasts the Trait, Learning and Social Cognitive Theories of personality in the chart below:

	Premise	Critique
Trait	*Traits are personality elements that are inferred from behavior and that account for behavioral consistency. Trait theory adopts a descriptive approach to personality.*	*Critics argue that trait theory is descriptive not explanatory and that the explanations that are provided by trait theory are circular in that they restate what is observed and do not explain it.*
Behavioral	*Behaviorists believe that we should focus on observable behavior rather than hypothesized psychic forces, and that we should emphasize the situational determinants of behavior. John B. Watson the "father" of modern behaviorism, rejected notions of mind and personality altogether. He also argued that he could train any child to develop into a professional or a criminal by controlling the child's environment. B.F. Skinner adopted Watson's view in the 1930's. B. F. Skinner opposed the idea of personal freedom and emphasized the effects that reinforcements have on behavior.*	*Behavioral theorists have highlighted the importance of referring to publicly observable behaviors in theorizing. However, behaviorism does not describe, explain, or suggest the richness of inner human experience.*
Social Cognitive	*Developed by Albert Bandura, this theory has a cognitive orientation and focuses on learning by observation. Bandura proposes a pattern of reciprocal determinism in which people influence the environment just as much as the environment influences them. To predict behavior, social-cognitive theorists consider situational variables (rewards and punishments) and person variables (competencies, encoding strategies, expectancies, emotions, and self-regulatory systems and plans).*	*Critics of social-cognitive theory note that it does not address self-awareness or adequately account for the development of traits It may also not pay enough attention to genetic variation in explaining individual differences in behavior.*

Answers to the Reading for Understanding about "The Humanistic-Existential Perspective: How Becoming?"

99. Humanism	106. self	112. personal experience
100. Existentialists	107. frame of reference	113. unscientific
101. personal meaning	108. actualize	114. circular
102. unconscious	109. unconditional positive	115. learning
103. self-actualization	regard	
104. Maslow	110. conditions of worth	
105. selves	111. genuine	

Answers to the Reading for Understanding about "The Socio-cultural Perspective: Personality in Context"

116. cultural	122. Eastern	128. retain
117. socioeconomic	123. Acculturation	129. blend
118. gender	124. assimilated	130. higher
119. Individualists	125. lose	131. sociocultural
120. Collectivists	126. separation	132. cultural
121. Western	127. bicultural	133. expectations

Reflection Break # 3:

Compare and contrast the Humanistic–Existential and Socio-cultural perspectives on personality in the chart below.

	Premise	Critique
Humanisitc-Exisitential	Humanism puts people and self-awareness at the center and argues that we are capable of free choice, self-fulfillment, and ethical behavior. Existentialism argues that our lives have meaning when we give them meaning. Whereas Freud wrote that people are motivated to gratify unconscious drives, humanistic psychologists believe that people have a conscious need for self-actualization, or to become all that they can be.	Humanistic–existential theories have tremendous appeal because of their focus on the importance of personal experience. Self-actualization, like trait theories yields circular explanations for behavior. Humanistic theories, like learning theories have little to say about the development of traits and personality types.
Socio-Cultural	The socio-cultural perspective encourages us to consider the roles of ethnicity, gender, culture, and socioeconomic status in personality formation, behavior, and mental processes.	The socio-cultural perspective provides valuable insights into the roles of ethnicity, gender, culture and socioeconomic status in personality formation. Without reference to socio-cultural factors we may not be able to understand generalities about behavior and cognitive processes. However, we will not be able to understand how individuals think, behave and feel about themselves within a cultural setting.

Answers to the Reading for Understanding about "Measurement of Personality"

134.	predict	141.	forced-choice	148.	ambiguous
135.	Behavior rating scales	142.	disorders	149.	Rorschach
136.	assessing	143.	validity	150.	Thematic Apperception
137.	adjustment	144.	clinical	151.	TAT
138.	aptitudes	145.	response sets		
139.	Objective	146.	empirically		
140.	multiple-choice	147.	Projective		

Reflection Break # 4:

1. d; 2. e; 3. c; 4. g; 5. f; 6. b; 7. a; 8. h

Answers to the Reading for Understanding about *"Life Connections*: Gender Typing—On Becoming a Woman or a Man"

152.	different	167.	women	182.	aggressiveness
153.	Biological	168.	men	183.	gender typing
154.	personality	169.	aggressively	184.	identification
155.	small	170.	Frodi	185.	Oedipus
156.	similar	171.	justified	186.	Electra
157.	verbal	172.	women	187.	Social-cognitive
158.	language	173.	physical allure	188.	identification
159.	Males	174.	gender-typing	189.	socialization
160.	math	175.	Biological	190.	aggressively
161.	computational	176.	natural selection	191.	Gender-schema
162.	women	177.	evolutionary	192.	lenses of gender
163.	men	178.	structures	193.	culture
164.	dominance	179.	organization	194.	gender roles
165.	shallower	180.	hormones	195.	labels
166.	supportive	181.	Testosterone	196.	schema

197. genetic

198. environmental

Answers to the Final Review Multiple Choice Questions:

1. c (p. 414)
2. c (p. 414)
3. c (p. 416)
4. c (p. 416)
5. c (p. 416)
6. d (p. 416)
7. b (p. 417)
8. c (p. 418)
9. d (p. 419)
10. a (p. 419)
11. d (p. 420)
12. a (p. 422)
13. b (p. 426)
14. a (p. 426-27)
15. c (p. 427)
16. c (p. 432)
17. d (p. 431)
18. c (p. 432)
19. c (p. 435)
20. c (p. 441)

Answers to Chapter 12:

Answers to the Reading for Understanding about "Historic Views of Psychological Disorders: "The Devil Made Me Do It"?"

1. spiritual intervention
2. Greeks
3. devil

Answers to the Reading for Understanding about "What are Psychological Disorders and Classifying Psychological Disorders."

4. disabilities
5. disorders
6. classification
7. observable symptoms
8. multiaxial
9. I
10. II
11. III
12. IV
13. V
14. diagnoses
15. no
16. was
17. vote
18. politically
19. health
20. more
21. disorder
22. Bailey
23. oppression
24. departure
25. prenatal
26. lifestyle

Reflection Break # 1:

1. II; 2. V; 3 I; 4. III; 5. IV

Answers to the Reading for Understanding about "Anxiety Disorders"

27. Anxiety
28. phobias
29. fears
30. panic
31. persistent anxiety
32. obsessions
33. compulsions
34. stress
35. Posttraumatic
36. acute
37. psychodynamic
38. repressing
39. unconscious impulses
40. learning
41. observational learning
42. Cognitive
43. Biological
44. genetically predisposed
45. Anxiety
46. concordance
47. biochemical
48. neurotransmitters

Answers to the Reading for Understanding about "Dissociative Disorders"

49. Dissociative
50. amnesia
51. fugue
52. identity
53. depersonalization
54. odder
55. skepticism
56. Psychodynamic
57. Learning
58. shame
59. sexual

Answers to the Reading for Understanding about "Somatoform Disorders"

60. Somatoform
61. conversion
62. la belle indifférence
63. hypochondriasis
64. hysterical
65. physical
66. Psychodynamic

Reflection Break # 2:

Compare and contrast the Anxiety, Dissociative and Somatoform Disorders by completing the following chart.

	Characteristic Symptoms	**Theoretical Origins**
Anxiety Disorders	Anxiety disorders are characterized by motor tension, feelings of dread, and overarousal of the sympathetic branch of the autonomic nervous system. These disorders include: ❖ Irrational, excessive fears, or phobias, or persistent fears of specific objects; ❖ Panic disorder, characterized by sudden	❖ The psychodynamic perspective tends to view anxiety disorders as conflicts originating in childhood. Generalized Anxiety disorder is explained as difficulty in repressing primitive impulses and obsessions are explained as

	attacks in which people typically fear that they may be losing control or going crazy. ❖ *Generalized or pervasive anxiety, in which the central feature is persistent anxiety;* ❖ *Obsessive-compulsive disorder, in which people are troubled by intrusive thoughts (obsessions) or impulses to repeat some activity (compulsions).* ❖ *Stress disorders, in which a stressful event is followed by persistent fears and intrusive thoughts about the event.* ❖ *Posttraumatic stress disorder can occur 6 months or more after the event, whereas acute stress disorder occurs within a month.*	*leakage of unconscious impulses.* ❖ *Learning theorists view phobias as conditioned fears.* ❖ *Social Cognitive learning theorists note that observational learning plays a role in acquisition of fears.* ❖ *Cognitive theorists focus on ways in which people interpret threats.* ❖ *Biological Factors also play a role in anxiety disorders. Some people may be genetically predisposed to acquire certain kinds of fears.* ❖ *Some psychologists suggest that biochemical factors-which could be inherited-may create a predisposition toward anxiety disorders. One such factor is faulty regulation of neurotransmitters.*
Dissociative Disorders	*Dissociative disorders are characterized by sudden, temporary changes in consciousness or self-identity.* ❖ *Dissociative amnesia involves loss of memory or self-identity.* ❖ *Dissociative fugue, involves forgetting plus fleeing and adopting a new identity;* ❖ *Dissociative identity disorder, otherwise known as multiple personality disorder, in which a person behaves as if more than one personality occupies his or her body;* ❖ *Depersonalization is characterized by feelings that one is not real or that one is standing outside oneself.*	*Dissociative disorders are some of the odder psychological disorders and there is some skepticism about their existence.* ❖ *Psychodynamic theory proposes that people with Dissociative disorders use massive repression to keep disturbing memories or ideas out of mind.* ❖ *Learning theories propose that people with Dissociative disorders have learned not to think about bad memories or disturbing impulses to avoid feelings of guilt and shame. Surveys find that the memories being avoided may involve episodes of childhood sexual or physical abuse.*
Somatoform Disorders	*People with Somatoform disorders exhibit or complain of physical problems, although no medical evidence of such problems can be found.* ❖ *In conversion disorder, stress is converted into a physical symptom, and the individual may show la belle indifférence (indifference to the symptom).* ❖ *In hypochondriasis people insist that they are suffering from a serious physical illness, even though no medical evidence of illness can be found.*	❖ *These disorders were once called "hysterical neuroses" and expected to be found more often among women. However, they are also found among men and may reflect the relative benefits of focusing on physical symptoms rather than fears and conflicts.* ❖ *Psychodynamic theory proposes that symptoms of Somatoform disorders protect the individual from feelings of shame and guilt, or another source of stress.*

Answers to the Reading for Understanding about " Mood Disorders"

67.	Mood	71.	Bipolar	75.	bipolar disorder
68.	Depression	72.	manic	76.	productive
69.	Major	73.	genius	77.	inspiration
70.	delusional	74.	depression	78.	Jamison

79.	creativity	84.	Leaning	89.	Genetic
80.	learned helplessness	85.	Cognitive	90.	serotonin
81.	attributional	86.	Self-blaming		
82.	serotonin	87.	global		
83.	psychodynamic	88.	biological		

Answers to the Reading for Understanding about "Schizophrenia"

91.	Schizophrenia	100.	Disorganized	109.	ban
92.	delusions	101.	social impairment	110.	M'Naghten
93.	hallucinations	102.	Catatonic	111.	understand
94.	stupor	103.	waxy flexibility	112.	wrong
95.	mood	104.	psychodynamic	113.	irresistible
96.	social interaction	105.	Learning	114.	1%
97.	schizophrenia	106.	Biologically	115.	institutionalized
98.	Paranoid	107.	dopamine	116.	longer
99.	delusions	108.	multifactorial		

Answers to the Reading for Understanding about "Personality Disorders"

117.	Personality	122.	antisocial	127.	Cognitive
118.	personality	123.	shame	128.	Genetic
119.	paranoid	124.	avoidant	129.	Antisocial
120.	schizotypal	125.	Psychodynamic		
121.	Social withdrawal	126.	Learning		

Reflection Break # 3:

Compare and contrast the Mood, Schizophrenic and Personality Disorders by completing the following chart.

	Characteristic Symptoms	**Theoretical Origins**
Mood Disorders	*Mood disorders involve disturbances in expressed emotions.* ❖ *Depression is the most common of the psychological disorders. Major depression is characterized by persistent feelings of sadness, loss of interest, feelings of worthlessness or guilt, inability to concentrate, and physical symptoms that may include disturbances in regulation of eating and sleeping. Feelings of unworthiness and guilt may be so excessive that they are considered delusional.* ❖ *Bipolar disorder, formerly known as manic-depressive disorder, is characterized by dramatic swings in mood between elation and depression; manic episodes include pressured speech and rapid flight of ideas.*	❖ *From the psychodynamic perspective, bipolar disorder may be seen as alternating states in which the personality is dominated by the superego and ego.* ❖ *Learning theorists, on the other hand, suggest that depressed people behave as though they cannot obtain reinforcement and point to links between depression and learned helplessness.* ❖ *Cognitive theorists note that people who tend to ruminate about feelings of depression are more likely to prolong them. And Seligman notes that people who are depressed are more likely than other people to make internal (self-blaming), stable, and global (large) attributions for failures; factors that they are relatively powerless to change.* ❖ *Researchers are also searching for biological factors in mood disorders. Genetic factors involving regulation of neurotransmitters may also be involved in mood disorders. For example, bipolar disorder has been linked to inappropriate levels of the neurotransmitter glutamate. Moreover,*

		people with severe depression often respond to drugs that heighten the action of serotonin.
Schizophrenic Disorders	*Schizophrenia is a most severe psychological disorder that is characterized by disturbances in thought and language, such as loosening of associations and delusions; in perception and attention, as found in hallucinations; in motor activity, as shown by a stupor or by excited behavior; in mood, as in flat or inappropriate emotional responses; and in social interaction, as in social withdrawal and absorption in daydreams or fantasy.* ❖ *Paranoid schizophrenia is characterized largely by systematized delusions and frequently related auditory hallucinations. They often have delusions of grandeur and persecution.* ❖ *Disorganized schizophrenia is characterized by incoherence, loosening of associations, disorganized behavior and delusions and flat or highly inappropriate emotional responses; extreme social impairment is common with disorganized schizophrenia.* ❖ *Catatonic schizophrenia is characterized by a striking motor impairment; often it is a slowing of activity into a stupor that may suddenly change into an agitated phase. Catatonic schizophrenic may also show a waxy flexibility in which the person maintains positions into which they have been manipulated by others and mutism.*	❖ *The pychodynamic view argues that schizophrenia occurs because the ego is overwhelmed by sexual or aggressive impulses form the id and the person regresses to an early phase of the oral stage.* ❖ *Learning theorists explain schizophrenia in terms of conditioning and observational learning.* ❖ *Biologically, schizophrenia is connected with smaller brains, especially fewer synapses in the prefrontal region, and larger ventricles in the brain.* ❖ *According to the dopamine theory of schizophrenia, people with schizophrenia use more dopamine than other people do, perhaps because they have more dopamine in the brain along with more dopamine receptors than other people.* ❖ *According to the multifactorial model, genetic vulnerability to schizophrenia may interact with other factors, such as stress, complications during pregnancy and childbirth, and quality of parenting, to cause the disorder to develop.*
Personality Disorders	*Personality disorders are inflexible, maladaptive behavior patterns that impair personal or social functioning and cause distress for the individual or others.* ❖ *The defining trait of paranoid personality disorder is suspiciousness.* ❖ *People with schizotypal personality disorders show oddities of thought, perception, and behavior but the bizarre behaviors of schizophrenia are absent.* ❖ *Social withdrawal, indifference to relationships and flat emotional response are the major characteristic of schizoid personality disorder.* ❖ *People with antisocial personality disorders persistently violate the rights of others and are in conflict with the law. They show little or no guilt or shame over their misdeeds and are largely undeterred by punishment.* ❖ *People with avoidant personality disorder tend to avoid entering relationships for fear of rejection and criticism.*	❖ *Psychodynamic theory connected many personality disorders with hypothesized Oedipal problems.* ❖ *Learning theorists suggest that childhood experiences can contribute to maladaptive ways of relating to others.* ❖ *Cognitive psychologists find that antisocial adolescents encode social information in ways that bolster their misdeeds.* ❖ *Genetic factors may be involved in some personality disorders.* ❖ *Antisocial personality disorder tends to run in families and may develop from some combination of genetic vulnerability (less gray matter in the prefrontal cortex of the brain, which may provide lower--than—normal levels of arousal), inconsistent discipline, and cynical processing of social information.*

Answers to the Reading for Understanding about "Life Connections: Understanding and Preventing Suicide"

130. suicide
131. hopelessness
132. Rathus
133. stressful
134. social support
135. sexuality
136. achieve
137. substance abuse
138. problem solving
139. genetic
140. environmental
141. warning
142. suicide
143. not true
144. psychosis
145. signals
146. sleeping
147. concentrating
148. decline
149. social relationships
150. mood
151. professional
152. listener
153. solutions
154. care

Answers to the Final Review Multiple Choice Questions

1. c (p. 455)
2. d (p. 455)
3. a (p. 459)
4. d (p. 459)
5. b (p. 459)
6. c (p. 459)
7. c (p. 460)
8. d (p. 461-2)
9. d (p. 463)
10. a (p. 463)
11. b (p. 464)
12. b (p. 465)
13. c (p. 465)
14. c (p. 466)
15. b (p. 466)
16. a (p. 468)
17. c (p. 470)
18. b (p. 471)
19. b (p. 478)
20. d (p. 475)

Answers for Chapter 13:

Answers to the Reading for Understanding about "What Is Therapy? The Search for a "Sweet Oblivious Antidote"

1. Psychotherapy
2. badly
3. possession
4. exorcism
5. Asylums
6. humanitarian
7. treatment
8. warehousing

Answers to the Reading for Understanding about "Psychodynamic Therapies: Digging Deep Within"

9. Freud
10. childhood
11. conflicts
12. libidinal
13. psychoanalysis
14. catharsis
15. free association
16. dream
17. repress
18. resistance
19. interpretation
20. transference
21. parents
22. dreams
23. unconscious
24. manifest
25. latent
26. wish fulfillment
27. phallic symbols
28. years
29. intense
30. directive
31. ego
32. id

Answers to the Reading for Understanding about "Humanistic-Existential Therapies: Strengthening the Self"

33. conflicts
34. unconscious
35. humanistic-existential
36. Client-centered
37. genuine
38. unconditional positive regard
39. empathic understanding
40. genuineness
41. popular
42. non-directive
43. Gestalt
44. social masks
45. directive
46. aware
47. accept
48. choices
49. dialogue
50. I take responsibility
51. projection

Reflection Break # 1:

Compare and contrast Psychodynamic, Client-centered, and Gestalt therapy by completing the table below.

Type of Therapy	Characteristics
Psychodynamic Therapy	*The goals of psychoanalysis are to provide self-insight in to the conflicts that are believed to be the roots of a person's problems; encourage the spilling forth, or catharsis of psychic energy; and replace defensive behavior with coping behavior. The main method is free association, in which the client is asked to talk about any topic that comes to mind; but dream analysis and interpretations are used as well. Freud felt that although repressed impulses clamor for release, the ego persists in trying to repress unacceptable urges and shows resistance, or the tendency to block the free expression of impulses and primitive ideas. Modem approaches are briefer, less intense, and more directive, and the therapist and client usually sit face to face. Additionally, the focus tends to be on the ego rather than the id.*
Client-Centered Therapy	*Whereas psychodynamic therapies focus on internal conflicts and unconscious processes humanistic-existential therapies focus on the quality of the clients' subjective, conscious experience. Client-centered therapy uses nondirective methods to help clients overcome obstacles to self-actualization. His method is intended to help people get in touch with their genuine feelings and pursue their own interests, regardless of other people's wishes. In client-centered therapy the therapist shows a respect for clients as human beings with unique values and goals, or unconditional positive regard; empathic understanding, or a recognition of the client's experiences and feelings; and genuineness, or an openness in responding to the client. Client-centered therapists do not tell others what to do; they help clients arrive at their own decisions.*

Gestalt Therapy	Like client-centered therapy, Gestalt therapy assumes that people disown parts of themselves that might meet with social disapproval. He also argues that they put on "social masks" and pretend to be things they are not. Perls highly directive method aims to help people integrate these conflicting parts of their personality. He aimed to make clients aware of conflict, accept its reality, and make choices despite fear. Perls ideas about the conflicting personality elements are similar to psychodynamic therapy; however in Gestalt therapy the emphasis is on the here and now.

Answers to the Reading for Understanding about "Behavior Therapy: Adjustment Is What You Do"

52. do
53. behavior modification
54. learning
55. Behavior
56. Flooding
57. Systematic desensitization
58. virtual reality
59. Modeling
60. Aversive conditioning
61. cigarette smoking

62. self injurious
63. alcoholism
64. extinguished
65. operant
66. reinforcement
67. economies
68. approximation
69. biofeedback
70. token economy
71. Successive approximation

72. decrease
73. skills
74. self-monitor
75. Biofeedback
76. functional analysis
77. antecedents
78. consequences

Answers tot he Reading for Understanding about "Cognitive Therapies: Adjustment Is What You Think (and Do)"

79. Cognitive
80. Beck
81. cognitive errors
82. cognitive triad

83. scientifically dispute
84. Ellis
85. beliefs
86. irrational

87. directive
88. argues

Reflection Break # 2:

Compare and contrast Behavior therapy, Beck's cognitive therapy, and Ellis's Rational-Emotive Behavior Therapy by completing the table below.

Behavior Therapy	In contrast to the focus of psychodynamic and humanistic-existential forms of therapy on what people think and feel, behavior therapy tends to focus on what people do. Behavior therapy, also called behavior modification, relies on psychological learning principles (for example, conditioning and observational learning) to help clients develop adaptive behavior patterns and discontinue maladaptive ones. Behavior therapy methods include flooding, systematic desensitization, and modeling. Aversive conditioning is a controversial form of behavior-therapy method used for discouraging undesirable behaviors by repeatedly pairing clients' self-defeating goals (for example, alcohol, cigarette smoke, deviant sex objects) with aversive stimuli so that the goals become aversive rather than tempting. Behavior therapists also use the principles of operant conditioning to change behavior. Operant conditioning behavior methods are behavior therapy methods that foster adaptive behavior through principles of reinforcement. Examples include token economies, successive approximation, social skills training, and biofeedback training.
Beck's Cognitive Therapy	Cognitive therapies aim to give clients insight into irrational beliefs and cognitive distortions and replace these cognitive errors with rational beliefs and accurate perceptions. Aaron Beck's therapy method focuses on the client's cognitive distortions and notes that clients develop emotional problems such as depression because of cognitive errors that lead them to minimize accomplishments and catastrophize failures. The cognitive errors that contribute to the client's misery include a selective perception of the world, overgeneralization and magnification of events and absolutist thinking, or seeing the world in shades of black and white. He found that depressed people experience cognitive distortions such as the cognitive

	triad; that is, they expect the worst of themselves, the world at large, and the future. Beck teaches clients how to scientifically dispute cognitive errors.
Ellis's Rational Emotive Behavior Therapy	*Cognitive therapies aim to give clients insight into irrational beliefs and cognitive distortions and replace these cognitive errors with rational beliefs and accurate perceptions. Originally Ellis called his approach Rational-Emotive therapy because his focus was cognitive. However, he has always promoted behavioral changes to cement cognitive changes; in keeping with this he changed the name of the therapy to rational-emotive behavior therapy. Albert Ellis originated Rational Emotive Behavior Therapy (REBT), which holds that people's beliefs about events, not only the events themselves, shape people's responses to them. Ellis points out how irrational beliefs, such as the belief that we must have social approval, can worsen problems. Ellis methods are active and directive, he literally argues clients out of irrational beliefs.*

Answers to the Reading for Understanding about "Group Therapies"

89.	economical	94.	harmful	99.	communicate
90.	social support	95.	Couple	100.	autonomy
91.	individual	96.	cognitive behavioral		
92.	group therapy	97.	family		
93.	Encounter	98.	systems approach		

Answers to the Reading for Understanding about "Controversy in Psychology: Does Psychotherapy Work?"

101.	Eysenck	107.	randomly	113.	Psychodynamic
102.	spontaneous remission	108.	blind	114.	client-centered
103.	meta-analysis	109.	nonspecific therapeutic	115.	cognitive-behavioral
104.	effective	110.	effectiveness	116.	type
105.	experiment	111.	meta-analysis	117.	particular
106.	control	112.	better		

Reflection Break # 3:

1. Under what circumstances would you recommend that someone go for group therapy rather then individual therapy? Why?
   Since the methods and characteristics of Group therapy reflect the needs of the members and the theoretical orientation of the group leader. Group therapy can be advantageous since it is more economical than individual therapy. Group therapy might be recommended if the problem is one in which the social support and experiences of other members would be beneficial to the individual. If the person is imagining that they are different from others; group therapy can help them by allowing them to affiliate with others with similar problems. However, group therapy is not for someone who cannot disclose their problems in the group setting or risk group disapproval.

2. Briefly summarize the difficulties that arise when psychologists try to access the effectiveness of therapy.
   The ideal method for evaluating the effectiveness of treatment is the experiment. However, experiments are difficult to arrange and control. It is difficult and perhaps impossible to randomly assign clients to therapy methods such as traditional psychoanalysis. Moreover, clients cannot be kept blind as to the treatment they are receiving. Further, it can be difficult to sort out the effects of nonspecific therapeutic factors such as instillation of hope from the effects of specific methods of therapy.

Answers to the Reading for Understanding about "Biological Therapies"

118.	psychological	124.	rebound anxiety	130.	Monoamine oxidase
119.	biological	125.	dopamine	131.	Tricyclic antidepressants
120.	medical	126.	Antipsychotic	132.	serotonin
121.	Antianxicty	127.	depression	133.	Serotonin–uptake
122.	Sedation	128.	serotonin	134.	tricyclics
123.	tolerance	129.	antidepressant	135.	Lithium

136.	Electroconvulsive therapy (ECT)	141.	Psychosurgery	147.	ECT
137.	antipsychotic	142.	prefrontal lobotomy	148.	Psychosurgery
138.	major depression	143.	drug therapy	149.	schizophrenia
139.	controversial	144.	psychotherapy		
140.	memory	145.	solve problems		
		146.	antidepressants		

Reflection Break # 4:

Compare the different types of biological therapy by completing the following table

	Description
Drug Therapy	• *Antianxiety drugs belong to the chemical class known as the benzodiaepines and act by depressing the activity of the central nervous system which in turn decreases sympathetic activity. Sedation is the most common side effect of antianxiety medication.* • *Antipsychotic drugs help many people with schizophrenia by blocking the action of dopamine receptors. Antipsychotic drugs reduce agitation, delusions and hallucinations.* • *Antidepressants often help people with severe depression, apparently by raising levels of serotonin available to the brain. There are several different types of antidepressant drugs.* • *Monoamine oxidase inhibitors block the activity of an enzyme that breaks down noradrenaline and serotonin.* • *Tricyclic antidepressants prevent the reuptake of noradrenaline and serotonin and selective serotonin-uptake inhibitors block the reuptake of serotonin.* • *Serotonin–uptake inhibitors appear to be more effective than tricyclics.* • *Lithium often helps people with bipolar disorder, apparently by regulating levels of glutamate and can be used to strengthen the effects of antidepressant medication.*
Electroconvulsive Shock Therapy	*In ECT an electrical current is passed through the temples, inducing a seizure and frequently relieving severe depression. ECT is controversial because of side effects such as loss of memory and because nobody knows why it works.*
Psychosurgery	*Psychosurgery is a controversial method for alleviating agitation by severing nerve pathways in the brain. The best-known psychosurgery technique, prefrontal lobotomy, has been largely discontinued because of side effects.*

Answers to the Reading for Understanding about "Life Connections: Alleviating Depression (Getting Out of the Dumps)"

150.	Depression	154.	asserting	158.	Exercising
151.	Cognitive behavioral	155.	relationship	159.	asserting
152.	pleasant	156.	feelings	160.	effective
153.	rationally	157.	cognitive errors	161.	frustrations

Answers to the Final Review Multiple Choice Questions

1.	b (p. 488)	11.	c (p. 497)
2.	b (p. 489)	12.	b(p. 497)
3.	c (p. 490)	13.	c(p. 499)
4.	b (p. 490)	14.	c (p. 500)
5.	c (p. 491)	15.	a (p. 502)
6.	d (p. 492)	16.	b (p. 504)
7.	b (p. 493)	17.	c (p. 505)
8.	c (p. 494)	18.	d (p. 509-510)
9.	b (p. 494)	19.	d (p. 514)
10.	a (p. 496)	20.	b (p. 516)

Answers for Chapter 14:

Answers to the Reading for Understanding about "Social Psychology Individuals Among Others""

1. Social
2. perception
3. attraction
4. influence

Answers to the Reading for Understanding about "Attitudes-The Good, the Bad and the Ugly"

5. Attitudes
6. learned
7. changed
8. consistent
9. attitudes
10. behaviors
11. A-B
12. specific
13. accessible
14. vested interest
15. acquired
16. conditioning
17. observation
18. direct experience
19. evaluate
20. persuasion
21. elaboration likelihood
22. central
23. Peripheral
24. Repeated
25. once
26. fear appeals
27. expertise
28. attractiveness
29. will not
30. stereotypes
31. avoidance
32. exposure
33. coincides
34. avoid
35. environment
36. self-esteem
37. foot-in-the-door

Reflection Break # 1:

Matching:
1. h; 2. b; 3. f; 4. c; 5. a; 6. e; 7. I; 8. g; 9. d

Answers to the Reading for Understanding about "Social Perception: Looking Out, Looking Within"

38. social perception
39. the primacy effect
40. recency effect
41. attribution
42. attribution process
43. Social
44. dispositional
45. situational
46. independent
47. fundamental attribution
48. interdependence
49. actor-observer
50. dispositional
51. situational
52. self-serving
53. consensus
54. consistency
55. distinctiveness
56. internal
57. Body language
58. closer
59. negative
60. Gazing

Answers to the Reading for Understanding about "Interpersonal Attraction: On Liking and Loving"

61. relationships
62. attraction
63. appearance
64. cross-cultural
65. men
66. slenderness
67. tallness
68. cultural ideal
69. good-looking
70. attitudes
71. socio-cultural
72. reciprocity
73. matching hypothesis
74. Reciprocity
75. triangular
76. Intimacy
77. passion
78. commitment
79. love
80. Romantic
81. Passion
82. Consummate
83. commitments
84. affective shift
85. positive
86. negative
87. end
88. promiscuous
89. number
90. selective

Reflection Break # 2:

1. Why do we tend to hold others accountable for their misbehavior and excuse our selves for the same behavior?

    The tendency to infer the motives and traits of others through observation of their behavior is referred to as the attribution process. Social psychologists describe two types of attributions: dispositional and situational attributions. In dispositional attributions, we attribute people's behavior to internal factors such as their personality traits and decisions. In situational attributions, we attribute people's behavior to their circumstances or external forces. In North American culture we view the self as independent and tend to attribute other people's behavior to internal factors. This error, or bias in the attribution process, is known as the fundamental attribution error and occurs because we tend to infer traits from external behavior rather then from social roles and obligations. According to the actor-observer effect, we tend to attribute the behavior of others to internal, dispositional factors and our own behavior to external, situational factors since we see them as willing participants. The self-serving bias refers to the finding that we tend to attribute our successes to internal, stable factors and our failures to external, unstable factors. In other words we take credit for our successes, but blame our failures on someone, or something else. This attribution of behavior to internal or external causes is influenced by three factors: consensus, or the number of people responding in a certain way; consistency, or the degree to which the person responds the same on other situations; and distinctiveness, or the extent to which the person responds differently in different situations.

2. Briefly describe the factors that contribute to attraction in our culture.

    Attraction is influenced by factors such as physical appearance and attitudes and any aspects of beauty appear to be cross-cultural.

    Physically, men seem to find large eyes and narrows jaws to be attractive in women. In our culture, slenderness is considered attractive in both men and women, and tallness is valued in men. Psychological aspects of attraction include: Similarity in attitudes and socio-cultural factors (ethnicity, education, and so on), and reciprocity in feelings of admiration. According to the matching hypothesis, we tend to seek dates and mates at our own level of attractiveness, largely because of fear of rejection. Reciprocity is a powerful determinant of attraction; we tend to return feelings of admiration.

3. Describe Sternberg's three components of love and compare the level of each component in short-term relationship, romantic love and consummate love.

    Sternberg's triangular theory of love suggests that love has three components: intimacy, passion, and commitment. Intimacy refers to a couple's closeness, Passion means romance and sexual feelings, and Commitment means deciding to enhance and maintain the relationship. Different kinds of love combine these components in different ways. Romantic love is characterized by the combination of passion and intimacy. Passion is most critical in short-term relationships. Consummate love has all three factors.

Answers to the Reading for Understanding about "Social Influence: Are You an Individual or One of the Crowd?"

91.	Social Influence	97.	norms	103.	self-esteem
92.	Milgram	98.	explicit	104.	self-consciousness
93.	complied	99.	implicit	105.	collectivist
94.	hurt	100.	Asch		
95.	obedience	101.	conform		
96.	conformity	102.	liked		

Answers to the Reading for Understanding about "Group Behavior"

106.	facilitation	113.	majority-wins	120.	risky shift
107.	facilitate	114.	truth-wins	121.	Groupthink
108.	evaluation apprehension	115.	two-thirds majority	122.	leader
109.	impair	116.	first-shift	123.	invulnerability
110.	diffusion of responsibility	117.	polarized	124.	discrediting
111.	loafing	118.	riskier	125.	out-group
112.	decision-making schemes	119.	polarization	126.	cohesiveness

127. Flawed	132. crowding	137. bystander
128. skeptical	133. Mob	138. Crowds
129. deindividuation	134. Altruism	
130. anonymity	135. empathy	
131. responsibility	136. responsibility	

Reflection Break # 3:

1. What is conformity, how is it different from obedience, and what makes us conform to group norms?
   Obedience occurs when people obey the commands of others, even when they are required to perform immoral tasks. Conformity, on the other hand involves the changing of our behavior in order to adhere to social norms, or widely accepted expectations concerning social behavior.
   Factors contributing to obedience include socialization, lack of social comparison, perception of legitimate authority figures, the foot-in-the-door technique, inaccessibility of values, and buffers between the perpetrator and the victim. Personal factors such as desire to be liked by group members, low self-esteem, high self-consciousness, and shyness contribute to conformity. Belonging to a collectivist society and group size also contribute to conformity.

2. Why does group membership sometimes enhance performance and sometimes lessen performance?
   Social facilitation refers to the effects on performance that result from the presence of other people. The presence of others may facilitate performance for reasons such as increased arousal and evaluation apprehension, or the concern that others are evaluating our performance. However, the presence of others can also impair performance. When we are anonymous group members, we may experience diffusion of responsibility in which each person feels less obligation to help because others are present, and task performance may fall off. This phenomenon is termed social loafing. Group decisions tend to be more polarized and riskier than individual decisions, largely because groups diffuse responsibility. Group polarization refers to the tendency of groups to take a more extreme position than the individuals in the group would individually. This tends to lead groups make riskier decisions, or show a "risky shift".
   Groupthink can also occur in group decision making. Groupthink is an unrealistic kind of decision making that is fueled by group cohesiveness and the perception of external threats to the group, or to those whom the group wishes to protect. It is facilitated by a dynamic group leader, feelings of invulnerability, the group's belief in its rightness, the discrediting of information that contradicts the group's decision, conformity, and the stereotyping of members of the out-group. In groupthink group members tend to be more influenced by the group cohesiveness and a dynamic leader than by the realities of the situation. Flawed decisions are frequently made as a result of groupthink. Groupthink can however, be avoided if the leaders encourage members to remain skeptical about options and feel free to ask questions and disagree with one another.

3. What factors affect decisions to help (or not to help) other people?
   Altruism, or the selfless concern for the welfare of others is connected with heroic behavior. A number of factors contribute to altruism. Among them are empathy, being in a good mood, feelings of responsibility, knowledge of how to help, and acquaintance with-and similarity to-the person in need of help. According to the bystander effect, or the failure to come to the aid of someone in need, we are unlikely to aid people in distress when we are members of crowds. Crowds tend to diffuse responsibility.

Answers to the Reading for Understanding about "Life Connections: Understanding and Combating Prejudice"

139. Prejudice	142. stereotypes	145. discriminatory
140. Discrimination	143. conflict	
141. denial	144. intergroup	

Answers to the Final Review Multiple Choice Questions

1. d (p. 529)
2. b (p. 529)
3. b (p. 531)
4. b (p. 532)
5. a (p. 534)
6. b (p. 534)
7. b (p. 535)
8. a (p. 535)
9. c (p. 536)
10. c (p. 536)
11. c (p. 536)
12. d (p. 537)
13. b (p. 537)
14. c (p. 542)
15. b (p. 544)
16. a (p. 545)
17. a (p. 547)
18. b (p. 550)
19. c (p. 551)
20. b (p. 555)